100 resorts
in the
PHILIPPINES

TRAVELERS' SELECTION OF 100 HOTELS, RESORTS
AND DESTINATIONS THAT WILL ALSO CHARM YOU

100 resorts
in the
PHILIPPINES

PUBLISHER
Encyclea Publications

An Imprint of Asiatype, Inc.
11th Floor, Columbia Tower
Greenhills, Mandaluyong City
1550, Philippines
Tel. No.: (63-2) 725-6262
Fax No.: (63-2) 727-6053
E-mail: contact@encyclea.com
Website: www.encyclea.com
3rd edition - April 2005

COLOR SEPARATION
Asiatype Incorporated

PRINTING
Paramount Printing Company Limited

On the cover: Isla Naburot, Lagen, Pansukian and Ravenala Beach Bungalows
were the authors' favorite places with a heart.

Photo credits on page 348.

Kalaw Place, Mindoro Oriental

*D*ominique Grêlé was born in Caen, Normandy, France. In 1979, she graduated from the Institut Commercial de Nancy, a French business school, and shortly thereafter married Bruno Grêlé. They moved to Cairo, then to Mumbai, and after five years of living abroad, they returned to France with their first child Mathieu. Dominique joined the Credit Lyonnais' headquarters in Paris, started her banking career and had two other children, Antonin and Alice. When Dominique's husband was assigned to the Philippines by a pharmaceutical company, the whole family moved to Manila and Dominique joined the Credit Lyonnais Manila Offshore Branch as Head of Commercial Department. During weekends or short vacations, she "investigated" the Philippines—most of the time with her three children and husband, sometimes with friends when the place to be explored was feared too adventurous for the whole family to join—or alone when time was running out and a few more places had to be visited prior to the completion of the book. She liked Palawan, Boracay and Puerto Galera and traveled extensively around Manila. Dominique hopes this book can also help promote some destinations which she believes are still relatively unknown, specially the island of Negros and Cebu's west coast. She says: "I have lived in three cities. The only way to survive in a megalopolis is to escape from it as often as you can. May this book help you go out of Manila more often."

*L*ily Yousry-Jouve is an artist who seems to have an ongoing romance with the Philippine landscape—from Sagada in the north to Siargao in the south. Born in Cairo to a French mother and an Egyptian father who is a well-known artist, she grew up in Paris. She learned to paint while she was still a child, but she studied law, specializing in city planning, at the Sorbonne.

She dedicated her time to painting when she settled with her husband Marcel in Nairobi, Kenya in 1992—Marcel's assignment prior to Manila.

The Jouves lived in Manila for close to five years, with Marcel Jouve taking care of cultural matters at the French embassy in Manila.

*M*arcel Jouve shares the same passion for nature and exploration of this captivating country. He is the main author of the pictures of the guide, photography being another facet of his talent.

Lily has had two successful solo exhibits in Manila. Visiting and painting "Philippines Hidden Landscapes," the theme of one of her exhibits, gave her the idea to give information about the places she had seen, realizing that despite their beauty and variety, the Philippine Islands are still largely unknown.

Lily visited Palawan, North and South Luzon, Samar and Leyte in the Visayas and Lake Sebu, Agusan and Surigao in Mindanao.

PLACES WITH A HEART

Whether you want to discover the Philippines or escape Manila for a few days, you will be confronted with the difficulty of deciding where to go. Existing guides are very general in principle and it is mainly by word of mouth that information may be usually obtained.

When we arrived some years ago, we were both faced with the same dilemma: where to go, how to get there and where to stay. As we share the same passion to discover this beautiful country, we traveled as much as we could to the different islands—and then decided to make available the information about the different places that we visited and enjoyed.

One of us is an economist, the other a painter. Our goal is not to add another guidebook to the list of existing ones, some of which are extremely helpful. Instead, we wish to share our most pleasant experiences by providing the necessary information that could help you in the planning of a holiday. We traveled separately to very diverse regions, yet found the time to link up, if only to compare notes and to see if our approaches were similar.

To our minds, the best places to go to are not necessarily the most expensive nor the most plush. We defined "first-class" according to a set of criteria: the beauty of the site where the resort is located; the quality of the physical arrangements around it, the architecture and interior décor; the excursions possible in the area; the service; the warmth of welcome—all of these elements that make a place appealing. We have mentioned places with particularly interesting natural sites, though only simple hotels with basic amenities are located there. In general however, the resorts and hotels selected have a standard of minimum comfort.

Places with a Heart, Philippines is a very subjective book. Even the places that we deem charming may have certain aspects less appealing to others. This guidebook is by no means exhaustive, as that was not our goal. We have certainly—by ignorance or difficulty of gaining access—missed some places that may have deserved mention. For this, we apologize.

The islands of the Philippines are beautiful—their hidden beauty often difficult to portray because it often necessitates a long journey to reach certain destinations. A trip often becomes a genuine expedition by plane, jeepney and even *banca*! But for those who make the trip, the reward is well worth the effort.

The Philippines is a country which is in truth captivating and regrettably, inadequately known. In the minds of foreigners, there may be certain images of the Philippines that do not do justice to this enthralling country. The archipelago offers a multitude of splendors—the rice terraces of Banaue; the magical cliffs of Palawan and Siargao; the colonial past of Vigan, Silay and Iloilo; the formidable volcanoes and the sea which is a haven for divers and snorkelers. And these are but to mention only a few! Adrift in luminous waters lie paradisiacal islands where you can be Robinson Crusoe for a day, contemplating coral gardens inhabited by fish of extraordinary forms, sizes and colors.

Our wish is that through this guide, readers will be able to discover and appreciate the beauty of the Philippines—and the *joie de vivre* of its people. Each one, whether alone or with company—full of energy and thirsting for adventure, or merely needing a moment to unwind and relax, with a substantial budget or with limited means, fond of secret hideaways or animated resorts—should be able to find something suitable.

So...*bon voyage* and happy hunting!

Lily Yousry-Jouve

Dominique Grêlé

CONTENTS

A practical data sheet can be found at the end of the review for each resort. It begins with the Contact Section and is followed by the How-to-Get-There Section, the Accommodation Section, Indoor facilities and Services Section, the Food and Beverage Section, the Watersports and Other Activities Section and the Price Section. Each section has its own icon.

THE CONTACT SECTION

You will find all the necessary information to make a booking by yourself in this section. The information in this section is arranged in the following order:

1. The resort's name, address, telephone, fax and e-mail details.
2. The resort's booking office address, its telephone, fax and e-mail details, if needed.
3. The resort's website, if any.

COMMUNICATIONS

In cases where the resort cannot be reached by telephone, alternative means of communication will be suggested such as radio contact, mail, nearest telephone, etc.

BOOKING OFFICE

In most cases, the resorts' booking offices are in Metro Manila. If not, they are usually located in the main city nearest the resort. Metro Manila encompasses 14 cities, including Makati, Quezon City, Mandaluyong, Pasay, Pasig. See the map on page 332.

BOOKINGS

Bookings made via e-mail do not always result in a quick response as e-mail service varies from one resort to another. If you need prompt confirmation of your booking, it is best to use the telephone or fax.

If you have not received a written confirmation of your booking prior to your departure, it is also recommended to check with the resort if it has your booking details on record.

PEAK SEASON

Plan your trips well ahead if you intend to travel during Philippine peak seasons such as Christmas, New Year's Eve, Chinese New Year, Easter, Fiestas/Festivals and Philippine summer vacations (late March to late May). Resorts are often fully booked months in advance on these dates.

Some hotels require a minimum stay of five to seven days during peak season.

TELEPHONE NUMBERS

Please note that the country code for the Philippines is 63. 7-digit numbers in Metro Manila must be preceded by 632 from abroad. Local time is GMT + 8h. Phone numbers frequently change. In case a phone number is no longer accessible, it is advised that you contact the Philippine Long Distance Telephone Company (PLDT) directory assistance number at: 187 for numbers in Manila and the provinces or call 109 and ask to be put through to the nearest telephone directory.

If these attempts remain unsuccessful, contact the Department of Tourism (DOT) office covering the concerned region. A listing of DOT offices is also provided in the annex of the guidebook.

Domestic Direct Distance Dialing is available in most public payphones and private subscriber telephones. To make a local long distance call, simply dial the National Access Code Number (0) + the area code (XX) + the Telephone Number you wish to dial. To call Montebello Villa Hotel in Cebu, for example, dial: 0+32+231-3681. From abroad, it will be 00+63+32+231-3681.

THE HOW-TO-GET-THERE SECTION

You will find the necessary information to make transportation arrangements by yourself in this section, in the following order:

A brief description of the different modes of transportation to be used followed by an estimate of the total travel time needed. The distance from Manila is usually indicated for places in Luzon accessible by land.

Example 1: By land (7–8 hours) 250 kilometers from Manila via Kennon Road.

Example 2: By air, land and sea (6 hours)

2. A step-by-step access guide detailing the type of transport to be used (plane, ferry, jeepney, car, bus, *banca*—a local small boat, etc.); the time needed; the name of the transportation company (airline, shipping or bus company, car rental company, etc.); the starting point and the arrival point; the frequency of service.

Travelers departing from cities other than Manila should refer to the transportation list where connections with other cities are indicated.

SEVERAL ACCESS OPTIONS
It will be indicated whether there are travel options that exist.

INDICATIVE TOTAL TRAVEL TIME
It is assumed that travelers depart from Manila's domestic airport or ferry/bus terminal, or from Makati if access is by land. An allowance of 30 minutes should usually be given prior to arrival at the airport or ferry/bus terminal. For trips involving a connection between two different modes of transport such as a plane and a ferry, the best possible connection has been retained. In most cases the best connection is obtained while taking the first morning flight out of Manila.

SCHEDULES OF TRANSPORTATION COMPANIES
Schedules and routes serviced by domestic airlines and shipping/bus companies frequently change. For this reason, the transportation list found at the end of this book does not indicate precise schedules but instead only indicates the frequency of service. It is best to update schedules each time you make a travel plan.

TRANSFER ARRANGED BY THE RESORT
Resorts arranging for the transfer of their guests from the nearest airport or ferry/bus terminal, or directly from Manila are especially mentioned.

THE ACCOMMODATION SECTION

UNITS
A brief description of the resort's room categories, including a mention of facilities available such as a bathroom (private or common, with shower or bathtub, with hot water), a refrigerator, air-conditioning or fan, a TV set, a telephone, a private terrace is written. For the more luxurious resorts, the availability of a coffee/tea maker, a hairdryer, bathrobes, slippers will likewise be mentioned.

THE FOOD AND BEVERAGE SECTION

FOOD AND BEVERAGE
A listing of the resort's restaurant(s) and bar(s) is provided.

TYPE OF CUISINE
A list of the different cuisines offered by the restaurant(s) is provided.

QUALITY
A subjective assessment of the quality of the food, if tested, is provided. It can be:

Average The food is of average quality and/or the selection of dishes is limited. In such cases, we personally would opt to go for grilled choices with plain rice.

Familial The food is not sophisticated but is home-cooked, family style and good.

Good There is a wide selection of dishes and the food is rather refined.

Excellent There are a number of resorts which serve a very sophisticated selection of food. Those who are very particular about their food will be pleased.

The food was not tried in resorts where there is no assessment of the quality of the cuisine.

THE INDOOR FACILITIES AND SERVICES SECTION

A list of indoor facilities and services offered by the resort is provided. These may include a business center, a foreign currency exchange, a car/van/jeepney/taxi rental desk, medical services, chapel, children's playroom, babysitting, library, games/game room, TV-video room, billiards, table tennis, massage and fitness center, spa and/or Jacuzzi, a gym and others which may be unique to the resort.

WATERSPORT AND OTHER ACTIVITIES SECTION

A list of watersport and other activities offered by the resort is provided. Special mention will be made in cases where activities are not directly offered by the resort, but by independent operators. The list usually includes hiking, trekking, mountain biking, horseback riding, outdoor sports facilities such as volleyball, tennis or badminton, children's playground/kids' room, pool(s) with mention of the size and existence of a kiddie pool, beach with mention of the sand, snorkeling with mention of the sites, diving with mention of the sites, island hopping, kayak, other boats for rent (without giving the list of all boats available for rent, we mean here that other boats such as a windsurf or a sailboat are available).

THE PRICE SECTION

THE PRICE ICON

The icon represents the burial jar of the Manunggul, which can be found on Php1,000 notes.

HOW TO DETERMINE THE PRICE CHARGED BY THE RESORT

It can be determined as follows:

One jar means that the price for accommodations is below Php1,000.
Two jars means that the price for accommodations is in the Php1,001–2,000 range.
Three jars means that the price for accommodations is in the Php2,001–3,000 range.
Four jars means that the price for accommodations is in the Php3,001–5,000 range.
Five jars means that the price for accommodations is in the Php5,001–10,000 range.
Six jars means that the price is Php10,001 and up.

PRICING POLICY

There are two main pricing policies used by the resorts: on a per room basis or on a per person basis. Sometimes, meals and/or other services are included in the price.

For the guidebook, we have adopted a per room per night price policy for the costs of stay.

Meals and/or any added services are also indicated.

PUBLISHED RATES VERSUS ACTUAL RATES

The rates given in this book are published rates applicable during the regular season, usually from November to May, to the cheapest room category. Prices charged in USD have been converted into Pesos using a conversion rate of Php55.50 to the USD. During low season (from June to October), rates can be discounted by 20% to as much as 50%. Likewise during peak season (Christmas, New Year's eve, Easter, Chinese New Year, Philippine Summer vacations), a surcharge of 20% to 50% may be added and a minimum stay period is frequently requested. Promotional packages are often extended at the resort/hotel's sole discretion.

OTHER DISCOUNTS

Children (up to a maximum of two), as far as lodging is concerned, may normally share their parents' room free of charge on condition that no additional bed/crib is requested. Additional beds are charged Pesos 500–1,000.

Children above 12 years are usually considered as adults and charged accordingly when it comes to food. Children below 12 are given a 50% discount. Discounts for long stays are a common practice. Special rates may be offered on weekdays and for bookings done via Internet.

DEPOSIT

For your booking to be confirmed many resorts require a deposit to be made. It can be anything between 30% to 100% of the price of your stay. Make sure that you are given a receipt for your payment and that you are aware of the cancellation policy of the resort. Sometimes, these policies can be very strict and you can easily lose a substantial part (or even 100%) of your deposit.

THE SPECIAL ICONS

CLIMATE ICON

The Philippines is endowed with a great variety of climates, rainy seasons being completely different from one island to the other, and sometimes even within a single island. It was therefore deemed useful to mention the rainy and typhoon seasons for each region. Thanks to this climactic variability, you will always find a place in the Philippines with the best weather conditions to make your trip a truly enjoyable one. Source: "PAGASA" climate map of the Philippines.

FESTIVAL ICON

The main festivals are mentioned on a regional basis. Filipinos love feasts and many occasions are an opportunity to celebrate. Festivals are often very colorful and inventive. Each town has its own festival, so only the most popular ones have been noted.

HEART ICON

All the resorts selected in this guidebook are attractive either on their own right or because they are gateways to places well worth a visit.

However, some of them stood out for us because of a particular charm. These are our *"coups de cœur"* and we have identified them with a curiously heart-shaped seashell of the *cardium* family. You may be surprised to observe that some small resorts with simple amenities yet brimming with allure were awarded a heart. Those that are located in remarkable sites were also given a similar distinction. The more banal five-star hotels were not. That was our deliberate choice. The very few hotels we have judged outstanding in all respects were awarded two hearts.

In the course of your reading, you will even notice that some of our awarded selections are inclined toward being more rudimentary. Though not too far from the beaten track, these resorts with charm are remembered more for their intrinsic qualities rather than their added amenities.

LEGEND TO MAPS

———	Major Road	●	Capital City
———	Secondary Road	◎	City
———	Rough Road	◉	Town
✈	Airport (all airlines)	○	Barangay / Sitio / Barrio
🏠	Resort		

Luzon and Mindor

Steps of Wisdom, Batad, Ifugao Province

Painting by Lily Yousry-Jouve

Luzon

Mabudis Is. · Amianan Is.
Itbayat Is. · Siayan Is.
· Dinem Is.
BATANES
· BASCO
Deguey Is. · Sabtang Is.
Ibujos Is.

Babuyan Is.

Calayan Is.

Dalupiri Is.

Fuga Is. · Camiguin Is.

Palaui Is.

PAGUDPUD
**ILOCOS
NORTE**
· LAOAG

**LUZON
SEA**

**KALINGA
APAYAO**

CAGAYAN

ABRA

· VIGAN

TUGUEGARAO ·

**ILOCOS
SUR**

**MOUNTAIN
PROVINCE**
· BONTOC
ILAGAN ·

ISABELA

· BANAUE
LAGAWE
IFUGAO

LA UNION

SAN FERNANDO
(La Union)
BENGUET
LA TRINIDAD ·
BAYOMBONG ·

QUIRINO

BAGUIO
CITY

LINGAYEN ·
**NUEVA
VIZCAYA**

PHILIPPINE SEA

PANGASINAN

AURORA

ZAMBALES

TARLAC
TARLAC
CITY
CABANATUAN ·

· IBA
**NUEVA
ECIJA**

PAMPANGA
SAN FERNANDO
(Pampanga)
SUBIC ·
OLONGAPO
BULACAN

SUBIC
BAY
FREE
PORT
MALOLOS
BALANGA
MANILA
BATAAN
CAVITE
CITY

RIZAL

STA.
CRUZ
**LUZON
SEA**
CAVITE
LAGUNA
STA. ELENA
DAET

TAGAYTAY CITY
LIPA CITY
CALAUAG
**CAMARINES
NORTE**

LUCENA
CITY

BATANGAS
CITY
BATANGAS
QUEZON
SIPOCOT · NAGA CITY
**CAMARINES
SUR**
PILI ·
CATANDUANES
VIRAC ·

IRIGA
CITY

LEGAZPI
CITY
SORSOGON
SORSOGON

N
W E
S

⊞ Asian Spirit
⊞ Cebu Pacific
⊞ Philippine Airlines

LUZON

0   50   100 km

LUZON, THE LARGEST ISLAND IN THE PHILIPPINES, has a surface area of 104,688 square kilometers, stretching over 850 kilometers from Ilocos Province in the north to the Bicol Province in the south. Northern Luzon is geographically dominated by the Cordillera mountain range in the center of the region and the Sierra Madre mountains along the east coast. South Luzon, much narrower, is home to several active volcanoes like Mayon and Bulusan.

Certain parts of Luzon are accessible from Manila within a day or over a weekend: the Bataan Peninsula and Subic Bay in the west; Tagaytay and Taal, Caylabne Bay and the Calatagan Peninsula in the south. These destinations, if not for the adventure, at least offer the possibility of relaxation not far from the capital without having to take a plane. You can also go diving in the waters of the shipwrecks of Subic Bay; discover the forests of Bataan, Subic and Mount Makiling; visit the old houses of Taal and the churches around Laguna de Bay; and play golf in the resorts south of Manila. There are also beaches—even if these are usually not the most attractive beaches in the Philippines.

In North Luzon you can discover the splendors of the rice terraces in the Cordilleras where Igorot, Ifugao and Kalingas maintain spectacular, centuries-old ricefields that account for the most beautiful sceneries in the Philippines. Along the coast of Ilocos Sur and Ilocos Norte are many baroque churches and the colonial town of Vigan, the best preserved in the Philippines.

Malegcong Rice Terraces in Bontoc

Around Manila–The North

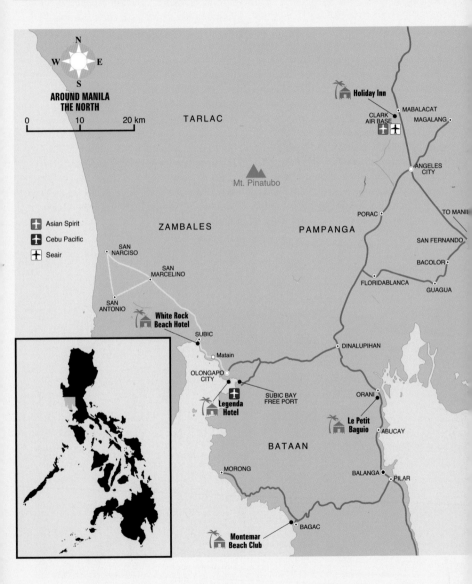

N
W E
S

AROUND MANILA
THE NORTH

0   10   20 km

TARLAC

Holiday Inn

CLARK
AIR BASE

MABALACAT

MAGALANG

ANGELES
CITY

Mt. Pinatubo

Asian Spirit
Cebu Pacific
Seair

ZAMBALES

PAMPANGA

PORAC

TO MANIL

SAN
NARCISO

SAN FERNANDO

SAN
MARCELINO

BACOLOR

FLORIDABLANCA

GUAGUA

SAN
ANTONIO

White Rock
Beach Hotel

SUBIC

Matain

DINALUPIHAN

OLONGAPO
CITY

Legenda
Hotel

SUBIC BAY
FREE PORT

ORANI

Le Petit
Baguio

ABUCAY

BATAAN

MORONG

BALANGA

PILAR

Montemar
Beach Club

BAGAC

Climate   Dry from November to April; wet during the rest of the year

Typhoons   June to November

Subic Bay Freeport, Clark Field and the Bataan Peninsula

SUBIC BAY FREEPORT IN ZAMBALES AND CLARK FIELD IN PAMPANGA were two former American military bases. After the troops left in 1992, the bases were transformed into large free economic zones, giving rise to ambitious development projects.

AT SUBIC BAY FREEPORT, you will be surprised to see former military structures transformed into hotels and industrial complexes. Luxurious residences constructed during the 1996 Asia-Pacific Economic Council (APEC) Summit to house the visiting heads of state, have since been converted into deluxe villas.

ABOUT 100 KILOMETERS FROM MANILA, Subic Bay Freeport and Clark Field offer attractions other than the duty-free shops and recreational facilities. The main attraction of the area is the Mount Pinatubo volcano, accessible by car from Subic or by trekking from Angeles City.

Subic Bay Freeport
Inside Subic Bay Freeport
(three hours from Manila, 124 kilometers)

CUBI BATS *(near the Legenda Suites)* Millions of bats suspended from the trees during the day take flight altogether around six o' clock every evening, forming an impressive black cloud that shrouds the sky.

THE SUBIC FOREST AND ECO-TOURS The Jungle Environment Survival Training (JEST Camp) on Appari Road, Upper Mau, was a training camp created during the 1960s in the Subic Forest to prepare the American soldiers for combat in Vietnam. Training was facilitated by members of the Aeta tribe, accustomed to surviving in the jungle. The children will be interested in survival techniques such as drinking water

collected in bamboo and making a fire from twigs of bamboo. A short trek through the jungle allows the discovery of trees with impressive trunks, different edible berries and plants with medicinal properties. A mini-zoo houses a small variety of animals. Longer random walks of a day or more may be organized on request. For more information, call Tel. No.: (047) 252-4123.

THE PAMULAKLAKIN FOREST TRAILS *(Binictican Drive)* The trails are a jump-off point for the discovery of the Subic Forest in two or three hours, with a guide from the Department of Tourism. You can also take part in a jungle survival demonstration and tribal dances. It is advisable to make advance reservations (minimum of 10 persons) with the Department of Tourism at Tel. Nos.: (047) 252-4123 or (047) 252-4242.

THE ROAD LEADING TO MORONG GATE *(beyond Corregidor Road)* This picturesque, seldom-traveled road leads into the forest. From here, there is a good view of the bay, and it is not difficult to see some birds and monkeys. Take note, however, that the road indicated on the map from Morong Gate to the town of Morong does not seem passable during the rainy season.

Casa San Miguel at San Antonio

WRECK DIVING *(from Waterfront Road)* Around 20 Japanese and American ships destroyed during the Second World War lie in the bay, as does a Spanish gunboat dating back to 1858. Subic Bay Aqua Sports on Waterfront Road is a good dive center and a hyperbaric chamber in Subic Bay Harbor. The gray sand beach, however, is quite unattractive.

Outside Subic Bay Freeport

CASA SAN MIGUEL AT SAN ANTONIO *(40 minutes from Subic)* In the serene, idyllic setting of a mango orchard created in 1920 by his grandfather, Coke Bolipata, a renowned Filipino violinist, created a superb building inspired by different architectural styles. Casa San Miguel was conceived as an open house for artistic endeavors. The Pundaquit concerts which take place every month should not be missed. For more information contact Tel. No.: 927-1043/903-8657 or e-mail: *colofino@hotmail.com.*

MOUNT PINATUBO HIDDEN TEMPLE SHRINE *(two and a half hours round trip from Subic)* The devastation left by Mount Pinatubo following its violent eruption in the early 1990s is evident when you visit the area and realize that the fumes rose up to 40 kilometers into the stratosphere, affecting areas far beyond the Philippines. The surrounding area, over a radius of more than 10 kilometers, was covered with layers of ash several meters thick. Typhoons, which are annually accompanied by heavy rains, transform this ash into mudslides—lahar—which aggravate the situation.

An excursion can be arranged. A four-wheel drive vehicle is necessary for the 45-minute drive on the dirt road. First, the track goes along Santo Tomas Dike, an imposing dike constructed to contain the lava flow—on the old riverbed of the Marella River. After San Rafael, before you reach Lake Pinatubo, the route climbs up

slightly and you can see, in all its poignant grandeur, the devastation caused by the eruption in June 1991. Formed as a result of the eruption, the lake engulfed the hamlets of Buhawen and Aglao, sparing only the rooftops and the belltower of the church. The road goes on in the direction of a dam.

From Subic Bay Freeport, exit from the Kalaklan Gate and, immediately after the bridge, turn left in the direction of Subic town. After passing through the town, continue in the direction of Iba and pass by Castillejos. At the welcome sign of the village of San Marcelino, note the road sign "Western Luzon Agricultural College" and "Nagbunga Barangay Hall." Turn right and follow the red arrow "MPHT Shrine." A little further at the fork of the road, go left in the direction of the Palan Shrine and continue following the arrows.

Clark Field

Clark Field is the jump-off point for trekking to the crater lake of Mount Pinatubo. Angeles City was badly hit by the eruption of Mount Pinatubo in June 1991.

TREKKING UP MOUNT PINATUBO *(weekend)* You need at least two hours by jeepney to get to the departure point, four hours of climbing and then three hours to descend. You therefore need to spend the night at the volcano. This uncomplicated excursion is organized by travel agents in Angeles City, who provide the necessary camping equipment, food, water and a guide. The services of a guide are recommended because of the inherent dangers of the unstable lahar and volcano activity. Do not attempt to climb if rain threatens or if temperature is too high. The best period to trek up is between February and March. Contact Ben at Cell No.: (0918) 655-3155 or e-mail: *laharben@mozcom.com.*

MOUNT ARAYAT *(20 kilometers east of Angeles City)* This extinct volcano, with an altitude of 1,030 meters is accessible by taking the Magalang exit on the North Expressway. After the tollbooth, turn left in the direction of Magalang and Mount Arayat National Park. Once you have completed the registration formalities at the park office, the ascent of Mount Arayat begins, quite steep sometimes, traversing a few secondary forests. It takes seven to nine hours of climbing to reach the peak.

MIMOSA LEISURE ESTATE *(1.5 kilometers from Angeles City)* A former military installation, the Mimosa Golf and Country Club is open only to members and their guests. There is an 18-hole golf course set with a magnificent view of Mount Pinatubo.

ANGELES FLYING CLUB *(approximately 20 kilometers east of Angeles City)* The aeronautic club is in Magalang, at the foot of Mount Arayat. The club offers beginners' courses in ultra light planes, as well as a flight over Mount Pinatubo. For information, call the Woodland Park Resort, Lizares Street, Dau, Tel. No.: (045) 892-1002 to 05 or e-mail: *woodland@mozcom.com*. Website: *www.woodland.ph*

BACOLOR *(5 kilometers from San Fernando)* The lahar at Bacolor, on the road that traverses San Fernando to Olongapo, has buried half of the church of the San Guillermo Parish, reconstructed in 1886. A small museum displays gripping photos taken during the eruption of the volcano.

The Bataan Peninsula

The Bataan Peninsula, whose tip in Mariveles forms part of the enclosure—with Cavite in the southern part and Corregidor in the middle—which protects the sea-bound entrance to Manila Bay, is steeped in history. It was the scene of the fiercest fighting between Allied and Japanese forces in 1942, as a prelude to the infamous Bataan Death March.

MOUNT SAMAT SHRINE *(half-day trip)* The circuitous steps that go up the mountain to the shrine may be too much exertion for the elderly. Along the way, you will pass by a museum, the Friendship Bell, the Zero Kilometer Marker where the Death March commenced, all fitting remembrances of the horrors of war. Mount Samat was the site where the bloodiest skirmishes were fought in World War II.

MOUNT NATIB *(one-day trek)* It is best to leave for the mountain early in the morning to make the first part of the ascent to Binutas in the shade. Leaving Binutas Pass, you continue along a good road via the national park up to Mount Natib, whose summit can be reached in two hours. The more energetic could actually make the ascent in an hour but the slope is steep and should actually be avoided during the rainy season.

TOMAS PINPIN MONUMENT AND THE FIRST ABUCAY CATHOLIC CHURCH *(day trip to Abucay town)* The monument was built in memory of the first Filipino printer while the church is one of the oldest in the Philippines. It was in the Abucay Church where Tomas Pinpin co-authored and printed the earliest books in the country, with Fr. Blancas de San Jose, in 1610. The church housed the first printing press in the country, outdating any single press in the United States.

Mount Natib, Bataan

Holiday Inn Resort

The Holiday Inn Resort opened in March 1996 in Clark Field, the former American military base. It is an immense hotel complex set in a 250-hectare site which includes a golf club. The eruption of Mount Pinatubo in 1991 caused a lot of damage but today, the area has still more than 7,000 trees, among them beautiful hundred-year-old mimosas. From the gardens, and even better from the rooftop, there is a superb view of Mount Arayat.

The hotel complex was designed by Jose Mañosa, the Filipino architect who also designed the Pearl Farm and Amanpulo resorts. He created a warm and intimate Filipino-Spanish ambience, which was not very easy given the vastness of the setting.

You can choose between two types of lodgings—either a bedroom in a five-story building or an individual villa. The villas are luxurious, very spacious and bright, thanks to large bay windows with venetian blinds. They include a kitchen, drawing-cum-dining room, two rooms with bathrooms, a private terrace, quarters for domestic staff and a garage.

In the rooms as well as in the villas, there is a cheerful atmosphere partly due to the warm green and yellow walls and the furnishings. Still-life paintings decorate the rooms. The furniture favors Philippine handicrafts from Pampanga, plaited wicker and wrought iron.

Near the main building is a swimming pool surrounded by a terrace filled with green plants, lounge chairs and parasols. A sunbathing area with a Jacuzzi is located on the rooftop.

The cuisine is excellent in the two restaurants: Café Mequeni on the ground floor, where you can dine in air-conditioned comfort, and the Mongolian Barbecue Restaurant on the rooftop, where you can dine outdoors.

Kid's Inn is a club reserved for children. They can also go to the Funhouse where they can play video games. It is also possible to rent bicycles and roller blades from the Mimosa Leisure Estate.

The hotel is also a popular venue for seminars and conferences. As the resort is near the Mimosa Golf and Country Club, people with a passion for golf will enjoy a holiday with the family.

HOLIDAY INN RESORT

Mimosa Leisure Estate, Mimosa Drive, Clark Field, Pampanga
Tel 845-1888
Fax 843-1363

Booking Office in Makati
Suite 300
Hotel Intercontinental Manila,
#1 Ayala Avenue, Makati City
Tel 752-8243 • 44 • 46 • 47
Fax 752-8245
E-mail *hircf@comclark.com*
Web
www.holiday-inn.com/clarkfield

1. By land (1½–2 hours) 90 km from Manila. Take North Expressway at Balintawak and get off at Dau exit. Take North Diversion Road to MacArthur Highway. In Angeles City, after about 1.5 km, turn right when you see the Holiday Inn Resort Clark Field sign.
2. By air (45 minutes) Thirty-minutes flight on Asian Spirit (3 weekly flights) and Seair (6 weekly flights) from Manila to Clark airport; 15 minutes by car from Clark airport to the hotel.

337 Units
188 Double-bedded Rooms • 85 Single-bedded Rooms • 30 Suites • 34 Two-bedroom Villas
All rooms and suites have individually controlled air-conditioning, cable TV, telephone, minibar, coffee/tea maker, hairdryer, and a private bathroom with hot water. Only junior suites have a bathtub and a safe. No connecting rooms. All villas offer the same facilities as the Junior Suites.

Indoor Facilities and Services
Business center • Car rental • Foreign currency exchange • Fully supervised Kid's Inn • Gym and fitness center • Medical services • Sundeck and Jacuzzi • Table tennis

Food and Beverage Outlets
Restaurants: Café Mequeni (buffet) • Mongolian Barbecue Restaurant
Cuisine Offered: International • Filipino
Quality: Excellent

Bars: 13th Lounge • Pool bar • Mequedeli

Watersports and Other Activities
Swimming pool (with kiddie pool) • Biking • Billiards • Limited golf arrangements at the nearby Mimosa Golf and Country Club

🛶🛶 🛶🛶 🛶🛶   Per room per night inclusive of breakfast

🛶🛶 🛶🛶 🛶🛶 🛶🛶   Per villa per night inclusive of breakfast

Legenda Hotel

If you are looking for a luxurious, elegant ambiance in Subic Bay, the Legenda Hotel along Waterfront Road will meet your expectations. The hotel belongs to a Malaysian chain that has several hotels in the Philippines, two of which are also located in Subic Bay Freeport—the Legenda Suites and the Four Seasons Hotel.

The hotel is composed of two, three-story buildings, which do not have a view of the sea as they are perpendicular to the avenues bordering the bay. The architecture of the hotel is resolutely Spanish—white buildings roofed by red tiles. From the road, you enter into a reception area suffused with light, due to large bay windows. There is an impression of luxury—marble black and white chequered floors, columns, the dome lit by an extravagant chandelier in the form of garlands of shining glass beads. Brightly-lit corridors link the rooms located on either side of reception.

The deluxe rooms are spacious, brightened by large bay windows. The décor is refined, both in the choice of furniture—a mix of wrought iron, bamboo and mahogany—as well as in the harmonious blend of colors: green, black and mahogany. Soft wall-to-wall carpeting accentuates the cozy aspect of the room. Superb marble bathrooms in different shades of gray have all the necessary elements of comfort.

The hotel does not have a beach but there is a small swimming pool behind the reception building. The hotel has also a large, formal Chinese restaurant, The Museum, and a simple, intimate coffee shop called Le Café. Both offer a wide range of dishes.

All the services and amenities expected of a rated hotel are provided: limousines that await your arrival at the airport, a fitness center, a discotheque, a casino and luxury boutiques of Lacoste, Gucci and Sachi. The hotel rates are very reasonable as compared to the other hotels where the level of comfort and amenities are quite inferior.

Note: *In terms of cost and quality, the Legenda Suites (102 suites, 2 restaurants) is in the same range as the Legenda Hotel. This is recommended for families preferring an apartment hotel with one or two rooms, a living room and an equipped kitchen. Legenda Suites is located in the Upper Cubi district, five minutes from the airport at the intersection of Tarlac and Sulu streets. The JEST Camp, Dungaree and All Hands Beaches and the Cubi Bats are all nearby. In addition, residents of the Legenda Suites have access to the swimming pool at Legenda Hotel.*

LEGENDA HOTEL

Legend International Resorts Limited, Waterfront Road, Subic Bay Freeport Zone, Zambales
Tel   732-9888
          (047) 252-1888
Fax   712-8575 • 712-1668
          (047) 252-7958
Web   www.subiclegend.com
Booking Office in Pasay
A. Soriano Aviation,
Andrews Avenue corner
Nichols Avenue, Pasay City
Tel   853-0325 • 28 • 30
Fax   853-7342

By land (3 hours) 124 km from Manila. Take North Expressway at Balintawak and get off at San Fernando, Exit No. 66. Take the Gapan-San Fernando-Olongapo road passing through Bacolor, Guagua and Lubao. After the "Welcome to Dinalupihan" sign, turn right to SBMA/Olongapo. Turn left at the sign indicating "Subic Bay Freeport 9 kilometers." At the intersection, look for the PTT gas station and turn right to Rizal Avenue. Turn left to Santa Rita Road (5th road on your left) which leads to Waterfront Road.

247 Units
33 Superior Twin • 34 Superior Double • 49 Deluxe Twin • 94 Deluxe Double • 37 Suites
All rooms have air-conditioning, bathroom with hot water, cable TV, telephone, minibar, hairdryer, bathrobes and slippers. Only the deluxe rooms are provided with a bathtub. Few rooms have a seaview.

Indoor Facilities and Services
Business center • Massage and fitness • Bowling center • Casino • Tour desk • Car rental • Foreign currency exchange

Food and Beverage Outlets
Restaurants: The Museum
Chinese • Le Café
Cuisine Offered: Chinese • Continental • Asian

Watersports and Other Activities
Swimming pool (small) • Diving at nearby Subic Bay Aqua sports (also on Waterfront Road) • Jet skiing • Parasailing • Fishing • Tennis • Equestrian center at El Kabayo • Golf arrangements at the nearby Subic Bay Golf and Country Club • Jungle trek at the JEST Camp • Eco-adventure (slides, wall climbing, paintball, war games, shooting range, island cruise, nature and marine tours) • Tours to Subic Bay Freeport, Mount Pinatubo

Per room per night inclusive of breakfast

White Rock Beach Hotel

After three long hours on the road, it is a relief to arrive at White Rock Beach Hotel, marked by magnificent travelers' trees. The hotel is set on a four-hectare property at the edge of Subic Bay, a lovely area with green lawns planted with coconut trees. The setting instantly gives you a leisurely feeling, quite unlike the aloofness of Subic Bay Freeport.

You have the pleasure of discovering a large beach though with gray sand. Here, there are deck chairs and parasols—and a nice view of the bay, Snake Island, and, in the distance, the mountain range of the Zambales province.

Opt for a room on the beachfront in a small, two-story building facing the beach. These rooms are bright and have a private balcony. Even those on the ground floor have direct access to the beach. It must be noted that the furniture, except for the white rattan in the living room, and the paint—need to be refurbished.

The standard rooms are in the main, four-story building. As there is no elevator, these rooms are not suitable for the elderly or for young children. Besides, only the two rooms which are set at an angle on the top floor and the family room have sea views. Although spacious and comfortable, these rooms are a bit dark and are lacking in warmth…functional and sober with wrought iron, wood and wicker furniture and a bright tiled floor.

The hotel caters to a clientele traveling "en famille." There is a large swimming pool reserved for children. In the evening, a string orchestra and a pianist serenade you while dining. It is better to dine in the patio opening onto the garden and the beach, rather than indoors, which is insufficiently ventilated.

If you want to try out other restaurants, you can drive to the Hungry Marlin Bar and Grill located adjacent to the Subic Bay Yacht Club or to Fishcado, a restaurant that serves seafood and Filipino cuisine from Mindanao. It is located near the western side of the Boardwalk along the waterfront area in Subic Bay Freeport.

WHITE ROCK BEACH HOTEL

Barrio Matain, Subic Bay, Zambales
Tel (047) 222-2398
(047) 232-2857
Fax (047) 222-2379
E-mail reservations@
whiterockresortsubic.com
Web
www.whiterockresortsubic.com
Booking Office in Quezon City
G/F Office Warehouse Building,
E. Rodriguez Jr. Avenue corner
Tital Street, Libis, Quezon City
Tel 421-2781 • 82
Fax 421-2785

By land (3 hours) 124 km from Manila. Take North Expressway at Balintawak and get off at San Fernando, Exit No. 66. Take the Gapan-San Fernando-Olongapo road passing through Bacolor, Guagua and Lubao. After the "Welcome to Dinalupihan" sign, turn right to SBMA/Olongapo. Turn left at the sign indicating "Subic Bay Freeport 9 kilometers." Exit at Kalaklan gate following the signs. Turn left immediately after the bridge following the direction of Subic town proper and watch for the White Rock sign after the Kilometer 134 post.

127 Units
Main building: 78 Standard Rooms including 2 corner rooms with bay-view • 8 Two-bedroom Family Room with beachfront view • 2 One-bedroom Suite
Beachfront annex building: 12 Beachfront Rooms (second floor) • 8 Beachfront Garden Rooms (ground floor)
Beachside: 15 Beachside Rooms • 4 Two-bedroom Beachside Cottage
All rooms have air-conditioning, bathroom with hot water, cable TV, and telephone. An extra bed can be added in all rooms.

Indoor Facilities and Services
Medical services • Foreign currency exchange • Table tennis • Billiards

Food and Beverage Outlets
Restaurants: Sunset Cafe • D'Rock KTV & Bar
Cuisine Offered: Filipino
Quality: Average

Watersports and Other Activities
Swimming pool (with kiddie pool) • Beach (gray sand) • Diving at nearby Subic Bay Aqua sports • Boats for hire • Cruising • Island hopping • Jungle trek at the JEST Camp • Golf arrangements with Subic Bay Golf and Country Club • Outdoor massage center with whirlpool • Children's playground

 Per room per night

Le Petit Baguio

Only two hours from Manila, Le Petit Baguio is a place with a casual, homey atmosphere. Located on the mountain at the edge of the national park of Bataan, it is recommended for those who are fond of nature and random walks. The resort is the "return to nature" dream of Frenchman Jean-Paul Chambouleyron who left France in 1994, and settled down here with his Lucie, who comes from Tala.

He built five bungalows on stilts, made from natural materials—bamboo and cogon—each with a nice terrace from where you can enjoy a view of the mountains. The interior decoration is personalized and pleasing, each room is wallpapered in different colors with hanging engravings of birds. Velvety carpeting, beds draped in snow-white quilts and enveloped in huge mosquito nets, all give the impression of comfort and well-being. Moreover, the nights are refreshingly cool. Each bungalow has a pretty bathroom. The main bungalow, where the meals are usually served, has a good view from its terrace. The cooking is done by Lucie who has mastered both French and Filipino cuisines. Meals are a moment to savor!

A little farm on the property supplies the resort's daily needs—eggs, chickens, ducks, geese and pigs. There is also a large orchard of calamansi, guava, banana, breadfruit and pineapple. You can gather yourself these farm produce and buy them.

The drawback, however, is the nearby cock-breeding area, responsible for the very early morning wake-up calls at the resort!

Jean-Paul is an ardent fan of orchids. He has installed a large greenhouse sheltering a number of species, some of which are quite rare. Domestic animals are ever present—when we last visited, we saw a cat, a dog, horses and three wild boars rescued from the hunters.

Le Petit Baguio also offers the opportunity for an excellent study of nature—an activity which will interest and amuse the children. Some schools organize nature study classes here at certain times of the year.

Aside from visits in the Bataan Peninsula, two short treks can be done from Le Petit Baguio:

Binutas Pass *(2 hours return trek) The view here of the mountains covered by forests and Subic Bay is superb. The route climbs up a bit but is wide and well-indicated.*

The Descent to the River *(2 hours trek) Just in front of Le Petit Baguio, a slightly sloping, though not very arduous track descends to the river. You pass by large erithrina trees and then carefully cross stepping-stones. Natural pools with crystal clear waters have been dug into the rocks. You can swim here but the water is cold. Finally, you reach a small gorge whose walls are covered in tree fern and philodendrons.*

LE PETIT BAGUIO

Tala, Orani, Bataan
Tel (0918) 935-4133
(0916) 304-2342
(Call early mornings
or during mealtimes)

 1. By sea and land (2.5 hours)
One hour by Mount Samat air-conditioned ferry from the PTA Bay Cruise Terminal, CCP Complex, Roxas Boulevard in Manila to Orion, Bataan (Tel. No.: 551-5290). Then one hour by Jean-Paul's own car (good for 4 only) or by van/jeepney arranged by the resort (for more than 4) from Orion-Tala-Orion.

Note: *The road can be slippery during rainy season and dusty in dry season.*

2. By land (4–5 hours) 110 km from Manila. Take North Expressway at Balintawak and get off at San Fernando, Exit No. 66. Take the Gapan-San Fernando-Olongapo road passing through Bacolor, Guagua and Lubao. At the junction of Olongapo/ Balanga, take Balanga. After approximately 15 km, turn right on a track to Tala (the track is facing the road to Orani on your left). There is a small sign "Le Petit Baguio" and a big sign "Orani Coffee" at the entrance of the track. Keep going straight for 30 minutes, pass Brgy. Pag-asa and Tala, then you will see on your right another sign marking the entrance of the resort.

 5 Units (Bungalows)
3 Bungalows (with double bed) •
2 Family Bungalows (with two bedrooms, good for 6 persons)

Indoor Facilities and Services
Collection of orchids on display (in a greenhouse)

 Food and Beverage Outlets
Restaurant on the terrace of the Main Bungalow
Cuisine Offered: French and Filipino
Quality: Excellent and plentiful

Watersports and Other Activities
Swimming (in the river) • Hiking • Trekking • Horseback riding (with local saddle) • Tour to Subic Rainforest (one hour by car)

 Per room per night
on full board basis

Montemar Beach Club

The great attraction of Montemar Beach Club is its accessibility from Manila. Without taking a plane or even your own car, you can reach it in two hours by ferryboat and then by van.

Montemar is a good place for relaxation. It is set in a rocky, wooded cove with a long beautiful beach surrounded by a garden of bougainvillea, flame trees, travelers' trees and coconut palms. The resort was completely renovated in 1996.

The rooms are in long, white, two-story buildings with red tile roofs. Curved balconies enclosed by railings, overflowing with flowers, pleasantly break the monotony of the façade.

The deluxe rooms are spacious and bright due to large bay windows. These open onto a private balcony with red flooring and a garden drawing room, some of which have direct access to the swimming pool. The gallery rooms in the buildings near the reception area are ideal for families as there is a loft accessible by a staircase. These rooms also have a balcony.

There is a relaxing, cozy atmosphere in every room. Everything is in soft, pastel tones, including the walls and the floral bedcovers. Bamboo furniture and handmade lamps make you feel at home. In the evenings, wooden shutters secure you in a snug cocoon. There is also a beautifully tiled bathroom with marble sinks in every room.

The two restaurants have pleasant settings although catering is not a strong point at Montemar. *El Meson* is the house restaurant on a paved terrace in the garden near the sea. Its white arcades, curved wooden windows, pretty red floors and bamboo furniture give it a warm, Spanish ambiance. The tables are set outdoors, under a large tree lit by little bulbs. It is pleasant to dine here in the evenings and enjoy the sea breeze. The other restaurant, *El Patio*, is also good for outdoor dining. Both restaurants offer Filipino and International cuisine.

The clear sand beach of Montemar is attractive; deck chairs and parasols are made available. The resort also has two swimming pools—the *Garden pool* for day-use guests, surrounded by coconut, bougainvillea and palm trees quite far from the rooms, and the *Blue-Tiled pool* with its circular bar at the surface of the water for the in-house guests.

While at Montemar, you can drive up to the summit of Mount Samat located near the resort. The area does not have any special attractions, but it does offer a scenic view of the Bataan Peninsula.

MONTEMAR BEACH CLUB

Barrio Pasinay, Bagac, Bataan
Tel (0919) 540-0626 to 27
Fax (0919) 547-0098

Booking Office in Makati
2/F Pacific Star Building,
Sen. Gil Puyat Avenue Extension
corner Makati Avenue, Makati City
Tel 892-6497 to 98
Fax 811-5235 • 811-5496
E-mail montemar@mindgate.net

1. By land (3 hours) 154 km from Manila. Take North Expressway at Balintawak and get off at San Fernando, Exit No. 66. Take the Gapan-San Fernando-Olongapo Road passing through Bacolor, Guagua and Lubao. After the "Welcome to Dinalupihan" sign turn left at the junction (you will see statues of soldiers). After kilometer 122 sign, turn right following the "Junction to Mt. Samat 3 kilometers" sign. From there follow the signages of Montemar Beach Resort.

2. By sea and land (2 hours)
One hour by Mount Samat, air-conditioned ferry from the PTA Bay Cruise Terminal, CCP Complex, Roxas Boulevard to Orion, Bataan, (Tel. No.: 551-5290). Thirty-five minutes by van from Orion pier to the resort.
Note: *Transfer from Manila may be arranged by the resort.*

87 Units
59 Deluxe (for 3 persons) • 18 Gallery Rooms (for 5 persons) • 4 Garden Rooms • 4 Suites • 2 Executive Suites (2 bedrooms)
All rooms have air-conditioning and fan, bathroom with hot water, private balcony.
Indoor Facilities and Services
Gym • Van rental • Billiards

Food and Beverage Outlets
Restaurants: El Meson • El Patio for dining al fresco
Cuisine Offered: International • Filipino
Quality: Average

Watersports and Other Activities
Swimming pool • Beach (gray sand) • Kayaking • Other boats for hire • Aqua cycling • Badminton • Pony riding • Excursions to Mount Samat if you bring your own vehicle

Per room per night

Note: *Full payment in advance.*
Cash payment only at the resort.

Around Manila–The South

AROUND MANILA THE SOUTH

0   10   20 km

MAKATI CITY
PASAY CITY
CAVITE CITY
ROSARIO
TANZA
GEN. TRIAS
NAIC
TERNATE
TRECE MARTIRES CITY
DASMARIÑAS
CARMONA
MUNTINLUPA
ANGONO
TO MANILA
MORONG
BINANGONAN
CARDONA
TANAY
MABITAC
SINILOAN
PAKIL
PAETE
Lake Caliraya
STA. ROSA EXIT
STA. ROSA
CALAMBA EXIT
LAGUNA DE BAY
JALA-JALA
LUMBAN
STA. CRUZ
PAGSANJAN
CAVINTI
Lagos Del Sol Resort
CALAMBA
LOS BAÑOS
LAGUNA
LUISIANA
MAJAYJAY
NAGCARLAN
U.P. LOS BAÑOS
Mt. Makiling
R&R Resort
SAN PABLO
CALAUAN
Villa Escudero
STO. TOMAS
ALAMINOS
Palimpan
SILANG
CAVITE
San Roque Beach Resort
TAGAYTAY CITY
TALISAY
Leynes
Club Estancia Resort Hotel
LAUREL
Hidden Valley Springs
NASUGBU
Coral Beach Club
TUY
BATANGAS
TAAL LAKE
Mt. Makulot
LIPA CITY
Bungahan
MATABUNGKAY
BALAYAN
AGONCILLO
STA. TERESITA
CUENCA
The Farm at San Benito
BALAYAN BAY
Punta
TAAL
Lago De Oro Beach Club
CALATAGAN
Eagle Point Resort
BAUAN
ROSARIO
Anilao
BATANGAS CITY
Sombrero I.
BATANGAS BAY
Cabán I.
MARICABAN ISLAND
Pisa
Culebra I.
Bonito Island Resort

Climate   Dry from November to April, wet during the rest of the year
Typhoons   April to May and October to November

Pahiyas, May 15, Lucban, Quezon Province. San Isidro Labrador, the patron saint of farmers, is honored during this superb and particularly creative harvest festival. All the houses are adorned with arrangements of fruits, vegetables, coconuts and kiping leaves, made from rice flour and water, dyed with food coloring—lavish creations depending on who has the most imagination. A jovial and hospitable mood reigns in the streets where sweets are distributed.

Taal Volcano and Tagaytay

The city of Tagaytay is on the upper reaches of the spectacular Taal caldeira, where lies Taal volcano, often hidden in the mist. Its proximity to Manila (56 kilometers) and its cool weather (altitude, 700 meters) make it a convenient destination for holiday seekers from the capital.

THE LAKE AND TAAL VOLCANO *(half day from Manila)* Taal Lake is in the crater of an ancient, extinct volcano. In the middle of the lake is a little island that constitutes one of the smallest active volcanoes in the world. Coming from Manila, after crossing the market place, you come to the crest of Tagaytay Ridge, on the edge of the caldeira. Go left and continue along

Taal Lake

the ridge until you see the sign indicating the road going down to Taal Lake in the direction of Leynes, Talisay and Laurel. Once on the lake at Leynes, the *banqueros* are quick to offer a trip to the old crater. The crossing takes approximately 45 minutes to an hour and the actual excursion between 30 minutes to one hour—depending if you go on foot or on horseback. It is recommended that you make the journey early in the morning as the waters become rough towards the afternoon and it can get quite hot due to the absence of shade. If you want to stay at Taal, you have a choice between San Roque Beach Resort at the edge of the lake and Estancia Resort Hotel higher up.

MOUNT MAKULOT *(one day from Manila)* This 947-meter high mountain is an easy climb and can be undertaken by any person in good health. From its summit, the view of the volcano, Taal Lake, as well as that of the city of Batangas and its bay, is spectacular. You must register at Cuenca before attempting the climb. Although this can be done in a day, as you only need a couple of hours to reach the summit, many climbers prefer to spend a night to enjoy the sunrise. To go to Cuenca from Manila, take the South Superhighway and get off at Exit No. 50A (Batangas, Lucena, Legaspi). Go through Santo Tomas, Tanauan, Malvar and Lipa City.

A newer and faster alternative route is the Star Tollway, the entrance of which is in Sto. Tomas. Signs along the road will guide you. Approximately eight kilometers after Lipa City, you will see a junction on the right going to Cuenca.

GOLF COURSES There are many golf courses near Tagaytay such as the Banyan Tree Evercrest Hotel and Country Club.

The Town of Taal

Overlooking the Bay of Balayan, the little town of Taal in the province of Batangas is 120 kilometers from Manila. At the Tagaytay rotonda, take the direction of Nasugbu and then turn left in the direction of Taal-Lemery. The road overlooks Taal Lake and the Bay of Batangas. After descending, at the crossroads, go left in the direction of Taal, Lemery, and Batangas City.

Taal is known for the active participation by some of its illustrious residents during the revolution of 1896–1898. Taal was already prosperous at the end of the 19th century and was populated by a sizeable number of aristocrats, shipowners, rich sugarcane and rice plantation owners. The number of Spanish colonial houses on Felipe Agoncillo Street and on the main road on the left of the Basilica of Saint Martin of Tours are testimony to this ostentatious past. Many of these were restored in the '70s.

THE BASILICA OF SAINT MARTIN OF TOURS   The imposing baroque-style basilica was constructed on the site of an old church in 1856. The original wood material has been preserved, which is evident in the Corinthian-styled upper parts and the Doric-styled lower portions of the columns.

The Basilica of Saint Martin of Tours, Taal

Interior of an old house in Taal

Houses open to the public
(along the main road)

AGONCILLO HOUSE This villa, constructed during the 1896 revolution, belonged to Felipe Agoncillo, revolutionary hero and diplomat. His wife, Marcela Marino de Agoncillo, sewed the Philippine flag, unfurled during the proclamation of the first Republic of the Philippines, on June 12, 1898, by General Emilio Aguinaldo. Take note of the large capiz windows and the dining room in narra and molave wood.

LEON APACIBLE MUSEUM AND LIBRARY This villa was named after Leon Apacible (1861–1901), the illustrious revolutionary who married the granddaughter of Maria Diokno, the woman responsible for its construction. In 1938, the house was redesigned by an architect who introduced the art-deco motifs. The house was transformed into a museum in 1970.

DOÑA GLICERIA "MARELLA" AND DON EULALIO VILLAVICENCIO HOUSE Overlooking the bay of Balayan, this recently-restored house had for its dwellers a shipowner and his wife, both ardent defenders of the nationalist movement. A suspension bridge linked the two houses, known as the Twin Houses. Admire the wood used in the construction—narra for the doors and molave for the pillars.

THE EMBROIDERY OF TAAL Taal, along with Lumban, is known for the quality of the embroidery created by its residents. You can buy beautifully embroidered tablecloths at prices much lower than those in Manila at the HME Embroidery workshop, a pink building in front of Don Gregorio Agoncillo House, at the end of Felipe Agoncillo Road.

Estancia Resort Hotel

The hills around Lake Taal are covered with pineapple plantations and coffee shrubs with white flowers that perfume the air. Estancia Resort Hotel is on Tagaytay Ridge, the coastal road that goes around a part of the lake. The resort is obscured by vegetation, but offers spectacular views of the lake and the volcano. Because of the altitude, the climate is delectably cool and the mist, which shrouds the lake at certain times of the day, gives it an air of a hill station.

The swimming pool stretches around the garden like a river. A wooden bridge spans the pool, much to the joy of children. Between December and February, the water can get quite cold.

One part of the rooms is housed in the main building but though they are quite comfortable, they are less pleasant than the *nipa* huts clinging to the foothills. It is recommended to stay here to take full advantage of the site's beauty. The huts, linked by little pathways, can be reached, either on foot or in a little vehicle resembling a golf cart—a quite convenient way to get to the more remote huts at the edge of the forest.

The style of the huts is typical traditional Filipino structures with bamboo walls, capiz windows and *nipa* roofs. The interiors are spacious, showcasing the different ways of using bamboo— little slats for the floor, thick poles for the walls, and plaited bamboo strips for the ceiling. The furniture is made of impeccably finished pale rattan and the bathrooms are made of marble. Each hut has a terrace, furnished with chairs and tables, where you can enjoy the view of the lush forest mirrored in the lake.

The design of the restaurant plays with contrasts. Large, semi-circular picture windows, accented by capiz, open in a spectacular fashion onto the forest and the lake. The rattan furniture warms the bleak glass and stone walls and floor. You feel relaxed in these surroundings where the only thing missing is a warm fireplace.

The place is ideal for relaxation— and for escaping the overwhelming summer heat of Manila. It can also be a stopover on the way to the beaches of the Calatagan Peninsula, Nasugbu or Anilao. Not to be missed are the trip across the lake to visit the crater of the volcano and the visit to the town of Taal and its old houses. You can also buy fruits and vegetables in the roadside stalls on your way back to the capital.

ESTANCIA RESORT HOTEL

Zone II, Barangay San Jose, Tagaytay City, Cavite
Tel (046) 413-1133 to 35
Fax (046) 413-1047

By land (1½ hours) 56 km from Manila. Take South Superhighway and get off at Santa Rosa, Exit No. 40. After the market of Tagaytay you reach Tagaytay Ridge. Turn right and follow the "Estancia" signs for about 2 km. The resort is on your left.

40 Units
4 Superior Rooms • 4 Deluxe Suites • 10 Executive Suites • 22 Nipa Hut Rooms and suites are air-conditioned, fully carpeted with TV (local channels only), telephone, minibar, marble bathroom with hot water and bathtub, piped-in music and balcony. Nipa huts are fan-cooled, with TV, shower, and telephone.

Indoor Facilities and Services
Sauna • Jacuzzi • Video games • Billiards (at Marina Bar) • Table tennis

Food and Beverage Outlets
Restaurant: Mob's Bar and Restaurant
Cuisine Offered: Filipino
Quality: Good

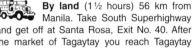
Watersports and Other Activities
Indoor and outdoor swimming pools • Children's playground

Per room per night

San Roque Beach Resort

The San Roque Beach Resort is the only resort directly on the banks of Taal Lake. Its owner, Lita Merkx, is a Filipina married to a Dutchman. After the construction of the resort in 1997, Lita, who was born here, acquired the neighboring property and expanded the resort that now has twelve rooms. The charm of San Roque lies in the beauty and serenity of the area, the magnificent view of the lake and its volcano, and the warmth and welcome of its owners.

If you are in a small group, you can rent the Guest House. Unlike the Kubo House and Nipa Huts, it is a concrete structure—without any particular charm—with three rooms, a furnished kitchen, a drawing room and a nice terrace looking out to the lake.

The Nipa Hut and the Kubo Houses were built in a more traditional style—*nipa* roofs, plaited bamboo walls. The tile floors are the only concession to modern comfort. The curtains and floral bedcovers are the only touch of fancy. Although the huts are small, the use of space was maximized to contain all the essentials. The twin rooms of the Nipa Hut are convenient for families with two children.

The resort has a homey atmosphere. Lita is ever ready to prepare your favorite dish on request, served in the small canteen (protected by mosquito nets) in the garden.

You can swim in the lake where the extremely clean water is tested twice a year by a team of foreign researchers and specialists from the University of the Philippines. A small corner of the beach is furnished with armchairs, deck chairs and parasols; the gray sand is raked and cleaned everyday.

The resort's banca is available for an excursion of the volcano, which is on the opposite bank. A small row boat is also made available for discovering the lake.

At the nearby Taal Lake Yacht Club, it is possible to rent a sailboat and kayaks, and take sailing lessons—without having to be a member. The club also organizes monthly regattas.

SAN ROQUE BEACH RESORT

Buco, Talisay, Batangas
Tel (043) 773-0271
(0919) 310-7976

 By land (2 hours) 82 km from Manila. Take South Superhighway and get off at Santa Rosa Exit No. 40. After the market of Tagaytay, turn left when you reach Tagaytay Ridge. After one kilometer, turn right, following the sign board indicating the directions of Talisay and Laurel. At the next junction, turn left following the direction of Talisay. Just before you reach the lake, turn right. Follow the road for about one kilometer— San Roque Beach Resort is on your left.

 12 Units
5 Kubo Houses • 4 Nipa Huts • 2 Guest House • 1 Mini Bungalow
The Kubo Houses and Nipa Huts have air-conditioning and fan, can accommodate two persons only.
The Guest House has three bedrooms with air-conditioning and fan. Two shower rooms with toilet; a kitchen with refrigerator and cooking facilities; a living room with lounge set, TV and stereo and a terrace. There are 2 toilets and 2 shower rooms for public use.

 Food and Beverage Outlets
Small canteen
Cuisine Offered: Filipino • Continental on request
Quality: Average

 Watersports and Other Activities
Beach (by the lake) • Rowboating • Kayaking • Sailing at the nearby Taal Lake Yacht Club • Tour to Taal Volcano with the resort banca or as arranged by the Taal Lake Yacht Club

 Per room per night

Caylabne Bay Resort

The Caylabne Bay Resort, only two hours away from Manila, is the seaside resort closest to Manila, along with Montemar Beach Club in Bataan. The last fifteen kilometers of the route go through a forest and offer superb panoramic views of the jagged coastline, Corregidor Island and the Bataan Peninsula further away. It is only after entering the premises and the Look-Out Café that you will discover the high wooded cliffs of the Bay of Caylabne and its marina. The resort is located in a wooded area, so vast that a map—distributed at the registration office—is necessary for finding your way around.

The rooms are set in a white building hidden behind a curtain of trees, against a backdrop of tropical vegetation. With its arched balconies and pink tile roof, the resort has a Mediterranean touch. The suites are very spacious, bright and comfortable with one room, a drawing room and a bathroom, both with marble flooring. The rooms are completely white with a polished, two-toned wood floor and elegant wrought iron furniture. However, the absence of wall décor gives a rather impersonal atmosphere.

A family resort *par excellence*, children are treated like royalty here. A superb river-shaped swimming pool with a slide, mini-golf and two playgrounds are for their exclusive use. The beach, sheltered by the pier of the marina, is completely safe. The water is quite shallow and a filtering net limits the swimming area. It is true that the sand is a mix of white and gray and the often rough waters strip the beach of any attractiveness, but every effort is made to compensate this: amusing, colorful tents shelter deck chairs and almost all sorts of watercraft are proposed, notably kayaks–although you can only use them up to the breakwater.

El Patio Restaurant offers fine dining by the sea and serves Filipino and Continental cuisines in a Mediterranean-inspired seafront ambiance. An orchestra serenades during meal times on some weekend nights. The Marina Bar, on the other hand, provides nightly entertainment with a Latin band during peak season.

CAYLABNE BAY RESORT
Caylabne Point, Ternate, Cavite
Tel 841-1318 to 26
Fax 841-1323

Booking Office in Makati
2/F Corporate Business
   Center Building
151 Paseo de Roxas corner
Pasay Road, Makati City
Tel 813-8519 to 26
Fax 840-1963
E-mail *salescb@caylabne.com.ph*
Web *www.caylabne.com.ph*

By land (2 hours) 75–90 km from Manila. There are two possible routes: The shorter one (75 km) starts at Roxas Boulevard and goes through the Cavite Coastal Road. The resort provides guests willing to take this route with a sketch. The longer (90 km) but faster route goes through South Superhighway. Exit at Biñan/Puerto Azul/Tagaytay/Carmona. Take Governor Drive from Carmona to Naic via Trece Martires. After Naic, you can follow the sketch given by the resort.

67 Units
13 Studio-type Rooms • 20 One-bedroom Suites (with Jacuzzi) • 22 Two-bedroom Suites • 12 Three-bedroom units All units/rooms have air-conditioning, TV, mini-bar, telephone, hairdryer, bathroom(s) with hot water, terrace.

Indoor Facilities and Services
Business center • Babysitting • Medical services • Massage • Shuttle service • Children's playroom • Billiards

Food and Beverage Outlets
Restaurant: El Patio
Cuisine Offered: Asian and International Buffet
Quality: Good

Bars: Marina Bar • Look-out Café and Bar

Watersports and Other Activities
Swimming pool (with kiddie pool) • Beach (almost white sand) • Island hopping • Kayaking • Fishing • Windsurfing • Other boats for hire • Hiking • Tennis • Mountain bike rental • Minigolf • Children's playground

Per room per night inclusive of breakfast

Laguna de Bay

Laguna de Bay is the name given by the Spanish to the largest lake in the Philippines. It occupies an area of 900 square kilometers and is well protected on the east by the Sierra Madre and on the south by Mounts Makiling and Banahaw. As you arrive in Manila by plane, you will be surprised by the odd geometric designs on the lake—arrows, rectangles, and circles—evoking cubist designs or strange writings. These are, in fact, fish-breeding pens, a major means of livelihood in the region.

THE TOUR OF THE LAKE FROM NORTH TO SOUTH The tour of Laguna comprises nice landscapes, churches and handicraft stalls. From Makati, take EDSA (Epifanio de los Santos Avenue) in the northern direction. At the Robinson's Galleria mall, take Ortigas Avenue on the right. At the first crossroads after Cainta Junction, turn right in the direction of Taytay. Follow the main road that goes through the province of Rizal before approaching the province of Laguna and rejoin the South Luzon Expressway at Calamba. Between Morong and Mabitac, along the coastal road, there are spectacular views of the lake and the vegetation.

Rizal   *(from Antipolo to Pililla)*

THE CHURCH OF SAINT JEROME, MORONG This baroque-style Franciscan church, constructed in 1615, was extensively renovated in 1852. It has a Mexican-baroque façade decorated with floral motifs. It has three stories with an octagonal belfry.

THE CHURCH OF SAINT ILDEFONSUS, TANAY This Franciscan church constructed in 1783, has an original façade with pillars capped by pineapples carved in wood. It has six altars and rococo-style baptismal fonts. The Stations of the Cross painted on wood in the nave of the church are remarkable.

Chapel at Villa Escudero

Laguna   *(from Mabitac to Calamba)*

MABITAC CHURCH This church from the 17th century rests on a hill overlooking the village and the lake. It was damaged by an earthquake in 1880 and has since been rebuilt. It is accessible by climbing 120 steps.

THE CHURCH OF SAN PEDRO DE ALCANTARA, PAKIL This church houses a statue of the Virgin of Turumba. The town of Pakil is famous for its wood filigree, the making of which you can observe in the handicraft shops. Every year after Holy Week, the Virgin's feast-day is celebrated during the Turumba festival.

PAETE CHURCH After an earthquake destroyed the original church dating back to 1646, a stronger church was built in 1717. Some renovations were undertaken in 1840; earthquakes damaged again the church in 1880 and 1937, and rebuilding took place in the 1880s and 1970s. The convent dates back to 1840. The baroque façade is adorned with carvings in ebony wood. In the church's

Pagsanjan Falls

vicinity are numerous handicraft shops selling woodcarvings and *papier-mâché* items.

LAKE CALIRAYA This artificial lake 300 meters above sea level was created in 1943 to supply a power station which is still in use. Swept by winds from the Pacific Ocean some 10 kilometers away, it is an ideal spot to windsurf. However, you must bring your own equipment. Enthusiasts of this sport come regularly to the Surf Camp at the edge of the lake. There are a number of resorts here, such as Lagos del Sol.

LUMBAN It is a town famous for its embroidery.

PAGSANJAN Pagsanjan has a church and some old houses but is mainly popular for the trip on the Pagsanjan rapids up to the Magdapio waterfalls. During the rainy season, the descent by boat is quite spectacular. Behind the magnificent waterfalls is a cave: being under the waterfalls is an unforgettable experience!

MAKILING NATIONAL PARK (*campus of the UPLB–University of the Philippines Los Baños*) About one kilometer before Los Baños, turn right at the roadsign saying "PCARRD," in the direction of the university campus. UPLB manages the well-preserved 24 square-kilometer park at the foot of the 1,100-meter high Mount Makiling. Go right up to the Forestry Department Nursery. Park your car and go on foot through a partly cemented, forested path. If you have a four-wheel drive vehicle, continue higher up to the climbing track, a four-hour return journey. You go through beautiful primary forest with remarkable flora—gigantic pandanus, tree ferns and orchids. On the way is a small trail leading to the much-visited mud springs. It is pleasant to spend a day in the forest, on a picnic, walking under the tall trees, and observing the birds. Mount Makiling is quite humid and can be quite cold. There may be leeches during the rainy season along the final stretch to the summit. A small museum within the campus exhibits local fauna and flora.

CALAMBA The house where Jose Rizal was born is located here and has been transformed into a museum. A church and hot springs can also be visited. You can stay at the R & R Resort if you want to be near the town's points of interest—although Calamba is only a day trip from Manila.

Makiling National Park

R & R Resort

For those who love walking—and the forest—the R & R Resort at the foot of Mount Makiling is a good place to stay. Although Mount Makiling is a day trip from Manila, just 55 kilometers away, it is nice to get away from the capital during the weekend and explore the forest.

The Makiling National Park is a forest reserve of 24 square kilometers surrounding the extinct 1100-meter-high volcano. It is under the management of the University of the Philippines Los Baños. The park's slopes are covered with superb primary forest where bird-watchers come early in the morning.

The little resort is quite pleasant with a good view of Mount Makiling. Lush vegetation surrounds the 10 two-story cabanas which make up the resort.

The cabanas are spacious and comfortable, with a drawing room on the ground floor, two little marble bathrooms, and two rooms, one on each floor. The rooms are very bright due to picture windows. The white and navy-blue walls, the blue lattice windows and the pale bamboo furniture give the place a happy atmosphere. Each cabana has its own terrace furnished with a table and chairs, and a small private swimming pool with hot sulphur waters from the volcano. The cabanas, however, are quite close to each other. The four rooms located in a separate building are not as pleasant.

The restaurant looks onto a large swimming pool through big windows. The pool, framed by lush greenery, is equipped with hydrotherapeutic hot water jets, making for a very relaxing swim after climbing Mount Makiling.

R & R RESORT

Maria Makiling Village,
Km 55, Barangay Pansol,
Calamba, Laguna
Tel (049) 545-2952

Booking Office in Quezon City
7816 Greenwood St. Marcelo
Green Village, Parañaque City
Tel/Fax 824-5258

By land (1 ½ hour) 55 km from Manila. Take South Superhighway until you reach the Calamba, Exit No. 50A (Batangas, Lucena, Legaspi). At Calamba Junction, turn right towards Los Baños. Pansol is the village just before Los Baños. Once in Pansol, you will pass by Pamana Hospital, Jose Rizal Provincial Hospital and turn right after Barretto Elementary School or Bato-Bato Resort. Then follow the signs indicating R & R Resort.

14 Units
10 Cabanas • 4 Rooms
All cabanas have air-conditioning, fan, intercom, and two bathrooms with hot water and a terrace with its own private hot spring pool.
The rooms have air-conditioning, fan and a bathroom with hot water.

Indoor Facilities and Services
Shiatsu massage • Table tennis • Videoke Room • Billiard

Food and Beverage Outlets
Restaurant overlooking the pool
Cuisine Offered: Filipino

Watersports and Other Activities
Swimming pool (with kiddie pool) • Hiking to Mount Makiling

Per room per night

Hidden Valley Springs

idden Valley Springs, located between Mount Makiling and Mount Banahaw, is hidden in the middle of a superb forest. A track goes into the jungle and, in half an hour, leads right up to the waterfalls crashing onto the mossy rocks below. There are at least six swimming pools naturally heated by volcanic waters.

The architecture of Hidden Valley Springs is very rustic, comfortable and yet in harmony with the natural surrounding forest. Wood is the main element of the different structures. The floorings of the cottages, the furniture of the restaurants as well as the pathways are made from molave railroad tiles recovered from tracks no longer in use.

The individual deluxe cottages, with or without attics, are grouped in fours. These are completely white, roofed with slate shingles made to look like wood. Spacious terraces provided with benches and armchairs, open onto green lawns and the surrounding forest. The interior is a pleasing harmony of beige and off-white tones. The superb molave flooring, ceilings covered with abaca fibers and country-style furniture, make for a very cozy setting. In the deluxe rooms without an attic, the ceiling beams were enhanced with red apitong wood while the deluxe rooms with attics have a sloping ceiling; the attic is accessible via a wooden spiral staircase with wrought iron steps. The slatestone bathrooms are particularly original, with walls decorated with sculpted leaves.

The standard rooms have been recently renovated to highlight the rustic style of the lodgings and other common areas. Also, the corrugated iron roof of the restaurant was replaced with material more in harmony with the surroundings.

It is at the open-air pavilion restaurant that lunch is served under a beautiful bamboo trellis; the other meals are served in the enclosed pavilion nearby. The two restaurants have a country look with their red clay floors. This is even more accented with its plaited bamboo walls and the bronze, ceiling lamps. It has a nice bar in the basement with large picture windows that open onto the swimming pools below.

HIDDEN VALLEY SPRINGS

Alaminos, Laguna
Tel (0919) 540-1766

Booking Office in Makati
G/F Cattleya Gardens
111 Carlos Palanca Jr. Street
Legaspi Village, Makati City
Tel 840-4112 to 14
Fax 812-1609
Web asiatravel.com/philippines/
other/hiddenvalley

 By land (1½ hour) 75 km from Manila. Take South Superhighway and get off at Calamba, Exit No. 50A (Batangas, Lucena, Legaspi). Turn left when you see Junction Inn Mansion. When you reach the Y-shaped intersection, take the left lane going to Lucena City/Alaminos. Turn left when you see Rural Bank of Alaminos. Before the church of Alaminos, turn right and follow the Hidden Valley Springs signs.

 32 Units
10 Regular Casitas • 10 Deluxe Casitas • 2 Regular Cottages • 10 Deluxe Cottages
All rooms have air-conditioning and a bathroom with hot water. Deluxe rooms have a private veranda overlooking the garden.

Indoor Facilities and Services
Babysitting • Medical services • Gym • Sauna • Handicapped-friendly Rooms • Table tennis

 Food and Beverage Outlets
Open-air restaurant • Enclosed restaurant
Cuisine Offered: Filipino
Quality: Average

 Watersports and Other Activities
6 Swimming pools (with 2 kiddie pools) • Trekking • Volleyball • Hiking to the Hidden Falls (30 minutes)

 Per room per night on full board basis

Villa Escudero
Plantations and Resort

Villa Escudero Plantations and Resort, named after the family of the owners for two generations, is set in the pastoral framework of a coconut plantation of almost 800 hectares—still under cultivation today. At the entrance is a beautiful Spanish church with a pink façade. It houses a museum which displays the unusual collection of its original owner,

Dr. Escudero: Chinese pottery, religious *objets d'art* and relics from the Second World War.

Mr. Escudero endeavored to recreate the ambiance which reigned in a plantation of the early 19th century. Carabao-drawn carts with guitarists and singers take you to your lodgings. The cement statues scattered around the property, representing personalities of the time, are quite baffling.

The part making up the resort is well separated from the places visited by tourists during the day. Plaited bamboo is the main element of the interior decoration of the pleasant, rustic wood structures with *nipa* roofs.

Two types of lodgings are suitable for families. The apartment type lodgings are set next to the other, each room with a small terrace looking out onto the garden. The river units are more pleasant as these have a view of the river. These are large duplex cottages with nice terraces furnished with armchairs and hammocks. On the ground floor is the main room that has an impressively high ceiling. The beds are provided with mosquito nets. A door opening onto a small corridor leads to the shower, toilets, washbasin and a cup-board. There are two small rooms on the upper floor.

The resort has two swimming pools surrounded by vegetation. The one which overlooks the river, will enchant children as it has its own waterslide. Bamboo rafts make it possible to explore the river. The midday meals, taken in a pleasant setting by the waterfalls—with your feet in the water—is a rather strange activity. Be careful not to slip! You can take home a souvenir of this moment, as there is a professional photographer to take photos. The other meals are served in the Coconut Pavilion, a beautiful well-ventilated bamboo structure overlooking the river. It is also here that a well-presented cultural show is performed by the resort staff.

VILLA ESCUDERO PLANTATIONS AND RESORT

San Pablo City, Laguna

Booking Office in Manila
1059 Estrada Street, Malate, Manila
Tel   521-0830 • 523-0392
       523-2944
Fax   521-8698
E-mail vespar@vasia.com
Web   www.villaescudero.com

By land (2 hours) 91 km from Manila. Take South Superhighway and get off at Calamba, Exit No. 50A (Batangas, Lucena, Legaspi). Turn left when you see Junction Inn Mansion. When you reach the Y-shaped intersection, take the left lane going to Lucena City/Alaminos. Head straight down, passing the town of Alaminos and San Pablo City. After the 91 kilometer sign, you will see the Laguna–Quezon boundary arch. Immediately after, look for the Villa Escudero sign and make a U-turn as advised.

31 Units

12 Apartment type with attic (good for 6 persons) • 17 River Units in Duplex Cottages along the river with an attic composed of 2 rooms (good for 12 persons) • 2 Air-conditioned Units

All rooms are fan-cooled and have a bathroom with hot water and separate toilet. The main bedroom on the ground floor is provided with one double bed and one single bed. Mattresses can be added in the attic rooms.

Indoor Facilities and Services
Business center • Medical services • Shuttle service (jeepney) • Museum • Cultural show • Wedding center • Chapel • Billiards • Table tennis

Food and Beverage Outlets
Restaurants: Coconut Pavilion • Labasin Waterfalls (lunch only)
Cuisine Offered: Filipino
Quality: Average

Watersports and Other Activities
Swimming pools (with kiddie pool and Jacuzzi) • Bird watching • Bamboo rafting • Fishing • Carabao cart rides • Mountain biking • Hiking • Tennis • Volleyball

Per room per night on full board basis

Lagos Del Sol Resort

At an altitude of 300 meters, Lagos del Sol Resort on the edge of Lake Caliraya is a pleasant spot, often quite cool and windy, as the Pacific Ocean is not far away. As such, it is an ideal place for different water sports—jet skiing, kayaking, water skiing and sailing. Regular clients come to the Surf Camp where, unfortunately, there is no place for renting the necessary sports equipment. It is also an excellent starting point for the descent to the Pagsanjan river and a visit to the villages of Lumban, Paete and Lucban, which is famous for its Pahiyas Festival.

The route goes through the traffic jams of Calamba and Los Baños, and it is only from Pagsanjan that you begin to feel the country air. The route then goes up towards Caliraya, the last 10 kilometers winding through the forest-covered mountain, providing superb views of Laguna de Bay.

Lagos del Sol Resort offers a tour of the lake by speedboat and you can rent fishing rods and try your luck from the floating raft or from a speedboat, as the waters of the lake are abundant with fish. The resort is surrounded by forest and there is an introductory route to get to know the different tree varieties—narra, molave, bamboo, Benguet and Caraibes pines.

Two types of lodgings are offered: the Cabanas, bungalows with two connecting rooms and the Banahaw rooms in a two-story building.

The Cabanas, quite set apart, are on the edge of the lake or higher up among the trees. Mounted on stilts, they are completely made of wood with capiz windows and are extended by spacious terraces. The tile roof is the only element that seems out of place. In the evening, all you can hear is the crackling of the branches and the rustling of the leaves. The interior is warm: beautiful multi-toned brown wood flooring, well-finished pale bamboo furniture, plaited wicker walls and ceiling. The cabanas are in fact furnished with all modern comforts.

The Banahaw rooms are in a building on a slightly elevated level and are designed mainly to house seminar groups. While offering the same level of comfort as the Cabanas, they are more simply furnished and decorated. The rooms on the upper floors benefit from large terraces, some of which have a view of the lake.

The large restaurant, Sierra Madre Dining Hall, is bright and pleasant, with large picture windows opening onto the forest and the lake. It has a warm atmosphere; its decor is mainly wood and bamboo. The large swimming pool with a Jacuzzi is separated from the lake by a strip of lawn where there are some deck chairs, tents, tables and chairs.

LAGOS DEL SOL RESORT

Lake Caliraya, Cavinti, Laguna
Tel   (0919) 540-0758 • 68
        78 • 88 • 98

Booking Office in Manila
Aloha Hotel, 2150 Roxas
Boulevard corner Quirino Avenue,
Malate, Manila
Tel   523-1835
        526-8088 loc. 133 and 152
Fax   526-0687
E-mail *lagosresort@yahoo.com*
Web   *www.asiatravel.com/
        philippines/lagosdelsol*

By land (2½ hours) 110 km from Manila. **Through South Superhighway.** Take South Superhighway and get off at Calamba exit no. 50A (Batangas, Lucena, Legaspi). At Calamba Junction, turn right towards Los Baños all the way to Pagsanjan Church. At Pagsanjan Church, turn left, passing through Palacol Bridge, going toward Barangay Bagong Silang, then start the ascent to Caliraya Lake. **Through Rizal.** From Edsa, take Ortigas Ave. Turn right at the first intersection after the Cainta Junction, towards Taytay. Follow the main highway bound for Laguna; pass through the 8 municipalities of Rizal. Make a U-turn at Barangay Bagong Silang, Lumban to start the ascent to Caliraya Lake.

56 Units
24 Cabana Rooms (Lakeview or Non-Lakeview) • 22 Banahaw Rooms • 10 Makiling Rooms
All rooms except Makiling Rooms have air-conditioning, TV, refrigerator, intercom, and a bathroom with hot water.

Indoor Facilities and Services
Gym and fitness center • Sauna • Car rental • Game room • Billiards

Food and Beverage Outlets
Restaurants: Sierra Madre Dining Hall
Cuisine Offered: International • À la carte (limited choices)
Quality: Average, but the steaks are good.

Watersports and Other Activities
Swimming pool (with kiddie pool and Jacuzzi) • Island hopping • Canoeing • Kayaking • Other boats for hire (lake tour) • Jet skiing • Sunset cruise • Floating hut • Fishing rods for hire • Children's playground • Trekking • Tennis

🚣🚣🚣🚣🚣   Per room per night

Coral Beach Club

oral Beach Club is the resort closest to Manila with a white sand beach, albeit artificial, the Matabungkay Beach. It is frequented primarily by golfers. It was launched by the owners of Lago de Oro Beach Club and was passed on several years ago to its current owners, Canadian Michael Hudson, an avid golfer and his Filipina wife—Carla. Michael created a golf club and organizes competitions every weekend. The Calatagan Golf Club is only 15 minutes away from the resort.

The resort is in the middle of a green lawn with palm trees. It has a pleasant Mediterranean look with immaculate white walls contrasting with the capiz windows and *nipa* roof.

There are two room categories: deluxe and standard. The deluxe rooms are in two, two-story buildings with a view of the garden. The rooms upstairs are linked by a long exterior corridor but do not have private terraces. The white interiors of the rooms contrast with the well-polished ochre red floors, the plaited rattan furniture and the basketry. The standard rooms make up the three family rooms at the entrance of the resort near the restaurant, and the two individual bungalows along the swimming pool. These bungalows are more suited to couples and are decorated with a Japanese theme.

The restaurant is a well-ventilated bamboo structure with a *nipa* roof that practically extends all the way to the beach. There are deck chairs in the garden where you can relax facing the beach. There is also a swimming pool and Jacuzzi.

Matabungkay Beach becomes quite lively on Sundays when people come to rent the roofed floating rafts, tables and chairs for picnics. On these days, it is better to go to White Sands Beach for a more peaceful and quiet atmosphere. This beach is on the other side of Nasugbu, in the direction of Cavite, and is accessible in half-an-hour.

CORAL BEACH CLUB

Matabungkay Beach,
Lian, Batangas
Tel　(0917) 901-4635
E-mail　admin@coralbeach.ph
Web　www.coralbeach.ph

By land (2 ½ hours) 110 km from Manila. Take South Superhighway and get off at Santa Rosa, Exit No. 40. After the market of Tagaytay, turn right when you reach Tagaytay Ridge. At the Tagaytay Rotonda, go straight and follow the direction of Nasugbu. After the kilometer 92 sign, turn right to Nasugbu and Lian. At the Shell gas station, turn left to Lian and Calatagan. Continue through Calatagan until you see the sign for Matabungkay Beach Resort and Hotel. Turn right. Proceed 1.5 kilometers and turn right on the cement road. Coral Beach Club is on your left side after you have gone 500 meters from the last turn you made.

20 Units
6 Standard Rooms (3 rooms good for two persons; 3 rooms good for four with one double bed and two single beds) • 14 Deluxe Rooms (good for three persons with 1 double bed and 1 single bed)
All rooms have a bathroom with hot water, air-conditioning, fan and satellite TV (except for standard rooms which only have local channels).

Indoor Facilities and Services
Gym • Billiards • TV/Video room • Library

Food and Beverage Outlets
Restaurant/bar
Cuisine Offered: Filipino • European
Quality: Good

Watersports and Other Activities
Swimming pool with Jacuzzi • Beach (white sand) • Fishing • Boats for hire • Golf arrangements in Calatagan Golf Course • Children's playground

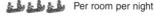　Per room per night

Lago De Oro Beach Club

Located not far from the tip of the Calatagan Peninsula, Lago de Oro Beach Club is under combined German, Australian and Filipino management. The present owners of Lago de Oro are not first-timers, as they had previously launched the Coral Beach Resort.

The route from Manila traverses coffee and pineapple plantations before the Tagaytay Ridge that overlooks Taal Lake, sugarcane fields near Nasugbu and fish breeding stations, and rice fields near the resort. Lago de Oro Beach Club is in the middle of the countryside facing the sea. It is a peaceful area, far from any construction, where you can spot the mountains in the background. It has a nice garden shaded by palm trees. Mangroves fringe the slightly muddy sea. At low tide, it recedes quite far off and uncovers a vast stretch of dark sand. These do not make for favorable swimming, but children will love to discover the marine life that collects in the shallow pools—striped multicolored worms, sea cucumbers, hermit crabs and starfish. They will enjoy the bullock-cart rides on the beach, offered free of charge by the resort. A seashell peddler offers beautiful shells at bargain prices.

The rooms are in two, two-story Mediterranean-style buildings with white façades, multiple arcades and pink tile roofs. The building near the swimming pool houses 26 rooms with a view of the sea from the terrace.

The interiors are remarkably well kept, bright, spacious and comfortable, with pale rattan furniture and marble bathrooms. There is a harmony of colors between the gray marble floors and the pastel shades of the fabrics. The other building, on the right as you enter the compound, has eight rooms whose balconies look out onto the fish breeding ponds and the countryside. These are family rooms that are absolutely functional. The interior is spacious and simple with tile flooring and ordinary wood furniture.

The restaurant is pleasant, with large picture windows, beautiful wrought iron and wicker furniture, and a circular, open-air terrace. It is possible to have dinner in the tent set up in the garden.

LAGO DE ORO BEACH CLUB

Balibago, Calatagan, Batangas
Tel (0917) 504-2685
Tel/Fax (043) 921-1617
E-mail
lago-de-oro@westlink.com.ph
Web *www.lago-de-oro.com*

By land (2 ½ hours) 115 km from Manila. Take South Superhighway and get off at Santa Rosa, Exit No. 40. After the market of Tagaytay, turn right, when you reach Tagaytay Ridge. At the Tagaytay Rotonda go straight and follow the direction of Nasugbu. After the kilometer 92 sign, turn right to Nasugbu and Lian. After the Shell gas station turn left to Lian and Calatagan. Continue through Calatagan until you reach kilometer 115. Turn right when you see the Lago de Oro sign. This is the access road to the resort.

26 Units
26 Rooms in two two-story buildings All rooms have air-conditioning, minibar, and bathroom with hot water, private patio.

Indoor Facilities and Services
Massage • Babysitting • Taxi rental • Game room • TV/Video room • Library • Billiards • Table tennis

Food and Beverage Outlets
Restaurant and bar (wines and cocktails)
Cuisine Offered: International • Italian • Filipino • Seafood
Quality: Good

Watersports and Other Activities
Swimming pool (with kiddie pool and Jacuzzi) • Beach (brown sand) • Cable waterski (the only one in the Philippines) • Island hopping (with barbecue) • Paddle boating • Fishing • Dive center • Golf arrangements in Calatagan Golf Course • Volleyball • Children's playground • Carabao rides

Per room per night

The Farm at San Benito

The Farm at San Benito, nestled at the foot of Mount Malarayat on the outskirts of Lipa City, sits amidst 47 hectares of lush fragrant greens, serene ponds and well manicured lawns. The spa resort was conceptualized and conceived in 2001 or 2002 primarily as the country's first alternative medical center that employs non-traditional healing techniques.

Upon entering the Farm, one is immediately enveloped by nature, green as far as the eyes can see. Visitors will notice that much thought has been placed into the landscaping of the South East Asian-inspired structures. All the facilities, be it the reception hall, the restaurant, library, spa, gym or villas, open up into the outdoors, maintaining a calming balance between human comfort and nature.

From the reception, guests instantly get a taste of the architecture used throughout, contemporary South East Asian. The health resort can accommodate up to 55 clients only. The Farm has a choice of 5 different kinds of accommodations, each differing in style, size and price: the Anahaw Villas, the Garden Villas, the Sulu Terraces, the Palmera Suites and a Master Villa. All rooms are fully air-conditioned, well-maintained and appointed, feeling cozy but not cramped. Each Garden Villa has a round bath tub in its own private garden out back. The Sulu Terraces, designed after rice huts of the Southern Philippines, have an open seating area on the ground floor. The Palmera Suites' shower opens up into the sky. The Anahaw Villas, the only ones that can accommodate more than three occupants, feature a loft with two beds that look out into the sky via the skylight. The Master Villa, only available through special arrangement, comes with an indoor garden and its own pool.

Guests venturing out through winding paths into the tropical gardens discover quaint little meditation corners scattered about in strategic places. Two of them stand out: an open *nipa* hut in the middle of the large pond by a sky-high, geyser-like fountain and a cozy deck lined with cushions, blanketed by a curtain of hanging vines by the Waterfall Pool.

The sole restaurant is the 85/15 Gourmet Restaurant, which serves all vegetarian fare and is a vital part of the whole wellness philosophy of the Farm. "85/15" refers to the food being served 85% raw and 15% cooked. The food here may very well dispel any notions that eating healthy is bland and boring. Indian samosas, Mexican burritos, five-layer quiche and non-dairy chocolate ice-cream are some of the delectable and often surprising flavors and aromas. The restaurant offers set meals which includes buffet breakfasts, 5-course lunches and 3-course dinners as well as *à la carte* dishes and numerous fruit drinks. The portions are large and filling.

Different wellness packages, from day trips to multiple-week health stays and detox programs, are available, the most popular being the Overnight Wellness Package which includes overnight accommodations, three meals, a live blood analysis, an hour's massage and a foot scrub or reflexology. Room-only arrangements are also available.

THE FARM AT SAN BENITO

119 Barangay Tipakan,
Lipa City, Batangas
Tel 696-3795
Tel/Fax 696-3175

Booking Office in Makati
Azalea Room, Mezzanine Floor,
The Mandarin Oriental Hotel
Makati Avenue, Makati City
Tel 751-3498
750-8888 loc. 72428
Tel/Fax 751-3497
E-mail info@thefarm.com.ph
Web www.thefarm.com.ph

 By land (2 hours) From Manila, take the South Superhighway and get off at Calamba Exit no. 50A. Down the road, turn right to the Star Tollway and get off at the Lipa/Tambo Exit at the end of the expressway and head towards Lipa City. Gear left at the fork with a Mc Donald's, and make a right when you see Max's Restaurant to your left. Turn left at A. Bonifacio Street, another left to Latag Study Camp, right to Barangay San Jose, left at Nicetas Katigbak sign, and finally a right by a telephone post to get to the Farm. There are signs to guide you once you get into Lipa City. The Farm also offers a shuttle service to and from Manila which can be arranged through their Makati booking office.

 25 Units
5 Sulu Terraces • 10 Palmera Suites • 3 Anahaw Villas • 6 Garden Villas • 1 Master Villa
All rooms are air-conditioned with private baths.

Indoor Facilities and Services
Massage/Therapies • Yoga/Meditation • Library • Gym

 Food and Beverage Outlets
85/15 Gourmet Restaurant
Cuisine Offered: Gourmet Vegetarian
Quality: Excellent

 Watersports and Other Activities
Swimming pools

 Per room per night on full board basis

Note: *Smoking is not allowed anywhere in The Farm. Bringing of food or snacks is also not allowed. Book at least two weeks in advance.*

Eagle Point Resort

Eagle Point is a dive resort managed by Filipinos and Americans. Leaning against wooded hills, it is set on three levels of very steep terrain, which it hugs unevenly at various points. All the rooms therefore have a view of the sea.

The biggest accomplishment of the resort is the main building, a superb, multi-leveled wooden structure housing the reception area, the restaurant, and the playroom. The restaurant and bar face the sea—in a huge and impressive room with exposed beams wrapped with corded rope. The tables are arranged along the length of the bay windows so that you can enjoy a view of the sea from any spot.

The Nipa Huts are perched high up on the property. They are a bit cramped, but have a fairly large, brightly-tiled bathroom and a small balcony.

The duplex and individual cottages are located below. These cottages, made of wood, including the roof's mossy panels, have a pleasing, rustic exterior. However, apart from the fine treatment on the ceiling, no effort has been made in decorating the interiors as the rough wooden furniture is not at all attractive. The rooms are spacious enough and comfortable with marble bathrooms and private balconies. The individual cottages have a little drawing room and two rooms, but are less spacious and not as bright than those of the duplex cottages.

On the neighboring islands of Sombrero and Maricaban, it is possible to dive and snorkel. Eagle Point has its own diving club that is quite expensive. You can also snorkel in front of the resort, but the reef is not that remarkable.

There is no sand beach at Anilao but the resort has two superb swimming pools: the Reef Pool, where you can swim among sharks, tortoise, and angel fish, and a freshwater swimming pool, with two levels linked by a slide, which is a great joy for children. The resort also has a walk-through aviary where you can observe *kalaws*, parrots and eagles.

EAGLE POINT RESORT

Bagalangit, Mabini, Batangas
Tel   (043) 986-0177
       (0917) 518-2568

Booking Office in Makati
G/F Summer Set Millennium
104 Aquino St. Legaspi Vill., Makati
Tel   813-3553
Tel/Fax 813-3560
E-mail *rsvm@eaglepoint.com.ph*
Web   *www.eaglepoint.com.ph*

By land (3 hours) 140 km from Manila. There are two possible routes, both accessible via South Superhighway. The **faster route** is to get off at Calamba, Exit No. 50A to Lucena. From the toll booth you have to reset the odometer counter to zero and follow the odometer readings. At 10.5 kilometers, turn right to the Star Tollway, to Batangas, get off at Lipa/Tambo exit at the end of the expressway. At 32.8 kilometers turn left to Batangas, 36.4 kilometers turn right to Cuenca/Alitagtag Road, 50 kilometer turn right (Landmark: Caltex Gas Station), 53.1 kilometers turn left to Bauan, 54.2 kilometers turn left to Bauan/Batangas City, 61 kilometers turn right to Mabini, 69.9 kilometers turn right to Anilao, 71.5 kilometers turn left to Barrio Bagalangit, 80.3 kilometers turn right to Eagle Point private road. The **more scenic route** is to get off at Sta. Rosa, Exit No. 40 and pass by Tagaytay and Lemery before reaching Batangas.

Note: *Transfer from Manila can be arranged by the resort.*

23 Units
16 One-bedroom Cottages • 1 Two-bedroom Cottage • 4 Executive Rooms • 2 Cabanas (non-air-conditioned cottages)
All rooms have air-conditioning (except for Cabanas), a bathroom, and private balconies all of which have seaside view.

Indoor Facilities and Services
Masseuse service • 24-hour stand-by generator • Car rental • Game room • Table tennis • Video room • Billiards

Food and Beverage Outlets
Cuisine Offered: Filipino • Continental • Seafood
Quality: Good
Bar: Col. Grimm's Bar

Watersports and Other Activities
Split-level swimming pools • Salt-water reef pool • Snorkeling (in front of the resort) • Island hopping to Sombrero and Maricaban Islands • Jet skiing • Diving • Dive center • Kayaking • Other boats for hire • Walk-thru aviary • Butterfly park • Children's playground

Per room per night
inclusive of breakfast

Bonito Island Resort

T his wooded five-and-half-hectare island, encircled by a golden sandy beach lined with coconut tress, is a little paradise for divers and lovers of peace and quiet. Bonito Island is on the eastern tip of Maricaban Island, midway between Batangas and Puerto Galera. At certain times of the year, particularly between November and February, the 45-minute *banca* trip can be quite bumpy and should be avoided if you have children traveling with you.

Before becoming a resort in the 1970s, the island—also known as Culebra Island—was the holiday home of its owner, Conrad C. Leviste (CCL), a dive enthusiast. The place progressively acquired a reputation among the diving clubs which became instrumental in convincing him to transform his home into a dive resort.

The resort offers lodgings either in the main building or in duplex cottages. The main building, known as the Long House, is a tile-roofed bamboo structure with five rooms in a row, linked by a common balcony facing the beach. It is also here that the terrace restaurant is located. The cottages have two rooms and are convenient for families.

CCL and Mabuhay cottages are nicely facing the sea. CCL is a cement structure with a *nipa* roof. Its interior is warm and comfortable, the bamboo walls contrasting with the marble floor. A sliding door separates the two bedrooms which is perfect for a family. A private balcony opens onto the sea. The last cottage is slightly off the beach.

The beach which encircles the island is enticing. One part near the main building is a wonderful area for snorkeling as the water is shallow and clear. Before venturing out to sea, be wary of the strong currents.

At the end of the afternoon, do not miss the chance to admire the sunset from the summit of the hill. In the evening, after diving, it is nice to have a drink at the bar facing the illuminated coastline of Batangas.

There are two dive sites at the nearby islands of Bonito and Malajibomanoc (*chicken feather*). The latter, also a good snorkeling site, has hot water springs 20 meters deep. Further on are two dive sites on Verde Island. You can also go there by speedboat for a half-day picnic to Malajibo-manoc or to Masasa, a beautiful white sand beach on Maricaban Island.

Note: *In case Bonito Island Resort is fully booked, try Pisa Divers Lodge on Maricaban Island. It is a small, unassuming diving resort managed by Paul Evans, an authority on diving. A former British marine soldier, Paul fought during the Falklands and Kuwait wars. You can contact him via e-mail:* paul@divepro.com.ph.

BONITO ISLAND RESORT

Bonito (Culebra) Island, Barangay Pisa, Tingloy, Mabini, Batangas

Booking Office in Makati
2/F LPL Mansions
122 L.P. Leviste Street,
Salcedo Village, Makati City
Tel   812-2292 • 94 • 95
         818-8064 • 894-0640
         818-5364
Fax   818-9754

By land and sea (4 hours)
Three hours by car from Manila to Mainaga pier in Mabini (near Batangas Harbor). From Manila there are two possible routes, both accessible via South Superhighway. The **faster route** is to get off at Calamba, Exit No. 50A, to Lucena, turn right to the Star Tollway, to Batangas, get off at Lipa/Tambo exit at the end of the expressway, turn left to Batangas. The **more scenic route** is to get off at Sta. Rosa, Exit No. 40, and pass by Tagaytay and Lemery before reaching Batangas Harbor. To reach Mainaga pier in Mabini, proceed through Bauan and after the 144 kilometers sign, turn right to Petron Terminal Mabini. Mainaga pier is near Petron's terminal. It is 45 minutes from Mainaga pier to Bonito Island by *banca*.

Note: *Transfer from Batangas Harbor is arranged by the resort.*

10 Units
6 Fan Rooms • 4 Beachfront Cottages (with air-conditioning)
All rooms have a private bathroom without hot water.

Food and Beverage Outlets
Open-air restaurant
Cuisine Offered: Filipino • Seafood Grill
Quality: Average

Watersports and Other Activities
Beach (white sand) • Snorkeling (by the resort) • Dive center • Island hopping • Kayaking • Other boats for hire • Fishing • Sunset cruise • Trekking

 Per room per night for 2 persons on full board basis including banca transfer from Batangas Harbor

Note: *Cash payment only. Special package for divers.*

Northern Luzon

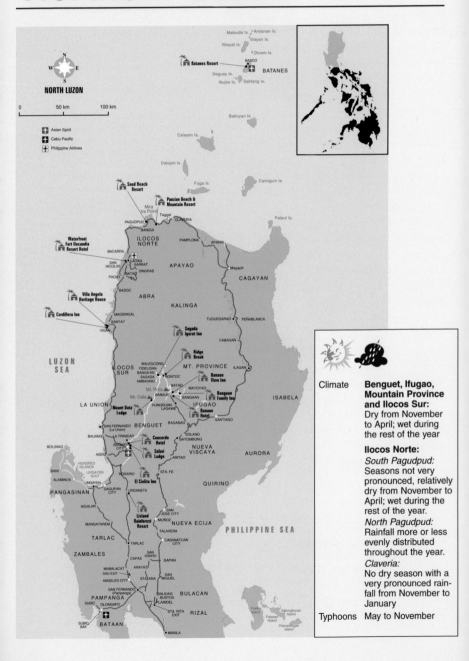

NORTH LUZON

0   50 km   100 km

✚ Asian Spirit
✚ Cebu Pacific
✚ Philippine Airlines

Mabudis Is. • Amianan Is.
Itbayat Is. • Siayan Is.
• Dinem Is.
BASCO
Batanes Resort ✚ BATANES
Deguey Is.
Ibujos Is. • Sabtang Is.

Babuyan Is.

Calayan Is.

Dalupiri Is.

Fuga Is.   Camiguin Is.

Palaui Is.

Saud Beach Resort
Panzian Beach & Mountain Resort
Mira Ira Point
PAGUDPUD   Taggat
BANGUI   CLAVERIA
Waterfront Fort Ilocandia Resort Hotel
ILOCOS NORTE   PAMPLONA   APARRI
BACARRA
LAOAG   SARRAT
SAN NICOLAS   BATAC   DINGRAS   Magapit
PAOAY   CAGAYAN
BADOC
Villa Angela Heritage House
ABRA   KALINGA
Cordillera Inn   MAGSINGAL
BANTAY   TUGUEGARAO • PEÑABLANCA
VIGAN
Sagada Igorot Inn   CABAGAN
Ridge Brook
LUZON SEA
MALEGCONG   MT. PROVINCE   ILAGAN
ILOCOS SUR   FIDELISAN
BANGA'AN   BONTOC
SAGADA   BANAUE
AMBASING   Banaue View Inn
BATAD
Mt. Polis   BANAUE   MAYOYAO   Banaan Family Inn
Mt. Data   BANGAAN
Mount Data Lodge   HUNGDUAN   IFUGAO   ISABELA
LA UNION   LAGAWE   Banaue Hotel
BAGABAG   SANTIAGO
SAN FERNANDO (La Union)   BENGUET
BAUANG   LA TRINIDAD
BOLINAO   BAGUIO CITY   Concorde Hotel   SOLANO
AGOO   Safari Lodge   BAYOMBONG
NUEVA VISCAYA   AURORA
BANI   HUNDRED ISLANDS   ARITAO
ALAMINOS   LINGAYEN GULF   ROSARIO
LINGAYEN   El Cielito Inn   STA. FE   QUIRINO
PANGASINAN   DAGUPAN CITY   URDANETA
AGUILAR   SAN JOSE CITY
Lislan Rainforest Resort   MUNOZ   NUEVA ECIJA
MANGATAREM   TALAVERA   PHILIPPINE SEA
TARLAC   CABANATUAN CITY
TARLAC   SAN ISIDRO
CAPAS   GAPAN
ZAMBALES   MABALACAT   ARAYAT
DAU EXIT   SAN MIGUEL
ANGELES CITY   STA. ANA
SAN FERNANDO (Pampanga)   BALIUAG   BUSTOS
PAMPANGA   PLARIDEL
SUBIC   OLONGAPO   BULACAN
SUBIC BAY   STA. RITA EXIT   RIZAL
BATAAN   MANILA
Polilio Island
Kalinghokan Island
Patnanungan Island
Palasan Island

Climate

Benguet, Ifugao, Mountain Province and Ilocos Sur: Dry from November to April; wet during the rest of the year

Ilocos Norte:
South Pagudpud: Seasons not very pronounced, relatively dry from November to April; wet during the rest of the year.
North Pagudpud: Rainfall more or less evenly distributed throughout the year.
Claveria: No dry season with a very pronounced rainfall from November to January

Typhoons May to November

Hundred Islands and the Province of Pangasinan

On a long weekend, a visit to the province of Pangasinan, 250 kilometers from Manila, may be combined with a trip to Ilocos. Known especially for its Hundred Islands National Park, this is a nice region whose jagged, wild coastline of black sand is fringed with swamps, marshes and fish breeding areas.

As there may be no attractive resort in the area close to the Hundred Islands, it is advisable to stay at the Lisland Rainforest, a little oasis of greenery in the town of Urdaneta.

The Hundred Islands National Park

The Gulf of Lingayen is punctuated with a chain of dark and sharply eroded coral islets — the Hundred Islands. These islets are accessible in 20 minutes by *banca* from the Lucap Pier, a few kilometers from Alaminos. The regular tourist itinerary involves a visit to Governor's Island, Quezon's Island and Children's Island. This tour takes about five hours but can be shortened if you wish. Snorkeling is possible in the area, but the reef is quite damaged.

UMBRELLA ROCKS (*Sabangan beach at Agno, 26 kilometers from Alaminos, 1 hour*) The black sandy beach of Sabangan may be somewhat disconcerting. A rocky layer covers it at certain places with deep, narrow crevices where sea worms thrive. But the highlight of the excursion is the sight of the limestone rocks on the beach resembling umbrellas, as these are extremely eroded at the base. En route, you can visit the 18th-century Agno Church.

BOLINAO (*36 kilometers from Alaminos, 1 hour*) A little archaeological museum presents 11th-century artifacts recovered from excavations done in the region. You can visit the impressive church built in 1609—its façade is well-preserved and the interiors are evocative of Aztec art.

Hundred Islands

Lisland Rainforest Resort

The Lisland Rainforest Resort is the perfect stopover on the long trip to Vigan. It is also the jump-off point for discovering the Hundred Islands National Park, which is just one hour away. There is no other hotel with such charm in the immediate vicinity of the national park.

After leaving the congested roads of Manila, you will be surprised to find this oasis of greenery and calm in the heart of the noisy town of Urdaneta.

The resort is in fact built on the remains of an old patch of rainforest—many trees as possible were saved during its construction. According to its owners, staunch protectors of the environment, about 788 adult trees still remain in the property.

The highlight of the hotel is the large swimming pool surrounding the main building like a bluish lagoon reflecting the silhouette of the trees. What a pleasure to take a dip in its cool waters! You can relax in deck chairs, listening only to the sound of birds that inhabit the little forest.

The main building, a nice structure with bay windows, houses the reception area and conference halls. The cottages are built only on one part of the property, in the middle of a green lawn. Painted entirely in white, these are tastefully decorated and are furnished with all the required comforts.

The pleasant, well-furnished restaurant is in a large building opening directly onto the swimming pool and the garden.

LISLAND RAINFOREST RESORT

182 San Vicente,
MacArthur Highway,
Urdaneta City, Pangasinan
Tel   (075) 568-2962
Fax   (075) 568-2938
E-mail *lisland_resort@hotmail.com*
            inquiries@lisland.com.ph

Booking Office in Parañaque
#6 Second Street, Villamar Court,
Tambo, Parañaque City
Tel   851-6531
Fax   852-8777
E-mail *mulawin@manila-online.net*
Web   *www.lisland.com.ph*

 By land (4 hours) 182 km from Manila. Take North Expressway at Balintawak and get off at exit. Take the North Diversion Road to MacArthur Highway. You pass by Angeles City and Tarlac, before reaching Pangasinan Province where Urdaneta is located.

 24 Units
6 Deluxe Rooms • 1 Deluxe Family Room • 5 Family Rooms • 12 Standard Rooms
All rooms have air-conditioning, a bathroom with hot water and cable TV. A minibar is provided in all rooms except in the standard rooms.

Indoor Facilities and Services
Car rental • Reflexology • Ballroom dancing lessons • Billiards • Table tennis • Aviary

 Food and Beverage Outlets
Cuisine Offered: Filipino • Continental
Quality: Familial

 Watersports and Other Activities
Swimming pools (with kiddie pool) • Children's playground • Swimming lessons

Note: *For excursions, see Pangasinan Province's points of interest.*

 Per room per night inclusive of breakfast

Baguio

Baguio is nestled in the middle of the Cordilleras, in the province of Benguet. The city was designed at the beginning of the 20th century by the American architect Daniel Burnham as a gateway for Americans burdened by the tropical heat. He favored green patches, which probably explains the delightful Burnham Park.

Monotony and tedium accompany you for the first seven hours of the eight-hour journey from Manila. Fortunately the last hour on Kennon Road is more rewarding: a well-maintained winding road allows the eyes to feast on a spectacular view of the mountains... despite their rather deforested slopes. You must check beforehand that the road has not collapsed and been cut off. Baguio is also accessible via Naguilian Road and Marcos Highway.

Baguio does not boast of any remarkable monument as it was destroyed successively by the Japanese in 1941, and by an earthquake in 1990. However, the pine-covered hills, parks, and the fresh mountain air—a stark contrast to the warm humidity of the capital—create an atmosphere hard to resist. The average temperature is 20 degrees and at night, the allure of a lighted fireplace and warm blankets are not at all unpleasant. Baguio, moreover, is the center of the region; a dynamic town with a university and even an international school, Brent School.

It is simply pleasant to take walks. A leisurely stroll along Session Road—the most animated street where most of the shops and restaurants are located—is enough to give you a feel of the town.

BAGUIO MARKET (*Magsaysay Avenue*) It is an extraordinary market where you can walk for hours through the stalls. Every aisle has its own specialty: flowers, meat, fish, rice, eggs, tobacco, jam, vegetables, fruits, fabrics, shoes. There is even an aisle specializing only in strawberries beautifully presented in pyramids or in little baskets. The market is open everyday.

THE MAHARLIKA CENTER Just beside the market, there are handicraft stalls, specializing in wood sculptures, silver jewelry, and baskets—all at very attractive prices. As it is in every market, it is necessary to be vigilant as theft can be an occurrence.

THE SAINT LOUIS UNIVERSITY Near the cathedral is a silversmith school run by Belgian nuns. The silver filigree work, a specialty of the region, cost nearly half the prices they fetch in Manila.

WOODWORK You will find a lot of wood sculptures and rustic furniture—a number quite similar to one another, although there are also originally-designed pieces. Some are also made from roots with astonishing shapes. These are sold by vendors along Asin Road, as well by shops in the city and at the market.

EASTER WEAVING SCHOOL Weavers work can be observed on Eastern Road, 20 minutes from the center of the city. Baguio is well-known for its weavework with designs ranging from ethnic to modern. You can buy these fabrics in the market as well as in other shops such as Narda's handicraft in Upper Session Road, which likewise has a workshop.

RESTAURANTS AND CAFÉS Do not miss having a drink or a delicious meal at the Café by the Ruins on Chuntug Street—an artists' café filled with charm, largely exposed to the outdoors and built on the ruins of an old house. Tasty Igorot cuisine is served here. Other restaurants are Barrio Fiesta, Star Café on Session Road, and Rose Bowl on Harrison Street. In the evening, you can listen to country music at Wild West on Chanum Street.

You have a choice among several comfortable lodgings. If you are lucky enough to know a member of the Baguio Country Club or of Club John Hay, it is easy to be sponsored and have a room. These two places are arguably the most pleasant in town, with vast gardens and golf and tennis courts. It is a pity that Club John Hay, previously open to the public, has now opted for a members-only policy.

Baguio Market

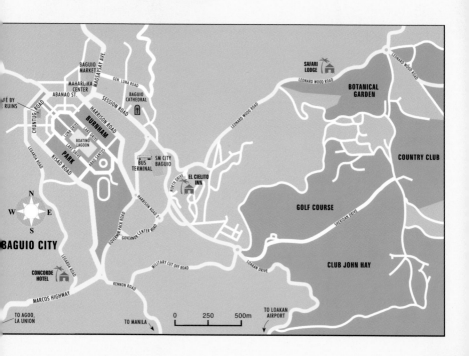

Concorde Hotel

The Concorde Hotel is in the hills, in a pleasant neighborhood on the outskirts of the town center. The large five-story brick building is well constructed, its red roofs emerging from the pine trees. The common areas are very congenial with superb dark, well-polished wooden floors, rustic furniture, statues and Ifugao basketry decorating the corridors of the different floors.

On the first floor, at the back of the reception area, is a large window-paned bar where a pianist plays in the evening. Also located here are the two restaurants of the hotel: a Chinese restaurant and the Denise Café. The latter has a warm atmosphere with its red terracotta tile floor, wood-beamed ceilings and its terrace with hanging plants and orchids. It has the added attraction of being open 24 hours a day.

A glass-enclosed elevator goes up to the labyrinth of corridors which lead to the rooms. The 138 rooms which make up the hotel are comfortable, although the furnishings differ, depending on the categories.

The Standard Rooms are not recommended as they don't have windows, only high slots directly opening onto the corridor which can be quite noisy. It is better to reserve a room at the back of the hotel, far from the bar, as the rooms are not soundproof.

The Classic Rooms are the best choice although these are more expensive than the Standard Rooms. More welcoming and cheerful, these rooms have French windows opening onto a pleasant wooden balcony with a view of the pine trees.

You also have to take a look at the Honeymoon Suite just for curiosity sake. It is furnished with beautiful antique furniture, including an impressive wood and red-brick alcove over the bed.

CONCORDE HOTEL

Europa Center, Legarda Road, Baguio City
Tel (074) 443-2058
Fax (074) 443-2060 • 61
E-mail concorde@mozcom.com
Web
www2.mozcom.com/~concorde

 By land (7–8 hours) 250 km from Manila via Kennon Road. Victory Liner (Tel. No.: 833-5019) has a terminal in Pasay City along Epifanio delos Santos Avenue (EDSA) for hourly departures in the morning. By car, take North Expressway at Balintawak and get off at Dau exit. Pass by Tarlac, Urdaneta, and Pozorrubio. Before reaching Rosario, take the junction to Baguio (Kennon Road).

Note: *If Kennon Road is not passable due to landslides, there are two other routes going to Baguio: Marcos Highway, accessible from Agoo, La Union or Naguilian Road, accessible from Bauang, also in La Union. Asian Spirit flies occasionally to Baguio. Check airline schedules.*

 148 Units
49 Standard Rooms (without a window) • 27 Superior Rooms • 51 Classic Rooms • 12 Deluxe Suite Rooms • 9 Suite Royale Rooms
All rooms have toilet bathrooms, cable TV, international access telephone, hairdryer (upon request) and a pullout bed.

Indoor Facilities and Services
Business center • Facial center • Car rental • Massage (by expert blind masseurs)

 Food and Beverage Outlets
Restaurants: Denise Café • Kingswood Villa • Hanasusi Restaurant
Cuisine Offered: Continental • Chinese • Japanese
Quality: Average
Bars: Symphony Bar (Pianist playing nightly) • Shadow Disco

 Watersports and Other Activities
City Tours
See Baguio's points of interest.

 Per room per night

Safari Lodge

S afari Lodge, set from the road on Leonard Wood Street, nestles high among the pine trees. This three-story stone house brings to mind a big mountain chalet.

The place was once a former residence. In contrast to the other modern hotels in Baguio, it is still full of traces of its past, a characteristic that gives it a particular charm. As the proprietor was once a dedicated amateur safari hunter in Africa, you will be surprised to discover that the big reception area is decorated with stuffed animals, some of which are quite unusual to the region: a lion, water buffaloes, and rhinoceros, alongside deer and birds. The room, a bit dark in the daytime, has beautiful, sparkling floors and high, wood-beamed ceilings. A magnificent fireplace at the end of the room is framed by two huge elephant tusks. The reception area is extended on one side by a veranda opening onto a garden and on the other by a glass patio opening onto a garden court. Meals are served in either area.

You enjoy an intimate atmosphere due to the limited number of rooms. Spacious and bright, the comfortable rooms are simply furnished and have a pleasant view of the pine forest. The blue and white tiled bathrooms are likewise big and pleasant. The apartments, suitable for groups, have the added advantage of a drawing room with a fireplace.

SAFARI LODGE

191 Leonard Wood Road,
Baguio City
Tel/Fax (074) 442-2419
Web www.safaribaguio.com

Booking Office in Parañaque
43 Florida Street, Merville Park,
Parañaque City
Tel 824-7388

By land (7–8 hours) 250 km from Manila via Kennon Road. Victory Liner (Tel. No.: 833-5019) has a terminal in Pasay City along Epifanio delos Santos Avenue (EDSA) for hourly departures in the morning. By car, take the North Expressway at Balintawak and get off at Dau exit. Pass by Tarlac, Urdaneta, and Pozorrubio. Before reaching Rosario, take the junction to Baguio (Kennon Road).

Note: *If Kennon Road is not passable due to landslides, there are two other routes going to Baguio: Marcos Highway, accessible from Agoo, La Union or Naguilian Road, accessible from Bauang, also in La Union. Asian Spirit flies occasionally to Baguio. Check airline schedules.*

10 Units
7 Family Rooms • 3 Standard Rooms All rooms are equipped with their own private baths with hot water. Additional mattress at P150.00 each.

Food and Beverage Outlets
Restaurant
Cuisine Offered: Filipino

Watersports and Other Activities
See Baguio's points of interest.

Per room per night

Note: *There are two other hotels on Leonard Wood Road: **Munsayac Inn,** Tel. No.: (074) 442-2451 and **Mountain Lodge,** Tel. No.: (074) 442-4544. These are more modest and cheaper, also in large houses with a pleasant family atmosphere.*

El Cielito Inn

El Cielito Inn is in a quiet area, set a little higher on one of the hills of Baguio. The three-story building housing the hotel is an assembly of pink cubes and rectangles, quite in disharmony with the surrounding area, but in terms of comfort and value for money, it is the best establishment in town.

The hotel is well-maintained, not surprising as its manager and the chef were formerly with the Hyatt Hotel that used to be in the area.

The reception area is pleasant and welcoming with comfortable sofas set in a décor blending wood, stone, red tile flooring, and green plants. At the end of the room, a bay window looks out into a little patio filled with bushy bamboo.

The rooms are on the upper floors and have views either of the road or the flagstoned interior patio adorned with some plants. All the rooms are quite comfortable, with marble bathrooms. The modern, functional furniture is pleasing; the décor in shades of pink, peach, and pale green is restful. The suites and deluxe rooms have a small veranda. The elegant apartments, ideal for families, have two bedrooms, a kitchen and a bathroom.

The restaurant on the ground floor is very bright due to the big bay windows that look out onto the street and the stained-glass ceiling. Its setting is luxurious, a blending of warm tones, from the inlay of the floor to the yellow-gold walls.

EL CIELITO INN

#50 North Drive, Engineer's Hill, Baguio City

Tel	(074) 250-6020
	(074) 443-2134
	(074) 443-5272
	(074) 443-4846
Tel/Fax	(074) 442-8743

Booking Office in Makati
804 Arnaiz Avenue (Pasay Road), San Lorenzo Village, Makati City

Tel	815-8951
Fax	817-9610
E-mail	stay@elcielitoinn.com
Web	www.elcielitoinn.com

By land (7–8 hours) 250 km from Manila via Kennon Road. Victory Liner (Tel. No.: 833-5019) has a terminal in Pasay City along Epifanio delos Santos Avenue (EDSA) for hourly departures in the morning. By car, take North Expressway at Balintawak and get off at Dau exit. Pass by Tarlac, Urdaneta, and Pozorrubio. Before reaching Rosario, take the junction to Baguio (Kennon Road).

Note: *If Kennon Road is not passable due to landslides, there are two other routes going to Baguio: Marcos Highway, accessible from Agoo, La Union or Naguilian Road, accessible from Bauang, also in La Union. Asian Spirit flies occasionally to Baguio. Check airline schedules.*

32 Units
11 Standard Rooms • 17 Deluxe Rooms (with TV) • 2 Superior Rooms (with TV and refrigerator) • 2 Apartelles (good for 4 to 6, with TV, refrigerator and kitchen) All rooms have a bathroom with hot water and telephone.

Note: *No elevator.*

Indoor Facilities and Services
Foreign currency exchange

Food and Beverage Outlets
Restaurant: Voyager Restaurant
Cuisine Offered: Filipino • International
Quality: Good

Watersports and Other Activities
City/Countryside tour
See Baguio's points of interest.

Per room per night inclusive of breakfast

Mount Data Lodge

The Mount Data region, about 100 kilometers north of Baguio, forms part of the Mountain Province. It is a relief to arrive at the Mount Data Lodge after an exhausting four-hour journey from Baguio or the two-and-a-half hour drive from Bontoc. The path is extremely rocky, and is prone to frequent landslides.

Mount Data Lodge is a long, single-story building, pleasantly set amid a pine forest, perched on a mountain 2,200 meters in altitude. Mount Data Lodge has the atmosphere of a mountain retreat and because it is rarely fully booked, the welcome is warm and attentive. The hotel was repainted recently.

A paneled corridor links the 22 rooms, some of which have balconies with a view either of the parking lot, or more pleasantly, of the pine forest. The rooms are spacious with light pinewood walls. The small adjoining bathrooms are tiled in white and have hot water. You might need it as the nights can get quite cold. You will also certainly appreciate the warm blankets on the beds.

A huge room, dominated by a double fireplace, functions as a restaurant and a lounge area. In the evening, it is good to snuggle in the sofas near the lighted fireplace. The bar, completely made of wood, is just alongside. The restaurant is pleasant with large bay windows looking out onto the pine forests. There is also a small separate room where you can watch television.

Mount Data is generally more of a stopover rather than a destination, but you can spend a day without getting bored. Some walks around the area are interesting, notably on the Mount Data plateau, where you can have a beautiful view of the mountain sides studded with vegetable gardens.

MOUNT DATA LODGE

Sinto, Bauko, Mt. Province

Booking Office in Manila
Marketing and Sales Department
Room 520, 5/F, DOT Building
T.M. Kalaw Street, Ermita, Manila
Tel   524-2502 • 524-2495
Fax   525-6490
E-mail *sales@philtourism.com*
              marketing@philtourism.com
Web   *www.philtourism.com*

 By land (12 hours) 250 km from Manila via Baguio. Victory Liner (Tel. No.: 833-5019) has a terminal in Pasay City along Epifanio delos Santos Avenue (EDSA) for hourly departures in the morning. By car, take North Expressway at Balintawak and get off at Dau exit. Pass by Tarlac, Urdaneta, and Pozorrubio. Before reaching Rosario, take the junction to Baguio (Kennon Road). From Baguio, it is a 4-hour-drive on a dirt road, very rocky, with frequent landslides. The funny thing is that the road's name is Halsema Highway!

Note: *From Bontoc it is a 2½-hour drive, also on a dirt road with frequent landslides.*

 22 Units
1 Single Room • 14 Twin Rooms • 5 Double Rooms • 2 Triple Rooms (3 single beds/rooms) 16 beds for males and females
There is no air-conditioning, but you would rather have a heater at night anyway…

Indoor Facilities and Services
Lobby with a display of artifacts of the different mountain tribes

 Food and Beverage Outlets
Restaurant and bar with a big fire place, lighted in the evening.
Cuisine Offered: International
Quality: Average

 Sports and Other Activities
For excursions, see Bontoc and Sagada's points of interest.

 Per room per night inclusive of breakfast

Sagada

Sagada is completely different from Bontoc and Banaue. It is a pleasant village nested among the pine forests at an altitude of 1,480 meters. It is a little less than an hour from the Bontoc track (18 kilometers) and six hours from the tedious Baguio road. The descent to Bontoc is steep, so check your tires before leaving Manila!

Sagada is known for its funeral rites—there are hanging coffins on the flanks of the limestone cliffs and in the grottos. It also boasts of picturesque mountain scenery and rice terraces. In Sagada, you can walk around without difficulty, as most of the sites are accessible by foot.

Do not miss a visit to Eduardo Masferre's studio while in town. Located at the entrance of Sagada as you arrive from Bontoc, the studio exhibits the master's black and white photographs. Go and dine at the Log Café, a charming, pine-walled little restaurant with a cozy ambiance. Stop by for a reservation (there is no phone).

A few of the hikes are described here, but there are others, as Sagada truly has many places you can walk to. Simplified maps of the area are readily available and you can, for the more difficult places, hire the services of a guide at the tourist information center.

THE VALLEY OF ECHOES *(2 hours walk)* It is located below St. Mary School and its adjoining church—both constructed in 1912—behind the cemetery that you are obliged to cross. You will note a few beautiful houses in the area, particularly the presbytery surrounded by garden with a melancholic charm. But even if you do not go right down into the valley, the view of the gray limestone cliffs amid the pine forests is strangely beautiful. You can

already see a few coffins hung high on the rocky spurs of the mountains. It takes two hours to visit the different caves, as the road is very steep. You can return by another route taking the other side of the valley on the main road. You will also find identical limestone formations with hanging coffins at Sugong (30 minutes on the road passing in front of Sagada Igorot Inn).

THE WATERFALLS OF BOKONG *(45 minutes from Sagada)* You must take the direction of the Bontoc Road, and, at the exit of the town, turn left on the road at the Masferré studio. A little after the Pines View Inn, a foot path on the left takes you to the waterfalls in 25 minutes.

THE RICE TERRACES OF BANGAAN *(1 hour from Sagada)* The beginning of the road is the same as when going to the waterfalls of Bokong, but you must stay on the main road. The route runs along the rice terraces with a view of the waterfalls in the distance, cascading onto the rocks against a backdrop of the pine forests. The rice terraces of Bangaan are outstanding, forming an entire circle with its walls of stone. A well-maintained small trail on the stone walls permits crossing one part of the terraces. You can continue on the road and go to the rice terraces of Fidelisan, 45 minutes from Bangaan. Without going down into the village, you can enjoy a spectacular view of rice terraces. The courageous can go right up to the big Bomodok waterfall (2 ½ hours). Jeepneys go to Bangaan, but it is a pleasant walk as the scenery is extremely beautiful, the road partly shaded by pine trees.

THE CAVES OF SUMAGING *(40 minutes from the road, 3 hours exploration)* and LUMIANG

(30 minutes by car)   You will need a guide and a torch to visit these caves. You can reach them from the main road by continuing on after Sagada Igorot Inn. The caves of Lumiang contain numerous sarcophagi piled one on top of the other.

THE CAVE OF BALANGAGAN *(3 hours from Sagada)*   This cave is very huge and does not contain any coffins but is composed of many room formations. Here too, you will need a guide and a torch.

THE RICE TERRACES OF KILTEPAN AND THE KILTEPAN MOUNTAIN *(1 hour exploration)*   To get to Kiltepan, you need to take the road in the direction of Bontoc and then turn left in the direction of the Mapiyaaw Sagada Boarding House. From the summit, at an altitude of 1,636 meters, there is a good view of the rice terraces, three and a half kilometers from town.

MOUNT AMPACAO *(half a day to one day exploration)*   The mountain of Ampacao has an altitude of 1,889 meters. It is a difficult climb (2–2 ½ hours), but you will be rewarded with a superb view of Sagada and the surrounding rice terraces. You can return in three and a half hours via the small Lake Danum. The road to the mountain parts from the school of Ambasin that you reach by continuing on the road passing in front of the Sagada Igorot Inn.

MOUNT POLIS *(4 hours from Sagada)*   It is necessary to take the old Spanish trail of Ambasin, crossing the pinewoods and several villages. The view of the Sagada valley is really superb.

Bokong Rice Terraces

Sagada Igorot Inn
and
Olahbinan Resthouse

Sagada Igorot Inn and Olahbinan Resthouse, the best hotels in town, are owned by Mrs. Hilda Piluden and her family. Mrs. Piluden knows her region well and can give you valuable information for organizing your excursions.

Sagada Igorot Inn, previously known as the Prime Hotel, is the best as far as comfort is concerned. Perched on a hill-side facing a partially inhabited valley of pine trees, it is an ordinary, white rectangular building with three floors. The hotel has just been renovated. Olahbinan Inn is close by, slightly on a lower level and can be reached by going a few steps down a rather steep stairway.

The 22-room Sagada Igorot Inn is larger than Olahbinan Resthouse which has only 11 rooms. The reception area is pleasant, its white walls charmingly decorated with the woodcraft of the mountain tribes. At the back of the reception is a spacious square dining area with large bay windows opening onto the pine forest and the valley below. No particular effort has been made in the décor, but the room is bright and neat. A counter which serves as a bar occupies one corner.

The simply-furnished rooms are either below or above the reception area. All have a window with a view of the valley.

The recently renovated Olahbinan Inn is the more congenial of the two hotels. You enter a pleasant dining room dominated by a fire place, which is lit in the evenings. A light pine counter looks into the kitchen through a wooden window. The paneled walls are decorated with black and white drawings. The tables are made of pinewood, but, the chairs, unfortunately, are plastic. On the ground floor is a very small double room with a newly-tiled bathroom. The other rooms are located upstairs on either side of the balcony with a view of the valley. The furnishings of the rooms are likewise basic and simple.

Do not hesitate to spend a few days at Sagada as the atmosphere of this small town in the midst of the pine-forest is truly very pleasant. You can enjoy the walk to many interesting places in the area.

SAGADA IGOROT INN AND OLAHBINAN RESTHOUSE

Poblacion Sagada,
Mountain Province
Tel (0919) 809-2448
The two hotels are next to each other and only a few meters from the Information Center, after the Masferré Country Inn.

By Car
1 hour from Bontoc (dirt road), 2 hours from Mount Data Lodge and 6 hours from Baguio (dirt road, very bad)

33 Units
Sagada Igorot Inn: 22 Rooms • Olahbinan Resthouse: 11 Rooms

Food and Beverage Outlets
Restaurants in both hotels
Cuisine Offered: Filipino • American • Continental
Quality: Average

Sports and Activities
For excursions, see Sagada's points of interest.

 Per room per night

Note: *Cash payment only.*

Bontoc

Bontoc, the capital of the Mountain Province, lies at an altitude of only 870 meters along a green mountain stream. The town is two and a half hours from the good Banaue road and you can make the return journey in one day. During the rainy season, landslides can cut off the road.

The view from the road is truly spectacular. The road goes into the mountain hollows which are still covered in certain areas by a canopy of luxuriant green forest, made up of mossy trees adorned with orchids.

A little before arriving in Bontoc, the scenery changes, the forest giving way to

Rice Terraces on the road from Bontoc to Banaue

the rice terraces. In Bay-yo, the square patchwork of terraces dominates an impressive precipice, evoking a citadel with the backdrop of mountains. The track leads to the pass of Mount Polis, obscured in the mist. In the surrounding area of Bontoc, the indigenous tribes now cultivate vegetables on the terraces, notably cabbages and potatoes on plots forming geometric patterns. The spiral designs of the vegetable gardens alone are astonishing.

The main interest in Bontoc is the visit to the rice terraces of Malegcong, an hour by car through a very steep track (three hours on foot!). The track goes right up to the village of Malegcong and you can see the rice terraces below without having to walk any further.

The rice terraces of Malegcong ascend like a staircase in the Mountain Side, near the Mainit Hot Spring. Unlike those of Banaue, the rice-fields here have the particularity of having stone walls. You can easily walk in the ricefields and go right up to the other slope of the circle—a narrow footpath follows the stone walls. The view of the rice terraces you have within the amphitheater is quite unusual and gives you a better understanding of their function. It takes an hour to walk through the area. The descent by car to Bontoc is faster than the going there (half an hour only).

If you spend the night in Bontoc, you will have time to visit the little museum dedicated to the mountain tribes, founded in 1911 by a Belgian missionary, Sister Basil Gekiere. It houses a collection of mountain tribe objects—tools, pottery, porcelain, jewelry, traditional costumes of beautifully woven cloth, and photographs. The museum garden likewise houses replicas of traditional dwellings.

On the road from Banaue to Bontoc

Ridge Brooke

There are no appealing hotels in Bontoc, only small establishments offering basic amenities. Ridge Brooke, the best in its category, is a small, unpretentious hotel, and spruced up in its own way. Moreover, its owners are pleasant and attentive.

The hotel is a four-story building at the entrance to Bontoc, just after the bridge, if you are coming from Banaue. It is therefore more quiet than the other establishments in town, although the rooms are not sound-proof. There is a small parking lot just in front.

The welcome here is warm and homey. The small reception area with its marble flooring and light pine walls has an air of welcome although its décor is debatable: walls painted in pale green; plastic chairs and tables. The area also serves as a restaurant and you can see the well-equipped kitchen from the little service window. A small television set and a music system are installed in a corner.

The 12 rooms comprising the hotel are in two floors. Though furnished simply, these are clean and bright. The view of the faraway mountains is not unpleasant. Only one of the rooms has its own bathroom. The others share two bathrooms per floor—one for men, the other for women. Only the latter has hot water, but it is possible to negotiate the sharing of the bathrooms with your neighbor.

Each floor is provided with a small, well-lit common terrace, equipped with tables and chairs. Here, you can enjoy a drink in the evenings.

Note: *If the Ridge Brooke is full, the second choice is Pines Kitchenette and Inn.*

RIDGE BROOKE

Bontoc, Mountain Province
Tel (0918) 738-1760
(0920) 229-2724

Booking Office in Baguio
Tel (074) 442-7014

 From Banaue 2½ hours in fairly good weather but during the rainy season, you need a 4WD. Check the condition of the road with Banaue Hotel or the tourist office of Baguio.
From Sagada 1 hour as the descent from Sagada is very steep.

 19 Units
12 Double Rooms • 7 Single Rooms
Only hotel in Bontoc with wide parking space and no water problem.

 Food and Beverage Outlets
Restaurant: Ridge Brooke Restaurant
Cuisine Offered: Filipino • International
Quality: Average

 Watersports and Other Activities
Swimming (Chico River) • Bontoc Museum • Tours to Malegcong rice terraces (1 hour by car or a 3- to 4-hour hike), Mainit Hot Springs (4 to 5 hours hiking from Bontoc; 18 kilometers)

Per room per night

The Banaue Rice Terraces

The rice terraces of the Ifugao Province which make up a part of the region around Banaue are the most spectacular of the Cordilleras. It is a breathtaking world of high mountain ranges with several peaks reaching heights of over 2,000 meters; of forests, waterfalls and valleys so deep that the ravines enchant and petrify all at once. The colors of the ricefields change with the seasons. Tender, green rice shoots dot the drenched brown earth at the onset of the planting season, burst into the bright green of the ripened crop, then turn into the golden hues of the harvest.

Bangaan Terraces

Few man-made landscapes can equal the splendor of these rice terraces. This overwhelming scenic beauty is awe-inspiring, as the Ifugaos constructed these ricefields more than 2,000 years ago—an undeniable feat of technical prowess. They are, for instance, shelved on a steep incline of over 1,000 meters spanning a surface of nearly 400 kilometers! The terraces are also listed on UNESCO's "World Heritage Site" as the first "combined cultural and natural site." This unique panorama is in danger of vanishing as many of the ricefields are no longer cultivated, having been deemed unprofitable.

The ricefields are irrigated by a system of bamboo pipes which gather the water of the mountain streams. The embankments here, some of which are over 15 meters, are made of soil. Those of Malegcong, Hapao and Hungduan are made of stone.

You can explore the ricefields during any season and since the road from Manila to Banaue is paved, the town is accessible throughout the year. During the rainy season, however, some parts may become impassable.

In Banaue, it is easy to rent a jeepney—indispensable if you do not own a four-wheel drive vehicle. The town itself may not be an endearing sight to some, with its undulating rooftops and entangled overhead electric wires. As it is at an altitude of 1,200 meters, Banaue can get quite cold at night. The few interesting handicrafts made here are hard to find as they are often sent to Manila or Baguio for sale.

BANAUE VIEWPOINT *(4 kilometers from Banaue)* The viewpoint is on the road from Banaue to Bontoc. The view is superb, the ricefields occupying a narrow, high spur in the mountain on a rather steep incline. As it is very near the town, the natural serenity of the surroundings is somewhat ruined by the sprouting handicraft stalls. From Banaue you can make a round trip (it can take between two to three hours) across the ricefields passing through the viewpoint.

THE VILLAGE AND THE RICEFIELDS OF BANGAAN *(one and a half hours from Banaue)* The track going to Bangaan may not be passable during the rainy season. The way up to Bangaan even now crosses spectacular ricefields. The vegetation is mostly sprawling ferns; there are waterfalls and mountain streams rippling down rocky slopes almost everywhere.

From the road, there is an exquisite view of the village of Poitan down below. A little farther, in the hollow of the valley amid the ricefields of Bangaan, is a traditional little village, quite pretty even though the rooftops, in general, are no longer thatched.

THE RICEFIELDS OF BATAD *(a four- to five-hour walk to and from Bangaan)* The ricefields of Batad are approximately 16 kilometers from Banaue with only 12 of these are possible by car. The trip from Bangaan to Batad is 24 kilometers on foot. You can cut this to 18 kilometers by driving back up to the junction leading to Batad. During the dry season you can drive right up to the viewpoint of Batad, four kilometers from Bangaan. If you have your own car, it is recommended that someone stay behind to look after it, as the children in the area have been known to amuse themselves by puncturing tires!

The road plods slowly up a shady track and after about an hour-and-a-half walk, you reach a superb vantage point where children are waiting with refreshments! From here you can go down in about an hour, either by steep stairways or by the main road, right up to the village of Batad. Along the road, you have a number of good vantage points to see the ricefields in their amphitheaters, still in the distance. To really explore them and go down to the waterfall below, you will have to spend the night at Bangaan or in one of the very basic lodges in Batad. The Hill Side View Inn, with a pleasant terrace looking onto the ricefields is a good place to rest.

THE RICEFIELDS OF MAYOYAO *(30 kilometers of road from Bangaan)* The road from Bangaan to Mayoyao can get very tedious and impractical during the rainy season. The ricefields are relatively flat compared to those

of Banaue or Batad, but are fairly sprawling. The houses are not grouped into hamlets but are isolated from one another in the middle of the ricefields. You must stay overnight at Bangaan to make the tour the following day.

On the road between Banaue and Bangaan

THE RICEFIELDS OF HUNGDUAN AND HAPAO *(one and a half hours from Banaue)* From Banaue Hotel, take the road going to Viewpoint and, before Viewpoint, turn onto the road on the left. At times, it may not be in a very good condition, but it crosses fertile ricefields at the bottom of the valleys before ending at Hapao, situated 15 km away (1 hour). The ricefields of Hapao are simply magnificent! They occupy an entire amphitheater and their high stone walls—quite unusual for Banaue—bring to mind certain European fortresses from the Middle Ages. One of the tracks has been maintained and you can go down by foot into the ricefields and go up at another end of town. If time is short, it is better to limit yourself to a walk in the ricefields of Hapao rather than to continue on to Hungduan, about 10 kilometers away, close to an hour of walking. These were the first ricefields, to be constructed by the Ifugaos and though picturesque, are less significant than those of Hapao.

Banaue Hotel

The Banaue Hotel is the only comfortable hotel in Banaue. It is perched on the hillside, slightly on the outskirts of this little town, which is not very pleasant with all its corrugated metal roofs.

Architecturally, the long rectangular building housing the hotel is not that charming, but the view of the mountains and the rice terraces is superb. Flowers, mostly pink daturas, brighten up the place.

The reception area with a few sofas and a television set is quite disproportionate and gloomy. A large fireplace could warm up the atmosphere but it is rarely lit. However, you can ask the management to light it at the onset of the afternoon. The restaurant, with its large bay windows dominating the view, is much more pleasant, even if the cuisine is without imagination. Next to the restaurant is a paneled bar.

The rooms, with their pine-covered walls, give the impression of a mountain shelter. Soberly furnished, the rooms are also provided with warm blankets and hot water, important as the nights can get cold. All the balconies face the rice terraces.

A swimming pool was constructed on the promontory dominating the view, but the water, often too cold, discourages swimmers. From the pool area, a small footpath goes down 240 steps towards the village of Tam-An, where you will find a number of handicraft stalls.

At the entrance of Banaue Hotel is the Banaue Youth Hostel, composed of four separate dormitories for girls and boys. Clients of the Youth Hostel have access to all the facilities of the Banaue Hotel including the restaurant and the swimming pool.

The staff of the Banaue Hotel are warm and efficient. They help in organizing your excursions; inform you of the state of the roads, and can help you rent a jeepney and a guide at very reasonable rates. A picnic basket can also be ordered the day before your tour.

BANAUE HOTEL

Banaue, Ifugao Province
Tel   (074) 386-4087
Fax   (074) 386-4088

Booking Office in Manila
Marketing and Sales Department
Room 520, 5/F, DOT Building,
T. M. Kalaw Street, Ermita, Manila
Tel   524-2502 • 524-2495
Fax   525-6490
E-mail *sales@philtourism.com*
Web   *www.philtourism.com*

By land (9–10 hours) 348 km from Manila. Take North Expressway at Balintawak and get off at Santa Rita, Exit No. 38, where signs indicate the road to Cabanatuan, Tuguegarao, Santa Rita, etc. The road goes through the provinces of Nueva Ecija and Nueva Vizcaya passing through Cabanatuan, San Jose, Santa Fe and Bayombong. After Solano, look for the turn-off to Banaue passing through Lagawe.

89 Units
Banaue Hotel: 45 Standard Rooms • 32 Deluxe Rooms • 4 Suites at 2 rooms per suite
All rooms and suites have air-conditioning, a bathroom with hot water, intercom and a private terrace. An extra bed can be added in all rooms.

Banaue Youth Hostel: 4 dormitories (2 girls' dormitories good for 11; 2 boys' dormitories good for 11)

Note: *As the rooms have communicating doors, it can be noisy.*

Indoor Facilities and Services
Jeepney rental (with picnic) • Guide • Transfer service

Food and Beverage Outlets
Restaurants: Imbayah Restaurant • Rooftop Coffee Shop • Guihob Cocktail Lounge • Cambulo Ballroom
Cuisine Offered: International
Quality: Average

Watersports and Other Activities
Swimming pool
For excursions around Banaue, see Banaue and Bontoc points of interest. Tours to Tam-An Village (down the pool), Banaue Viewpoint, Batad Village and Rice Terraces and Cambulo Village, Bangaan Village and rice terraces, Hapao and Hungduan rice terraces, Bontoc and Malegcong rice terraces

Per room per night inclusive of breakfast

Banaue View Inn

The Banaue View Inn is a small quiet family hotel. Set in the middle of a flower garden with an orchid greenhouse, it is perched on a promontory overlooking the town. En route from Manila, the hotel is on the main road just before the entrance to the city center.

A remarkable museum traces the life of Dr. Henry Otley Beyer, an American anthropologist who came to study the Ifugao tribes at the beginning of the 20th century, and who, after marrying a young Ifugao woman, settled and died in the region. He published a number of books and collected many Ifugao items such as handicrafts, clothes, jewelry and tools. All of these objects are exhibited in this museum, thanks to one of his sons, Gerry. It is he who owns the Banaue View Inn and lives there with his wife Lily and their children. The remains of Dr. Beyer, enveloped in a shroud in accordance with Ifugao tradition, are also on view in a building located behind the town hall.

The hotel is composed of a main building and an annex at the end of the courtyard. Amenities are simple and basic but the welcome is hospitable and the rates are moderate.

The main building, which also serves as the owner's residence, shelters a big reception area with a reading and television corner. It becomes particularly animated when the whole family gathers there. A terrace links the rooms on the second floor. In the two-story annex are five other rooms, including a large family room.

Banaue View Inn does not serve any meals aside from breakfast, but as the hotel is close to the city, you can walk to the nearby restaurants. Also from the hotel, it is easy to go to the tourism office as well as to the market, where you can find a few handicraft shops. Compared to those of Baguio, however, these shops are not very appealing.

The Banaue View Inn can provide a guide to accompany you on your exploration of the region. The tourism office can also give you assistance.

BANAUE VIEW INN

Barangay Poblacion, Bontoc Road, Banaue, Ifugao Province
Tel (074) 386-4078

Booking Office in Makati
8384 Mayapis Street,
San Antonio Village, Makati City
Tel 729-3448
(0920) 531-4070
(0919) 409-4080

By land (9–10 hours) 348 km from Manila. Take North Expressway at Balintawak and get off at Santa Rita, Exit No. 38, where signs indicate the road to Cabanatuan, Tuguegarao, Santa Rita, etc. The road goes through the provinces of Nueva Ecija and Nueva Vizcaya passing through Cabanatuan, San Jose, Santa Fe and Bayombong. After Solano look for the turn-off to Banaue passing through Lagawe.

11 Units
In the main building:
4 Rooms with bathroom on the first and second floors (good for 3) • 2 Rooms with common bathroom on the third floor (good for 3)
In the annex building:
4 Rooms with a bathroom (good for 2) • 1 Family Room with a bathroom (good for 4)

Food and Beverage Outlets
Only breakfast is served.
There are many restaurants nearby such as People's Lodge, Las Vegas and Eden Valley.

Watersports and Other Activities
For excursions around Banaue, see Banaue and Bontoc points of interest. Tours to: Banaue View Point, Batad Village and Rice Terraces and Cambulo Village, Hapao and Hungduan rice terraces, Bangaan Village and rice terraces, Bontoc and Malegcong rice terraces

Per room per night inclusive of breakfast

Note: *Cash payment only.*

Bangaan Family Inn

Bangaan Family Inn is in a choice location along the trail from Banaue to Mayoyao, overlooking the rice terraces of Bangaan. It is from here that you can go on foot to visit the famous rice terraces of Batad. If you wish to continue along this road (very bad during the rainy season) to the rice terraces of Mayoyao another 30 kilometers away, it is necessary to make a stopover here.

The site of this little inn is fantastic, with a superb view on the little village of Bangaan with its red-painted rooftops, tucked away in the middle of the green rice terraces. It is the only place, moreover, where you can have the opportunity to sleep in an Ifugao hut! It is for all these reasons that a stay of at least one night is recommended here, even though the inn only offers simple comfort.

The inn is in fact spread out on different parts of the trail. Above the trail is the restaurant as well as an adjoining building surrounded by flowers that houses eight of the rooms. The restaurant, made of wood, is pleasant and largely open to the view. Below the trail, accessible by a rather steep flight of steps, are five huts in the Ifugao style. These huts are quite rustic; alongside each is a smaller hut which serves as a bathroom with only a huge drum filled with cold water! You may, however, request for hot water for a small fee.

The Ifugao huts are quite set apart, each with a terrace from where you can admire the spectacular view. The last hut is like a big wooden bungalow, more comfortable with a little drawing room, two double rooms with woven bamboo walls and a mini-tiled bathroom. The view from the large bay window over the abyss is breathtaking.

BANGAAN FAMILY INN

Bangaan, Banaue, Ifugao Province
Owner Florencio Laroco
For reservations you have to send a letter to the owner.

From Banaue
One and a half hours by jeepney or 4WD vehicle. From Banaue Town Proper, take the road going to Mayoyao. After the turn-off to Batad, it is only 2 km before reaching Bangaan Family Inn.

14 Units
8 Rooms in the main building sharing one common bathroom • 5 Ifugao huts with a small separate hut used as a bathroom • 1 Cottage with a small bathroom There is only cold water, but you can ask for a bucket of hot water.

Indoor Facilities and Services
Guide

Food and Beverage Outlets
Restaurant
Cuisine Offered: Filipino
Quality: Average

Watersports and Other Activities
For excursions around Banaue, see Banaue points of interest. Trekking to Batad rice terraces, Mayoyao rice terraces

Per room per night

Note: *Cash payment only.*

Ilocos Sur

The entire Ilocos region, a long and narrow coastal plain northwest of Luzon, is rich in history. Vigan is the main attraction of Ilocos Sur, whereas many old churches are found in Ilocos Norte. These churches are constructed in the "earthquake baroque" style—massive façades reinforced with flying buttresses to resist any potential damage caused by earth tremors. The belfries, which also served as watch towers, were usually built apart. You can spend a few pleasant days in Vigan, discovering some of the historic monuments. But, if you have a bit more time to spare, you can combine a historical tour with a nature trek by continuing on to Pagudpud, 60 kilometers from Vigan.

Vigan

Vigan, 400 kilometers from Manila, is the only town in the Philippines with so many preserved historic sites—more than 180 edifices have been catalogued. In 1999, Vigan was added to the list of World Heritage sites of UNESCO. Legend has it that Vigan was saved from destruction by the Japanese due to a romantic liaison between a Japanese officer and a lady from the region.

Thanks to its prime location at the mouth of the Abra River four kilometers from the sea, Vigan was an important trading port back in the 15th century: ships from China, Japan, Korea and other Asian countries stopped here and trading took place with the mountain tribes. This town also saw the arrival of the Chinese traders who eventually made Vigan their home.

Vigan then became the center of politics and religion. In 1572 Juan de Salcedo became the governor and Vigan was made the capital of the Ilocos province. In 1758, the seat of the archdiocese of Nueva Segovia was transferred here. The Spanish clergy began constructing churches in the baroque Hispano-Mexican model, notably St. Paul's Cathedral.

Vigan has preserved its old-world atmosphere. The length of the main road is lined with the houses of rich Chinese traders. These are two-story houses with red tile roofs: the ground floor served as a warehouse while the second floor the living quarters. You enter through imposing wooden doors and see rooms with superb *narra* floors and immense high ceilings. One can find there an odd mixture of Chinese cabinets and chests, Filipino furniture made of beautiful local wood and European chandeliers, porcelain objects and crystal. It is a pity that the owners, who mostly reside in Manila,

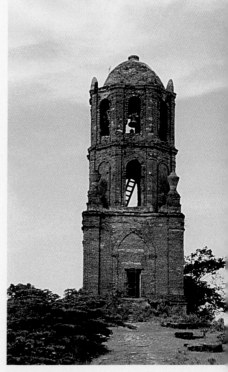

Bantay Church

seem to have neglected and abandoned the superb houses.

The charm of Vigan lies in exploring it, walking down its narrow alleys, which sometimes open onto old plazas such as Burgos and Salcedo. The streets resound with the clip-clopping of the horse-drawn carriages that are still used today by the townsfolk as a means of transport. Do not miss the chance to browse in the antique shops along Crisologo and Plaridel roads. You will find well-made, inexpensive copies of antique furniture.

The best time to walk around Vigan is towards the end of the afternoon when the roads are bathed in the warm light of the setting sun and when at 5 p.m. you can attend a sung mass in the Cathedral of St. Paul.

Apart from the old houses, other interesting monuments to visit are:

THE CATHEDRAL OF ST. PAUL Constructed in the earthquake baroque style, it was started in 1574 and completed in 1800. It is located on the Burgos Plaza.

THE ARCHBISHOP'S PALACE Adjacent to the cathedral, houses a museum dedicated to religious objects. It was completed in 1783.

THE AYALA MUSEUM Located on the Plaza Singson Encarnacion is the former residence of Father Jose Burgos, considered one of the fathers of Philippine nationalism. The two-story museum exhibits archaeological and ethnological objects, antique furniture, jewelry and costumes.

THE CRISOLOGO MUSEUM In the residence of Flor Crisologo, displays family souvenirs.

THE SYQUIA MANSION On Quirino Avenue is a huge house built in 1830 by a Chinese trader. It later became the residence of former Philippine President Elpidio Quirino. The mansion contains beautiful antique furniture.

GOVERNOR MANSION On the corner of Mabini and Ventura delos Reyes streets is a private residence with a superb facade.

THE POTTERY WORKSHOPS Vigan is known for its earthen jars, baked in a long, wood-fired oven using century-old techniques. You can visit a number of pottery shops along Rizal Avenue.

BANTAY *(1 kilometer from Vigan)* This restored 18th-century church is particularly visited for its bell.

MAGSINGAL *(13 kilometers north of Vigan)* The town church, constructed in 1827, has a beautiful baroque façade. It has exquisite sculptured altars, one of which has the unusual representation of two mermaids. A museum nearby has an interesting collection of Ilocano handicrafts, pottery and porcelain.

 Vigan celebrates a number of festivals: The festival of Vigan which takes place around the 25th of January lasts a week and includes a carnival, parades and concerts; Holy Week is marked by processions; the art festival of Vigan, with its parades of carriages, roadside spectacles and exhibitions, takes place in the first week of May.

Villa Angela Heritage House

Located in the central part of Vigan, Villa Angela is a charming, beautiful old house built in the middle of the 18th century. It is still filled with traces of the past, as it was not subjected to major renovations since its construction. The two-story house nestles at the end of a small, quiet garden. A stone staircase leads to a terrace, then to a vast entrance hall divided into several rooms: a spacious and bright music-cum-reading room and four other rooms. A part of the entrance hall was transformed into a dining room. Everywhere, the plank floors are made from magnificent, gleaming dark wood.

The high-ceilinged salon, with pale blue *trompe-l'œil* walls, opens onto the street through large *capiz* windows. Wood and wicker sofas, planters' chairs, rocking chairs, and wooden chests inlaid with mother-of-pearl, jostle alongside musical instruments, pianos and harps. Family portraits hang on the walls, as well as a large Venetian mirror.

The large rooms with four-poster beds are very romantic, though only one is air-conditioned with its own bathroom. As such, it must be reserved in advance. However, this is of little importance given the great opportunity of staying in an old villa such as this one.

The kitchen is welcoming, with its well-polished wooden table, white walls adorned with an odd assortment of kitchen utensils, green-colored crockery and an original collection of wood and wicker hats.

Depending on your mood, you may chose to eat your meals in the garden, in the kitchen or in the dining room… though why not try all three? It may be interesting, if you are with a large group, to rent the whole villa, and take advantage of the available special rates.

The manager, knows Vigan perfectly well; Villa Angela belongs to her family. She can help you in your discovery of Vigan, notably by providing a guide, enthusiastic about the history which you will encounter in the old houses that are normally not open to the public. She can also arrange to take you in a carriage—a pleasure in itself—to visit her workshop that makes reproductions of antique furniture and a pottery shop producing baked earthenware—a specialty of the region.

VILLA ANGELA HERITAGE HOUSE
25 Quirino Boulevard, Vigan, Ilocos Sur
Tel (077) 722-2914
(0917) 891-9711
E-mail candyverzosa@yahoo.com
candyverzosa@edsamail.com.ph
clverzosa@msn.com
Web www.villangela.com
Booking Office in Marikina
177 Libra Street, Cinco Hermanos, Marikina City
Tel/Fax 681-9994

 1. By air and land (3 hours)
Fifty-five-minute flight on Philippine Airlines (4 weekly flights) from Manila to Laoag. One and a half hours by the hotel's chartered van from Laoag to Vigan (80 km).

2. By land (8 hours)
407 km from Manila. Take North Expressway at Balintawak and get off at Dau Exit. Take North Diversion Road to MacArthur Highway. Before reaching the coastal road along which Vigan is located, you will pass by Angeles City, Tarlac, Urdaneta, Pozorrubio and Rosario. Then proceed further north passing by San Fernando (La Union) before reaching Vigan.

 6 Units
1 master bedroom with bathroom and air-conditioning • 1 south wing room with common bathroom and air-conditioning • 1 north wing room with common bathroom and air-conditioning • 1 Cuarto Paqueño with common bathroom and fan
There is no hot water. The hotel also has 2 air-conditioned dormitories at the basement. It can accommodate 22 people. Each dormitory has its own bathroom.

 Food and Beverage Outlets
The hotel serves only breakfast. Other meals are served on request and must be ordered in advance.
Quality: Familial

Restaurants in Vigan: Café Julia (familial) • Aniceto Mansion (cozy restaurant but poor quality) • Vigan Hotel's Cool Spot Restaurant (buffet type) • Café Leona

Watersports and Other Activities
The hotel can provide a guide for excursions. See Vigan's points of interest.

 Per room per night inclusive of breakfast

Note: *Special package if you rent the entire house. Cash payment only.*

Mena Crisologo Street

Cordillera Inn

The Cordillera Inn is an old Vigan house. Unfortunately the interior was completely renovated in a modern style, its charm now lost, given up for more comfortable amenities.

It is well located on Mena Crisologo, the restored main road of the town. You enter directly from the street into a large, pleasant reception area with stone floors, a huge, round center table and antique lamps on the walls. This area adjoins the small restaurant with a congenial family atmosphere here.

A large staircase leads to the rooms on the upper floors. The original rooms have been divided to create smaller ones. This is true especially with the standard rooms. The décor is simple and sober but nearly all the rooms have air-conditioning with private bathrooms.

CORDILLERA INN

U.N. Heritage Village,
Mena Crisologo Street
corner Gen. Luna Street,
Vigan, Ilocos Sur
Tel/Fax   (077) 722-2727
Web *www.ilocossur.net/Cordillera*

1. By air and land (3 hours)
Fifty-five-minute flight on Philippine Airlines (4 weekly flights) from Manila to Laoag. One and a half hours by the hotel's chartered van from Laoag to Vigan (80 km).

2. By land (8 hours)   407 km from Manila. Take North Expressway at Balintawak and get off at Dau Exit. Take North Diversion Road to MacArthur Highway. Before reaching the coastal road along which Vigan is located, you will pass by Angeles City, Tarlac, Urdaneta, Pozorrubio and Rosario. Then proceed further north passing by San Fernando (La Union) before reaching Vigan.

25 Units
20 Deluxe Rooms • 4 Family Rooms • 1 Suite Room
All rooms have air-conditioning, bathroom with hot water. The family room also has a TV.

Indoor Facilities and Services
Car rental

Food and Beverage Outlets
Restaurant: Cosina Ilocana
Small restaurant near the reception serving only breakfast.

Restaurants in Vigan: Café Julia (familial) • Aniceto Mansion (cozy restaurant but poor quality) • Vigan Hotel's Cool Spot Restaurant (buffet type) • Café Leona

Watersports and Other Activities
See Vigan's points of interest.

Per room per night inclusive of breakfast

Note: *Of slightly lower quality, in the same category, are the following hotels, also in old houses: Aniceto Mansion, Grandpa's Inn, Tel. (077) 722-2118, and El Juliana Hotel, Tel. (077) 722-2383/2994 (has a swimming pool but is devoid of any charm).*

Ilocos Norte

The province of Ilocos Norte, 486 kilometers from Manila, is located in the northernmost part of Luzon. Sparsely populated, its topography is mountainous and its climate harsh.

The province is rich in history as well as nature sites of great beauty in the area of Pagudpud. It is to be noted that Sarrat, the birthplace of former President Ferdinand Marcos, is in this province as is the former Malacañang Palace of the North with its private golf course. The network of roads in this province is excellent. The provincial capital is Laoag.

Laoag and its Environs

THE CATHEDRAL OF SAINT WILLIAM THE HERMIT Completed in 1700, this church constructed in the earthquake baroque style has undergone many restoration works. Its white and cream façade is quite extravagant, with massive crown-topped columns. Its belfry, the Bantay Bell Tower, is 100 meters away. Constructed in 1783 on sandy soil, the belfry is sinking into the ground because of the effect of seismic tremors. The bottom half of its door, completely buried, is evidence of that.

THE MUSEUM The Ilocandia Museum of Traditional Costumes exhibits traditional ethnic costumes of the mountain tribes in Tabacalera, an old tobacco warehouse. It was in use during the colonial days when tobacco cultivation was a monopoly of the region.

THE SAND DUNES You can see fairly impressive sand dunes, 10 to 30 meters high, in different places: in La Paz, north of the Laoag river, as well as south of the river where the Fort Ilocandia Resort and Casino is located. The highest dunes are those at Suba Beach.

SAN NICOLAS (3 kilometers from Laoag) The church, as well as its bell tower and convent, dates back to 1584. It was completely restored in the 19th century.

SARRAT (8 kilometers southwest of Laoag) The house where former president Ferdinand Marcos was born in 1917, is now the Marcos Museum. Also in the town is the Church of Santa Monica and its convent, constructed by the Augustinians in 1779.

BACARRA (8 kilometers north of Laoag) The Church of Saint Andrew, dates back to 1783, has a square bell-tower directly adjacent to the church. It was partially destroyed by an earthquake in 1930.

DINGRAS (22 kilometers west of Laoag) This beautiful church, set in the melancholic atmosphere of ruins, suffered damage several times. The Spaniards built the church in 1776 and it was destroyed by fire in 1838.

PAOAY (16 kilometers south of Laoag) The Church of Saint Augustine and its adjoining coral stone bell tower were constructed by the Augustinians in 1694. It is one of the most famous and magnificent churches in the region and is listed in the World Heritage Sites of UNESCO. It is an imaginative blend of earthquake baroque and oriental architecture. Its astounding façade displays an immense theatrical décor with its massive flying buttresses. The two sides of its façade are extended by curved buttresses, giving it a graceful air. The ensemble emerges from a beautiful open space, unlike many other churches located within urban settings.

Paoay Church

Mira Ira Point

BATAC *(17 kilometers south of Laoag)* The town was once an important center for tobacco production. You can visit Balay Ti Ili, a villa which belongs to the Marcos family, and the former "Malacañang Palace of the North." Overlooking Paoay Lake, this superb, Spanish style building, completed towards the end of the 1970s, is a luxurious replica of the Malacañang Palace in Manila. The late president owned a private golf course, which has since been transformed into the Paoay Lake Golf Course, a private club.

BADOC *(38 kilometers from Laoag)* This is the birthplace of the painter Juan Luna, who was born in 1857. A beautiful stone villa in the colonial Spanish style, it was restored and transformed into a museum exhibiting reproductions of the artist's works. A church with a blue and cream façade, with massive flying buttresses and adjacent bell tower, also deserves a visit.

THE LIGHTHOUSE OF BURGOS (CAPE BOJEADOR) *(50 kilometers north of Laoag)* Swept by violent, roaring winds, the red brick lighthouse of Burgos or Cape Bojeador was constructed in 1892 by the Spaniards. Despite the ravages of time and natural elements which have damaged it severely, the building must once have had a certain elegance. Do not miss the chance to chat with the keeper, a poet who will show you his works written in Iloko then translated into English and disseminated on the Internet. From the summit of the lighthouse

you will discover magnificent views of the jagged coastline and the South China Sea.

PAGUDPUD, THE VIADUCT OF PATAPAT AND MIRA IRA POINT *(60 kilometers north of Laoag)* Superb sceneries, far away from the tourist path, lie hidden in the vicinity of Pagudpud and Mira Ira Point, farther up north. Both are possible excursions from Vigan (3 hours) or from Laoag.

PAGUDPUD In the beautiful and peaceful bay of Bangui is Pagudpud, with its vast and magnificent gold sand beaches. There are a few little resorts scattered along the beach where an atmosphere of peace and tranquility is guaranteed.

THE VIADUCT OF PATAPAT The landscape changes if you continue along the northern road leading to Claveria. The viaduct of Patapat, built on the mountainside, is practically deserted and in excellent condition. It overlooks the sea, offering spectacular views of the area.

MIRA IRA POINT At 15 kilometers from Pagudpud, Mira Ira is the northernmost point of Luzon. You will need a four-wheel drive vehicle to reach the point, a wild amphitheater torn apart by the winds. At the beginning of the trip, stop at White Beach, a little beach hidden in a cove below the road. Here, you can swim in complete peace. A cliff riddled with holes can be found in the neighboring beach.

PANNZIAN *(75 kilometers, 1 hour from Laoag)* Its long, black sand beach, often beaten by strong winds, is set amidst spectacular surroundings of forested mountains plunging into the sea. It is a good base for walking tours. Pannzian Beach and Mountain Resort provides a guide for treks up the mountain behind the resort. It takes five hours to reach the summit, but tall trees hide the view. In just 30 minutes, you can reach a little waterfall concealed in the vegetation.

Fort Ilocandia Resort
and Casino

The hotel was constructed just to accommodate the guests at the wedding of Irene Marcos, daughter of the late President Ferdinand Marcos. Spread on a 77-hectare area on the edge of Suba beach, it is the only rated hotel in the entire Ilocos Norte which offers comfortable accommodations for travelers between Vigan and Pagudpud.

Before the Waterfront Hotel chain took over its management, this hotel essentially targeted a clientele from Taiwan, assuring direct flights between Kaoshiung and the international airport of Laoag. It was a bit disconcerting as you could only use Taiwanese dollars at the automatic beverage dispensers. The new management has changed that. It made the necessary renovations for the improvement of the hotel's facilities.

The hotel, with its red brick façade and roofs contrasting with the white round windows, is clearly inspired by the colonial Spanish architecture. There is a huge, impressive fountain in the impeccably maintained gardens with palm trees.

The main building houses the lobby, a number of restaurants, as well as some of the rooms. The rest of the rooms are spread out in four other two-story buildings. Each room has its own balcony with a pleasant view of the sea.

You will appreciate the Olympic-sized swimming pool—set on the edge of the beach—after a long day exploring the vicinity. The beach, though quite vast with well-equipped *nipa* huts, is not very tempting as the sand is gray and the sea is often rough. However, it is pleasant to take a walk along the sand dunes.

The hotel offers a number of recreation and sports activities. Golf lovers can play on the golf course overlooking Paoay Lake, which used to be the private golf course of Ferdinand Marcos. The hotel offers a number of excursions to the neighboring areas.

FORT ILOCANDIA RESORT AND CASINO

Barangay 37, Calayab, Laoag City
Ilocos Norte
Tel (077) 772-1166 to 70
Fax (077) 772-1411
E-mail firc@compass.com.ph
info@jimeihotel.com
Web www.laoagforfun.com

Booking Office in Pasay
Unit 202, Antel Seaview Tower A
2626 Roxas Boulevard, Pasay City
Tel 834-7219 • 833-9596
833-9601
Fax 834-7221

1. By land (11–12 hours) 486 km from Manila. Take North Expressway at Balintawak and get off at Dau exit. Take North Diversion Road to MacArthur Highway. Before reaching the coastal road along which Laoag is located you will pass by Angeles City, Tarlac, Urdaneta, Pozorrubio and Rosario. Then proceed further north passing by San Fernando (La Union) and Vigan before reaching Laoag.
2. By air (1 ½ hour) Fifty-five-minute flight on Philippine Airlines (4 weekly flights) from Manila to Laoag. 10 minutes by car from Laoag International Airport to the resort.

279 Units
163 Standard Rooms • 50 Deluxe Rooms • 8 Seaview Suites • 9 Sunset Suites • 47 Superior Rooms • 1 Presidential Suite • 1 Junior Suite
All rooms have air-conditioning, cable TV, telephone, and a bathroom with hot water, a private balcony.

Indoor Facilities and Services
Spa • Fitness center • Car rental • Medical services • Casino • Video games • KTV • Billiards • Tour and travel agency

Food and Beverage Outlets
Restaurants: Courtyard Cafe • Garden Cafe • Golden Pavilion • Every House Restaurant (Chinese Restaurant)
Cuisine Offered: Chinese • Seafood • Continental
Quality: Average

Bars: Ice Cream • Sunset Bar • Bench Bar

Watersports and Other Activities
Swimming pools (Olympic size and kiddie pool) • Beach (gray sand) • Jet skiing • Windsurfing • Canoeing • Fishing • Diving • Golf arrangement with nearby 18-hole Lake and Side golf course • Driving range • Shooting range • Horseback riding • Paint ball • Beach volleyball • Archery • Children's playground • Tours to: Laoag City, Vigan and Pagudpud

Per room per night inclusive of breakfast

Saud Beach Resort

Saud Beach Resort is probably the most pleasant of the few resorts on this part of the coast, far away from the tourist track. The property is located between a beautiful marsh of majestic trees and a beach bordered by palm trees. The hotel is owned by a Filipino, and managed by a German-Filipino couple.

A big building with a high *nipa* roof houses the restaurant facing the sea and some rooms at the rear. The rooms are in two floors, grouped around an interior patio. Those on the first floor are much more pleasant as they have a lovely view of the marsh while the others may seem boxed in. However, all the rooms are very comfortable and the décor is sober and pleasant—white walls, beautiful floors and capiz windows. Each room has its own little private terrace.

A bit further down the beach, a big wood and stone house with a roof resembling the prow of an overturned ship, shelters other rooms on three floors. These are the best as they are larger and more private than those in the main building.

There are two superb suites on the second floor that can easily accommodate a family. These are spacious and very bright, with large bay windows that provide a view not only of the marsh but also of the sea. The rooms by the sea have a private terrace.

The interiors of the rooms are attractive, with beautiful wood floor contrasting the whiteness of the walls. Antique wood and wicker sofas are arranged in a corner. Apart from all the necessary comforts, these room also have beautiful marble bathrooms.

The restaurant, which opens out to the beach, is very pleasant, with an original checkered flooring made up of assorted black, green and white pebbles taken from the beach. It has also pretty bamboo furniture.

The magnificent, almost-deserted beach of Pagudpud is conducive to relaxing and swimming. Here you can be completely alone, as the hotel owns the part of the beach facing the resort. There is no coral reef accessible from the beach, but you can be taken by banca to one close by.

SAUD BEACH RESORT

Pagudpud, Ilocos Norte
Booking Office in Quezon City
No. 29, E. Mayaman Street,
Teacher's Village,
Diliman, Quezon City
Tel/Fax 921-2856

 1. By air and land (3 hours)
Fifty-five-minute flight on Philippine Airlines (4 weekly flights) from Manila to Laoag. One and a half hours by car from Laoag to Pagudpud (60 km).

Note: *The resort can arrange for airport transfer.*

2. By land (11 hours) 548 km from Manila
Take North Expressway at Balintawak and get off at Dau exit. Take North Diversion Road to MacArthur Highway. Heading for the coastal road you will pass by Angeles City, Tarlac, Urdaneta, Pozorrubio and Rosario. Once on the coastal road proceed further north going through San Fernando (La Union), Vigan (Ilocos Sur) and Laoag (Ilocos Norte) before reaching Pagudpud.

 33 Units
16 Deluxe Rooms • 9 Beachfront Rooms (with Veranda overlooking Saud and Natural Lake) • 2 Double Suite Rooms • 2 Honeymooner's Suite • 4 Family Suite Rooms
All rooms have air-conditioning, refrigerator, and a bathroom with hot water, a private terrace.

 Food and Beverage Outlets
Restaurant: Saud Beach Resort Restaurant
Cuisine Offered: Chinese • Seafood • International
Quality: Good

 Watersports and Other Activities
Beach (white sand) • Snorkeling (in other places) • Excursions to Mira Ira Point (30 minutes)
See also Ilocos Norte's points of interest.

 Per room per night inclusive of breakfast

Pannzian Beach
and Mountain Resort

Over the vast stretch of black sand, the mist on certain mornings cascades down the mountains overlooking the sea. The wind has twisted the surrounding trees —such is the superb and strange setting of Pannzian Beach and Mountain Resort. The resort is located along the little coastal road from Pagudpud to Claveria, between the beach and the forested mountain.

The resort is composed of a main building and several cottages, set on a vast slightly sloping terrain facing the sea. A little one-story house is near the coastal road. Though it does not have a view of the sea, it is bright and pleasant. This house may be rented in its entirety or by room only.

It has a covered terrace, a drawing room with a bow-window, a kitchen and several rooms. The five rooms are comfortably air-conditioned and three of them have their own bathroom. If you are with a large group, supplementary mattresses are also provided.

Below the house are two comfortable—but not very appealing—stone bungalows. There is also a large open building which houses the restaurant. Further down below, an older bungalow made of old wood has a nice terrace. It has a pleasant view of the sea across the fields. Unfortunately, during the summer, a campsite set up on the field, obstructs this view.

Access to the wide, black sand beach is not very convenient. Strong winds battering the shore discourage swimming, but you can walk along the shore or hike (with a guide) through the mountain trail just behind the resort.

PANNZIAN BEACH AND MOUNTAIN RESORT

Pansian, Pagudpud, Ilocos Norte
Booking Office in Marikina City
11A, E. Quirino Street, Vista Valley
Marikina City
Tel 646-9020
Fax 682-7844

 1. By air and land (3 hours)
Fifty-five-minute flight on Philippine Airlines (4 weekly flights) from Manila to Laoag. One and a half hours by car from Laoag to Pansian (75 km).

Note: *Pannzian Resort can pick you up from Laoag airport or you can take a public bus headed for Claveria. Pannzian Resort is off the main road.*

2. By land (11 hours) From Manila take North Expressway at Balintawak and get off at Dau Exit. Take North Diversion Road to MacArthur Highway. Heading for the coastal road you will pass by Angeles City, Tarlac, Urdaneta, Pozorrubio and Rosario. Once on the coastal road, proceed further north going through San Fernando (La Union), Vigan (Ilocos Sur), Laoag (Ilocos Norte) until you reach Pagudpud. Pannzian is 15 km away from Pagudpud, along the road going to Claveria.

 10 Units
4 Air-conditioned Cottages • Private House with living room and small kitchen • 3 Air-conditioned bedrooms with bathroom and 2 other air-conditioned bedrooms with bathroom and terrace. There is also a campsite; tents can be rented.

 Food and Beverage Outlets
Restaurant
Cuisine Offered: Filipino (according to what is available from the market); order in advance
Quality: Average

 Watersports and Other Activities
Beach (gray sand) • Swimming (in the river) • Hiking • Tours to Mira Ira Point and Pagudpud. See also Ilocos Norte's points of interest.

Per room per night inclusive of tour and resort guide

Note: *Cash payment only.*

The Batanes Archipelago

If you overcome your anxiety of being stranded by a typhoon for a few days and venture to the archipelago of Batanes, you will not regret it. The best season to visit the archipelago of Batanes is from March to June. This archipelago, to the extreme north of Luzon, is a timeless place, unique and spellbinding, possibly one of the most beautiful discoveries in the Philippines.

The "House of Winds" is a completely harmonious archipelago, where the scenery, architecture and inhabitants of extreme graciousness are in symbiosis with one another. It was precisely the winds that contributed to the particular architecture of the stone villages and fashioned the landscape.

The archipelago is composed of 10 islands and islets, of which Batan, with its small airport in the capital of Basco and Sabtang are the most accessible. Itbayat, the largest of the islands, is less visited, being a four-hour crossing away from Batan on an often-choppy sea. Sporadically a small plane ensures the liaison between Basco and Itbayat.

The Isle of Batan

The archipelago of Batanes is a protected landscape and you must register at the DENR office upon arrival at Basco, where you will be delivered a permit. The isle is still very wooded and forms an ideal place

Sabtang — Village of Chavayan

for trekking with a number of footpaths lining the hollows of the vales and the crests.

THE COASTAL ROUTE AND A VISIT TO THE VILLAGES *(half a day)* A spectacular coastal road allows you to wander through half the isle by jeepney. You will discover a jagged coastline where the high black cliffs are lashed by waves, long, inhospitable, deserted sandy beaches trimming a somber sea, a changing skyline where clouds run swiftly by. In the interior, the countryside is by contrast cheerfully green, with an undulating landscape.

Along the road are the villages of Mahatao, San Vincente, Ivana and Uyugan. To withstand the effects of typhoons and other climatic hazards, the sturdy dwellings were constructed in days gone by with gray stone walls whose thickness could measure up to a meter. They are often whitewashed, have narrow openings and are covered with very dense thatched roofs. Today, many inhabitants prefer constructing the houses in cement and the traditional houses are beginning to be left in abandon. Nevertheless, the further away you go from Basco, the more the ancient habitations have been preserved. The lanes and alleys of the villages are gaily planted with low, well-trimmed bushes and flowers and in the courtyards of the houses, stand enthroned trees with knotted trunks and polished foliage. Fishnets dry by the doorway.

Batan — Marlboro Country near Mt. Matarem

MARLBORO COUNTRY *(half a day)* The "Marlboro Country" with the more poetic local name of "Payaman," (wild pasture lands) is an extremely beautiful landscape of green pastures or groves and hedges of high graminaceae forming astonishing and original geometric designs. White Brahmin cows, buffaloes and goats are left to graze at liberty. In places, a shelter of low tortuous trees forms an impenetrable carpet of closely woven vegetation. Numerous pathways run along the pastures and to discover this unusual landscape it is preferable to set aside half a day.

MOUNT IRAYAT *(One day—Five hours ascent and 3 hours descent)* The silhouette of this 1000-meter high volcano, with its summit often in the clouds, dominates the island. The track begins behind the airport but a guide to show the way is keenly recommended. After crossing the orchards and traversing innumerable ridges you penetrate, at an altitude of 700 meters, a mossy forest. It is here that flourishes the medinila with heavy pink grapes and that the green pigeons nest. The last part of the ascent is very steep and the funnel of the volcano is covered with reeds.

The Isle of Sabtang

The boat with a small, rounded bottomed hull, seems fragile in the waves, but the crossing is short. On the isle of Sabtang, a pretty little blue and white church stands

Ivatan woman

out in profile with a slightly surrealistic allure in this isle at the other end of the world. There are no tricycles or public jeepneys in Sabtang. In fact, there are only two jeepneys on the isle. If you come to Sabtang for the day, it is essential to hire one to visit the different villages. In principle, you can rent it at the grocery shop, next to the pier. You can also easily find lodgings.

SABTANG ISLAND *(day excursion, 30 minutes by tricycle from Basco and 30 minutes crossing by boat)* It is even more untamed than Batanes with better-preserved traditional villages. There you will not fail to see an Ivatan woman wearing the traditional, long and thick headdress made of vegetable fibers.

SAVIDUG It is the first village you will come across with beautiful ancient stone houses. The landscapes you cross to get there are as spectacular as Batan, the coastal road allowing vertiginous views of the sea below. Palm trees punctuate the cliffs covered with short green grass.

CHAVAYAN It is the most striking of the villages and the best preserved. Here, the Ivatans still live in their stone dwellings. You have nice walks through the narrow alley and discover, situated at the end of an impassé in an attractive interior courtyard, a little white chapel. A lone street stall has drinks to offer.

Batan — view towards Mt. Iraya

Batanes Resort

atanes Resort is located on the edge of the cornice facing the South China Sea. As a result, it benefits from a superb view of the wild, jagged, wave-beaten coastline and the cliffs covered by green pastures. From the hotel you can see a beach down below, but it is without direct access.

Batanes Resort is a government hotel and, in terms of comfort and location, it is the best choice in the area, and this at very reasonable rates.

The resort is on a piece of land enclosed by a stonewall. It is planted with a thick lawn brightened with massifs of different varieties of multi-colored flowers.

It comprises six duplex bungalows aligned facing the ocean, constructed on terraces with pebbled buttresses. Two bungalows stand independently on a small rise.

The bungalows are scarcely in the traditional architectural style of the country, but are nevertheless pleasant with their walls in gray pebbles and their windows and doors with little tiles painted in white. Unfortunately, a red corrugated iron roof covers them.

Each room is clean and attractive with their flooring and pink walls and enjoy a pleasing view of the garden and the distant sea.

The reception area is slightly lower down, also facing the sea. The restaurant is brightened by numerous openings, pleasantly lulled by the sea breeze. From the high ceiling, two crystal chandeliers, are suspended in a slightly incongruous manner, in stark contrast with the plastic tables. They are however, covered with white tablecloths at mealtimes. You may indicate your culinary preferences, but provisions on the island are hard to come by. In May, try the delicious mabolo fruit whose trees are abundant on the island.

The hotel is a good starting point for visiting the island, only three kilometers from Basco. Tricycles pass frequently on the coastal road either in the direction of Basco or in the direction of the wharf for the Isle of Sabtang. Moreover, the hotel can reserve a jeepney for you, with a driver for the day.

Going down the road, 200 meters to the left and after a little bridge, a tranquil path leads to a meteorological station. It is a worthwhile promenade in the heart of the prairies and you will discover the beautiful views of Payaman and the coast.

BATANES RESORT

Kaychanarianan, Basco, Batanes
No phone at the resort.
Tel (078) 533-3444
       (078) 533-3456
Tel (Manila) 927-2393
Note: *Your message will be delivered to the resort*

By air and land (3 hours)
One-hundred-and-twenty-minute flight on Asian Spirit (4 weekly flights) from Manila to Basco. Chartered plane: CHEMTRAD, in Tuguegarao City. Tricycle: 20 minutes from Basco airport to the hotel.

6 Units
6 Duplex-type Cottages with bathroom and water heater

Watersports and Other Activities
Beach • Trekking • Bird Watching • Fishing • Tours to Ivatan houses and Marlboro country (Payaman), Isle of Sabtang

Per room per night

Note: *Cash Only*

Southern Luzon

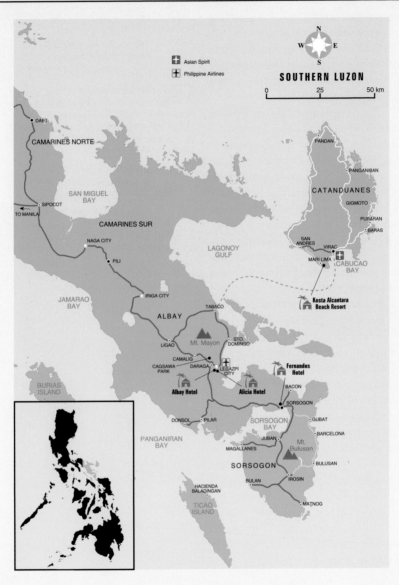

✈ Asian Spirit
✈ Philippine Airlines

SOUTHERN LUZON

0   25   50 km

N
W   E
S

DAET

CAMARINES NORTE

SAN MIGUEL
BAY

SIPOCOT
TO MANILA

CAMARINES SUR

NAGA CITY

PILI

LAGONOY
GULF

JAMARAO
BAY

IRIGA CITY

TABACO

ALBAY

LIGAO

Mt. Mayon

STO.
DOMINGO

CAMALIG

CAGSAWA
PARK

DARAGA

LEGAZPI
CITY

Albay Hotel

Alicia Hotel

**Fernandos
Hotel**

BACON

SORSOGON

BURIAS
ISLAND

DONSOL

PILAR

SORSOGON
BAY

GUBAT

PANGANIRAN
BAY

JUBAN

Mt.
Bulusan

BARCELONA

MAGALLANES

SORSOGON

BULUSAN

HACIENDA
BALADINGAN

BULAN

IROSIN

TICAO
ISLAND

MATNOG

PANDAN

PANGANIBAN

CATANDUANES

GIGMOTO

PURARAN

BARAS

SAN
ANDRES

VIRAC

MARI LIMA

CABUCAO
BAY

**Kosta Alcantara
Beach Resort**

Climate **East Albay, East Sorsogon and Catanduanes:** No dry season
with a very pronounced maximum rainfall from December to
January
West Albay and Sorsogon: Rainfall more or less evenly
distributed throughout the year
Ticao Island: Not very pronounced, relatively dry from
November to April; wet during the rest of the year
Typhoons May to November

Albay

A mere 55-minute flight takes you to Legaspi, the capital of Albay, located 547 kilometers from Manila. The province boasts of old, well-preserved churches and Mayon volcano. Mayon's majestic silhouette, seen from as far off as the islands of Catanduanes and Ticao, towers above the plains.

MAYON VOLCANO The volcano's local name "magayon" means beautiful and it really is captivating with its perfect cone of 2,421-meter high incessantly coughing up smoke and gas. Different lava flows can be observed on its slopes. It is an active volcano, which most recently erupted in 1993; but it was the eruption of 1814 that was most destructive. Until late 2002, some volcanic activities were detected. The volcano is constantly monitored by The Philippine Institute of Volcanology and Seismology.

The challenging climb to Mayon is usually begun from Buyoan and takes at least two days—after getting authorization from the Tourism Office of Legaspi. It will provide you with a guide and necessary equipment as well as give you information regarding the climb including potential risks. The first night is spent in a little hut with basic amenities, and at an altitude of 1,800 meters, it can get quite chilly. The base of the volcano is forested with tortured, twisted trees. After this, you reach an arid zone. The last 250 meters are the most tedious and exhausting. Rocks and gravel roll under your feet—and onto those following behind you.

THE RUINS OF CAGSAWA (*6 kilometers northwest of Legaspi*) The village of Cagsawa was completely destroyed by the eruption in 1814. Overshadowed by the Mayon, nothing is left but ruins from which emerges the salvaged tower of the 18th-century church.

THE CAMALIG CHURCH (*14 kilometers northwest of Legaspi*) The town of Camalig was also destroyed in 1814 and only the massive, lava-stone 19th-century church remains.

Albay Church

The caves of Hoyop-Hoyopan are eight kilometers from the surroundings.

THE CHURCH OF DARAGA (*5 kilometers northwest of Legaspi*) This 18th-century baroque church of black volcanic stone is decorated with beautiful sculptures on its main façade. Perched on a promontory, it has the formidable Mayon in the background.

SANTO DOMINGO (*coastal road from Legaspi to Tabaco, 11 kilometers from Legaspi*) The route from Legaspi to Tabaco, which is the departure point for ferries to the island of Catanduanes, is quite spectacular. It twists and turns around the volcano. You will see green rice fields interspersed with lava flows and fallen rocks, and pass through the town of Santo Domingo, which has a church dating back to 1789. The church was built from lava blocks.

THE CHURCH OF SAINT JOHN THE BAPTIST AT TABACO (*27 kilometers from Legaspi*) In the town center, make a stopover to see the well-preserved, beautiful coral church and its detached bell tower. If you need to take the early morning ferry to Catanduanes, it is a good idea to spend the night at Tabaco.

THE CUISINE OF BICOL The region of Bicol is known for its spicy culinary specialties, cooked in coconut milk. The *Bicol Express* leaves an indelible fiery impression in your mouth! *Pili* nuts, another specialty, which taste like almonds, are made into delicious sweets.

Albay Hotel

In the chaotic town of Legaspi, Albay Hotel is the best possible choice. It is a large, white, five-story building in the city center, brighter than the other hotels.

On the ground floor are the large reception hall with marble flooring, a restaurant and a coffee shop. The rooms are bright and spacious, offer-ing all the necessary comforts and amenities. The furniture is sober and functional; the tapestry, beige curtains, and the clean wooden floors are an absolute contrast to the worn-out car-peting you find in most of the other hotels. There is a little drawing room of lacquered bamboo; the large bath-rooms are tiled in white. All the rooms, with the exception of two that have no windows at all, have bay windows offering a good view of Mayon Volcano. Some rooms at the back of the hotel have a view of a river and an amusing restaurant on stilts.

The hotel has two restaurants. Café Ola is more pleasant as its windows look out onto a small garden. Comfortable benches are set near the windows around bistro tables; a variety of specialities from Bicol is offered. At the back is a quiet area with an outdoor bar and swimming pool which was not appealing when we last visited.

Notes: *An alternative to the Albay Hotel is the Alicia Hotel on the outskirts of the city, just two minutes away from the airport. The hotel's reception area and the restaurant-bar have a quiet air and a subtle elegance, with soft colors, marble floors, beautiful wrought iron furniture and comfortable armchairs. The rooms are pleasant and do not cost as much as those at the Albay Hotel, being generally smaller. Alicia Hotel, Capt. F. Aquende Drive, Legaspi. Tel. Nos.: (052) 481-4444 • 481-0801*

You can also stay at the Casa Eugenia Hotel in Tagas. This is a fairly new and pleasant hotel whose owners also own one of the ferry companies that offers trips to Catanduanes. Tel. Nos.: (052) 830-0425 • 558-2307

ALBAY HOTEL
88 Peñaranda Street,
Legaspi City, Albay
Tel/Fax (052) 480-8660
(052) 481-3223

Booking Office in Makati
Eagle Crest Building,
Sen. Gil Puyat Avenue corner
Pasong Tamo, Makati City
Tel 816-2373
Fax 815-4730

 1. By air and land (1 ½ hours)
Fifty-five-minute daily flights on Philippine Airlines from Manila to Legaspi. Fifteen minutes by car from Legaspi airport to the hotel.

2. By land (9–11 hours) 547 km from Manila. Take South Superhighway and get off at Calamba, Exit No. 50A (Batangas, Lucena, Legaspi). You will go through the province of Quezon (passing Lucena), then through the Bicol Peninsula, passing two provinces and their capitals: Camarines Norte (Daet) and Camarines Sur (Naga). Another route, which is also a shortcut to Naga and Legaspi is the Quirino Highway. Saving one and a half hours travel time, it is made by making a right turn before reaching Sta. Elena and meets the National Highway at Sipocot.

Note: *If you arrive by bus, the hotel is located five minutes from the bus station. Free transfer from Legaspi airport is arranged by the hotel.*

 75 Units
56 Deluxe Rooms • 19 Junior Suites
All rooms have air-conditioning, a bathroom with hot water, telephone, TV.

Indoor Facilities and Services
Babysitting • Car rental

Food and Beverage Outlets
Restaurants: Cafe Ola (coffee shop open 24 hours) • Miraya (function room for fine dining)
Cuisine Offered: Filipino • Chinese
Quality: Average

 Watersports and Other Activities
Swimming pool • Tours to Albay's points of interest

 Per room per night

Sorsogon Province and Ticao Island in Masbate

Located at the southernmost point of Luzon, Sorsogon exudes a feeling of subtle joyfulness. You are instantly seduced by the scenic charm of this rural region of green hills and cascading springs dominated by the Bulusan volcano. Whale sharks also frequent the waters off Sorsogon, making it an ideal location for spotting these giants of the sea. The churches of Sorsogon, badly renovated as cement now covers the volcanic stone façades, are less remarkable than those in Albay.

The island of Ticao belongs to the province of Masbate, but since it is very accessible from Sorsogon (Pilar or Bulan), it is mentioned in this section.

Sorsogon

DONSOL AND THE WHALE SHARKS (*1 hour from Legaspi or Sorsogon*)   The best season to observe the whale sharks is between December and May, especially in March before the water temperature rises. These whales are not aggressive, living on plankton, little fish and shrimps. They can grow up to 18 meters in length, but those sighted at Donsol range between 4 and 12 meters. The whale shark is characterized by a bluish-gray body marked with white spots and streaks, a large flat head and a massive mouth with minuscule teeth. Upon your early-morning arrival at Donsol, go to the visitor's center at the Municipal Tourism

Palogtoc Waterfalls

Council, where you will pay an entrance fee and then be directed to your boat.

THE TOWN OF SORSOGON (*62 kilometers from Legaspi*) This little town and its hotel, Fernandos Hotel, is a good base from which to discover the province. Moreover, the owners know the region perfectly well and are interested in developing eco-tourism.

BACON (*10 kilometers from Sorsogon*) This little town faces the Bay of Sugot. It has a nice beach two kilometers away, from where you will see the mountains on the island of Rapu-Rapu. Its church was partially renovated.

THE BARCELONA CHURCH (*27 kilometers from Sorsogon*) This is one of the few churches in the province that have kept its original features including its façade of black coral.

THE BEACH OF DANCALAN (*42 kilometers from Sorsogon*) This is a very pretty beach facing the Pacific Ocean, widening at low tide, as is the case of many of the beaches in the region. If you wish to stay near the beach, the Villa Luisa Celeste Resort is quite suitable. (Tel. No.: (056) 211-2991 • (0919) 593-4939).

THE RIZAL BEACH AT GUBAT (*19 kilometers from Sorsogon*) This is a long stretch of pretty white sand beach facing the Pacific Ocean. Stop and lunch at the Veramaris Resort—a tall building on the beach (Tel. No.: (056) 311-1824 at Gubat).

THE WATERFALLS OF PALOGTOC (*about 30 kilometers from Sorsogon*) Below a superb coconut grove with its well-maintained green lawn, you will see the aquamarine waterfalls enveloped in tree ferns. Children love to swim here, and in the warm waters of the Masacrot Waterfalls.

THE BULUSAN VOLCANO (*42 kilometers from Sorsogon*) The scenic beauty of Sorsogon is evident in Bulusan, an active volcano with an altitude of 1,560 meters. The little crater lake located at an altitude of 600 meters is accessible by car. An archway of trees shades the little track that takes you there. A forest with a well-marked track—you can go around it in one hour—surrounds the dark, emerald green waters of the lake. The climb to the volcano starts from the lake through a dense forest and takes at least one day.

MATEO HOT SPRINGS (*43 kilometers from Sorsogon*) The noisy resort located nearby, unfortunately, spoils the site of the waterfalls at the foot of Bulusan.

The Island of Ticao in Masbate

The Island of Ticao is about one and a half hours from Pilar, near Donsol. Hacienda Baladingan, set on a 600-hectare coconut grove bordered by a gold-sand beach, is the place for those seeking a quiet and charming place with simple comforts. The three-room house is rented for a modest sum along with the services of a cook and a maid. The trip from Legaspi to Pilar can be done by jeepney and then by private *banca*. The staff of the Hacienda can organize this for you. You can combine your stay with a whale shark excursion, as Donsol is 10 minutes away from Pilar. One and a half hours from the Hacienda by *banca*, a fossilized limestone waterfall, 40 meters high, pours directly into the sea. You can also go walking in the 50-hectare second growth forest close by.

For more information, contact Francis Ho – globecare@manila.com.ph

Fernandos Hotel

ocated in the heart of Sorsogon, the hotel's owner, Gina Duran, is its good fortune. She knows the region well, loves it, and takes pains to acquaint visitors with the area, in an effort to promote eco-tourism. She is full of good advice and can even organize a variety of excursions.

In a region that does not have many tourists, such concern merits making Fernandos Hotel a base from which to visit the province. Its central location is convenient for visiting the different attractions of Sorsogon. Aside from the usual places to visit, Fernandos recommends a series of excursions mentioned in the practical page.

The hotel is a simple two-story building with a small garden patio. The ground floor has a reception area and a restaurant that looks onto this patio through large French windows left open on fine days.

This is the best place to unwind, as the ambiance is warm and bright. The wicker and wood sofas, pink sandstone floor, green plants and fans with opaline lamps give it a quaint, antique style. You can have an idea of the the region by viewing video cassettes in the drawing room. The restaurant and bar are in the extension of the reception area. In the evening, bamboo tables and chairs are set up on the patio.

Some rooms on the ground floor near the restaurant can get quite noisy. The others are on the second floor and are linked by a corridor overlooking the restaurant. These rooms are large and clean with a gray sandstone floors and simple, functional furniture.

All the rooms have a view of the garden, which is left somewhat untended on the other side of the building.

FERNANDOS HOTEL

N. Pareja Street, Bitan-o, Sorsogon City
Tel (056) 211-1357
Tel/Fax (056) 211-1573
E-mail
fernandohotel@hotmail.com
cecilia_h_duran@yahoo.com
Web www.sorsogontourism.com

1. By air and land (2½ hours)
Fifty-five-minute daily flight on Philippine Airlines from Manila to Legaspi. One hour by car/bus (62 km) from Legaspi to Sorsogon.
2. By land (10–12 hours) 609 km from Manila. Take South Superhighway and get off at Calamba, Exit No. 50A (Batangas, Lucena, Legaspi). You will go through the province of Quezon (passing by Lucena) and then through the Bicol Peninsula passing provinces and their capitals, Camarines Norte (Daet), Camarines Sur (Naga). Another route which is also a shortcut to Naga and Legaspi is the Quirino Highway. Saving one and a half hours travel time, it is made by making a right turn before reaching Sta. Elena and meets the National Highway at Sipocot.

16 Units
8 Standard air-conditioned rooms • 5 Executive Rooms (3 with bathtub & refrigerator) • 3 Mabuhay Rooms (2 with common bathroom and 1 with bathroom)
All rooms have air-conditioning, a bathroom with hot water and TV. The suites have bathtubs.

Indoor Facilities and Services
Car rental • Massage

Food and Beverage Outlets
Restaurant: Kalundan Seafood
Restaurant
Cuisine Offered: Filipino • Seafood

Watersports and Other Activities
Car rental to Sorsogon • Mountain biking • Tennis • Island hopping to Paghuliran Island in Sawanga, Tikling Island in Matnog, Juag Island near Matnog • Whale shark interaction in Donsol • Diving in Bacon • Snorkeling • Dive center • Fishing • Sunset cruise • Trekking • Bulusan volcano climbing • Tours to PNCO waterfalls near Sorsogon, Bulusan Lake, Hot Springs and Churches • Birdwatching in mangroves of Puerto Dias (one hour from Sorsogon) • See also Sorsogon's points of interest with a rented car

Per room per night inclusive of breakfast

Catanduanes

Off Tabaco, on the Pacific Ocean, Catanduanes is an island totally bypassed by the tourists—a fact that is certain to please those who prefer something off the beaten track.

It is a fairly large island with a surface area of 1,511 square kilometers. The countryside is permanently green as even during the dry season, Catanduanes is prone to sudden passing showers. Its exposure to typhoons has given the island its name, "The Land of the Howling Winds."

The poor state of the road network and the lack of hotel infrastructure limit

Catanduanes Coast

the discovery of this beautiful island. A few hotels are located along the southeast coast of the island, east of Virac, the capital. Kosta Alcantara is the only resort with a certain appeal, as the others are not well maintained or have closed down.

BEACHES

The jagged, rocky, southeast coast of Catanduanes between Igang and San Andres is composed of several bays with golden sand. Igang, Bosdak, and Batag with its limestone arch; Marilima, where Alcantara Resort is located, and Palauig are also beautiful white sand beaches where you can be taken by *banca*. This side of the coast faces Luzon and you have a spectacular view of Bulusan Volcano and Mayon Volcano close by. Unforgettable is the view of Mayon's perfect cone—rising from the waves in the slight blue morning mist, then turning red and purple at dusk.

THE "MINI CHOCOLATE HILLS"

Behind Palauig, also on the southeast coast, you will get a glimpse of little, round forested hilltops lying in the middle of the rice fields. These bring to mind the Chocolate Hills of Bohol—on a small scale. It is pleasant and easy to walk or bike around the area.

SURFING

Puraran, about 30 kilometers from Virac on the east coast, is renowned for this sport. There is no existing resort making it necessary to camp or be accommodated by the local residents. Given the condition of the road network, it is not possible to go from the Alcantara Resort to the surfing area, in a day.

Kosta Alcantara Beach Resort

The Kosta Alcantara Beach Resort is located between two rocky promontories at one end of the white, kilometer-long Marilima Beach. The residence of Severo Alcantara who retired here with his wife and opened it to the public a few years ago. The atmosphere of the resort is a reflection of the graciousness of Mr. Alcantara and his staff.

The house is surrounded by a garden where Mrs. Alcantara lovingly tends some magnificent species of orchids. The beach is bordered by coconut trees and the back of the resort leans against a hill, giving it an air somewhat of the Chocolate Hills of Bohol. The resort is made up of only one low concrete building, parallel to the beach. A large sheltered terrace on the ground floor, which occupies nearly the whole length of the building, and ends with a bar. This sheltered terrace is largely open and offers a splendid view of the sea. You can see the elegant silhouette of Mayon Volcano and its neighbor, Bulusan Volcano, in the distance. At sunset, soft clouds which sometimes drape the volcanoes evoke the fragility of a Japanese etching.

The locally inspired furniture, the bar and the covering of certain walls, are made largely from the beautiful speckled anahaw wood. The interior décor exudes a sober elegance, reinforced by the gray-pink tone of the floor tiles. Overlooking the terrace, which is transformed into a dining room during meal-times, are two rooms with a view of the garden at the back. On the first floor, linked by a gallery over-looking the terrace, are four other rooms. These are quite charming, largely due to the sloping ceiling covered with anahaw leaves intertwined to form overlapping fans. These rooms with pretty blue flooring have simple, dark wood furniture. The only inconvenience is that there is only one adjoining bathroom to be shared by two rooms.

At low tide, the sand is laid bare for miles as the water recedes; you have to walk quite far out to swim. At high tide, however, the waves roll at the foot of the terrace, completely covering the shore. Visitors sometimes come to rent the huts on the beach for a couple of hours.

It is possible to explore the surrounding countryside on foot, with tricycle or by a car belonging to the resort. You can also hire a *banca* to discover the rocky coast and the other bays rimmed with turquoise waters.

KOSTA ALCANTARA BEACH RESORT

 Marilima, Virac, Catanduanes
No phone. Radio communications only.

Booking Office in Virac
Fax (052) 859-7001 • 8010445
(052) 811-1459

 1. By air and land (2 hours)
Seventy-five-minute daily flights on Asian Spirit from Manila to Virac. Thirty minutes by car from Virac airport to the resort.

2. By air, land, sea (7 hours)
Fifty-five-minute daily flight on Philippine Airlines from Manila to Legaspi. 1 hour by bus from Legaspi. Four hours by ferry from Tabaco to Virac. Two companies service this route: MV Bicolandia Lines Inc. leaves at 6:30 a.m. (Tel. No.: (052) 830-1187); Regina Shipping Lines, San Andres, Catanduanes, leaves at 1 p.m. (Tel. No.: (052) 811-1345). Thirty minutes by car from Virac harbor to the resort.

Note: *Transfer from Virac airport to the harbor can be arranged by the resort.*

 6 Units
Ground floor: 2 Double Rooms (each with a bathroom) • Second floor: 4 Double Rooms (with 2 bathrooms; 2 rooms share a bathroom)
All rooms have air-conditioning; no hot water.

 Food and Beverage Outlets
Restaurant on the terrace
Cuisine Offered: Filipino • Seafood (depending on the catch of the day)
Quality: Good

 Watersports and Activities
Beach (white sand) • Snorkeling (in other places—try Bosdak, but snorkeling is not the best here) • Island hopping • Boats for hire • Fishing (by arrangement)

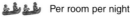 Per room per night

Note: *Cash payment only.*

Mindoro

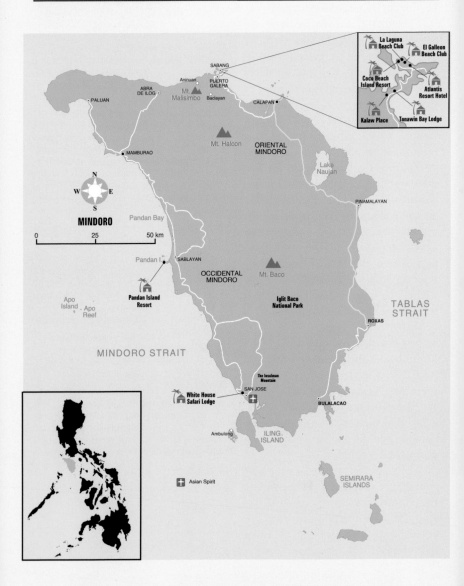

La Laguna Beach Club
El Galleon Beach Club
Coco Beach Island Resort
Atlantis Resort Hotel
Kalaw Place
Tanawin Bay Lodge

SABANG
Aninuan
PUERTO GALERA
Mt. Malisimbo
Baclayan
ABRA DE ILOG
PALUAN
CALAPAN
Mt. Halcon
ORIENTAL MINDORO
MAMBURAO
Lake Naujan
N
W · E
S
MINDORO
Pandan Bay
PINAMALAYAN
0   25   50 km
Pandan I.
SABLAYAN
OCCIDENTAL MINDORO
Mt. Baco
Pandan Island Resort
Apo Island
Apo Reef
Iglit Baco National Park
TABLAS STRAIT
ROXAS
MINDORO STRAIT
The Insulman Mountain
SAN JOSE
White House Safari Lodge
BULALACAO
Ambulong
ILING ISLAND
Asian Spirit
SEMIRARA ISLANDS

Climate   Seasons not very pronounced, relatively dry from
           November to April; wet during the rest of the year

Typhoons   February to April and November to December

Mindoro

Mindoro, about 10,000 square kilometers in size, is the nearest big island to Manila. A mountain range whose highest points are Mount Halcon (2,586 meters) and Mount Baco (2,488 meters) runs across it from north to south and serves as a natural boundary between the two provinces that make up the island: Mindoro Oriental, famous for Puerto Galera, and Mindoro Occidental.

Mindoro is endowed with many attractions: rainforest-clad mountains where the rare, endangered tamaraw dwells, the Mangyan Tribes, and the spectacular diving and snorkeling sites around Puerto Galera. Surprisingly though, the island has been well preserved, as tourism is very much managed in the area.

There are limited airline connections to the island. Travel time takes about five hours from Manila. Most of the area is owned by wealthy Filipino families who wish to keep the island as it is. The other important towns of Calapan and, on the Occidental coast, Mamburao and San Jose, are less visited—although San Jose has flights from Manila. The road network is very poor, with some sections even impassable during the rainy season.

Muelle Bay

Oriental Mindoro: Puerto Galera

The crossing from Batangas to Puerto Galera, between Maricaban and Verde Islands, is already a pleasure. The arrival itself is amazing, as the site is truly exceptional: hilly peninsulas and islets encircle Muelle Bay, its calm and transparent waters accessible through the two narrow channels of Batangas and Manila. Puerto Galera lies at the far end of the bay and is one of the best natural harbors in the Philippines. It once served as a refuge for Spanish galleons en route to India and other parts of Asia and Mexico. Today, it shelters sailboats. Puerto Galera offers many lodging possibilities in resorts that rarely have a capacity higher than 30 rooms. Most are built and decorated with natural local materials. Here, you are far from Mactan's heavy urbanization and the frenetic development that Boracay is faced with at the moment.

Main areas of lodging

SABANG and its hectic routine—every square meter of ground or sand is practically occupied by a house, a bar or a *banca* — is what you will definitely avoid if you want peace and quiet. Atlantis Resort is nonetheless a little apart from this commotion. Sabang is accessible by *banca* or by car from Puerto Galera.

BIG LA LAGUNA AND SMALL LA LAGUNA are very narrow white sand beaches that sometimes disappear at high tide. This is where many comfortable resorts, generally specializing in diving, are located. Big La Laguna has the advantage of having good snorkeling directly from the beach. These beaches are accessible only by *banca* or on foot from Sabang (30 minutes to get to Big La Laguna).

THE BEACHES OF WHITE BEACH AND ANINUAN Located west of Puerto Galera, these beaches are accessible by car or *banca*. These are beautiful white sand beaches, but it was not possible to select any place of particular charm as the development of the beachfront was done in a disorderly manner and most resorts are too basic and not very well-maintained. However, it is but fair to note Tamaraw (Cell No.: (0917) 324-7061) on Aninuan Beach, with its peaceful atmosphere and Mindorinne Oriental (Cell No.: (0917) 857-8425) on White Beach. In Aninuan, you can stop and have lunch in one of the small huts on the beach.

SECLUDED RESORTS

Lovers of more secluded places have the option to stay at Coco Beach Resort, set apart in a cove with its own beach, or even better, at the wonderful small resort of Tanawin, perched on its hill overlooking Varadero Bay. There is also the romantic Kalaw Place, hidden in an enchanting forest park facing Muelle Bay.

Puerto Galera

As the area is superb and has many interesting attractions, there is so much to choose from. It will be necessary to come back, time and again, to be able to see everything—and again with the same pleasure.

THE VILLAGE OF PUERTO GALERA

It is a small, quiet village with flower-lined streets where you will find some handicraft shops, notably those with the beautiful, fine basketwork of the Mangyan tribes. There is also the Excavation Museum in front of the church, which showcases porcelain and artifacts found in the wrecks of Chinese junks and Spanish galleons that sank in the region. Do not miss having a drink at the harbor at the Coco Point Café, while viewing the sailboats and colored *bancas*.

THE BEACHES

The mountainous coastline of Puerto Galera, 42 kilometers long, is composed of numerous beaches and deserted, secret coves of white sand, bordered by crystal-clear waters. It is very pleasant to go island hopping—all the resorts offer trips—and have a swim or a picnic at Long Beach, Halige Beach, Aninuan Beach, Talipanan Beach and Paradise Beach, just to mention a few of the most well-known. The finest is, without doubt, Bayanan Beach.

Mindoro Coast

DIVE SITES *(5 minutes to 1 hour from the main beaches)* Puerto Galera's reputation as a diving destination took off in 1983. It is still one of the most important diving destinations today and its reputation has become quite international. There are about 15 dive centers and about 30 diving sites recorded as of this writing. The coral reefs are protected and marine life is of great diversity and beauty. If all you do is snorkel, you will certainly have your fill as well: Big La Laguna Beach, Long Beach, and Coral Garden with its dense carpet of pink and yellow corals are feasts for the eyes. Big La Laguna is the ideal place for children who snorkel, as the water is shallow and calm.

PONDEROSA GOLF *(20 minutes)* Ponderosa was created by Tony Taylor, a golf enthusiast. It is set at an altitude of 600 meters in a beautiful mountainous area covered with rainforest, overlooking the bay of Puerto Galera. The resorts can register you for a game.

View from Ponderosa Golf

But even if you do not play golf, go and have a drink just the same at the terrace of the bar that offers a fantastic view of the bay.

MOUNT MALISIMBO *(day tour)* Mount Malisimbo, with an altitude of about 1,400 meters, is in Aninuan, 15 kilometers from Puerto Galera. Ask the resort way in advance to organize the climb for you with a guide. From Ponderosa Golf, you can walk to the beautiful forest next to Mount Malisimbo.

CALAPAN CITY *(2 hours and 30 minutes)* Calapan, the administrative capital of Oriental Mindoro, has a colorful market and an arena where cockfights are held every Sunday at 3 o'clock p.m. To get there, you will cross rice fields, calamansi plantations and waterfalls lost in the vegetation, affording several majestic panoramas of the coastline.

SAN RAFAEL RIVER *(1 hour by banca, 1 hour and 30 minutes by car)* If you go by car, take the route to Calapan. You can rent a small *banca* to go upriver from the village located at the river's mouth.

THE VILLAGES OF THE MANGYAN IRAYA TRIBE *(30 minutes for the nearest tribe)* The back country and the tribes are also interesting to discover. The resorts can organize visits to the villages, but do hire a guide and try not to disturb this already endangered population. The Mangyans, kin to the aboriginal tribes of Mindoro, are composed of several ethnic groups, one of which is the Irayas who live around Puerto Galera. Originally, they were peaceful nomads who were forced to seek refuge in the mountains. Today they live on land reserved for them by the government. The Mangyans live simply in modest *nipa* and bamboo huts, cultivating the land for livelihood. They also make exquisite, finely-woven baskets with geometric motifs of black, beige and brown. Certain villages are easily reached—Baclayan is a 30-minute jeepney ride from Puerto Galera.

TAMARAW FALLS *(45 minutes)* The waterfalls can be seen from the road and, down below, a path leads to natural rock pools where you can swim amid lush vegetation.

Tanawin Bay Lodge

Perched like an eagle's nest on the peak of a hill overlooking Varadero and Muelle Bays, Tanawin is only two kilometers from Puerto Galera. Far from the bustle of Sabang Beach, Small La Laguna or Big La Laguna, it is the ideal resort for those seeking secret and serene places.

The resort is surrounded by a magnificent tropical garden with stone paths lined with santan and hibiscus. Coconut and fan palm trees dot the green, their trunks hosting orchid plants. An old jasmine tree has fleeting blossoms in April that perfume the pool area with its persistent fragrance. The gray marble pool has a pavilion that houses the bar. The view from the resort is both spectacular and dramatic.

The houses, each one is unique in its own way, with stone walls and imposing thatched roofs evoking a fairy tale-like atmosphere, are standing around the garden.

The Snail House is the most impressive of the guesthouses with its turret, topped with a pointed roof, dominating the precipice. Its rounded interior is composed of two levels, a ground floor with a mini-kitchen and a living room, and a second floor that houses the bedroom and a gray marble bathroom.

The rooms have big picture windows that look out to the sea. The wide terrace of braided bamboo is a lovely place to sit and watch the enchanting view of Varadero Bay and the changing seascape. At night, the lights of fishing boats seem to besiege the tower.

Higher up along the pathway, on the other side of the crest, is the two-story Circular House. It has a thatched roof that reaches down to the ground. It is made up of two suites in a half-moon pattern. Each suite has two floors, with a small living room and a bathroom on the ground floor, and a bedroom upstairs. All rooms have a view of Muelle Bay. A semi-circular terrace links the two suites, making it very convenient for a family.

The Sunset House is suffused with the warm light of the setting sun on Muelle Bay. You enter the house through a small bamboo bridge. Its interior, though smaller and simpler, is nevertheless very pleasant and cozy. Everything is either made of wood or braided bamboo. A French window opens to a small terrace.

The main house is where the owner—Herbert Wunnemann, a former civil engineer who designed the resort, and his Filipina wife, Vangie—stay. It also shelters the restaurant, the sitting room-cum-library and three bedrooms. Meals are taken on the terrace where there is a fabulous view of the garden and Varadero Bay. However, on windy evenings, dinner is served in the interior patio. Service is always elegant, and the bamboo tables are set with bowls of lovely flowers.

There is no beach at the resort, but it is possible to go swimming in a cove just below it. However, as the cove can only be accessed via a 200-step staircase, it may be difficult for the children or the elderly. An alternative is to rent a *banca* to go diving in the bay or explore other beaches, like the one in nearby Encenada.

TANAWIN BAY LODGE
Puerto Galera, Oriental Mindoro
Tel/Fax (043) 442-0112 • 287-3337
(0916) 221-9647
E-mail sales@tanawinbayresort.com
Web www.tanawinbayresort.com

By land, sea and land
1. (4 ½ hours) Three hours by car/van from Manila to Batangas Harbor. The resort can arrange for a private vehicle to pick you up from the airport or your residence/hotel in Manila, or you can take your own car. The route is via South Superhighway. Get off at Exit 50A to Lucena, turn right to the Star Tollway, to Batangas, get off at Lipa/Tambo exit, turn left to Batangas. At Batangas Harbor, leave your car at the parking area. **Resort Banca** One hour from Batangas Harbor to Muelle Pier. **Resort Minibus** 5 minutes from Muelle Pier to the resort.
2. (5 hours) Sikat Ltd., operates a daily bus and ferry service from Manila to Puerto Galera. The bus departs from City State Tower Hotel and has a direct connection with a ferry in Batangas Harbor. For information/reservations call Tel. No.: 521-3344 • Fax: 526-2758. **Resort Minibus** 5 minutes from Muelle pier.
3. (5 hours) CCL Shipping Lines also operates a daily van and ferry service from Manila to Puerto Galera. The service van departs from the Swagman Hotel and has a direct connection with the Island Cruiser in Batangas Harbor. Tel. No.: 523-8545. **Resort Minibus** 5 minutes from Muelle Pier.
4. (5 ½ hours) Three hours by car from Manila to Batangas Harbor. See option 1. In Batangas Harbor you have to complete the formalities (allow 30 minutes) for being allowed to ship your car on board the Montenegro Shipping Lines car ferry. You need to show your car documents. **Car ferry** One and a half to 2 hours by Montenegro Lines from Batangas Harbor to Balatero Pier (4 km from Puerto Galera). 15 minutes by car from Balatero pier to the resort via Sabang village. Montenegro Shipping Lines has two daily services. Tel. No.: (043) 723-8294.

6 Units
The Snail House (good for 2; with a kitchenette and minibar) • 2 Executive Circular Houses • 2 Superior Sunset Rooms (good for 2) • 1 Triangle House
Except for the rooms in the main house, which share a common bathroom, all rooms have a bathroom with hot water and fan.

Indoor Facilities and Services
Massage • Car rental • Foreign currency exchange • Babysitting • Library

Food and Beverage Outlets
Restaurant: Al Fresco Dining
Cuisine Offered: International
Quality: Good

Watersports and Other Activities
Swimming pool • Snorkeling (in other places) • Diving arrangements with nearby dive shops • Island hopping • Kayaking • Other boats for hire • Fishing • Sunset cruise • Trekking to Mountain Malisimbo • Mountain biking

 Per room per night

Kalaw Place

I solated on one of the promontories dominating Muelle Bay, Kalaw Place brings to mind the setting of "Sleeping Beauty" as soon as you walk through its large iron gate. The area is filled with molave trees, bougainvillaea, cycas, fan palms, narra trees and wild orchids, all growing over wild grass. The main house, constructed more than 20 years ago by Mr. Kalaw — owner of the resort, is perched on a platform facing the sea, completely hidden by the vegetation.

Mr. Kalaw put his whole heart into this beautiful, romantic old house. Twisted tree trunks serve as columns and balustrades, bamboo as staircase ramps. Glass and *capiz* bay windows punctuate the façade made of huge bamboo brackets. On a slightly elevated terrace, as well as in the interior of the house, you discover attractive antique furniture, rocking chairs, pedestal tables, oil paintings, cabinets inlaid with mother-of-pearl and tables with thick wooden tops. Aside from the dining room where the meals are prepared by Mrs. Kalaw, the house also contains four guest rooms, two per level. One of the rooms on the second floor is an apartment composed of two bedrooms and one large living room with a built-in kitchen. All the rooms have spacious interiors with bamboo walls and pretty marble bathrooms.

Aside from the rooms in the main house, another house a few steps below, with a sumptuous view of the bay, has three very spacious rooms with a kitchenette. The rooms open onto a terrace through large *capiz* panels. What a pleasure to wake up in the morning with a wonderful view of the sea and the iridescent flight of the kingfishers!

A stone staircase goes down towards the shore to a little jetty. There is no beach here as the coast is fringed with mangroves. But it is here that you wait for the *banca*, which takes you to discover the coast and the nearby beaches. Puerto Galera, Coral Garden or White Beach are less than 15 minutes away. Mr. Kalaw can contact the diving clubs and provide you with a guide if you prefer to trek in the mountains.

KALAW PLACE

Palangan, Puerto Galera, Oriental Mindoro
Tel (0917) 532-2617
Tel/Fax (043) 442-0209
E-mail kalaw@kalawplace.com.ph
Web www.kalawplace.com.ph

 By land and sea
1. (4 ½ hours) Three hours by car/van from Manila to Batangas Harbor. The resort can arrange for a private vehicle to pick you up from the airport or your residence/hotel in Manila, or you can take your own car. The route is via South Superhighway. Get off at Exit 50A to Lucena, turn right to the Star Tollway, to Batangas, get off at Lipa/Tambo exit, turn left to Batangas. At Batangas Harbor, leave your car at the parking area. **Resort Banca** One hour from Batangas Harbor to Muelle Pier. **Resort Minibus** 5 minutes from Muelle Pier to the resort.
2. (5 hours) Sikat Ltd., operates a daily bus and ferry service from Manila to Puerto Galera. The bus departs from City State Tower Hotel, 1315 Mabini Street, Ermita, Manila and has a direct connection with a ferry in Batangas Harbor. For information/reservations call Tel. No.: 521-3344 • Fax No.: 526-2758. **Resort Minibus** 5 minutes from Muelle pier.
3. (5 hours) CCL Shipping Lines also operates a daily van and ferry service from Manila to Puerto Galera. The service van departs from the Swagman Hotel, Flores Street, Ermita, Manila and has a direct connection with the Island Cruiser in Batangas Harbor. Tel. No.: 523-8545. **Resort Minibus** 10 minutes from Muelle Pier.
Note: *The resort does not arrange transfer from Batangas Harbor or Puerto Galera.*

 6 Units
Main House: 2 Bedrooms (with bathroom) • 1 Apartment (with two bedrooms—1 in attic, kitchen, living and bathroom) • Second House (with sea view): 1 Apartment (with kitchenette, bathroom and balcony; good for 6) • 1 Apartment (with kitchenette, bathroom and balcony; good for 2) • 1 Apartment (with kitchenette, bathroom and balcony; good for 3)
All rooms have hot water, fan, mosquito nets, and intercom.

Indoor Facilities and Services
Table tennis • Billiards

 Food and Beverage Outlets
Restaurant in the Main House
Cuisine Offered: Filipino • International
Quality: Familial

 Watersports and Other Activities
Snorkeling (5 minutes) • Diving can be arranged • Island hopping • Jungle trekking • Golf arrangements with Ponderosa Golf • Tennis

 Per room per night

Note: *Cash payment only.*

Atlantis Resort Puerto Galera

Atlantis Resort stands out because of its Mediterranean architecture evoking a Greek village with its gleaming white structures. It is managed by Georg Bender, a German national. The hotel is slightly off Sabang Beach from which it is separated by a small public path. Because of the steep terrain, the buildings are literally clinging to the hillside, their shapes hugging the land's contours. This location allows you to escape the bustle of Sabang and to enjoy the view of the sea.

A rather surrealistic flight of stone stairs with white carved railings leads to the rooms that become more sumptuous, cozy and have grander views as you go higher up the hill.

Designed and decorated in a very original manner, all rooms are very pleasant with curved walls, rounded bathrooms and bed alcoves. The brown limestone floors, the braided bamboo ceilings and the flowery printed bedspreads in bright colors are in contrast with the whiteness of the walls and furniture. The wooden lattice windows open widely either to the sea or the surrounding vegetation.

The Standard Rooms are located in a two-story building near the pool. These are the least spacious of the rooms and the only ones without air-conditioning. The deluxe rooms are spacious and bright, with beautiful bathrooms. The rooms located higher up the hill have terraces. The suites atop the hill are the most attractive, with wide terraces outfitted with garden furniture, and some even with their own bar. From here, you enjoy an unimpeded view of the sea and the sunset in total privacy.

The restaurant, which serves quality cuisine, is where Franco, the Italian chef, presides. It is along the path that runs through Sabang Beach in a big, open bamboo structure. Unfortunately, the sea cannot be seen from here.

Atlantis offers an exceptional degree of comfort, charging the same rates as the neighboring hotels that offer much simpler accommodations. The quality of its facilities, the small moon-shaped swimming pool and the professionalism of its diving club compensate for the unattractiveness of Sabang Beach.

For swimming and snorkeling, you should walk to the nearby beaches of Small and Big La Laguna. On the other hand, if you wish to enjoy Sabang's nightlife, you are close by. It is relatively easy to find jeepneys for excursions, but Atlantis can likewise arrange this for you.

ATLANTIS RESORT PUERTO GALERA

Sabang Beach, Puerto Galera, Oriental Mindoro

Tel	(0917) 562-0294
	(0973) 497-503
Tel/Fax	(043) 287-3066 to 69
E-mail	andy@atlantishotel.com
	info@atlantishotel.com
Web	www.atlantishotel.com

Booking Office in Makati
Tel 817-2883

 By land and sea
1. (4 ½ hours) Three hours by car/van from Manila to Batangas Harbor. The resort can arrange for a private vehicle to pick you up from the airport or your residence/hotel in Manila, or you can take your own car. The route is via South Superhighway. Get off at Exit 50A to Lucena, turn right to the Star Tollway, to Batangas, get off at Lipa/Tambo exit, turn left to Batangas. At Batangas Harbor, leave your car at the parking area. **Resort Banca** One hour from Batangas Harbor.
2. (5 hours) **Bus and Ferry** Sikat Ltd., operates a daily bus and ferry service from Manila to Puerto Galera. The bus departs from City State Tower Hotel, 1315 Mabini Street, Ermita, Manila and has a direct connection with a ferry in Batangas Harbor. For information/reservations call Tel. No.: 521-3344 • Fax No.: 526-2758. 20 minutes by resort *banca* from Muelle pier.
3. (5 hours) CCL Shipping Lines, also operates a daily van and ferry service from Manila to Puerto Galera. The service van departs from the Swagman Hotel, Flores Street, Ermita, Manila and has a direct connection with the Island Cruiser in Batangas Harbor. Tel. No.: 523-8545. **Resort Banca** 20 minutes from Muelle Pier.

 40 Units
20 Deluxe Rooms • 11 Superior Deluxe Rooms • 1 Flintstone Gardenview House (family room) • 2 Flintstone Seaview House • 1 Coconut Suite • 1 Seaview Suite • 1 Honeymoon Suite • 3 Executive Suites
All rooms have TV, minibar, queen-size bed, bathroom with hot water, separate toilet and air-conditioning—except for standard rooms which are fan-cooled and do not have separate toilets.

Indoor Facilities and Services
Foreign currency exchange • Babysitting • Billiards

 Food and Beverage Outlets
Restaurant: Franco's Restaurant
Cuisine Offered: Italian • International
Quality: Good

Watersports and Other Activities
Swimming pool • Snorkeling (in other places) • Atlantis Dive Center • Island hopping with picnic • Sunset Cruise • Kayaking • Picnics • Jungle and river trip (with barbecue) • Mountain bike and motorcycle rental • Golf arrangements with Ponderosa Golf • Tours to Puerto Galera, Calapan, Tamaraw Falls, Mangyan Valley

 Per room per night inclusive of breakfast

Coco Beach Island Resort

On an isolated 10-hectare property, the Coco Beach Resort was the brainchild of a Danish-Italian, a furniture-buyer who frequently traveled to the Philippines. He fell in love with the site. It had all the necessary ingredients for a dream resort: white beach, tropical vegetation, crystal clear waters swarming with fish and fabulous corals. In 1986, Coco Beach Island Resort came into being. To accentuate the natural beauty of the surroundings, only traditional local materials were used in the construction and furnishing of the resort and to showcase the traditional warm hospitality of the islanders, a local family would be assigned to cater to the needs of the visitor. The innovative idea of a service family catering to your needs, the possibility of discovering the environment and the Mangyan tribes living in the countryside, and the daily transport service from Manila by the Coco Beach Express also add to its attraction. The resort is very much in demand during peak season.

The rooms are divided among several structures. The remarkable deluxe rooms and suites are housed in separate *nipa* bungalows scattered around a vast flower garden filled with bougainvillea and orchids. These are all tastefully furnished in an island motif and use natural materials. Giant clams that serve as washbasins, shell lamps, white bamboo beds and a hammock on a balcony where you can relax while enjoying the view of the sea. The less spacious standard rooms are in a one-story structure not far from the sports grounds. The furnishings, although in the same style, are simpler. Except for standard rooms, all rooms have a view of the sea.

One of the most fascinating features of the resort is the family that is assigned to look after your comfort. They are in charge of the maintenance of the rooms and are usually at hand throughout your stay—discreet and assuring in their being helpful. You can even have three hours of free babysitting if you need this kind of service. Without any hotel training, these families offer Philippine hospitality at its best.

Dining is another attraction at the resort, since the number of restaurants available offer a wide variety of choices. For exclusive dining, do not miss the picturesque Doña Lina, a revolving *nipa* and bamboo restaurant, which emerges from the treetops. It offers a panoramic view of the sea and is particularly splendid at sunset. At the Carabao Restaurant, breakfast is served buffet-style. The food is good and the service is fast and dependable. This restaurant is actually moved around either to the beach or in the garden depending on theme dinners that are organized each night.

Boredom is unheard of in Coco Beach as there is a wide selection of recreational activities available: morning jogging, swimming in a playfully-designed and magnificently huge pool, daily excursions to different beaches, trekking for one or several days to discover the countryside.

COCO BEACH ISLAND RESORT

Brgy. Bihija Sabang, Puerto Galera, Oriental Mindoro
Tel (0919) 540-0000
Fax (0919) 547-0347
E-mail resort@cocobeach.com
Web www.cocobeach.com

Booking Office in Manila
G/F Baywatch Tower,
2057 M.H. del Pilar Street,
Malate, Manila
Tel 521-5260 • 526-4594
Fax 526-6903
E-mail info@cocobeach.com

By land and sea
1. (5 ½ hours) The Coco Beach Express departs daily from Manila at 6:30 a.m. Pick up points include several hotels in Makati and Manila. It connects with large Coco Beach *bancas* which leave Bauan Pier (near Batangas) three to four hours later. Arrival time at the resort is around noon. The Coco Beach Express departs from the resort daily at 7:30 a.m. (extra service sometimes arranged on Sunday afternoons). Arrival time in Manila is around 1 p.m.
2. (4 hours) Three hours by car/van from Manila to Batangas Harbor The resort can arrange for a private vehicle to pick you up from the airport or your residence/hotel in Manila, or you can take your own car. The route is via South Superhighway. Get off at Exit 50A to Lucena, turn right to the Star Tollway, to Batangas, get off at Lipa/Tambo exit, turn left to Batangas. In Batangas Harbor, leave your car at the parking area. **Resort Banca/Speedboat** 45–60 minutes from Batangas Harbor.

Note: *As there is no road between Puerto Galera and Coco Beach, the car ferry service option is not practical.*

96 Units
10 Suite Rooms (each room with a living room and a bed room) • 78 Deluxe Rooms (most with sea view) • 8 Standard Rooms (no sea view)
None of the rooms have air-conditioning or hot water but all have a bathroom, fans, and mosquito nets.

Indoor Facilities and Services
Medical services • Car rental • Foreign currency exchange • Babysitting • Billiards • Library • TV/Video room

Food and Beverage Outlets
Restaurants: Palmera Café • Doña Lina (by reservations only) • Japaoki
Cuisine Offered: Filipino • International • Japanese
Quality: Good

Bars: Barracuda Bar and Music Lounge

Watersports and Other Activities
Swimming pools (with kiddie pool) • Beach (white sand) • Snorkeling (different beach) • Dive Center • Island hopping • Kayaking • Other boats for hire • Fishing • Dolphin watching • Trekking (overnight) • Mountain biking • Golf arrangements with Ponderosa Golf • Children's playground • Tours to: Calapan, Mangyan Village, San Rafael River, Puerto Galera

Per room per night inclusive of breakfast and round trip transfer from Manila

El Galleon Beach Club

El Galleon Beach Club is ably managed by Allan Nash, an Australian national who took over in 1994, when the resort only had seven rooms. Today, the resort has 31 rooms set in a vast, steep area covered with lush vegetation. The property is at one end of Small La Laguna Beach just beside Sabang Beach—a location which offers wide views of the Bay of Batangas, facing the setting sun.

The traditional architecture of the buildings, using mainly *nipa*, bamboo and rattan is particularly well done, integrating the surroundings and distinguishing the resort from its neighbors. At the entrance, near the sea, is a building with stone pillars and *nipa* roofing that houses the reception, the restaurant, a conference hall, a reading corner and a billiard table. A lone coconut tree, saved during the construction of the resort passes through the ceiling.

Behind the main building, in a tiled patio by the pool and a nice fan tree, is a two-story building with 20 rooms. There are bamboo cottages bordering Small La Laguna, some of which have nice views of the ocean. Stone steps under an arch of foliage lead to two rooms with private terraces, another two spacious rooms that are connected to each other by a balcony, a family room that is a little cramped and the honeymoon suite. An elevated structure perched at the hill's summit houses four more rooms. It is naturally not recommended for the elderly.

A circular balcony overlooks the garden and the ocean. Despite the absence of air-conditioning, these rooms are very popular because they open out on two sides. The interior decoration is simple but pleasant: whitewashed walls with fish paintings, wicker-braided ceiling and furniture in bamboo, rattan or wood.

The cuisine, deliberately French, is excellent and Antoine, the French chef from Marseille, is quite a personality. He will surely tell you about his Mindoro Island tour on foot and by bicycle.

The hospitality and service at El Galleon is of high quality and Asia Divers, the dive school is very professional. Even if a beach is almost non-existent on the resort, you can swim and snorkel just the same. Moreover, the sheltered cove of Big La Laguna, known to be exceptional for snorkeling, is just 10 minutes away on foot. The resort can also arrange for a *banca* to go to the white beaches dotting the coastline, or to snorkel at Coral Garden or Long Beach. Reservations for a jeepney to go to the countryside can be arranged from Sabang, 10 minutes away on foot.

EL GALLEON BEACH CLUB

Small La Laguna, Puerto Galera, Oriental Mindoro
Tel   (0917) 814-5107
Tel/Fax (043) 287-3205
E-mail   admin@asiadivers.com
Web   www.elgalleon.com

Booking Office in Makati
Abimir Place, 1741 Dian Street, Palanan, Makati City
Tel   834-2974
Tel/Fax 551-8063
E-mail   manila@asiadivers.com
Web   www.asiadivers.com

By land and sea
1. (4 ½ hours) 3 hours by car/van from Manila to Batangas Harbor. The resort can arrange for a private vehicle to pick you up from the airport or your residence/hotel in Manila, or you can take your own car. The route is via South Superhighway. Get off at Exit 50A to Lucena, turn right to the Star Tollway, to Batangas, get off at Lipa/Tambo exit, turn left to Batangas. In Batangas Harbor, leave your car at the parking area. **Resort Banca** One hour from Batangas Harbor.
2. (5 hours) Sikat Ltd., operates a daily bus and ferry service from Manila to Puerto Galera. The bus departs from City State Tower Hotel, 1315 Mabini Street, Ermita Tel. No.: 521-3344 and has a direct connection with a ferry in Batangas Harbor. **Resort Banca** Twenty minutes from Muelle Pier.
3. (5 hours) CCL Shipping Lines also operates a daily van and ferry service from Manila to Puerto Galera. The service van departs from the Swagman Hotel, Flores Street, Ermita, Manila and has a direct connection with the Island Cruiser in Batangas Harbor. Tel. No.: 523-8545. **Resort Banca** 20 minutes from Muelle Pier.

31 Units
Main building at the poolside: 12 Dolphin Rooms • 4 Sweetlip Rooms • 3 Turtle Rooms (family rooms) • Along Small La Laguna beach: 2 Whitetip Rooms (with balcony overlooking the pool) • 2 Pilot Rooms • 1 Honeymoon Suite • On top of the hill: 4 Manta Rooms • 1 Moray Room • 1 Eagle Room • 1 Emperor Room
All rooms have air-conditioning, a bathroom with hot water, minibar and queen-size bed.

Indoor Facilities and Services
Jeepney for hire

Food and Beverage Outlets
Restaurant: El Galleon Restaurant
Cuisine Offered: French • European
Quality: Excellent

Bar: Point Shooter Bar

Watersports and Other Activities
Swimming pool • Snorkeling (by the resort and at Coral Garden) • Asia Divers Dive Center • Island hopping with picnic/barbecue • Kayaking • Fishing • Sunset cruise • Golf arrangement with Ponderosa Golf • Tours to Puerto Galera's point of interest with hired jeepney

 Per room per night inclusive of breakfast

La Laguna Beach Club
and Dive Center

Right on Big La Laguna Beach in a small sheltered cove, this resort is managed by Australians Michael Donaldson and his partner. The resort has 33 rooms tightly laid out, without any green spaces, but nonetheless pretty and well-maintained. Its location in the middle of a nice white-sand beach where snorkeling is great is definitely an advantage. The area is considered one of the best sites for snorkeling and one of the rare places where you can do that right in front of your resort. Walking on the sandy portions to avoid the flowering corals at low tide, you will effortlessly descend into crystal-clear turquoise waters to observe the enchanting display of fish and corals in all shapes and colors. On condition that you take certain precautions and you keep watch of the comings and goings of *bancas*, the shallow waters and undisturbed beach is perfect for children.

Most of the rooms are located behind the beach in a two-story bamboo and wood structure with *capiz* windows. The façade is decorated in a rather lively way with many hanging plants. The rooms look out to the pool surrounded by grass and a few coconut trees.

No particular effort has been put in the rooms' interior decoration and the amenities are simple. There is bamboo furniture and the bathrooms are tiled in checkered black and white. Some rooms are in cottages with only the basic necessities. These have the added inconvenience of being too close to the restaurant.

The bamboo restaurant is right in front of the beach and offers simple but tasty meals at reasonable prices. If you want to have an extra choice, good eating places are not lacking in the area: the Italian restaurant of Portofino on the same beach, El Galleon on Small La Laguna and the Atlantis on Sabang.

The diving club is reputable. You can rent kayaks, a pleasurable way indeed to visit the cove before going on a discovery tour of the coastline and—perhaps—a river trip. The resort can likewise organize treks to the countryside.

LA LAGUNA BEACH CLUB AND DIVE CENTER

Big La Laguna, Puerto Galera, Oriental Mindoro
Tel (0917) 794-0323
Tel/Fax (043) 287-3181
E-mail lalaguna@llbc.com.ph
Web www.llbc.com.ph

 By land and sea
1. (4½ hours) Three hours by car/van from Manila to Batangas Harbor. You can ask the resort to arrange for a private car/van to pick you up from the airport or your residence/hotel in Manila, or you can take your own car. The route is via South Superhighway. Get off at Exit 50A to Lucena, turn right to the Star Tollway, to Batangas, get off at Lipa/Tambo exit, turn left to Batangas. In Batangas Harbor, leave your car at the parking area. **Resort Banca** One hour from Batangas Harbor.
2. (5 hours) Sikat Ltd., operates a daily bus and ferry service from Manila to Puerto Galera. The bus departs from City State Tower Hotel, 1315 Mabini Street, Ermita, Manila Tel. No.: 521-3344 and has a direct connection with a ferry in Batangas Harbor. **Resort Banca** Twenty minutes from Muelle pier.
3. (5 hours) CCL Shipping Lines also operates a daily van and ferry service from Manila to Puerto Galera. The service van departs from the Swagman Hotel, Flores Street, Ermita, Manila and has a direct connection with the Island Cruiser in Batangas Harbor. Tel. No.: 523-8545. **Resort Banca** 20 minutes from Muelle pier.

 33 Units
22 Double Deluxe Rooms • 2 Twin air-conditioned rooms • 1 Cottage Twin with air-conditioning • 2 Cottage Twin w/o air-conditioning • 2 Deluxe Family Rooms • 4 Regular Family Rooms
Standard rooms and cottages are fan-cooled and do not have hot water. Other rooms are air-conditioned and have a bathroom with hot water.
Note: *Family Rooms have a double bed and a set of bunk beds. Twin Rooms have a double bed and a single bed. In other rooms, one extra bed can be added.*

Indoor Facilities and Services
Foreign currency exchange • Babysitting

 Food and Beverage Outlets
Beachfront Restaurant and Bar
Cuisine Offered: International
Quality: Good

 Watersports and Other Activities
Swimming pool • Beach (white sand) • Snorkeling (in front of the resort) • 5-Star Padi dive shop • La Laguna Dive Center • Island hopping • Kayaking • Other boats for hire • Fishing • Sunset cruise • Jungle trekking (with picnic) • Golf arrangements with Ponderosa Golf

 Per room per night

Occidental Mindoro

Although San Jose has regular flights to and from Manila, tourism in Occidental Mindoro is far from developed. Yet, landscapes around San Jose are very attractive. To the north in Pandan Bay, off Sablayan village, lies the pretty island of North Pandan. A small resort ideal for divers is located here. A stay in Pandan can easily be arranged along with a stopover in San Jose.

SAN JOSE San Jose is the most important town of Occidental Mindoro, only one hour by plane from Manila. The place itself has

countryside is totally untamed and in the horizon, you will unexpectedly discover strange red-ochre cones right in the heart of greenfields dotted with acacia trees. To explore the area at your own pace, the best mode of transportation is a motorcycle.

THE MANGYAN HANUNO'O TRIBE IN IGLIT BACO NATIONAL PARK *(1 or 2 days minimum)* The Hanuno'os have a distinct tradition of writing and music. They produce lovely basketwork with geometric motifs. You will have to contact White

Mindoro Beach

little to offer, but the countryside, particularly the mountainous hinterland, is well worth a visit. You can discover this region from the White House Safari Lodge.

THE INSULMAN MOUNTAINS *(half day tour, 1 hour by jeepney or motorcycle from San Jose on a dirt road)* The mountainous

House Safari Lodge way in advance if you want them to organize your trip there, since authorizations are required. If you limit yourself to the fringes of the National Park, where landscapes are already superb, a day is enough. The government has set up a conservation project of the tamaraw in captivity in this part of the park. How-

Insulman Mountains

ever, if you wish to meet the Mangyan tribe or go further into the park and see tamaraws in the wild, you will have to plan a two-day trip.

THE ISLANDS OF WHITE BEACH, AMBULONG AND ILIN *(plan for a whole day)* These islands are located south of San Jose and can be visited easily in a day by *banca*. With beautiful gold sand beaches bordered with coral reefs, these are ideal for swimming and snorkeling. The vegetation is very interesting on the coastlines, with numerous cycad trees and mangrove swamps in some bays. White Beach is closest, a 20-minute ride by *banca* from White House Safari Lodge. It is ideal for children. The best snorkeling is on the western coast of Ambulong, an hour and a half from the lodge.

APO REEF *(2 days)* San Jose is also a jump-off point for the very beautiful Marine National Park of Apo Reef, located between Occidental Mindoro and Busuanga. The best way to go there from San Jose is to rent the Riva, the yacht of White House Safari Lodge. Apo Reef is also readily accessible from Pandan island via Sablayan. Travel time from San Jose to Pandan island via Sablayan is two and a half hours by jeepney and *banca*.

PANDAN BAY
Although off the beaten track, the small resort of Pandan Island in Pandan Bay is the only one which boasts of a dive center close to Apo Reef—a major advantage. Apo Reef has been declared a Marine National Park and has been under tight protection for several years. Along the walls which drop off into the depths, you can observe remarkable fan coral, gorgonians, huge sponges as well as numerous fish species. Along Shark Ridge, there are sightings of manta rays, sea turtles, tunas, mackerels jacks, and along Barracuda Ridge, barracudas and some very rare species such as frog fish, pilot fish and crocodile fish.

White House Safari Lodge

White House Safari Lodge, 45 minutes away by plane from Manila, is a good place to start discovering Occidental Mindoro, a region that has remained untamed and exceptionally beautiful.

David Anthony "Tony" Parkinson, an Englishman who lived 28 years in Kenya, built this small hotel. He came to the Philippines when the Calauit Animal Reserve in Palawan was created in 1977. If you ask him, he will surely tell you stories about the trans-location of eight species of big Kenyan mammals to a Philippine island. He perfectly knows the region around San Jose that curiously resembles the Kenyan countryside in certain areas. No wonder he settled here. Tony can also organize activities for you if you advise him of your plans well in advance.

White House Safari Lodge is a perfectly maintained two-story house with a casual atmosphere. It is surrounded by a small flower garden on a black sand beach, in a quiet community of San Jose.

The rooms are quite comfortable with marble bathrooms. Some of them have a terrace overlooking the sea. Meals are taken downstairs in a small dining room with a lounging corner. Whitewashed walls with picture frames of birds and sailboats, well-polished parquet floors, wood furniture and the flower-printed material covering the beds and sofas give an English touch—surprising in this remote place. You can either rent a jeepney or a motorbike to discover the countryside's mountain scenery, notably the Insulman Mountains with their reddish fairy-cone forms contrasting with the green plains dotted with acacia trees. If you have a few days, the owner can organize a trek for you to the National Park of Iglit/Baco to see the Mangyan tribe and, if you are lucky, the rare tamaraw.

You can likewise rent a *banca* for the day for island hopping, coasting along deserted islets, mangrove-filled bays and shores with cycad trees. You can go snorkeling at White Island, a mere 20-minute ride by *banca* or around Ambulong Island, an hour away.

WHITE HOUSE SAFARI BEACH HOTEL

San Jose, Occidental Mindoro
Tel/Fax (043) 491-1656
E-mail *edithpark@yahoo.com*

By air and land (1 hour)
Fifty-minute daily flights on Asian Spirit or Air Philippines from Manila to San Jose City. Five minutes by tricycle from San Jose airport to the lodge.

5 Units
3 Deluxe Rooms • 2 Family Suites
All rooms and suites have air-conditioning, minibar, TV, a bathroom with hot water.

Food and Beverage Outlets
Restaurant: White House Restaurant
Cuisine Offered: Filipino • International
Quality: Average

Watersports and Other Activities
Beach (not very attractive as the beach is in the city proper and the sand is black) • Snorkeling (in other places) • Diving (in other places) • Island hopping • Fishing • Trekking to Mangyan tribes • Motor-biking • Tours to the countryside with jeepney (Insulman)

🛶🛶🛶🛶 Per room per night

Note: *Cash payment only.*

Pandan Island Resort and Dive Camp

Distant bells ring across the sea from the village of Sablayan on the west side of Mindoro Island. It is Easter Sunday morning on Pandan Island.

Clear sea laps against the white sand beach, calm and glowing with the reflected colors of the rising sun. Mahal, the diving *banca*, is being prepared by the Whitetip Divers for a day trip to Apo Reef, while the larger Amas rests, picturesquely silhouetted, after its five-day diving safari to Busuanga.

The palm-thatched roof of our bungalow rises steeply. Outside, yellow-breasted bulbuls fly busily through the leaves and a green-winged ground dove, its bright emerald green-colored wings with glossed bronze, rustles through the grass. In the lush forest behind, coucal and fruit doves call, while the brilliantly yellow, black-naped oriole, dashes over the tree tops. Walking along the narrow path through the forest to Wild Lagoon and Spanish Nose, the now rare, Mindoro imperial pigeons can be heard, but are seldom seen.

The large, open-sided thatched dining room is silent but for a few divers, sleepily munching on breakfast, amid the chatter and activity in Tess' prodigious kitchen. Breakfasts are ordered à la carte, while lunches and dinners are served, buffet-style. The fare is simple, tasty, and plentiful.

Dominique Carlut and his energetic, vivacious wife, Marina, came to Pandan Island in 1986. They were joined a couple of years later by Denis Godart and their partnership has been the force behind the careful development of the resort, the only one in the island. The resort has 17 reasonably-priced bungalows surrounding the central bar and dining area. It can accommodate about 40 people. The mixed sounds of German, Swiss-German, French, Tagalog, and English reflect the resort's international clientele.

During the day, children's laughter echoes along the beach. In the evenings, lively conversation over card games and billiards drift across the cool sand to dreamers contemplating the night sky.

The impressively equipped and efficiently run Whitetip Divers is a focal point of the resort and offers a range of sporting activities apart from dive safaris and diving in the protected reefs around the island. Kayaks and windsurfing boards are available and there are boat excursions offered for those who wish to explore the nearby coasts and villages. Radek Jaeger and Peter Treadwell started the diving operation in 1992, later joined by Swiss divemasters Monika Ditle and Andy Himmelsbach. They have trained an excellent group of Filipino divemasters and mechanics. They also offer PADI dive courses for visitors to the island.

The long and dusty trip back, either to Abra del Ilog and the ferry to Batangas, or to San José and a flight to Manila, is punctuated with vivid images of underwater vistas—bright coral reef, glimpses of graceful green turtles and the myriad colors of the fish. Among the favorites are the long-nosed butterfly fish, spirited clownfish, golden sergeants, moorish idols and magnificent emperor angel fish. Most memorable of all were the dolphins leaping around the prow of our *banca* in the last rays of the sun as we returned from Apo Reef, a world away from reality.

(With the kind contribution of Susan McLaren)

PANDAN ISLAND RESORT AND DIVE CAMP

Pandan Island, Sablayan,
Occidental Mindoro
Tel (098) 281-0050
Web *www.pandan.com*
Booking Office in Manila
Asiaventure Tours and Travel
Tel 526-6929 • 523-7007
Fax 525-1811
E-mail *asiaventure@attglobal.net*
Web *www.asiaventureservices.com*

1. By air, land and sea (4 ½ hours) Fifty-minute daily flights on Asian Spirit or Air Philippines from Manila to San Jose City. Two-and-a-half to three hours by jeepney from San Jose airport to Sablayan. Twenty minutes by *banca* from Sablayan to Pandan Island.
2. By land and sea (15 hours) Three hours by car from Manila to Batangas Harbor. The route is via South Superhighway. Get off at Exit 50A to Lucena, turn right to the Star Tollway, to Batangas, get off at Lipa/Tambo exit, turn left to Batangas. In Batangas Harbor, you will leave your car at the parking area. **Ferry** Eleven-hour night trip by Montenegro Lines (Tel. No.: (043) 723-2834 • 723-9302) from Batangas to Sablayan. Trips are only on Mondays; departure at 5 p.m. **Banca** Twenty minutes from Sablayan to Pandan Island.
3. By land, sea, land and sea (12 hours) Three hours by car from Manila to Batangas Harbor. (See option 2) 4 hours by Montenegro Lines (Tel. No.: (043) 723-8294) from Batangas Harbor to Abra de Ilog, 4 daily trips, last trip at 4 p.m. For information, call the Passenger terminal in Batangas. Three-and-a-half to 4 hours by bus/jeepney from Abra de Ilog to Sablayan. Twenty minutes by *banca* from Sablayan to Pandan Island.
Note: *Transfer from San Jose airport can be arranged by the resort.*

17 Units
5 Budget Rooms (with 2 common bathrooms) • 11 Standard Bungalows • 1 Deluxe Bungalow
All bungalows have a bathroom. There is no generator but a solar system is installed on each bungalow.

Indoor Facilities and Services
Foreign currency exchange • Babysitting • Table tennis

Food and Beverage Outlets
Restaurant: Pandan Restaurant
Cuisine Offered: Continental • French • Filipino – Buffet Style
Quality: Good and plentiful

Bar: Beach Bar

Watersports and Other Activities
Beach (white sand) • Snorkeling • Whitetip Divers Dive center (dives to Apo Reef and around Pandan Island) • Island hopping • Kayaking • Other boats for hire • Excursion to Mindoro and Apo Reef Busuanga • Hiking • Horseback riding (in Mindoro) • Volleyball

Per room per night on full board basis
Note: *Cash payment only*

Palawan

ne Remote Bay, El Nido, Tapiutan

Painting by Lily Yousry-Jouve

Palawan

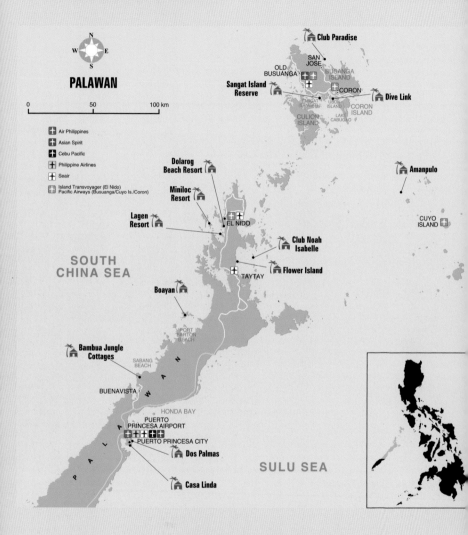

PALAWAN

0   50   100 km

- Air Philippines
- Asian Spirit
- Cebu Pacific
- Philippine Airlines
- Seair
- Island Transvoyager (El Nido)
  Pacific Airways (Busuanga/Cuyo Is./Coron)

Club Paradise

SAN JOSE

OLD BUSUANGA

Sangat Island Reserve

BUBANGA ISLAND

CORON

Dive Link

CULION ISLAND

LAKE CABUGAO

CORON ISLAND

Dolarog Beach Resort

Amanpulo

CUYO ISLAND

Miniloc Resort

Lagen Resort

EL NIDO

SOUTH CHINA SEA

Club Noah Isabelle

Flower Island

TAYTAY

Boayan

PORT BARTON BEACH

Bambua Jungle Cottages

SABANG BEACH

BUENAVISTA

HONDA BAY

PUERTO PRINCESA AIRPORT

PUERTO PRINCESA CITY

Dos Palmas

SULU SEA

Casa Linda

P A L A W A N

Calamian Islands, Taytay, El Nido, Cuyo Islands, Sabang:

Climate   Seasons not very pronounced; dry from December to May; wet during the rest of the year

For Puerto Princesa and Honda Bay climate, refer to Puerto Princesa and Honda Bay chapter

Typhoons   June to November

Palawan

PALAWAN PROVINCE, SOUTHWEST OF MINDORO, IS COMPOSED OF MORE THAN 1,700 ISLANDS. Busuanga, Culion, Calauit and Coron located north, are the most notable of the Calamian Group. Palawan, the main island is in the center with Puerto Princesa, the provincial capital. In the south are the islands of Balabac and Bugsuk. The province is largely formed by a mountainous ridge, still covered with rich vegetation that harbors endemic animal species despite deforestation and occasional fires.

CORON ISLAND Part of the Calamian Group of islands in northern Palawan, Coron Island is a dream of phantasmagoric stones, with vertical limestone cliffs encircling the hidden lagoons and fjords. Here lie shipwrecks, which guard their secrets, far from the clutches of human intervention. The bays of Taytay and Honda, northeast of Palawan, near Puerto Princesa, boast of spectacular sea gardens strewn with different blossoming corals and colorful fishes.

SABANG It is a world of stalactites and stalagmites, surrounded by vine-draped, orchid-filled forests, concealing birds, butterflies and insects. The natural wealth of Palawan—certainly its greatest attraction—has not yet been fully developed for tourism. The number of charming luxury or family resorts is still limited. One hopes that for the islands' preservation, it will stay this way.

The Calamian Islands

Tourism in the Calamian Islands has only been developed in the northern part of Busuanga Island and around Coron town and Coron Island, the major focus southeast of Busuanga. You can hardly combine a visit to both coasts in a long weekend.

Miniloc Blossom, El Nido

North Busuanga

Barracuda Lake, Coron

The two destinations are superb, with the most striking sceneries in Coron. The landscapes in northern Busuanga, though less spectacular, are enchanting too.

CORON It is the best known of the islands, rises southeast of Busuanga. Walled by particularly high cliffs, it hides two beautiful lagoons and fantastic lakes. Leaving Busuanga by *banca* from the little uninspiring village of Coron, it takes 30 minutes to reach Coron Island's massive silhouette is shaped like a black fortress against the sky.

Coron Island

You pass immense limestone cliffs just before the entrance of the lagoon, a bizarre landscape of protruding cone-like shapes. Then, entering a narrow gap in the rock you are astounded to discover a lagoon of transparent, emerald waters. The cliffs, whose sharp-edged walls are covered with strange plants and trees, encompass the lagoon. You can dock at a small landing at the far end of the lagoon

and take an easy 10-minute climb up a hilly path to a freshwater lake. The magnificent view is certainly worth the effort! Swimming and scuba-diving are a must and with a little luck, you may meet the barracuda, which gave the lake its name and which, as the legend goes, willingly accompanies divers on their adventures.

Coron Island

A few minutes from here, a little farther along the coastline, nestling in the hollow of the cliffs, is a second lake, Cabugao. The second lagoon, about 30 minutes away from the first, is more extensive, and, being less visited, more mysterious. The lagoon is largely open to the sea but also reveals smaller, secondary

Coron Lagoon

lagoons. You can cross it by kayak, appreciating in silence the untouched beauty and grandeur of the scenery. Here and there, you can spot a Tagbuana dwelling, lost in the cliffs' immensity.

The gurgling Maquinit Hot Springs are near the village of Coron. But here, the scenery is undeniably less spectacular. Mount Tundarala, on Busuanga coast, at an altitude of 640 meters, offers beautiful views of Coron Island. It is an easy six-hour trek from Coron town. Coron Bay is equally renowned among divers for the Japanese shipwrecks, sunk by the Americans in 1944. The depths of the sea have taken possession of them, creating a strange and surrealist atmosphere.

For practical reasons, you can stay in the little Dive Link Resort or in the more

North Busuanga

Palawan. The mangroves, exceedingly high and old, shelter a variety of birds. Their tangle of aerial roots form intricate wood sculptures.

It is also from this area that you can visit the animal reserve on the island of Calauit, created in 1977 on the initiative of former president Marcos. African animals, such as the giraffe, the impala, the zebra, the buffalo and the gazelle were brought in from Kenya. Also sheltered here are Palawan's own rare and endangered species: the Philippine bear cat, the Palawan peacock, the Calamian deer, and the mouse deer—although it is difficult to observe them. Understandably, this transplantation, which led to the displacement of the local population, is still a subject of controversy. If you have had the chance to go to Africa and observe these animals in their original environment, the visit to Calauit is a little disappointing—even more so as the trip is done in groups, by truck.

North Busuanga

pleasant Sangat Island Reserve, on magnificent Sangat Island, 45 minutes by *banca* from Coron Village.

THE NORTHERN COAST OF BUSUANGA AND CALAUIT It includes small islands and deserted islets rimmed by coral reefs. You can go island hopping, stopping as you please on deserted islands and play Robinson Crusoe at least for a day.

Club Paradise on the little island of Dimakya is reached after a boat ride along an arm of the river lined by mangroves, among the best preserved of

North Busuanga

Dive Link

If you want to visit Coron Island or dive the many Japanese war ships sunk in the region during the Second World War, Dive Link is an interesting alternative to the uncomfortable and noisy lodges in the town. This low-key resort, established by the Matta family in 1999, is only five minutes away from Coron Village. It is on the little wooded island of Uson on the other side of the bay.

The resort is a direct contrast to the placidity and splendor of the area. The structures are painted in a variety of bright colors, like those in a child's coloring book: there is a yellow jetty with red railings, blue corrugated iron roofing on the bungalows, and walls tinged with the same shade, accented by the red-framed windows. This play of colors is again rendered in the interiors of the bungalows—bamboo-braided walls with blue borders, red flooring, yellow curtains and bedcovers. The initial shock of these intense colors subsides, as you realize that the place is actually very pleasing.

The resort is nestled in a natural garden of coconut trees right at the foothills. The majestic view of Coron Bay, open to most of the cottages, is particularly enchanting at sunset.

Bungalows, well spaced from each other, are grouped in two rows on a hill facing the ocean. These are very well maintained and furnished with simple bamboo furniture. Each bungalow has a balcony that offers an excellent view of the surroundings. The windows shut only with screens.

The bamboo restaurant overlooks the sea. Here, the home-cooked dishes are placed within a miniature multi-colored *banca*. The *talakitok*, or Jack fish, are very fresh, brought in regularly from the Coral Bay Resort, which is also owned by the Mattas.

It is a little muddy in the area, hence the absence of a beach, but there is a big swimming pool not far from the sea.

The resort offers an extensive *banca* tour of Coron and its lagoons, complete with snorkeling atop a ship-wreck and lunch served buffet-style.

DIVE LINK

Uson Island, Coron, Palawan
Tel (0919) 475-2696
E-mail *info@divelink.com.ph*
f_b@divelink.com.ph
Web *www.divelink.com.ph*
Booking Office in Quezon City
Unit 15C Atherton Place
Tomas Morato, Quezon City
Tel 412-0644 • 375-2561
376-2048
Tel/Fax 371-9928
E-mail
chona_alejan@divelink.com.ph

1. By air, land and sea (2 ½ hours) Sixty-five-minute flight on Seair or Asian Spirit; or ninety-minute flight on Pacific Air from Manila to Busuanga. All air-lines have daily flights. Forty-five minutes by van from Busuanga Airport to Coron town. A shuttle van awaits passengers and takes them to Bayside Divers Lodge in Coron. Time of departure from Busuanga airport depends on flight schedules. Fifteen minutes by *banca* from Coron town to the resort.
2. By sea, land and sea (14 hours) Fourteen-hour night trip from Manila to Coron on WG&A Superferry (Tel. No.: 528-7000 Web: *www.super-ferry.com.ph)* **Manila-Coron:** Departure Friday, 5:45 p.m., arrival Saturday, 5 a.m. **Coron-Manila:** Departure Sunday, 8:45 p.m. arrival Monday, 7:30 a.m. Fifteen minutes by tricycle/jeepney from the ferry terminal to the municipal pier. Fifteen minutes by *banca* from Coron town to the resort.
Note: *Transfer from Bayside Divers Lodge in Coron is arranged by the resort.*

20 Units
7 Bungalows (with bathroom) • 6 air-conditioned Bungalows • 4 Garden Suites (with 2 bedrooms and 1 bathroom; good for families) • 3 Family Cottages
All rooms are fan-cooled and limited air-conditioned, have a balcony and twin beds. Coffee service on veranda. Extra beds are also available.
Indoor Facilities and Services
Massage

Food and Beverage Outlets
Restaurants: Coconut Grove • Rock Islet
Cuisine Offered: Filipino • Asian
Quality: Familial

Watersports and Other Activities
Swimming pool • Diving (arrange-ments with dive shops based in Coron such as Dive Calamianes near Bayside Divers Lodge) • Island hopping to Coron Island, CYC Beach, Banol Beach, Twin Lagoons, Skeleton Wreck • Western Busuanga Tours: Malajon (Black) Island, South Cay, North Cay, Maltatayok, Pamalican, Culion Island, Calauit Wildlife Sanctuary

 Per room per night

Club Paradise

Club Paradise is located on the 19-hectare Dimakya Island in the northeastern part of the Calamianes, northern Palawan.

The resort's appeal lies in its 700-meter beach of beautiful, fine white sand and its turquoise waters, which shelter a coral reef.

Part of the island's forest was preserved when the resort was built, and a 30-minute walk through a path will take you up to Eagle's Point where one can possibly observe some birds, monitor lizards and, if you are lucky, a Calamian deer.

The resort itself is well-hidden in lush tropical plants. Upon arrival, the only glimpse that can be seen is the restaurant's nipa-thatched roof. The spacious and airy restaurant, with white walls and parquet flooring is part of the central building of the resort. It opens out to the sea. A nearby swimming pool, bordered with multi-colored bougainvillea, separates the restaurant from the Beach Club.

The comfortable rooms of the resort are to be found in various other buildings, which vary considerably in location and styles.

The Beachfront Cottages, made of wood, bamboo and nipa are our favorite. They are separated from the main buildings and are surrounded by tropical plants. The cottages have a nice view of the sea from a small terrace, which is furnished with a hammock. The interiors of the rooms are bright and pleasant. All the rooms have marble bathrooms.

The Island View Rooms are in a two-story building on a promontory overlooking the garden. The nicest rooms—with private terraces—are on the second floor. All rooms are spacious with big picture windows.

The Hillside Cottages are composed of four different buildings consisting of two floors with a room on each floor. The nicest rooms are on the first floor which has a good view of the ocean. However, because these rooms are quite far from the main building and can be accessed only through a rather steep stairway, they are not recommended for the elderly.

The Sea View Cottages are semi-detached bungalows found on Sunrise Beach on the other side of the Island. These bungalows are recommended for families as the rooms are interconnected. However, only the rooms overlooking the beach, which is surrounded by rocks, have a pleasant view. A suspended stairway leads toward the restaurant a little further away.

From Club Paradise, it is possible to take a banca to the nearby islands. You can go from one golden beach to another, snorkel in lagoons encircling the islands, dive to the nearby shipwrecks (the Dimalanta shipwreck can be reached in 40 minutes), or better yet, visit the Calauit Animal Reserve with African and endemic species, which is just an hour away. A visit to the Coron lagoons is possible in good weather. A little nature museum educates about the fauna, flora and conservation projects.

Snorkeling and diving are possible from the beach itself. It is also possible to see some dugongs that frequent this area, and turtles that lay their eggs on the resort's beaches every year.

CLUB PARADISE

Dimakya Island, Coron, Palawan
Tel (0920) 911-9704
Booking Office in Manila
Regent Building, Malunggay Road,
FTI Complex, Taguig, Metro Manila
Tel 838-4956 to 60
Fax 838-4462
E-mail clubpara@info.com.ph
reservation@clubparadisepalawan.com
Web www.clubparadisepalawan.com

1. By air, land and sea (3–4 hours) Sixty-five-minute flight on Seair or Asian Spirit; or ninety-minute flight on Pacific Air from Manila to Busuanga. All airlines have daily flights. Thirty minutes by car from Busuanga airport to the Decalachao mangrove area. Thirty to forty-five minutes by *banca* from the mangrove to the resort.

2. By sea, land and sea (15 hours) Thirteen hours (night trip) from Manila to Coron on WG&A Superferry (Tel. No.: 528-7000 Web: *www.super-ferry.com.ph*) **Manila-Coron:** Departure Friday, 3:45 p.m.; Arrival Saturday, 5 a.m. **Coron-Manila:** Departure Sunday, 8:45 p.m.; arrival Monday, 7:30 a.m. Fifteen minutes by tricycle/jeepney from the ferry terminal to the municipal pier. Forty-five minutes by van/shuttle service to Busuanga airport from Bayside Divers Lodge. Time of departure from Bayside Divers Lodge depends on flight schedules.

Note: *Transfer from Busuanga airport is arranged by the resort.*

60 Units
20 Island View Air-conditioned Rooms • 13 Beachfront Deluxe Cottages • 8 Hillside Air-conditioned Cottages • 6 Beachfront Air-conditioned Cottages • 6 Seaview Deluxe Cottages • 6 Gardenview Air-conditioned Cottages • 1 Beachfront Fan Cottage
All units have a bathroom with hot water, a refrigerator and private terrace.

Indoor Facilities and Services
Library • Videoke Room • Conference Room • Table tennis • Dart • Billiards • Babysitting • Dugong Bar • Jungle Bar • Sattelite TV Room • Reflexology Center • Sari-Sari Gift Shop • Business Center

Food and Beverage Outlets
Restaurants: Kamalig Restaurant
Cuisine Offered: International • Filipino/Local
Quality: Good

Watersports and Other Activities
Swimming pool • Jacuzzi • Beach (white sand) • Tennis • Hiking Trail • Diving • Snorkeling • Sunset Cruise • Kayaking • Island Hopping • Bottom Fishing
Tours to: Coron Island, Maricaban Bay, Calauit Safari, Apo Reef.

Per room per night on full board basis

Sangat Island Reserve

This idyllic little resort is nestled in a spectacular site on Sangat Island off the south coast of Busuanga, just 45 minutes by *banca* from Coron Village.

The resort's site has tall limestone cliffs encircling a small cove of golden sand, lined with coral reefs. The owners, Englishman Andy Pownall and his Filipina wife Edith, designed the resort so as to minimize its impact on the island's environment. The area has been declared a natural reserve. This makes it a pleasant and tranquil place with a casual atmosphere.

In Sangat, there is no telephone, air-conditioning or hot water. You go there for its magical beauty—not for luxurious accommodation.

Eight bungalows made of bamboo and cogon grass are scattered at the foot of the cliff along a flowered path, some of them directly on the beach; the others just behind. Each bungalow is different, the most beautiful being the last one near the cliff. They are secluded, spacious, bright and airy, thanks to large windows and doorways. A big bamboo bungalow, largely open toward the ocean lies in the center of the resort. It houses the reception area, a bar with a lounge and a restaurant.

The beach is narrow but nice, and you can swim, snorkel or canoe in the sheltered lagoon just in front of the resort. Do not miss going along the coastline by canoe to discover secret coves. The resort also organizes longer hikes to neighboring islands.

Behind the resort is a hilly path (a 30-minute walk) that leads to a small rainforest. Sangat is rich in wildlife: tropical birds, monkeys, and impressive monitor lizards hunting for food at the back of the kitchen.

The resort has a dive center and is an ideal base for diving the wrecks of the Japanese fleet that found refuge in Busuanga during the Second World War. There are 14 magnificent shipwrecks covered with corals and colonized by fishes. Detailed descriptions of the different shipwrecks are available in the resort's website. Six of these shipwrecks are only 10 minutes away from the resort.

From Sangat, you can easily visit Coron Island just an hour away by resort *banca*.

SANGAT ISLAND RESERVE

Sangat Island, Coron Bay, North Palawan

Tel   (0919) 205-0198
        (0919) 617-5187
        (0919) 299-5469
E-mail resort@sangat.com.ph
        info@sangat.com.ph
Web   www.sangat.com.ph

1. By air, land and sea (3 ½ hours) Sixty-five-minute flight on Seair or Asian Spirit; or ninety-minute flight on Pacific Air from Manila to Busuanga. All airlines have daily flights. Forty-five minutes by van from Busuanga airport to Coron. A shuttle van awaits the passengers to take them to Bayside Divers Lodge in Coron. Time of departure from Busuanga airport depends on flight schedules. Forty-five minutes by *banca* from Bayside Divers Lodge to the resort.

2. By sea, land and sea (15 hours) Fourteen-hour night trip from Manila to Coron on WG&A Superferry (Tel. No.: 528-7000 Web: *www.super-ferry.com.ph*) **Manila-Coron:** Departure Friday, 5:45 p.m., arrival Saturday, 5 a.m. **Coron-Manila:** Departure Sunday, 8:45 p.m., arrival Monday, 7:30 a.m. Fifteen minutes by tricycle/jeepney from the ferry terminal to the municipal pier. Forty-five minutes by *banca* from Bayside Divers Lodge to the resort.

Note: *Transfer from Bayside Divers Lodge in Coron Town is arranged by the resort.*

11 Units
10 Cottages (with bathroom—no hot water—and terrace) • 2-bedroom Villa on its own private beach next to the resort beach. There is no air-conditioning or fan.

Indoor Facilities and Services
Babysitting • Massage • Nitrox Filling Station

Food and Beverage Outlets
Restaurant and Small Bar
Cuisine Offered: Asian and Western
Quality: Familial

Watersports and Other Activities
Beach (white sand) • Snorkeling (by the beach) • Dive center (The main attraction for divers is the 14 Japanese WWII shipwrecks very close to Sangat) • Kayaking • Trekking • Rock climbing (various routes identified) • Island hopping and other Tours (scheduled)

 Per room per night on full board basis including round trip *banca* transfer

Note: *A special package is available for divers.*

La Esperanza

La Esperanza is a stylish wood schooner, built the traditional way. On windy days, it is very good-looking with its five sails spread out.

Captain Jacob Bakker built La Esperanza in 1974. This Dutchman, after crisscrossing the Carribean, has been based in Palawan for the last 20 years. He knows these waters by heart and is full of stories. His wife Crisna, who is originally from Cebu, is particularly warm and full of life. She is also a fabulous cook and her bread is irresistible!

The sailboat is 15 meters long and is spacious. The deck allows comfortable movement for the occupants. A table and chairs can be installed under a canopy during meals for sun protection or you can snuggle up in cozy cushions while watching the sumptuous scenery as you cruise. The sailboat has two cabins, one with a big double bed and another one with two single beds. The dining nook, used only on rainy days, can be transformed into a room by simply taking the table down and installing a double bed in its place. On warm nights, it is always possible to pick up your mattresses and sleep on deck under a starry night. The sailboat has an interior bathroom, but showers are taken on deck from buckets of fresh water.

The kitchen is well equipped with a refrigerator and freezer, so drinking ice-cold beverages is possible. You can bring refreshments if you wish, but you can always find beer, rum and soft drinks on board.

The sailboat is indeed the ideal way to discover this fantastic region of hundreds of deserted islets. La Esperanza goes from one golden beach to another; from one blue lagoon to another, and it anchors in a different bay every night. You can discuss the itinerary with the captain, as the possibilities are endless. You can limit yourselves to a Busuanga tour if you have little time (count a minimum of three days) and discover Black Island, Calauit and the mysterious lagoons of Coron. (The three days can be spent on Coron Island alone.) With more time on your hands, you can take the Coron route to El Nido and its fabulous limestone cliffs. (Count a minimum of five days.)

With even more time, you can go up to the National Park of the Sabang Underground River. (Count a minimum of one week.) In the last two options, the return trip to Coron by boat has to be paid. Other alternatives are, of course, possible. On board, you get this impression of total independence. You hit ground when you wish; you can walk along deserted beaches, swim and snorkel in the most favorable places.

Although the boat is equipped with tanks and a compressor for scuba diving, you have to bring your own equipment. These can be rented in Coron. Note that the captain is not a diver. Among the most interesting sites are the shipwrecks around Busuanga.

Note: *As of press time, there was a change of ownership. Kindly check the website from time to time for any update.*

LA ESPERANZA

Capt. Jacob Bakker,
La Esperanza Sailing Charters
R.C.P. I. Box 04B-02,
Coron 5316, Palawan
E-mail *sailpalawan@yahoo.com*
Web *http://dgte.mozcom.com/ esperanza*

 1. By air, land and sea (2½ to 3 hours)   Sixty-five-minute flight on Seair or Asian Spirit; or ninety-minute flight on Pacific Air from Manila to Busuanga. All airlines have daily flights. Forty-five minutes by jeepney from Busuanga airport to Bayside Divers Lodge in Coron town. Time of departure from Busuanga airport depends on flight schedules.

2. By sea (14½ hours)   Fourteen-hour night trip from Manila to Coron on WG&A Superferry (Tel. No.: 528-7000 Web: *www.superferry.com.ph*) **Manila-Coron:** Departure Friday, 5:45 p.m., arrival Saturday, 5 a.m. **Coron-Manila:** Departure Sunday, 8:45 p.m., arrival Monday, 7:30 a.m Fifteen minutes by tricycle/jeepney from the ferry terminal to the municipal pier.

Note: *The captain will wait for you in Coron where La Esperanza is anchored.*

 Units
La Esperanza is a schooner-rigged yacht, 15 meters overall, 4.5-meter beam, 2.2-meter draft, equipped with a 120 HP diesel motor. It has a big cabin with a double bed and another cabin with two single beds. The settee in the saloon forms another double bed. There is one toilet; shower is on the deck.

 Food and Beverage Outlets
Type of Cuisine: Filipino • International
La Esperanza has exceptional deck space with a permanent shade where the meals are usually served. When it rains, meals are served in the saloon. The kitchen is well-equipped with freezer and refrigerator.
Quality: Excellent and plentiful

 Watersports and Activities
Snorkeling • Dive center • Island hopping (There is also a motorized dinghy to explore the shores) • Kayaking (1 only) • Windsurfing • Fishing

 For 2 persons per night on full board basis

Taytay Bay

The small town of Taytay is on the north-eastern coast of Palawan. Taytay Bay shelters many islets, some of which are composed of high limestone cliffs like in El Nido, but they are less spectacular. Nevertheless, it is a beautiful region, untamed to this day and worth being discovered. Taytay was the Spanish capital of Palawan until the 18th century. It has kept the ruins of a 300-year-old church and Fort Puerto de San Isabelle, dating back to 1622. There are only two resorts in Taytay Bay: the luxurious Club Noah Isabelle on Apulit Island, frequented by Japanese and Koreans, and the small and charming Flower Island Resort. The two resorts are an hour away from each other.

LAKE DANAO Lake Danao is only 30 minutes from Taytay. It is surrounded by a lush forest

Flower Island Bay

fishes like jacks and napoleons are of considerable size and can be observed by merely snorkeling. There are several caves on the opposite side of the resort, notably the Saint Joseph Cave.

SILANGA ISLAND *(25 minutes from Club Noah)* This is the island where you are likely to be brought for a picnic and barbecue if you stay in Club Noah. It is a nice place for swimming and there is a small spot for snorkeling.

SMALL SILANGA *(25 minutes from Club Noah)* It has a small golden sandbar that surfaces only at low tide.

ELEPHANT AND CASTLE ISLANDS *(45 minutes from Club Noah and 1 hour 30 minutes from Flower Island)* These islands are protected as a nesting site for swallows. Visiting these islands is impossible during the nesting period or when the winds are strong. Hidden in the cliffs' hollows is a natural pool with clear waters ideal for swimming.

QUIMBALUDAN ISLAND *(30 minutes from Club Noah)* It has a pretty, white sandbar shaped like a semi-circle. The coral reef is beautiful, especially at the drop-off.

DINOT ROCKS *(30 minutes from Club Noah)* This is a marine reserve which has a vast coral reef known for snorkeling and night diving. With luck, you can even see sea turtles.

RIO VERDE *(45 minutes from Club Noah)* This is a branch of the Tamisan River. You can visit this area by canoe, and observe bird life along the 1.2 kilometer stretch lined by mangroves.

FLOWER ISLAND *(1 hour from Club Noah)* This small paradise island fringed by a white sand beach, shelters a charming resort. It is surrounded by islets where snorkeling and diving are possible.

and strewn with islets. It can be visited more easily from Club Noah Isabelle than from Flower Island. You can walk in the forest and go bird-watching, or go kayaking in the lake.

APULIT ISLAND The luxurious Club Noah Isabelle is on Apulit Island. Its cove has a magnificent coral reef with quite a variety of fishes. The seeming fireworks display of colored fishes is a feast for the eyes. Some

Club Noah Isabelle

Club Noah Isabelle has a spectacular location in a cove of the 40 hectare-wide Apulit Island, surrounded by forested limestone cliffs. In the cove's hollows lies a small beach of fine, almost white sand. The huge bay's extraordinary waters of turquoise and emerald green shelter a coral reef that is exceptionally rich in colorful fishes. You can stay here for hours without tiring of the scenery—the marine life is just so varied. On the other end of the bay is a large beach, accessible by foot during low tide.

Two types of very comfortable accommodations are offered: the cabanas and the family houses, both constructed on stilts above the sea and aligned a little too near each other on a narrow path along the cliff.

The *nipa* and wood cabanas have a beautiful view of the cliffs, but they are a little small. The two-story concrete family cottages are more attractive, with one bedroom on each level and the bathroom on the first floor. The rooms are spacious and nicely decorated with sea-inspired white and blue-gray interiors. The picture window opens out onto the terrace where you can directly dive into the lagoon after breakfast—served right on your terrace. You can even have a shower right there for rinsing out.

There are two restaurants where you can dine… depending on the mood of the manager. The first one constructed on stilts, advances on to the sea like a ship. It is very pleasant, opening in a certain way to the winds of the sea through the open picture windows. The second restaurant faces the beach. Tables lit with small lanterns are installed there in the evening.

The ambiance in Club Noah is definitely romantic. The majority of its clientele are young Korean and Japanese couples on their honeymoon. Intimate dinners by candlelight, on the small cliffside terraces overlooking the bay can be requested in advance. Surprise cocktails—with the sound of Mozart and the glimmer of numerous candles set on the cliff's walls—can also be organized in a cave on the other side of the island.

The bar close to the pier is the meeting point for all activities, very well organized by the resort. While dining, you are asked what you want to do the next day: snorkeling or diving just in front of the resort (a must because you can see big jacks and napoleons at only three meters), island hopping, going on a picnic in one of these deserted islands around Apulit, visiting caves, or even sailing a sunset cruise.

CLUB NOAH ISABELLE

Apulit Island, Taytay,
Northeastern Palawan
Tel (0918) 909-5583

Booking Office in Palawan
Goodwill Building, Rizal Ave., Ext.
Puerto Princesa City, Palawan
Tel (048) 434-8476 • 434-8478
Fax (048) 434-8477

Booking Office in Makati
6/F Multinational
Bancorporation Center,
6805 Ayala Avenue, Makati City
Tel 844-6688 • 844-6166
844-7786 • 843-6037
Fax 845-2380 • 845-1990
E-mail info@clubnoah.com.ph
Web www.clubnoah.com.ph

By air, land and sea (3 ½ hours)
Ninety-minute daily flights on Seair from Manila to Sandoval. Fifteen minutes by jeepney from Sandoval airport to a nearby river. **Dinghy** 10 minutes down to the river's mouth. Thirty to sixty minutes by *banca* depending on the tide.

Note: *Transfer from Sandoval airport is arranged by the resort.*

50 Units
30 Single Detached Water Cabanas (good for 2) • 20 Family Water Cabanas (with 2 double rooms fronting the sea; good for 4–5 persons)
All units have a private balcony, intercom, minibar, air-conditioning, toilet and shower facilities.

Indoor Facilities and Services
Babysitting • Medical services • Table tennis • Billiards

Food and Beverage Outlets
Restaurants: Tropicana Restaurant • Café Isabelle (Water Restaurant)
Cuisine Offered: International • Seafood • Filipino • Japanese
Quality: Good
Bars: Serena Bar • El Capitano Bar • Rock Bar

Watersports and Other Activities
Swimming pool (small) • Beach (white sand) • Snorkeling (from the cottage) • Diving • Kayaking • Other boats for hire • Fishing • Island hopping • Cave exploration • Village tours • Sunset cruise • Beach volleyball • Trekking Lake Danao

 Per room per night on full board basis including round trip airport transfers, resort-programmed activities

Flower Island

Flower Island is an enchanted hideaway in the vast and remote Taytay Bay. The resort was built behind a golden beach encircled by a coral reef. With a homey and casual atmosphere that comes being at home with nature, the resort gives you the chance to get away from the busy city lights. Moreover, the quality of service you get here is well worth the price you pay.

Seven non air-conditioned bungalows and a two-story house with four air-conditioned rooms are well-conceived. They are spread out along a pristine beach, far enough from each other, among bougainvilleas, frangipani trees and red lilies. The terraces at the front of the bungalows are very attractive, with hammocks facing the sea, assuring complete privacy.

The restaurant sits in a big round bungalow opening onto the beach with a small lounge for reading or listening to music. The place is pretty with red tile floors, handmade bamboo, wood-

and cast-iron furniture. Everything is bathed in a subdued light. You may feel as if you are in the south of France. Indeed, you would give your hosts great pleasure by bringing them a bottle of pastis, an alcoholic specialty from Marseilles.

You can, in under an hour, tour the island on foot across a cobblestoned path, but its interior is impenetrable. The beach is perfect for swimming or snorkeling in the small coral reef fronting the resort. There is a beautiful mangrove patch at one end of the beach. A small promontory, evoking some Balinese temple was fitted in. It is only accessible at low tide.

Canoes are available and the resort's *banca* can bring you around in search of islets. You can also go fishing if you may choose—and taste your day's catch in the evening.

In Flower Island, you lose all sense of time. It is the ideal place to rest, read in your hammock or walk along the serene shoreline collecting seashells.

FLOWER ISLAND

Taytay, Sandoval, Palawan
Satellite No.: (0985) 409027
E-mail
flowerisland_ph@yahoo.com
Web
www.flowerislandresort.com

Booking Office in Makati
605 National Life Insurance Building
Ayala Avenue, Makati City
Tel/Fax 893-6455

 By air, land and sea (3 ½ hours)
Ninety-minute daily flights on Seair from Manila to Sandoval. Ten minutes by jeepney from Sandoval airport to the pier. Seventy-five minutes by the resort's *banca* (cabins inside) or forty-five minutes by speedboat from Sandoval pier to Flower Island.

Note: *Transfer from Sandoval pier is arranged by the resort.*

 8 Units
7 very private Double Beachfront Cottages (with fans, bathrooms—cold water only—and verandas facing the sea) • 1 House (with 4 air-conditioned rooms, with bathrooms — cold water only — and common verandas)

 Food and Beverage Outlets
Beachside Restaurant
Cuisine Offered: Filipino • French • Mediterranean • Seafood
Quality: Excellent

 Watersports and Other Activities
Beach (white sand) • Snorkeling (by the beach or at Club Noah Isabelle) • Diving • Kayaking • Other boats for hire • Fishing • Island hopping (with picnic) • Sunset cruise

 Per room per night on full board basis inclusive of three meals a day

Note: *Cash payment only*

El Nido

Few sceneries have the almost mythical beauty of the El Nido archipelago. Leaving the frenzy of Manila and its cacophony of noises, you are suddenly transported to a world of stone and silence, whose splendor is staggering. Wherever you set your sights on, limestone islands raise their high and enigmatic silhouettes over the sea. The rocks take surreal forms, evoking a world of magicians, ogres and fantastic creatures.

Lagoons of crystal-clear turquoise and emerald waters hide beneath the stone depths. During the rainy season, from the months of May to the end of August, it does rain, but rarely for days on end. As soon as the sun shines, the drying cliffs take on astonishing shades of color, from very pale gray to black.

The rocks are always adorned with flowers, wild begonias punctuating the cliff as if with small, red lanterns. You can stay for a week at El Nido without having discovered everything there is to see.

The most essential trips around the vicinity are described here. Whichever resort you might be staying in, all these islands can be visited by *banca*.

THE MINILOC LAGOONS

Miniloc Island, where the comfortable El Nido Resorts Miniloc is located, must be the most visited of the Bacuit Archipelago. Within Miniloc Island are two lagoons: Big Lagoon and Small Lagoon. **Big Lagoon** is 15 minutes away from the resort. You enter it after crossing a rather narrow canyon, surrounded by high limestone cliffs that seem to cut the sky with their sharp edges. **Small Lagoon** is a little farther on the island's coast. The crossing can be rough at times, but the contrast as you enter the lagoon's silent world is captivating. At its far end, accessible only by canoe or swimming, is an opening in the rocks that leads to even smaller and more enchanting lagoons imprisoned by immense cliffs. One

Matinloc Island, El Nido

of these is cone-shaped and aptly named "the cathedral." Residing in El Nido Resorts Miniloc, you can easily be dropped off by kayak in any of the two lagoons and comb these magical places at your own pace.

PAYONG-PAYONG (*5 minutes from Miniloc*) The beach with a small reef is on the right

side of El Nido Resorts Miniloc. You can also have wonderful snorkeling along the coast.

PANGALUSIAN (*20 minutes from Miniloc*) The island is rather flat and boasts of a nice beach. Its principal attraction is the 30-minute climb through a well-indicated

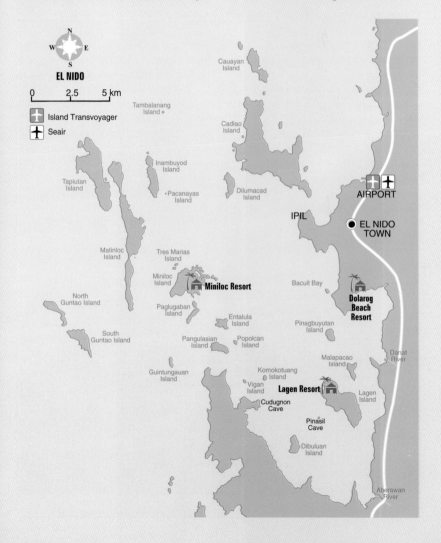

EL NIDO

0   2.5   5 km

✈ Island Transvoyager
✈ Seair

Cauayan Island

Tambalanang Island ○

Cadlao Island

Inambuyod Island

Tapiutan Island

Pacanayas Island

Dilumacad Island

AIRPORT

IPIL

● EL NIDO TOWN

Matinloc Island

Tres Marias Island

Miniloc Island

Miniloc Resort

Bacuit Bay

Dolarog Beach Resort

North Guntao Island

Paglugaban Island

Entalula Island

Pinagbuyutan Island

South Guntao Island

Pangulasian Island

Popolcan Island

Danat River

Malapacao Island

Guintungauan Island

Komokotuang Island

Vigan Island

Lagen Resort

Lagen Island

Cudugnon Cave

Pinasil Cave

Dibuluan Island

Aberawan River

path on the hill, which allows a breathtaking view of the archipelago.

TAPIUTAN *(1 hour 15 minutes from Miniloc)* Facing Matinloc, the island of Tapiutan shelters a vast and deep bay framed by cliffs. A golden beach lined by weatherbeaten trees lies in its hollows. Because a large part of the bay is shallow, snorkeling is easy.

CADLAO *(1 hour from Miniloc)* Cadlao is a big, forested island with many attractive beaches and a hidden lagoon. It is quite open to the sea and can only be reached by canoe because of the coral reefs. The chalky cliffs are particularly striking, evoking some surrealist sculptures, mirrored in emerald waters.

TURTLE ISLAND *(40 minutes from Miniloc)* This rocky and arid island is completely off the coast, solitary and somehow surreal. It has a coral reef fronting its nice beach.

ENTALULA The island has a lovely golden beach lined with coconut trees, giving it the perfect tropical image. It has a lovely coral reef.

MATINLOC It is a big island, still wild and beautiful, with many points of interest. **Secret Beach** *(30 minutes from Miniloc)* It is a fascinating place. A *banca* can get there through a narrow passage between cliffs in an emerald lagoon of corals, at the end of which lies a pretty beach of white sand. You can swim for hours, walk along the coast, observe the coral reefs

View from Pangalusian Island

Big Lagoon, Miniloc Island

and rest in its many sandy creeks. **Hidden Lagoon** *(45 minutes from Miniloc)* On the other side of the island, on the way to Matinloc's circular bay, you can catch a glimpse of a hole in a high cliff. It is only accessible through swimming, and it leads to a tiny lagoon with a narrow beach, completely surrounded by cliffs. **The Bay of Matinloc** *(1 hour from Miniloc)* Cruising along the strait, between Matinloc and Tapiutan Islands, you enter into a vast circular bay surrounded by cliffs. A small coral reef allows you to observe a large variety of fishes.

Snake Island *(30 minutes from Lagen)* Visits to the island are interesting at low tide. It is then that the long and narrow strip of sand—in the form of a snake—becomes visible.

Manlalic River and the Rainforests *(1 hour from Dolarog)* This trip can easily be organized from Dolarog. The hike starts after a 20-minute *banca* ride on Manlalic River, through mangroves. You can see many kingfishers along the way. The forest can be reached after a 30-minute hike, passing through a small village.

Lagen *(20 minutes from Miniloc)* Lagen Island, where the luxurious El Nido Resorts Lagen is to be found, is also gorgeous. Its superb limestone cliffs are covered with a very well preserved rainforest. A path leaving the resort through a shortcut—and after a steep climb—brings you to the other side of the island, to a pretty and solitary beach.

Pinasil *(15 minutes from Lagen)* The island has a cathedral-like cave with its interior slightly illuminated by an opening at the summit. It is one of the many caves where swallows' nests are gathered from a dizzying height.

El Nido Resorts Lagen Island

Lagen Island is magnificent. Its high cliffs are covered with a beautiful forest that rolls almost all the way down to the beach of very fine, almost white sand.

You may reach the resort by air and by sea. Upon arrival at the small El Nido airport, you are warmly welcomed by a solicitous and smiling staff member with cold drinks, hot coffee or tea, and native rice cakes. After a brief rest, you are then seated in a comfortable *banca* that takes you on a 30-minute trip through a length of incredible limestone cliffs.

Owned by Ten Knots, which also owns the El Nido Resorts Miniloc Island, 20 minutes away by boat, the resort was brilliantly designed by architect Nestor David to exude an impres-

sion of harmony, simple elegance and oneness with nature.

The resort occupies three sides of the cove of Lagen Island. The entrance is lined with battered forms of rock, reminding one of sentinels. A stone dike limits the expanse of calm waters. Just behind the beach lies an elegant, lagoon-shaped pool, which reflects the surrounding trees. The wooden lounging chairs nearby, arranged to face the bay, invite you to sit down and relax against their ecru throw pillows.

The high-ceilinged wood and glass clubhouse contains the reception area. White stone floors, beautiful wood furniture, tomb markers (wooden sculptures) from Mindanao; plants in terracotta jars and modern paintings by Dan Raralio,

Elizabeth Siojo and Ramon Diaz accentuate the elegance of the room. Huge bay windows open to the pool and a nice bar lies at one end. The restaurant is also located inside the clubhouse. Interestingly decorated with musical instruments, it is usually used only on rainy days, as dinners are generally served by candlelight beside the pool.

The Water Cottages are bungalows with the most attractive views of the island. These are constructed on stilts and can be found on both sides of the bay, with superb terraces that extend over the ocean and the cliffs; the Beachfront Cottages behind the beach likewise have a view of the sea, though from a further distance; the Forest Rooms, located in a two-story building, face toward the forest as their name implies.

The rooms are superb, no matter which type you choose. They are spacious and wisely extended with vast terraces furnished with a sofa and throw pillows. Each room has a small entrance hall with ample cabinets and big marble and wood bathroom. All the amenities for comfort are available: a minibar, a telephone, a CD player (don't forget to bring your favorite compact discs!) and remote control air-conditioning. The interior design is simple but chic, the furniture is modern but made from bamboo and wood. The cabinets, floors, and sliding shutters are made of a magnificent redwood.

Note: *Lagen or Miniloc?*
The price range can make the difference. Lagen is architecturally much more elegant and more expensive, whereas Miniloc is more laid back. Miniloc has the advantage of being nearer the lagoons, where activities can be organized at your leisure. By comparison, Lagen excursions are usually done in groups.

EL NIDO RESORTS LAGEN ISLAND

Lagen Island, El Nido,
Northern Palawan
Tel   759-4050

Booking Office in Makati
Ten Knots Development Corporation
2/F Builders Center Building
170 Salcedo Street,
Legaspi Village, Makati City
Tel   894-5644
Fax   810-3620
E-mail *sales@elnidoresorts.com*
Web   *www.elnidoresorts.com*

 By air and sea (2 ½ to 3 hours)
Seventy-five-minute flight on Island Transvoyager, Inc. (daily morning and afternoon flights) or one hundred fifteen minutes on Seair (3 weekly flights) from Manila to El Nido. Forty-five minutes by *banca* from El Nido airport to the resort.

Note: *Transfer from El Nido airport is arranged by the resort.*

 51 Units
20 Forest Rooms • 18 Water Cottages • 9 Beachfront Cottages • 4 Forest Suites
All rooms have a terrace, air-conditioning, minibar, CD player, telephone, hairdryer.

Indoor Facilities and Services
Clinic • Babysitting • Massage • Medical services • Billiards • Table tennis • Library

 Food and Beverage Outlets
Lobby Bar, Pool Bar
(*In the evening, tables are set near the pool*)
Cuisine Offered: Local • International
Quality: Good

Watersports and Other Activities
Swimming pool • Beach (white sand) • Snorkeling (in front of the resort) • Diving for certified divers (e-card required) • Kayaking • Other boats for hire • Island hopping (with picnic) • Windsurfing • Hobie cat sailing • Water skiing • Fishing • Mangrove tours • Sunset cruise • Tours to the Big and Small Lagoons • Hiking

 Per room per night on full board basis including round trip airport transfer, one welcome dive for non-divers and all activities

El Nido Resorts Miniloc Island

Miniloc Island is one of the loveliest in the El Nido archipelago, with its high, sharp limestone cliffs and mysterious lagoons: Big Lagoon and Small Lagoon. You arrive at the resort after crossing El Nido Bay, dotted by many limestone islands.

The ragged cliffs above the village of El Nido that you see at the beginning of the short trip are particularly imposing. The resort's surroundings are spectacular, nestled in a narrow bay of golden sand, encircled by dark cliffs.

Coconut trees with bright yellow fruits adorn the small beach. Comfortable bamboo lounging chairs and parasols are there for the taking, a circular bar right behind. A small pigeon loft that houses white doves and pink bougainvillea plants add a happy note to the scenery. A jetty brings you to the counter that serves as the hotel's reception area.

The small bungalows are made of wood with *nipa* rooftops. These have all the amenities for a certain level of comfort. The interior design is simple yet in good taste: braided bamboo walls, wicker cabinets, wood floors and beds covered in white.

Despite the wide difference in the quality each type of cottage offers, they are all surprisingly within the same price range.

The Water Cottages are set apart from the rest and have the most beautiful view of the sea from their terraces.

The Sea View Cottages, located near the restaurant fronting the beach, are slightly less expensive but share a common bath.

The Cliff Cottages are ideal for families. These are two-story cottages behind the beach at the foot of the cliff. The view from their terraces is superb. However, they are not more expensive than the other cottages.

The Garden Cottages are specifically less pleasant, with smaller rooms and narrow unfurnished terraces. These cottages are located behind the beach.

The less spacious Family Cottages are bungalows interconnected with one another.

The restaurant is in a big round *nipa* hut where tables are arranged in the veranda for a good view of the sea and nearby islands. The buffet tables are set inside in order to ensure some privacy. In the evenings, the lights are filtered and the music is soft.

Note: *In comparison to El Nido Resorts Lagen Island, which is more elegant but expensive (managed as well by Ten Knots), El Nido Resorts Miniloc Island was built using natural materials befitting its surroundings. Here, the atmosphere is informal. Activities are well-organized by a very attentive staff. You are even asked about your plans for the next day while dining.*

EL NIDO RESORTS MINILOC ISLAND

Miniloc Island, El Nido,
Northern Palawan
Tel   759-8482

Booking Office in Makati
Ten Knots Development Corporation
2/F Builders Center Building
170 Salcedo Street,
Legaspi Village, 1229 Makati City
Tel   894-5644
Fax   810-3620
E-mail *sales@elnidoresorts.com*
Web   *www.elnidoresorts.com*

 By air and sea (2½ to 3 hours) Seventy-five-minute flight on Island Transvoyager, Inc. (daily morning and afternoon flights) or one hundred fifteen minutes on Seair (3 weekly flights) from Manila to El Nido. Forty-five minutes by *banca* from El Nido airport to the resort.

Note: *Transfer from El Nido airport is arranged by the resort.*

 31 Units
16 Garden Cottages • 3 Cliff Cottages • 7 Water Cottages • 5 Sea View Rooms (built over the water)
All cottages and rooms have private verandas, air-conditioning, day bed, minibar, private toilet and shower facilities, hot water, hairdryer, telephone with international access.

Indoor Facilities and Services
Clinic • Babysitting • Massage • Billiards • Table tennis

 Food and Beverage Outlets
Restaurants: Clubhouse Restaurant (tables are set-up in the veranda providing views of the sea and nearby islands.
Cuisine Offered: Local • International
Quality: Good
Bar: Pavilion Bar

 Watersports and Other Activities
Swimming pool • Beach (white sand) • Snorkeling (in front of the resort) • Diving for certified divers (e-card required) • Kayaking • Other boats for hire • Island hopping (with picnic) • Windsurfing • Hobie cat sailing • Water skiing • Fishing • Mangrove tours • Sunset cruise • Tours to the Big and Small Lagoons • Hiking

 Per room per night on full board basis, including round trip airport transfer, one welcome dive for non-divers and all activities

Dolarog Beach Resort

The Dolarog Beach Resort is in a deserted beach seven kilometers from El Nido. The view from the resort, which opens to the bay of Bacuit is particularly beautiful. One can contemplate on the mammoth-like form of Binagbayoton Island with a tiny rounded beach just facing the resort. The outlined silhouette of Lagen is in the distance. Malapacao Island, whose two high rocks on both extremes are stationed like sentries on both sides of a golden beach are bordered by coconut trees.

The resort has an informal and family-oriented atmosphere. An Italian named Edo built the resort over 20 years ago. He lives here with his Filipina wife and children, his monkey and cats.

The resort is composed of five bungalows on a one and a half-hectare property. It sits on a field of coconut trees surrounded by grass, facing a long and narrow white sand beach, where swimming can be most enjoyable. The beach sinks into a soft slope where children can swim without much risk. Some shells that are brought willy-nilly to the shore by the tides.

The wood and bamboo bungalows on stilts, directly on the beach, are simple and relatively spacious. They have wooden floors, tiled connecting bathrooms, and the beds are provided with mosquito nets. There are three individual bungalows by the restaurant's right side. On its left are two connecting cottages which cater more to families, as they share a terrace.

Each bungalow has its own terrace, furnished with armchairs and hammocks for viewing the fabulous limestone cliffs. The arrival of rains and storms can also be viewed here, in total tranquility. At the end of a beautiful day, the setting sun offers its décor of orange and pink hues.

The restaurant is housed in a big wooden structure at the center of the resort. Generously opening toward the sea, it has a small bar behind which is a wall painted with fishes—souvenirs of a local artist.

The resort provides a *banca*, so excursions can actually be done from here. One can even ask to be brought to the rainforests through the Manlalic River, crossing mangroves where various kinds of birds can also be observed. The trip takes one hour by *banca* and another 20 minutes on foot until the forest.

DOLAROG BEACH RESORT

 El Nido, Palawan
Tel (0919) 867-4360
E-mail *dolarog@mysmart.com*
(send the e-mail a week before)
Web *www.dolarog.com*

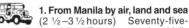

1. From Manila by air, land and sea
(2 ½–3 ½ hours) Seventy-five-minute flight on Island Transvoyager, Inc. (daily morning and afternoon flights) or one hundred fifteen minutes on Seair (3 weekly flights) from Manila to El Nido. Passengers holding a confirmed booking at Lagen or Miniloc resorts are given priority on Andres Soriano Aviation. Twenty minutes by tricycle from El Nido airport to the town proper. Thirty minutes by *banca* from El Nido pier to the resort.

2. From Manila by air, land and sea
(8 hours) Ninety-minute daily flight on Seair from Manila to Sandoval. Twenty to thirty minutes by jeepney from Sandoval airport to Taytay City. Twenty minutes by tricycle from Taytay City proper to Embarcadero. Three hours by *banca* from Taytay Embarcadero to El Nido pier. Thirty minutes by *banca* from El Nido pier to the resort.

3. From Puerto Princesa by land and sea
(10 hours) The road may be impassable during rainy season. It will take you three and a half hours from Puerto Princesa to Roxas; Two hours from Roxas to Taytay. From Taytay there are two options. **By land**: Four hours from Taytay to El Nido **By land and sea:** Twenty minutes by tricycle from Taytay City proper to the Embarcadero. Three hours by *banca* from Taytay Embarcadero to El Nido pier. Thirty minutes by *banca* from El Nido pier to the resort.

11 Units
6 Single Front Beach Cottages •
2 Double Front Beach Cottages •
1 Balcon Family (connecting to 2 more rooms) All cottages have a private bathroom (no hot water). There is no air-conditioning or fan. The beds have mosquito nets. The generator is on until 10 p.m.

Indoor Facilities and Services
Babysitting

 Food and Beverage Outlets
Restaurant: Beachfront Restaurant (small bar at the back)
Cuisine Offered: Italian • Filipino • International
Quality: Familial, depending on the day's catch

Watersports and Other Activities
Beach (white sand) • Snorkeling (in other places) • Diving (arrangements with a Dive Shop in El Nido) • Island hopping (with picnic) • Boats for hire • Windsurfing • Fishing • Forest trekking • Volleyball

 Per room per night on full board basis

The Cuyo Islands

The archipelago of the Cuyo Islands is located north of the Sulu Sea, far out in the open sea of Palawan and yet still part of it. The archipelago is composed of about 40 islands and islets, most of which are uninhabited. It is known because of the internationally renowned Amanpulo Resort on the island of Pamalican, one of the many in the Aman chain of hotels. The archipelago is divided into two island groups.

Up north is the Quiniluban group to which Pamalican Island belongs. The 89-hectare island houses the ultra-exclusive Amanpulo Resort. The marine environment around the island was declared a protected zone. Fishing and docking are prohibited. Pamalican has a superb beach, five-and-a-half kilometers long on the side where the resort is located. It is wilder and windier on the other side.

To the south are the Cuyo Islands, where the village of Cuyo is located, together with its Spanish fort constructed in 1677 to protect its population from Moro pirates. It shelters a church, a convent and a chapel in its high stone walls.

In the Cuyo Islands, what is most surprising are the extraordinary colors of the coral reefs and the beaches, which are either in gold or dazzling white powder sand. Here, the sea has all the possible hues of blue and green—azure, turquoise, beryl, aquamarine and emerald all mixed together in a fabulous palette of colors. Places endowed with such intensity of colors are rare. The coral reefs encircling the islands are favorable for snorkeling.

Amanpulo

Amanpulo

If you want to splurge, why not try the luxurious Amanpulo Resort on ultra-exclusive Pamalican island? Amanpulo is the idyllic retreat for a rich and famous clientele who seeks peace and privacy. The resort, designed by Filipino architect Francisco Mañosa, was built in such a way as to give its privileged few the impression that they are alone on the island.

After an hour by private plane, you will arrive at a small and elongated green island, set on an iridescent beryl and azure sea, fringed with the purest of sands. The welcome upon arrival is warm and personalized: champagne and canapés are served and a personal golf cart—to be used for going around the resort—is placed at your disposal. Your own personal attendant appears as soon as you call him; you will be constantly reminded that there are 250 people here ready to serve a mere 100 guests!

Within the Club House are the reception area, the bar, and the restaurant. The reception area, immense and impressive, is all in wood with narra floors and *lauan* columns and ceilings. It opens out to a terrace with sliding panels, facing the ocean. Rattan and coconut wood furniture enhance the surroundings, while ornate wood pieces from Mindanao and wicker from Palawan decorate the adjoining rooms.

The casitas or guesthouses, discreetly hidden in vegetation, are perfectly private. You can choose to stay in the beach casitas which have the best location along the beach; in the tree top casitas nestled in the branches of large trees; or in the hillside casitas perched on the hill's summit, offering a spectacular view of the sea.

All the accommodations are extraordinary in terms of both size and luxury. The rooms are huge—at least 65 square meters—and bright because of immense picture windows. Beige walls, polished wood floors, interior shutters, designer rattan furniture and beautiful accessories crafted locally, complete the interior design.

The casitas have two comfortable divans at an angle along the picture windows of the dining room—where you can have your meals served—while listening to music. A vast bedroom, with a king-sized bed, has all the possible amenities that you can think of. A dream bathroom of marble and wood is complete with a dressing room, two sinks, a bathtub and a separate shower.

The picture windows open onto a slightly elevated wooden deck. Soft mattresses are strewn here, inviting you to watch the sunset—as spectacular as everything else in Amanpulo. Each casita looks out to a private garden, where a hammock swings gently between two coconut trees. A private path leads to a part of a fabulous deserted beach where two deck chairs and a parasol await you.

The resort has a superb, lagoon-type swimming pool bordered with bougainvillea. After a swim, you can lie down on huge mattresses scattered in the open-air cabanas.

Snorkeling in the beautiful coral reef encircling the island is breathtaking. The spot is accessible from the beach and visibility in the water is excellent. Diving, however, is less interesting.

To have a perfect end to a perfect day, you can have a romantic candle-lit dinner accompanied by soft, soothing music in the resort's excellent restaurant.

AMANPULO

Pamalican Island, Palawan
Tel 759-4040 • 851-0295
Fax 759-4044
E-mail
amanpulo@amanresorts.com
Web *www.amanresorts.com*

 By private charter arranged by the resort (Island Aviation - Tel. No.: 833-3855) (1 ½ hours). Guests are met at Manila's international airport and taken by complimentary car transfer to Amanpulo's lounge, from where they are flown directly to Pamalican Island in 90 minutes. Daily departure from Manila at 1:30 p.m. or 4:30 p.m. (2 flights on Monday/Friday). Daily departure from Pamalican at 10 a.m. or 3 p.m. (2 flights on Tuesday/Thursday/Sunday)

 40 Units
29 Beach Casitas • 7 Hillside Casitas • 4 Treetop Casitas
All casitas are air-conditioned and have satellite TV, minibar, CD player, a separate living room, a bathroom with bathtub, shower, bathrobes and a private terrace. Each casita is provided with a club car.

Indoor Facilities and Services
Babysitting • Library • Internet and e-mail • Massage • Beauty parlor • Meeting facilities • Medical services • Foreign currency exchange

 Food and Beverage Outlets
Restaurants: The Restaurant • The Beach Club
Cuisine Offered: Filipino • International
Quality: Excellent

Note: *Breakfast is served only in the casitas. All meals can be taken in the casita. Barbecues are held at the seaside picnic grove.*

 Watersports and Other Activities
Swimming pool • Beach (white sand) • Snorkeling (50–300 meters offshore) • Dive center • Island hopping (with picnic) • Kayaking • Other boats for hire • Fishing • Water skiing • Windsurfing • Laser boat sailing • Sunset cruises • Tennis (with lessons) • Mountain biking • Guided nature walk • Children's playground and lounge

 Per room per night

Sabang

Sabang is a small and timeless village devoid of any real tourist infrastructure. The place is known by virtue of the Underground River National Park close by. But Sabang's attraction also lies in its tranquility; its superb, untamed beaches dominated by high cliffs; and its mountains covered by jungle. Several days can be devoted to a Sabang visit.

THE UNDERGROUND RIVER NATIONAL PARK *(one day on foot and a half-day if you go by banca)* The National Park covers 5,000 hectares of well-preserved forest. The underground river is about eight kilometers long beneath the cliffs, four kilometers of which can be covered by *banca* with a guide, equipped with a kerosene torch so you can admire the stalactites and stalagmites. The river can be reached from Sabang by *banca* (one hour), but if you have the time, the walk across the National Park is quite pleasant and relatively easy.

After having bought your ticket at the park's office, at the one and only village

Saint Paul Underground River National Park, Sabang

street just before the jetty, take the path directly across that runs along the beach. At its end is a sign indicating the entrance to the National Park. You then take the "Monkey Trail." The climb is rather steep, but a makeshift wooden railing has been installed. The path, always perfectly indicated, crosses the jungle, affording beautiful views of the cliffs and the sea. You cross a marvelous beach before arriving at the rangers' station. From there, you can go deeper into the jungle through a less maintained path, or continue along the beach. Arriving at the cave's entrance, you simply rent one of the *bancas* awaiting visitors.

CABAYUGAN *(9 kilometers from Sabang)* The village of Cabayugan is in a spectacular setting of cone-shaped cliffs in the middle of rice paddies. You can visit the small caves of Kawili and Lion (bring your flashlight). Unless you catch the jeepney at 8:00 a.m., you have to take the route on foot. Nonetheless, walking through rice paddies and forests is pleasant.

Bambua Lodge and Restaurant

Bambua Lodge and Restaurant, the nicest among the small hotels of Sabang, is a kilometer away from the village. It is located in a beautiful area surrounded by mountains and rice paddies, just beside the St. Paul Underground River National Park. The resort is on a dirt road that connects Puerto Princesa to Sabang.

The resort is perched on a small hill, a five-minute walk from the road through a well-maintained path that leads to a wooden bungalow set at treetop level. This serves as the restaurant and reception area. In summer, tables are set in the garden.

Andre and Rosalie Dartmann, a German-Filipino couple, who are full of ideas in extending their property and improving its comforts, own and manage the resort. Note that Sabang is still remote and it is this isolation that gives its particular charm.

The atmosphere is informal. Several tiny and very simple bungalows are scattered in the garden. The interiors are very basic and common as well with showers and toilets outside. Andre has also constructed four detached and delightful bungalows.

These four bungalows are spacious with a bathroom, a double bed with a mosquito net and a small lounge corner. The view that you get from the terrace is exquisite, overlooking rice paddies and mountains from a distance.

From Sabang, you can also hire a *banca* at the pier, and go to the unspoiled and serene beach of Panagumian, 30 minutes away, and 10 minutes away from the Underground River National Park.

Panagumian Beach

BAMBUA LODGE AND RESTAURANT

Sabang, Palawan
Booking Office in Puerto Princesa, Palawan
Purok Maunlad, Brgy. San Pedro, Puerto Princesa City, Palawan
Tel (048) 434-3887
E-mail bambua@pal-onl.com
Web www.bambua-palawan.com

 By air and land (5 hours with a car rental) Seventy-five-minute daily flights on Philippine Airlines, Cebu Pacific, Asian Spirit or Air Philippines from Manila to Puerto Princesa. Three hours by car/van from Puerto Princesa airport to Sabang. The air-conditioned bus departing from Trattoria Inn on Rizal Avenue leaves at 7:30 a.m. It takes longer than the car/van ride. You also have to spend the night in Puerto Princesa. From Sabang, the bus leaves at 3 p.m.

Superferry (Tel. No.: 528-7979) and Negros Navigation (Tel. No.: 245-4395) also operates ferry service from Manila to Puerto Princesa.

 16 Units
4 Village-type Cottages (with private bathroom and electric fan) • Lodging House (8 rooms with double-deck beds) • Duplex Cottages (4 rooms with common bathroom)

 Food and Beverage Outlets
Restaurant
Cuisine Offered: Filipino
Quality: Average, but the best restaurant in town

 Watersports and Other Activities
Swimming and snorkeling is possible near Sabang village (You need to rent a boat for snorkeling) • Tours to St. Paul Underground River National Park • Cabayugan cliffs day walk • Trekking in the jungle and countryside

 Per room per night on full board basis

Cabayugan cliffs

Puerto Princesa and Honda Bay

Puerto Princesa is a necessary stop-over to the south or north of Palawan. All things considered, it is a pleasant and restful city; clean and adorned with flowers. If you have a few hours to spend, go and see its small museum in the old City Hall Building where you will experience a good overall view of Palawan culture. You will also find an interesting collection of pottery found in sunken Chinese junks discovered in the region.

A stay in Puerto Princesa is never complete without a visit to Honda Bay, only 30 minutes away by boat. It is a beautiful natural site, with numerous coral reefs framed by distant mountains.

To visit the bay, you can take a *banca* from the jetty at St. Lourdes, in the municipality of Tagburos, 10 kilometers away. The different islets are accessible in 15 to 45 minutes. The best known is Arreceffi Island. The islets of Honda Bay have superb, long white beaches surrounded by a crystal clear sea. These also have lush tropical vegetation extending into vast mangrove forests that at times are double the size of the islands. The mangroves are teeming with birdlife of many migratory species.

PANDAN ISLAND Pandan Island is named after the pandan trees that line the beach with their heavy, yellow fruits. If it is not too hot, go to the other end of the beach, on the other side of the island which is wilder. Its waters are bordered with mangroves.

SNAKE ISLAND Snake Island is named after the form of its long beach of white sand. It is sad to see the dying coral reef here. You can listen to the songs of the birds from the neighboring mangrove swamps.

WHITE SANDBAR White Sandbar, property of Dos Palmas Arreceffi Island Resort, is a simple sandbar emerging from the water. Here, you will enjoy a panoramic view of the bay and mountains.

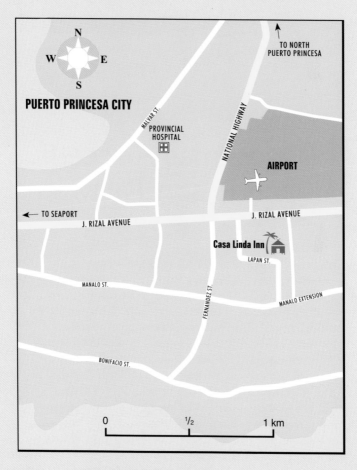

Puerto Princesa and Honda Bay:

Climate   Seasons not very pronounced; wet during July and August

Typhoons   Never affect Puerto Princesa; it happens only in the North of Palawan, El Nido, during November to December

Dos Palmas Arreceffi Island Resort Palawan

Dos Palmas is on Arreceffi, a paradise island of 20 hectares lost in the middle of beautiful Honda Bay. The island's natural beauty is breathtaking: crystal clear waters, with a long, white sand beach shaded by coconut trees. The island is extended by marshlands where numerous species of local and migratory birds thrive. Upon arrival, you get the impression of entering into a real oasis. A profusion of giant gumamelas and multicolored bougainvillea swell into a magnificent garden where verdant grass, meticulously maintained, carpet the ground around the trees.

From the architectural point of view, it is rather surprising to see stark white structures devoid of any indigenous material. The white, corrugated iron roofs, more weather-resistant than *nipa* roofing, nevertheless follow the form of the typical Badjao Tribe houses. Bamboo and wood, on the other hand, are used in the interior of cottages and common areas.

The Single Detached Bay Cottages on stilts, located at the resort's entrance are ideal for couples, assuring them of complete privacy and tranquility. The Duplex Garden Cottages are ideal for families because of a loft which can accommodate three or more occupants.

Bright, spacious and quiet, the rooms are simply furnished in white wood and the high ceilings are made of beautiful braided wicker. The bright bathrooms are clean and comfortable.

All the rooms have a balcony from where you can enjoy the splendid panorama of sea and mountains.

The restaurant, which opens to both the sea and the garden, is very pleasant because of the generous use of bamboo. Tables are set around the pool, on the beach, or, in the evenings, in the garden. Make sure to ask to have your breakfast served on a floating raft anchored 500 meters from the beach, however. After the meal, you can simply dive into the water and do some fabulous snorkeling.

Since the sea around the resort is not too deep, visibility underwater is excellent. The corals are varied and multicolored, taking many forms. Fishes are abundant and of very diverse species. Another excellent place for snorkeling and diving is Helen's Garden, 500 meters from the beach, marked by a floating raft equipped with a ladder.

At dusk, you can ask to be brought to a sandbar emerging from the water and have a drink there, watching the sunset. At the end of the day, it is very pleasant to leave on a kayak and tour the island. You may spend about 45 minutes if you stay out at sea, more if you enter deep in the swamps to observe the birds.

At Dos Palmas, much attention is given to the quality of service—always warm and dependable. The beauty of the site and its tranquility will seduce you. Here, there is no intrusive music nor jet skis. The silence is broken only by the lapping of the waves, bird songs and the occasional *banca* passing by in the open sea.

DOS PALMAS ARRECEFFI ISLAND RESORT PALAWAN

 Arreceffi Island, Honda Bay, Puerto Princesa City, Palawan

Booking Office in Pasig
Unit 1005 Antel Global Corporate Center, Julia Vargas Avenue, Ortigas Center, Pasig City
Tel 637-4226 • 637-4236
Fax 637-4230
E-mail *info@dospalmas.com.ph*
Web *www.dospalmas.com.ph*

 By air, land and sea (3 hours) Seventy-five-minute daily flights on Philippine Airlines, Cebu Pacific, Asian Spirit or Air Philippines from Manila to Puerto Princesa. Thirty minutes by mini-bus from Puerto Princesa Airport to Santa Lourdes Wharf. Fifty minutes by *banca* from Santa Lourdes Wharf to the resort.

Note: Airport transfer is arranged by Dos Palmas.

Superferry (Tel. No.: 528-7979) and Negros Navigation (Tel. No.: 245-4395) also operates ferry service from Manila to Puerto Princesa.

 48 Units
10 Bay Cottages • 38 Duplex Garden Cottages
All rooms have air-conditioning, fan, and private bathroom with hot water, minibar, intercom, private balcony, and extra bed.

Indoor Facilities and Services
Spa services • Billiards • Table tennis

 Food and Beverage Outlets
Restaurant: Kara-e-nan Restaurant
Cuisine Offered: International • Filipino
Quality: Good

Watersports and Other Activities
Swimming pool with Jacuzzi • Beach (white sand) • Mountain biking • Jogging trail • Snorkeling (450 meters off the beach) • Dive center • Island hopping • Kayaking • Other boats for hire • Fishing • Children's playground

 Per room per night

Casa Linda

This small family hotel, ten minutes by tricycle from Puerto Princesa Airport in a quiet dead end, is a good bargain.

Inspired by traditional architecture in wood and bamboo, it is constructed on a level a little bit above the ground. All the structures built on three sides of the property encircle a pretty, small inner garden filled with plants and flowers. A kiosk lies in the middle of the garden where you can have a drink or simply read.

Upon arrival, you first enter a wooden building that houses a small reception hall, a lounge and a restaurant. This area opens to the garden and has a warm atmosphere, with its beautiful, polished wooden floors and bamboo sofas covered with comfortable throw pillows. This is where avid TV lovers watch their favorite shows in the evenings.

The bedrooms along the passageway overlooking the garden, are clustered around the reception area. These are rather dim and lighting at night is poor. The interiors are simple but very clean with bamboo-covered walls and small, tiled bathrooms. Only some of the rooms are air-conditioned.

The hospitable receptionists can help you organize your Palawan trip, especially car rentals or reservations for *bancas* or hotels within the province.

CASA LINDA

Trinidad Road, Rizal Avenue,
Puerto Princesa City, Palawan
Tel (048) 433-2606
Fax (048) 433-2309
E-mail *casalind@mozcom.com*

By air (2 hours)
Seventy-five-minute daily flights on Philippine Airlines, Cebu Pacific, Asian Spirit or Air Philippines from Manila to Puerto Princesa. Ten minutes by tricycle from Puerto Princesa airport to the hotel.

Superferry (Tel. No.: 528-7979) and Negros Navigation (Tel. No.: 245-4395) also operates ferry service from Manila to Puerto Princesa.

12 Units
2 Air-conditioned Family Room • 8 Standard Air-conditioned Rooms • 2 Standard Fan Rooms
All rooms have a bathroom with cold water only.

Indoor Facilities and Services
Tour desk • Transportation hiring

Food and Beverage Outlets
Restaurant: Casa Linda Restaurant
Cuisine Offered: Filipino
Quality: Average

Sports and Activities
See Puerto Princesa's points of interest.

Per room per night inclusive of breakfast

Boayan

Nestled in the idyllic surroundings of a forested bay in clear emerald waters, the house of Boayan, a little isle in the South China Sea, is an ideal spot for those in search of secluded comfort.

Boayan is not a resort, but the home of Philippe, Ditchay and their daughter Amélie. It becomes yours for the duration of your stay. In fact, they literally move out into another house nearby. Domestic help is on call and you can indulge in the services of an incomparable cook—Ditchay herself! Given that provisions cannot be obtained easily on the isle, you will be amazed by the excellent variety of culinary dishes she cooks up in Franco-Philippine style—duck (preserves, soufflés, curry, rillettes), pâtés, cheese toasts, chocolate cake and delicious home-made bread. Vegetables and herbs are grown in the garden and the hen house assures fresh eggs for breakfast!

Six years ago, in their search for another way of life, Philippe and Ditchay said goodbye to their respective professions as photographer and actress and came to settle here. They live on the isle like modern Robinson Crusoes—no television, electricity or telephones, but the magnificent spectacle of the bay, solar panels, the clarity of the digital satellite radio, a satellite telephone in case of an emergency and Internet! They are attentive but discreet hosts who will provide you with interesting political, cultural or tourist information on the Philippines that they know so well.

The house is a large wooden pavilion on stilts, surrounded by a planked terrace facing a lagoon. It has two rooms and a bathroom. The kitchen is in a separate pavilion, very nice and inviting with wicker-work and kitchen utensils decorating the walls.

The terrace, with its fabulous view of the surrounding hills, is the place where you will spend most of your time. Mealtimes are the highlights of the day and are tuned to the sounds of the waves. You are only a hop, skip and a jump from the crystal waters of the lagoon, which you can consider your own private swimming pool, where no mortal will come to disturb your tranquility. The lagoon boasts of an easily accessible beautiful coral reef. You can also admire the multi-colored fish of this sea garden with the help of snorkeling equipment.

The powdery white-sanded beach stretches out in front of the house. At low tide, it is pleasant to wander about in search of seashells. However, do restrain from destroying the fragile surroundings of the reef.

You can go fishing in a motorboat driven by an experienced boat man, on an excursion or a picnic on the golden deserted beaches, explore the little forest on the hills opposite or simply laze on your terrace and dream.

You will feel as if you're in another world here, where time is of no consequence and where peace and tranquility are omnipresent. It is a tricky task returning to the hustle and bustle of the capital, but the memory of this paradise lost will remain with you for a long, long time.

BOAYAN

 Yellow House, Boayan Island, San Vicente, Palawan
Tel 00 873 762 279 951 (satellite INMARSAT)
E-mail boayanfree@free.fr boayan@chinaseaisland.com
Web www.chinaseaisland.com
Note: *The house is closed from July to mid-December*

 By air, land and sea (5 hours)
Seventy-five-minute daily flights on Air Philippines, Cebu Pacific, Asian Spirit or Philippine Airlines from Manila to Puerto Princesa. Two hours by car from airport to Port Barton. Forty-five minutes from Port Barton to Boayan Island.

Note: *Transfer from airport is usually included in the package.*

Superferry (Tel. No.: 528-7979) and Negros Navigation (Tel. No.: 245-4395) also operates ferry service from Manila to Puerto Princesa.

 1 Unit
Private house (with spacious terrace, 2 bedrooms, bathroom, electric fans)

Note: *Electricity is provided by solar panels and a back-up generator.*

The house comes with a staff of 5 people made up of the host, cook, chambermaids and all around utility men (languages spoken: English, French and the local language)

Indoor Facilities and Services
Worldspace radio and data system • Satellite phone • Stereo • Computer

 Food and Beverage Outlets
Prepared by the owner. They serve excellent culinary dishes.
Cuisine Offered: Franco-Filipino
Quality: Excellent

Note: *Alcoholic beverages can be provided at cost or you may bring your own.*

Watersports and Other Activities
Beach • Snorkeling • Fishing • Boats for hire • Island Hopping

Price on request, depending on the number of people.

Note: *Minimum stay of one week is recommended.*

Visayas

he Sentry, Isla Naburot, Guimaras

Painting by Lily Yousry-Jouve

Visayas

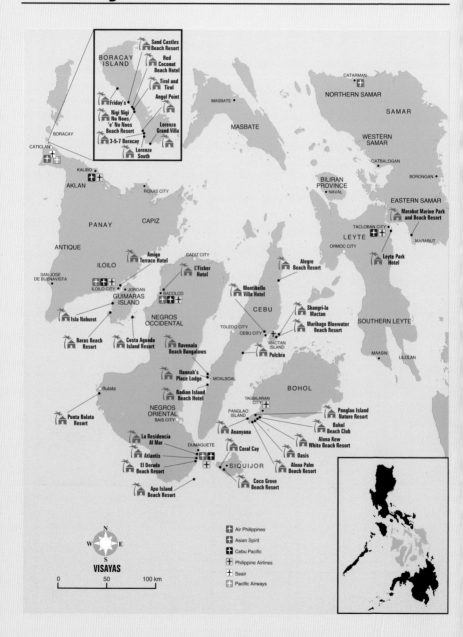

BORACAY ISLAND
- Sand Castles Beach Resort
- Red Coconut Beach Hotel
- Tirol and Tirol
- Angol Point
- Friday's
- Nigi Nigi Nu Noos/ 'e' Nu Noos Beach Resort
- Lorenzo Grand Villa
- 3-5-7 Boracay
- Lorenzo South

BORACAY
CATICLAN
KALIBO
AKLAN
ROXAS CITY
PANAY
CAPIZ
ANTIQUE
ILOILO
- Amigo Terrace Hotel
SAN JOSE DE BUENAVISTA
ILOILO CITY • JORDAN
GUIMARAS ISLAND
- Isla Naburot
- Baras Beach Resort
- Costa Aguada Island Resort
CADIZ CITY
- L'Fisher Hotel
BACOLOD
NEGROS OCCIDENTAL
- Ravenala Beach Bungalows
- Hannah's Place Lodge
MOALBOAL
- Badian Island Beach Hotel
Bulata
NEGROS ORIENTAL
BAIS CITY
- Punta Bulata Resort
- La Residencia Al Mar
DUMAGUETE
- Atlantis
- El Dorado Beach Resort
- Apo Island Beach Resort
SIQUIJOR
- Coral Cay
- Coco Grove Beach Resort

MASBATE
MASBATE
- Montibello Villa Hotel
TOLEDO CITY
CEBU
CEBU CITY
- Alegre Beach Resort
- Shangri-la Mactan
- Maribago Bluewater Beach Resort
MACTAN ISLAND
- Pulchra
BOHOL
TAGBILARAN CITY
PANGLAO ISLAND
- Panglao Island Nature Resort
- Bohol Beach Club
- Alona Kew White Beach Resort
- Ananyana
- Alona Palm Beach Resort
- Oasis

CATARMAN
NORTHERN SAMAR
SAMAR
WESTERN SAMAR
CATBALOGAN
BORONGAN
BILIRAN PROVINCE
NAVAL
EASTERN SAMAR
- Marabut Marine Park and Beach Resort
TACLOBAN CITY
LEYTE
ORMOC CITY
MARABUT
- Leyte Park Hotel
SOUTHERN LEYTE
MAASIN
LILOLAN

Legend (airlines)
- Air Philippines
- Asian Spirit
- Cebu Pacific
- Philippine Airlines
- Seair
- Pacific Airways

N
W E
S
VISAYAS
0   50   100 km

THE VISAYAS, THE LARGEST CENTRAL GROUP OF ISLANDS BETWEEN LUZON AND MINDANAO, is made up of the main islands of Bohol, Cebu, Leyte, Samar, Negros, Panay, and the smaller islands of Boracay, Siquijor, Guimaras, Romblon, and a number of islets. In general, the Visayas is accessible from Manila and there are a number of fast, comfortable ferry services connecting the islands. If you have time, it is pleasurable and economical to go from island to island via ferry.

The region actually covers very different islands, each with its own character. But the islands share a common sense of festivity with exuberant, colorful festivals such as the Sinulog of Cebu, the Ati-Atihan of Kalibo, the Dinagyang of Iloilo and the Masskara of Bacolod.

- Cebu occupies a central position in the Visayas, making it the region's most dynamic center. There you can find luxury hotels in Mactan, interesting vestiges of the past on the southern coast and the lovely beaches of Moalboal on the west coast where you can go diving and snorkeling.

- Bohol is famous for its intriguing Chocolate Hills—hundreds of rounded hillocks emerging from the plain, brown or green depending on the season. It is also home to many beautiful old churches and good dive sites.

- Boracay possesses a summery, casual atmosphere and golden beaches.

- Panay may have the most beautiful church in the Philippines, the fortress-church of Miag-ao. Iloilo, the capital, contains many interesting old houses set in the middle of urban developments.

- Negros Occidental offers the fascinating old houses of Silay, some of which are open to the public. Negros Oriental is famous among divers for Apo reef in the small island of Apo, near Dumaguete.

- Siquijor is a pleasant little island well-known for its faith healers.

- Samar and Leyte are still covered, in some parts, with virgin rainforest. Nature lovers will like it here, as the islands remain relatively unexplored by tourists.

Miag-ao Church

Cebu

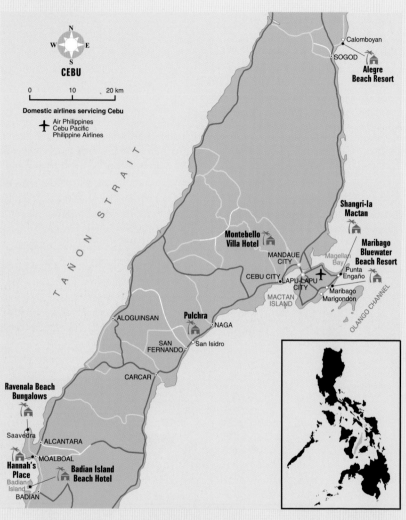

CEBU

Domestic airlines servicing Cebu

Air Philippines
Cebu Pacific
Philippine Airlines

  Climate **South coast:** Seasons not very pronounced, relatively dry from December to April; wet during the rest of the year
North coast: Rainfall more or less evenly distributed throughout the year

Typhoons   May to December

Sinulog, Cebu City, third week of January. The festival honors the Santo Niño, the patron of Cebu, whose image, offered by Magellan to the Rajah Humabon, is preserved in Saint Basilica Minore of San Augustin. The Sinulog refers to the dance-like motions of women holding candles while praying to the Santo Niño, usually in front of the Basilica. Parades, processions and street dancing mark this famous festival.

Cebu and Mactan

The island of Cebu, with a population of 3 million, stretches over 200 kilometers and is 40 kilometers at its widest point. Cebu is the region's center of commerce, industry and education. The two main centers of attraction are the Island of Mactan where the big hotels are concentrated and Moalboal on the west coast, renowned for diving. However, the city of Cebu itself, as well as the southeast coast, still preserves some vestiges of the past.

Cebu City

Cebu is the oldest city in the Philippines, founded in 1565 by Spaniard Miguel Lopez de Legazpi. Today, Cebu, with Davao, are the most important cities after Manila. The atmosphere is without doubt more agreeable than that of the capital, even if at peak hours, Cebu is also plagued by traffic jams. The city attracts many businessmen from Korea, Japan, Taiwan, Singapore and Hongkong. There are, in fact, international air links between Cebu and these countries. The airport is on the island of Mactan, 13 kilometers from the city. If you want to make a complete city tour, you will need one full day as the different sites of interest are fairly dispersed.

FORT SAN PEDRO Constructed by Legazpi in 1565, it is one of the oldest fortresses in the Philippines. Today, it houses the province's tourism office.

THE BASILICA MINORE DEL SANTO NIÑO ON LUNA STREET Constructed in 1565 and reconstructed in 1735, it houses the relic of the statue of the Infant Jesus given by Magellan to the wife of the Rajah Humabon, as well as other religious art objects.

CASA GORORDO MUSEUM ON LOPEZ JAENA STREET A beautifully restored 19th-century Spanish house, it has been transformed into a museum of paintings and antique furniture.

MAGELLAN'S CROSS In 1521, Ferdinand Magellan himself marked the site of the first communal baptisms, erecting the wooden cross on Plaza Santa Cruz.

SHOPPING The shops, malls, restaurants and cinemas are concentrated on Colon Street, within the commercial artery of the town. Cebu displays considerable creativity as far as bamboo furniture goes. It also specializes in shellcraft and the guitars, the fabrication of which can be observed in Mactan, in the district of Maribago.

Mactan

If you are in Cebu for pleasure, it is clearly more pleasant to stay on the island of Mactan—now linked to Cebu city by two bridges—than in the city center. Mactan is, in fact, a succession of hotels, often enormous and luxurious, located mostly on the east coast, 20 kilometers from the city and only eight kilometers from the airport. The beaches in front of these hotels are small, covered with artificial white sand and the waters are not always clear. On the other hand, if you like comfortable, plush hotels, you have the luxury of choice. After all, it is sometimes nice to indulge one's self and Cebu is easily accessible from Manila.

PUNTA ENGAÑO It is the monument to Lapu-Lapu, the local chieftain who, in 1521, resisted the troops of Magellan. Magellan was killed in combat, in this area of the southeastern coast where the monument was eventually erected.

OLANGO WILDLIFE SANCTUARY From February to May and from August to November of each year, the 920 hectares that make up this island are a haven for a large concentration of migratory birds. You can also dive and snorkel on the northwest part of the island. *(30 minutes)*

DIVING Most of Mactan's hotels have dive centers. As the nearby coral reefs have been badly damaged by pollution and dynamite fishing, you have to go further away to dive—on Hilutangan Island (1 hour), Sandbar (1½ hours) and Danajon Bank where the white sandbank can only be observed at low tide. Some resorts take you to the island of Cabilao where the diving is exceptional and snorkeling is possible (2½ hours by boat).

Montebello Villa Hotel

Montebello Villa Hotel is 20 minutes away from the city center, in what was once a hacienda, now a vast landscaped garden of five hectares. Though the city has big and very comfortable hotels, this is the only one possessing any real charm. This is largely due to the surrounding vegetation and the peaceful, family atmosphere despite its 145 rooms.

The hotel is quite pleasant with its low, white Spanish-style buildings, the red tile roofs and the arcades at the entrance. The wide, high-ceilinged reception area with its red brickwork is welcoming, with its curved archway and white rattan sofas.

Some of the rooms are located at the back of the reception area around a large outdoor patio that has access to the garden. The other rooms are in separate two-story building linked together around a swimming pool.

The rooms are furnished with functional furniture, fitted carpeting, and small tiled bathrooms. The standard rooms, though smaller and without a balcony, are pleasant. The three standard rooms located in a separate wing by the main pool are the best choice as these rooms have separate entrance halls.

The Poolside Restaurant, opening onto a second bigger swimming pool, is a nice place to hang around. The magnificent, old bougainvilleas with their knotted trunks cling to the building in a tight embrace and drape the roof with fuchsia flowers, which also creep up right under the arches—where the tables are arranged—all along the swimming pool. From here you can catch a glimpse of the garden and its well-maintained lawns shaded by beautiful trees. A bridge over the pond is the perfect backdrop for the many wedding ceremonies that are held at Montebello.

Note: *If you prefer to stay in the city center, the following two hotels are recommended:*

- *Waterfront Cebu Hotel and Casino is an extravagant, gigantic 560-room complex, whose high, massive dome-crowned silhouette dominates the surroundings (a combination of the Arabian Nights and Disney World).*
  Tel   (032) 232-6888
  Fax   (032) 232-6880
  E-mail wcch@waterfronthotels.net
  Web   www.waterfronthotels.net

Manila Sales Office:
Tel   687-0888
Fax   687-5970

MONTEBELLO VILLA HOTEL
Banilad, Cebu City
Tel   (032) 231-3681 to 89
Fax   (032) 231-4455
E-mail
info@montebellovillahotel.com
Web
www.montebellovillahotel.com

Booking Office in Makati
Suite 201, Greimel Building,
7838 Makati Avenue corner
Valdez Street, Makati City
Tel   890-3194
Fax   890-3192
E-mail   *montemla@info.com.ph*
info-monte@montebellovillahotel.com

 By air and land (2 hours)
Seventy-five-minute daily flights on Philippine Airlines, Air Philippines or Cebu Pacific from Manila to Cebu. Twenty minutes by car from Cebu Mactan Airport to the hotel.

Note: *Transfer from Cebu Mactan Airport can be arranged by the hotel.*

Superferry also operates ferry service from Manila to Cebu. For more information, you can call tel. nos. 528-7979 or 528-7171.

 150 Units
33 Standard Rooms • 96 Deluxe Rooms • 8 Executive Rooms • 6 Superior Deluxe • 4 Doña Mercedes Suites • 1 Penthouse • 2 Honeymoon Cottages
All rooms have air-conditioning, telephone, cable TV and a bathroom with hot water system. Some deluxe, executive and suite rooms have a terrace. All rooms except standard rooms have a minibar and bathtub.

Indoor Facilities and Services
Business center • Babysitting (on request) • Car rental • Bowling

 Food and Beverage Outlets
Restaurants: Café Bougainvillea • El Jardin • La Terrace
Cuisine Offered: Filipino • International
Quality: Average

Watersports and Other Activities
Two swimming pools • Tennis

 Per room per night inclusive of breakfast

Shangri-La's Mactan Island Resort

The Shangri-La Mactan is no exception to the high quality one associates with this chain of hotels. It is an outstanding five-star hotel set in a large, 13-hectare property on a slight promontory facing the sea.

The tone of elegance and luxury is felt as soon as you step into the immense, lavish reception area—shining marble floors toned down by wood inlay, a magnificent floral arrangement on the huge center table, a light breeze stirred up by the numerous ceiling fans, as the light flows in from the garden, potted plants set everywhere—a superb setting at sunset.

The reception area opens onto a vast terrace which looks onto the garden below and offers a view of the swimming pool and the sea. Comfortable rattan armchairs invite you to stop and have a drink while listening to the music of the resident pianist.

Two wide, pale wooden staircases, on each side of the reception lead down to the garden and restaurants.

The Garden Patio, as its name suggest, opens onto the garden via large sliding doors. Asiatica which serves Asian specialties, is done entirely in wood and has a gentle, quiet air. The Cantonese restaurant, Shang Palace has elegant oriental décor; Paparazzi, which offers Italian cuisine, has a modern and comfortable ambiance. Finally, Cowrie Cove, a romantic, outdoor seafood restaurant, overlooks the sea.

The rooms are in the Atrium and the Ocean Wing, constructed in 1997. The Atrium is a square, eight-story building with a central patio. Bougain-villeas line the banisters of the aisles leading to the rooms. Plush marble and glass elevators take you to the rooms. The Ocean Wing is in harmony with the rest of the structures, particularly bright with the same combination of wood, marble, and furniture in wrought iron and glass. The Horizon Club offers certain privileges such as a complementary breakfast and cocktails.

The hotel has more than 500 rooms. The rooms are of a reasonable size, with a marble bathroom equipped with a bathtub and a balcony, which is furnished with terrace furniture. The décor is classic, elegant—bright colors, wall-to-wall carpeting and rattan furni-ture. The Deluxe rooms are more sump-tuously decorated. The suites, with their reproduction of antique furniture are absolutely superb.

The garden is magnificent with flowers and shady green lawns. The 1,500 square-meter swimming pool is quite spectacular. The small cream sand beach is in a private cove, charm-ingly hemmed in by coconut trees. Indeed, all the communal areas of the Shangri-La Mactan are superb and the service is impeccable.

SHANGRI-LA'S MACTAN ISLAND RESORT

P.O. Box 86, Punta Engaño Road, Lapu Lapu City, Cebu
Tel (032) 231-0288
Fax (032) 231-1688
E-mail *mac@shangri-la.com*
Web *www.shangri-la.com*

Booking Office in Makati
Makati Shangri-La, Manila
Ayala Avenue corner Makati Avenue, Makati City
Tel 818-0952
Fax 818-0833 • 893-8503
E-mail
mactansales-slm@shangri-la.com
Web *www.shangri-la.com*

 By air and land (2 hours)
Seventy-five-minute daily flights on Philippine Airlines, Air Philippines or Cebu Pacific from Manila to Cebu. Fifteen minutes by car from Cebu Mactan airport to the resort.
Note: *Transfer from Cebu Mactan airport can be arranged by the resort.*

Superferry also operates ferry service from Manila to Cebu. For more information, you can call tel. nos. 528-7979 or 528-7171.

547 Units
179 Deluxe Seaview • 151 Garden View • 129 Bayview • 2 Shangri-La Suites • 1 Presidential Suites • 26 Executive Suites • 13 Panorama Suites • 41 Horizon Suites • plus 5 connecting rooms All rooms have air-conditioning, cable TV, IDD telephones with bathroom extension, minibar and refrigerator, in-room locker, tea- and coffee-making facility, hairdryer; offer valet services.

Indoor Facilities and Services
Business center • Supervised children's play-ground • Babysitting • Spa • Health club • Medical services • Shuttle service • Car rental • Tour desk • Game room • Table tennis

 Food and Beverage Outlets
Restaurants: Garden Patio • Asiatica • Shang Palace • Paparazzi • Cowrie Cove
Cuisine Offered: International • Asian • Thai • Indian • Filipino • Cantonese and Dimsum • Italian • Seafood

Bars: Buko Bar and Grill • Coco Loco • Lobby Lounge • Beach Bar • Paparazzi

Watersports and Other Activities
Swimming pools (with kiddie pool) • Beach (artificial sand) • Snorkeling (in other places) • Diving • Parasailing • Water skiing • Jet skiing • Windsurfing • Kayaking • Other boats for hire • Island hopping • Island for private dining • Tennis • Bike rental • Golf (6 holes) • Tour to Cebu countryside, Bohol, Sumilon

 Per room per night inclusive of breakfast

Maribago Bluewater
Beach Resort

Maribago Bluewater Beach Resort does not have the sumptuous allure and romantic air of the Shangri-La Mactan but it does offer comfortable lodgings. Its architecture blends the use of hard materials with *nipa*, resulting in a more laid-back look than the other resorts.

The resort is located between the White Sands and Tambuli resorts, on an area bordering Maribago Beach. You enter a large tree-lined courtyard with a pond decorated with statues of dolphins. A lovely reception hall with a high ceiling and exposed wood beams is largely open. The wall painting of clouds on the sea at the rear end of the reception is quite amusing.

The owner obviously wanted to get the most from his property and so cottages are a little too compact. Fortunately some of the beautiful trees have been preserved. The cottages are in two sections, one on either side of the reception area. Each section has a nice swimming pool spanned by a little bridge.

In the section to the right of the reception are the two-story cottages that surround the swimming pool. To the left of the reception area are a series of individual cottages set next to each other and a second set of duplex cottages facing the sea.

Regardless of location, the rooms all relatively small but quite comfortable. The decoration is pleasantly sober—wooden floors, white walls and sliding doors in *capiz* that open onto a small furnished terrace. The rooms also have marble bathrooms with bathtubs.

In the middle of the garden, more independent, spacious and convenient for families are the Royal bungalows with *nipa* roofs. These are quite attractive with one room, a drawing room, two bathrooms and a large terrace furnished with tables, chairs and hammocks. The drawing room has wood floors and walls, bamboo sofas covered with brightly colored material and an alcove decorated with shells. The interior may be a bit dark due to the trees outside, but in the evening, the lighting gives the place a warm ambiance.

Maribago has several restaurants and bars. The most pleasant are those constructed on a little edge that juts out onto the sea, giving a lovely view of the bay: Sunset Cove Live Seafood restaurant, a large high-ceilinged building, with bistro-style tables and chairs, and the Pier 7, a circular bar in stone with a wooden roof.

Little *nipa* huts and lounge chairs are scattered on the beach. On the tiny islet of Alegrado, a few minutes away, there are deck chairs available to laze in. The sea is slightly hemmed in by a bay and the water is not very clear. This, and the presence of many fishing boats, does not make it very conducive to swimming.

MARIBAGO BLUEWATER BEACH RESORT

Maribago, Buyong,
Mactan Island, Cebu
Tel (032) 232-5411 to 14
(032) 492-0100
Fax (032) 492-0128
E-mail bluwater@pworld.net.ph
bluwater@mozcom.com
Web www.bluwaterresort.com

Booking Office in Makati
Room 1120, Cityland Herrera Tower
#98 Herrera corner Valero Streets
Salcedo Village, Makati City
Tel 817-5751 • 887-1348
Fax 845-0680

 By air and land (2 hours)
Seventy-five-minute daily flights on Philippine Airlines, Air Philippines or Cebu Pacific from Manila to Cebu. Fifteen minutes by car from Cebu Mactan airport to the resort.

Note: *Transfer from Cebu Mactan airport can be arranged by the resort.*

Superferry also operates ferry service from Manila to Cebu. For more information, you can call tel. nos. 528-7979 or 528-7171.

 90 Units
82 Deluxe Rooms • 8 Royal Bungalows (good for 4)
All rooms have air-conditioning, minibar, cable TV, and a bathroom with hot water, telephone and private terrace.

Indoor Facilities and Services
Babysitting • Medical services • Gym • Sauna • Jacuzzi • Limousine • Car rental • Foreign currency exchange • Billiards • Table tennis • Library

 Food and Beverage Outlets
Restaurants: Allegro Restaurant • Halo-Halo • Sunset Cove Live Seafood
Cuisine Offered: Filipino • Japanese • International
Quality: Good
Bars: The Pier 7 • Poolside Bar

 Watersports and Other Activities
Swimming pools • Beach (white sand) • Diving • Island hopping • Boats for hire • Fishing • Yacht cruising • Mountain biking • Children's playground • Tennis

 Per room per night inclusive of breakfast

Pulchra

Pulchra gets its name from the Latin word "beautiful"—and beautiful it certainly is. After an hour and a half trip on the monotonous road along Cebu suburbs, you reach a beautiful, peaceful garden filled with the songs of birds.

The reception area is big and elegant, with a high *nipa* and wood ceiling, white marble floors and very attractive armchairs made of plaited wicker. You are welcomed politely and efficiently. The area seems deserted, though occupied by a discreet Japanese clientele. The resort has joint Filipino and Japanese ownership and was designed by the Filipino architect Joe Canizares.

The large swimming pool begins right outside the reception hall then lazily meanders up to Ventus, the main restaurant which it encircles. You can swim and then have a drink without leaving the pool—there is a bar on the edge of the water. The main restaurant opens onto the beach, which is unfortunately is made of gravel and not very pleasant to walk on. A much smaller restaurant, the Opus, is reserved for more intimate dinners. Another bar, the Luna Bar, recreates an atmosphere of outer space with its interior in shining pebbles—black on the floor, gray on the walls and blue on the ceiling—illuminated with hundreds of little lights. It is the only place where you will find a television set, as the primary aim of Pulchra is to maintain peace and quietness.

The Lagoon Suite Rooms face another swimming pool. The interiors are extremely elegant with white marble floors, beige sofas and attractive modern furniture. The rooms have adjoining terraces.

The Garden Side Villas and the Family Villas are cleverly concealed in individual gardens. These are big—and have even the luxury of a private swimming pool! The Family Villas with two rooms each, have no doors to separate the rooms, yet privacy is maintained. The rooms are slightly lower on either side of the living room and each has its own bathroom and a large terrace looking onto the swimming pool. The Jacuzzi Villas facing the sea not only have a private swimming pool but a private Jacuzzi and a massage kiosk as well!

Special mention must be made of the bathrooms: completely circular in the Garden Villas, almost maze-like in the Family Villas with showers and toilets found in nooks and corners. The bathtub, on the other hand, is in a lush, outdoor patio.

Apart from the high rates, the flaw of Pulchra is its setting in an unattractive urban environment with an artificial gravel beach. But spending a weekend in Pulchra is a bit like living inside a lovely picture of an interior decorating magazine!

PULCHRA

San Isidro, San Fernando, Cebu
Tel	(032) 232-0823 to 25
Fax	(032) 232-0816
Cebu City	(032) 232-0823 to 25
(Reservation)	(032) 232-7667
Tel	(032) 233-4215 to 16
Fax	(032) 233-4213
E-mail	info@pulchraresorts.com
Web	www.pulchraresorts.com
	www.pulchra.co.jp

 By air and land (3 ½ hours)
Seventy-five-minute daily flights on Philippine Airlines, Air Philippines or Cebu Pacific from Manila to Cebu. One and a half hours by car from Cebu Mactan airport to resort.

Note: *Transfer from Cebu Mactan airport (43 km) can be arranged by the resort.*

Superferry also operates ferry service from Manila to Cebu. For more information, you can call tel. nos. 528-7979 or 528-7171.

 37 Units
21 Lagoon Suites (Double or Twin) • 7 Pool Garden Villas • 5 Seafront Jacuzzi Villas • 4 Two-bedroom Pool Villas
All rooms have veranda, air-conditioning, CD player, minibar, coffee and tea maker, telephone, bathrobes, and hairdryer.

Indoor Facilities and Services
Babysitting • Massage • Free shuttle • Foreign currency exchange • Massage and aesthetic services • C D/Book library

 Food and Beverage Outlets
Restaurants: Ventus Restaurant • Opus restaurant • Beach Grille
Meals can also be served in the villas and in the suites.
Cuisine Offered: Filipino • Euro-Asian • Seafood
Quality: Good

Bars: Luna Bar and Fons Bar

Watersports and Other Activities
Swimming pool (huge) • Snorkeling (in other places) • Diving (Casai Reef, Cabilao Island—1.5 hours, Balicasag Island—2 hours, Sumilon) • Windsurfing • Tennis • Island tours

 Per room per night

Alegre Beach Resort

North of Cebu City, the Alegre Beach Resort offers exclusive and high-quality service in a tropical setting—27 hectares of green oasis overlooking a cove of white sand bordered by the sea. The resort is managed by Pathfinder Holdings, which also owns the Cebu Plaza Hotel.

The restaurant, which also incorporates the bar, is the central point of the resort. It is in an extremely charming, low building with an original double *nipa* roof and offers an outstanding panorama view of the sea and the neighboring islands. You can have your meals either indoors, in air-conditioned comfort, or outside on the terrace, open to the sea breeze. The food, served buffet style, is excellent. Singers perform during the evening meals. The restaurant also offers a nice view of the swimming pool through the bay windows. The attractive three-tiered pool, brightly lit in the evenings, is surrounded by plants and shrubs and is spanned by little bridges.

The cabanas with *nipa* roofs are scattered over the pretty, green lawns amidst the trees and flowers. The most stunning of these, the Ocean View

Cabanas, are perched on top of a cliff and have a spectacular view of the beach and the sea. One of them even has its own private garden. The others look out onto the gardens where it is not unusual to get a glimpse of monitor lizards scurrying by.

Each cabana has two rooms, both of which are remarkably furnished and the level of comfort is exceptional. The décor, focused on beautiful wood, creates a congenial atmosphere. The innovatively-designed furniture is sophisticated and sober. The frosted glass lamps diffuse soft light, creating a feeling of well-being. Plants, wicker baskets, fabrics and carpets in pastel shades make for more intimate and personal rooms.

The marble bathrooms, done in warm tones, are a particular success. Separated from the room by Venetian blinds, these are immense and luxurious, with a shower and a shining white bathtub, which even includes a jacuzzi! The light pours in blissfully through bay windows. Each cabana has a private terrace with lounge chairs.

The beach, accessible via a staircase, is fringed by palm trees. You can snorkel in the coral reef in front of the beach or you can be brought further out by *banca*. Many other activities are offered at rates relative to the prestige of the hotel. The sunset cruise, included in the package, is a privileged moment even if the dolphins are not always on cue. Calanganman Island, with its white sand and turquoise-blue waters, is paradise. Divers can visit the House Reef before venturing out to the nearby islands of Talong or Capitancillo.

ALEGRE BEACH RESORT

Calumboyan, Sogod, Cebu
Tel   (032) 231-1198 • 254-9800
         (032) 254-9811
Fax   (032) 254-9833
E-mail
cbusales@alegrebeachresort.com
Web *www.alegrebeachresort.com*

Booking Office in Pasig
10/F, The Centerpoint Condominium
corner Julia Vargas Avenue
and Garnet Street,
Ortigas Center, Pasig City
Tel   634-7505 to 08
Fax   633-1833

 By air and land (4 hours)
Seventy-five-minute daily flights on Philippine Airlines, Air Philippines or Cebu Pacific from Manila to Cebu. Two hours by mini-bus from Cebu Mactan airport to the resort.
Note: *Transfer from Mactan Cebu airport (75 km) is arranged by the resort.*
Superferry also operates ferry service from Manila to Cebu. For more information, you can call tel. nos. 528-7979 or 528-7171.

 40 Units
10 Ocean View Rooms in 5 duplex cabanas (2 rooms have a private garden) • 30 Deluxe Rooms in 15 duplex cabanas with garden view
All rooms have air-conditioning, fan, cable TV, CD players (on request), telephone, minibar, coffee/tea maker, hairdryer, a bathroom with hot water, shower and bathtub with Jacuzzi, separate toilet, private terrace.

Indoor Facilities and Services
Business center • Mini-library • Babysitting • Medical services • Car rental • Foreign currency exchange • Massage • Scheduled city shuttle service • Billiards

 Food and Beverage Outlets
Restaurant: Pavilion restaurant
Cuisine Offered: International
Quality: Excellent food and service

Watersports and Other Activities
Swimming pool (huge with kiddie pool) • Beach • Diving • Dive shops • Island hopping (with picnic) • Jet skiing • Snorkeling • Fishing • Kayaking • Other boats for hire • Sunset cruise (with whale and dolphin watching) • Trekking (half day or full day) • Mountain biking • Golf arrangements with nearby golf courses (1 to 1 ½ hours) • Tennis • City tours

 Per room per night including round trip airport transfer and sunset cruise with dolphin watch

South Cebu and Moalboal

Moalboal is a dive site on the southwest coast of the Island of Cebu, about 90 kilometers from Cebu City. You will need three hours of driving if you go directly, leaving Carcar on the east coast to cross the mountains, to Barili and then to Moalboal on the opposite coast. The mountain road is very picturesque. If you have time, it is interesting to combine a seaside holiday with a visit to the churches and some old houses located on the east coast.

Carcar

South Cebu

THE CHURCHES BETWEEN CEBU AND BOLJOON *(70 kilometers, from Cebu City)* You need at least one hour to get out of Cebu City and the suburbs. The first interesting church you come across, set on the edge of the road, is Naga (18th century). It has a white and light gray façade embellished with angels, flowers and leaf sculptures. The town of Carcar, 33 kilometers from Cebu City, has some old colonial houses. Beside the church, Saint Catherine School is in a huge and beautifully renovated house with fine wrought iron balconies. Balay na Tisa on Santa Catalina street, built in 1859, is an interesting house open to the public. It has a tiled roof with a peculiar shape evoking a pagoda. Inside are antique furniture and beautiful *calados*, wooden panels with openwork design.

Church enthusiasts can continue along the southern road beyond Carcar and go on up to Argao (33 kilometers from

Naga Church

Carcar), where an 18th-century baroque church is located and further on, to the superb church of Boljoon (dating back to 1783), whose elegant silhouette overlooks the sea. To reach Moalboal after the visit to Boljoon, the simplest way is to come back up to Carcar and cross the mountain.

Moalboal

The west coast is a surprising palette of blue, turquoise green, aquamarine and indigo. The waters not only have extraordinary colors but magnificent corals as well. Although a strong typhoon swept through Panagsama in September 1984 and entirely destroyed the coral reef, it has been able to regenerate rapidly. Other neighboring sites were fortunately spared. There are several incredible sites for diving and snorkeling in the region. Most dive centers organize dive safaris to Bohol, Balicasag, Cabilao, Pamilacan and Apo Island.

Moalboal

PESCADOR ISLAND MARINE PARK *(2 kilometers from Panagsama Beach)* It is considered the "Jewel of the Crown" by divers.

WHITE BEACH *(15 minutes by banca or car from Moalboal)* It is a charming, peaceful white sand beach with two resorts. A drop off, easily accessible from the shore, descends down to 50 meters. Snorkeling is also ideal here. On Sundays, the beach is a popular picnic area.

PANAGSAMA BEACH *(3 kilometers from Moalboal)* It is one of the original dive centers of the Philippines developed in the early '80s. The beach is almost non-existent due to the typhoons, but the reef is superb with a sloping wall that descends down to 35 meters. You only have to swim a mere 50 meters to reach it. It is an ideal spot for night dives. Panagsama Beach is a bit crowded nowadays, as lodges, dive shops, stores and restaurants have sprung up. Hannah's Place and the Italian Corner, both located next to the Seaquest Dive Center at the northern end of Panagsama Beach, offer excellent food.

THE ORCHID FARM *(in Moalboal town proper, 15 minutes from Panagsama Beach)* You can spend an hour or more admiring the many varieties of orchids on display. It also has a nice pool.

KAWASAN FALLS *(Matutinao, 17 kilometers south of Moalboal)* You take a jeepney ride for 45 minutes until Matutinao, then walk for 20 minutes. The start of the trail to the falls is next to the church. The first 12-meter high waterfalls are surrounded by lush tropical vegetation and have a natural pool where it is possible to swim. Two other waterfalls can be visited in the area but as the ascent is pretty steep, it requires a bit more effort.

White Beach, Moalboal

Ravenala Beach Bungalows

This charming little resort gets its name from the Latin for the travelers' tree "ravenala." It is tucked away on the magnificent white sands of White Beach, 15 minutes from the famous Panagsama Beach at Moalboal. It blends all the necessary elements that guarantee a relaxing holiday: privacy, a pleasant architecture, a beautiful landscaped garden, crystal clear waters and a superb 50-meter deep ridge running parallel to the shore. Even children can swim here in complete safety.

You are warmly greeted upon arrival by the resort's owners: Eddie, a Dutchman and Teresita, a Filipina. When they constructed the resort a couple of years ago, the owners were also its architects and landscape artists. Passionately fond of their property, they were pioneers in developing diving in the Philippines over 20 years ago and have trained instructors who have now settled in the region. Concerned about environmental protection, they will tell you about the damage wreaked by the terrible typhoon that swept through the beach of Panagsama in 1984, the return of the whale sharks that were mercilessly massacred on Pamilacan Island and the absolute necessity of eliminating the starfish with poisoned spikes that devour the corals.

The rooms are in two big bungalows opposite each other, perpendicular to the beach. These have been designed, furnished and decorated by the owner and have a comfortable "cottage atmosphere." They have imposing *nipa* rooftops, stone walls, and many semi-octagonal lattice windows. Two rooms have more recently been added, facing the beach and especially suitable for children.

The guestrooms on the ground floor have neat and harmonious interiors, with pink and green as the main colors. The furnishings include an imposing bamboo bed with a brightly colored floral bed covers, armchairs and low tables. Bedside lamps, mirrors and cone-shaped hats complete the decor. Deck chairs on the terrace invite you to relax, while you enjoy the breeze.

A lovely stone staircase on the outside leads to the apartments on the upper floors meant to accommodate close friends.

The restaurant is very well ventilated—a magnificent, octagonal, bamboo structure with multicolored orchids suspended from a stone pillar in the center. The food is delicious. In the evening, you will see in the distant dark horizon a chain of lights formed by the countless tiny lamps on the fishing boats out at sea.

Note: *If Ravenala Beach Bungalows is fully booked, the Dolphin House is located on the same beach. It is a nice house overlooking the sea. It has six little rooms offering basic comforts. Dolphin House takes its name from the "dolphin ballet" that takes place regularly at sunset in front of the resort.*

For reservations call Tel. No.: (032) 474-0073 or (0919) 321-6533 or Fax: (032) 474-0074.

RAVENALA BEACH BUNGALOWS

White Beach, Barangay Saavedra, Moalboal, Cebu

Tel	(032) 474-0075
	(032) 424-7533 (Booking)
	(0917) 324-8680
Fax	(032) 232-5452
E-mail	*ttschaap@yahoo.com*
Web	*www.ravenala.net*

 By air and land (4 ½–5 hours)
Seventy-five-minute daily flights on Philippine Airlines, Air Philippines or Cebu Pacific from Manila to Cebu. Three hours by car from Cebu Mactan airport to the resort. Two possible routes: **1.** through Carcar and Barili; **2.** through the Transcentral Highway which starts at Nivel Hills (the road going to Cebu Plaza Hotel) going to Busay hills then to the mountain roads of Taptap, Sibugay and Cantimpla. The next big municipality you would pass through is Balamban. After Balamban, you will pass through Toledo City then Borbon, Pinamungahan and Mantalongon. Once you get to Mantalongon Market, you can turn right to the direction of Barili proper and follow the road that will lead you to Moalboal.

Note: *Transfer from Cebu Mactan airport can be arranged by the resort.*

Superferry also operates ferry service from Manila to Cebu. For more information, you can call tel. nos. 528-7979 or 528-7171.

 9 Units
7 Standard Rooms • 2 Beachfront Rooms
All rooms are fan-cooled and have mosquito nets. No hot water.

 Food and Beverage Outlets
The resort serves food on request. **Cuisine Offered:** Filipino • International
Quality: Excellent

Watersports and Other Activities
Beach (white sand) • Snorkeling (by the beach) • Diving (50 meters deep reef in front of the resort) • Tours to: Pescador Island, Tongo Point, Kawasan Falls and Orchid Farm

 Per room per night including breakfast

Note: *Indicate upon check-in if you plan to use a credit card so that authorization can be secured in advance.*

Hannah's Place

In 1983, a German national, Hannah, who was a passionate diver, settled on Panagsama Beach and opened a restaurant named Hannah's Place near the Seaquest Dive Center where she taught diving. The restaurant became a great success—inspiring her to build her own house near the restaurant. In 1997, she decided to convert her house into the warm and intimate guesthouse that it is today.

The resort's location at the extreme north of the beach—at the end of the track used by all the establishments in the area—gives it the dual advantage of peace and quiet. It was Eddie, the owner of Ravenala Beach Bungalows, who designed the house that immediately strikes you with its white, metal sheet roof. The climbing plants and flowers that color the façade make a break in the structure's neat lines. Inside, a gleaming red-tiled corridor leads to the three standard rooms with Japanese-styled sliding doors. The corridor also leads to a large and pretty covered terrace, which leads to the two family rooms that open onto it. There is a little drawing room furnished with white rattan chairs, where complimentary coffee or tea is served. From here, you can have a view of the sea down below and in the foreground, a beautiful red and brown tree.

The terrace is literally invaded with plants and climbing flowers—hibiscus, bougainvilleas and orchids. A huge tree with a twisted, tortured trunk goes right through the ceiling. The rooms are bright, comfortable and tastefully decorated, with white walls and marble floors contrasting with the warmth of the wood ceiling and furniture. Indonesian batik bedcovers give a touch of color and cheer. Each bedroom also has its own marble bathroom.

A staircase descends from the terrace to the beach below. This pleasant second terrace is furnished with deck chairs where you can sit and catch a bit of sun. Since the typhoon in 1984, the beach has unfortunately been reduced to a small strip of sand. But in just a few strokes, you can reach a deep ridge where snorkeling is possible. Furthermore, the nearby Seaquest Dive Center offers scuba diving courses. It also organizes excursions to the attractions of Moalboal.

Only breakfast is served in the guesthouse, but for the other meals, you can walk to Hannah's restaurant just a stone's throw away. The mouthwatering aroma of the garlic-flavored cuisine and the essence of the cocktails continue to attract an enthusiastic clientele. The nice view of the Straits of Tañon also makes the restaurant an extremely pleasant place to relax in.

HANNAH'S PLACE

Panagsama Beach, Moalboal, Cebu Island
Tel (032) 474-0091
Fax (032) 346-0592
E-mail
hannah@hannahs-place.com
hannah@seaquestdivecenter.com
Web *www.hannahs-place.com*

 By air and land (4 ½–5 hours)
Seventy-five-minute daily flights on Philippine Airlines, Air Philippines or Cebu Pacific from Manila to Cebu. Three hours by car from Cebu Mactan airport to the resort. Two possible routes: **1.** through Carcar and Barili; **2.** through the Transcentral Highway which starts at Nivel Hills (the road going to Cebu Plaza Hotel) going to Busay hills then to the mountain roads of Tap-tap, Sibugay and Cantimpla. The next big municipality you would pass through is Balamban. After Balamban, you will pass through Toledo City then Borbon, Pinamungahan and Mantalongon. Once you get to Mantalongon Market, you can turn right to the direction of Barili proper and follow the road that will lead you to Moalboal.

Note: *Transfer from Cebu Mactan airport is arranged by the resort.*
Superferry also operates ferry service from Manila to Cebu. For more information, you can call tel. nos. 528-7979 or 528-7171.

 5 Units
2 Family Rooms • 3 Standard Rooms
All rooms have air-conditioning, a minibar and a marble bathroom with hot water.

 Food and Beverage Outlets
Restaurant: Hannah's Place Restaurant
Cuisine Offered: International
Quality: Good

 Watersports and Other Activities
Beach (narrow, white sand) • Snorkeling • Diving with Seaquest Dive Center • River Climbing • Canyoning and other activities with Planet Action Adventure [Tel.: (032) 474-0024; e-mail: *planet@solnets.com*; Web: *www.action-philippines.com*] also on Panagsama Beach • Caving • Horseback riding • Trekking • Biking • Tours to Moalboal's points of interest

Per room per night on full board basis

Badian Island Resort and Spa

This luxury hotel, under German management, is located on an island in the Bay of Badian. The resort is set on an eight-hectare property, 15 minutes by boat from the village of Badian on the southwest coast of the Island of Cebu. One part of the area is landscaped with magnificent, perfectly maintained flower gardens. The other has been left in its natural state.

You will first discover a lagoon and the mangroves with aerial roots, and an attractive white sand beach, recreated artificially after a typhoon destroyed the beach. From the beach you have a nice view of the mountain range on the west coast of Cebu, and further away on the right, the coastline of the island of Negros. As a welcome gesture, you are greeted by the sound of music and given the traditional shell necklace.

The 50 rooms, divided into 25 duplex villas with *nipa* roofs, are set in the middle of the gardens to take full advantage of the view of the mountains and the sea. Very spacious and bright, thanks to large bay windows, the rooms are furnished to provide maximum comfort. The use of *capiz* for windows, doors and the ceiling to diffuse a soft light; the pretty wood floor and the impeccably-finished pale-bamboo furniture, all contribute to create a warm and cozy atmosphere. All rooms have luxurious marble bathrooms with bathtubs. The hammocks on the balcony invite you to relax and admire the view.

The main restaurant, located near the swimming pool, is a beautiful bamboo structure. The excellent meals are served buffet style. In the evening, musicians or folk dancers add a lovely ambience to the setting.

The large, white sand beach, bordered by coconut trees is pleasant with its *nipa* parasols and its hammocks.

Children will love playing in the mangroves, accessible by walking on the stretch of sand where the water is shallow. A section of the beach, cleaned daily, is reserved for swimming.

Many other activities, including water sports, golf, and tours are offered, but at rates commensurate to the standard of the hotel. The many diving and snorkeling sites near Badian are well-known. A glass-bottomed boat will take you to Coral Garden on the other side of Badian, facing Negros Island. The snorkeling is fabulous at Moalboal, along the ridge 40 meters away from White Beach. Pescador Island, also in Moalboal, is well-known as a dive site.

BADIAN ISLAND RESORT AND SPA

Badian, Cebu Island
Tel (032) 475-1103 • 475-1106
(032) 253-6364
Fax (032) 475-1101 • 253-3385
E-mail *badiancebu@aol.com*
Web *www.badianhotel.com*

Booking Office in Cebu
Cebu Capitol Complex-A
N. Escario Street, Cebu City
Tel (032) 253-6452
(032) 416-6159
Fax (032) 253-3385

 By air, land and sea (5 hours)
Seventy-five-minute daily flights on Philippine Airlines, Air Philippines or Cebu Pacific from Manila to Cebu. Three hours by car from Cebu Mactan airport to Badian pier. Five minutes by speedboat from Badian pier to the resort

Note: *Transfer from Cebu Mactan airport is arranged by the resort.*

Superferry also operates ferry service from Manila to Cebu. For more information, you can call tel. nos. 528-7979 or 528-7171.

 44 Units
2 Single Suites • 10 Family Suites • 18 Junior Suites • 14 Badian Suites
All rooms have air-conditioning, minibar, telephone, radio, hairdryer, tea/coffee maker, a bathroom with hot water and bathtub and a private terrace.

Indoor Facilities and Services
Foreign currency exchange • Car rental • Babysitting • Billiards • Video room • Table tennis

 Food and Beverage Outlets
Restaurant: Panorama Restaurant
Cuisine Offered: Asian • International
Quality: Excellent but exorbitantly expensive

 Watersports and Other Activities
Swimming pool • Beach (white sand) • Snorkeling (Coral Garden/White Beach) • Dive center • Boats for hire • Windsurfing • Hobie cat sailing • Outdoor spa • Island hopping (with picnic) • Sunset Cruise • Coral Garden Picnic • Tours to Kawasan waterfalls • 3-hole golf course • Driving range • Children's playground • Tennis • Badminton

 Per room per night inclusive of breakfast

Panay–Guimaras

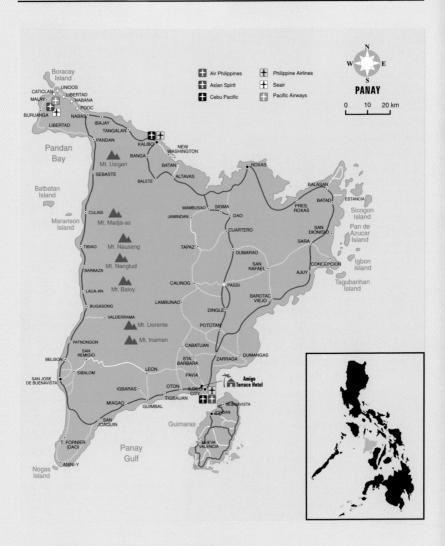

Air Philippines
Asian Spirit
Cebu Pacific
Philippine Airlines
Seair
Pacific Airways

PANAY

0   10   20 km

Boracay Island
CATICLAN
MALAY
BURUANGA
UNIDOS
LIBERTAD
HABANA
POOC
NABAS
LIBERTAD
IBAJAY
TANGALAN
PANDAN
KALIBO
BANGA
BATAN
SEBASTE
BALETE
ALTAVAS
NEW WASHINGTON
Mt. Usigan
Pandan Bay
Batbatan Island
Mararison Island
CULASI
Mt. Madja-as
JAMINDAN
MAMBUSAO
SIGMA
DAO
CUARTERO
TIBIAO
Mt. Nausang
TAPAZ
DUMARAO
BARBAZA
Mt. Nangtud
SAN RAFAEL
LAUA-AN
Mt. Baloy
CALINOG
PASSI
BUGASONG
LAMBUNAO
DINGLE
VALDERRAMA
Mt. Llorente
POTOTAN
PATNONGON
Mt. Inaman
CABATUAN
BELISON
SAN REMIGIO
STA BARBARA
ZARRAGA
DUMANGAS
SAN JOSE DE BUENAVISTA
SIBALOM
LEON
PAVIA
IGBARAS
OTON
ILOILO CITY
MIAGAO
TIGBAUAN
GUIMBAL
SAN JOAQUIN
T. FORNIER (DAO)
ANINI-Y
Nogas Island
Panay Gulf
Guimaras
JORDAN
BUENAVISTA
NUEVA VALENCIA
ROXAS
BALASAN
BATAD
ESTANCIA
PRES. ROXAS
SAN DIONISIO
SARA
CONCEPCION
AJUY
BAROTAC VIEJO
Sicogon Island
Pan de Azucar Island
Igbon Island
Tagubanhan Island
Amigo Terrace Hotel

Climate	Dry from November to April; wet during the rest of the year	
Typhoons	June to October	

Dinagyang at Iloilo City, fourth weekend of January. The festival is held in honor of the Infant Jesus and comprises a religious procession, colorful street dances and a competition organized to choose the most beautiful costume and choreography.

Ati-Atihan, Kalibo, third week of January, culminating on the weekend: Refer to Boracay chapter.

Iloilo

Iloilo shelters a number of beautiful old houses that once belonged to the Sugarcane Barons and the Spanish elite of the time. But unlike those in Vigan or Silay, these are scattered in the urban framework of the town and are not open to the public. Jaro, in the northern part of the town, has a few houses but it is generally during a random exploration that you come across an elegant house with a melancholic charm—often abandoned in its garden.

JARO *(3 kilometers from the center of Iloilo)* The old houses are in the vicinity of the renovated Cathedral of Jaro. Acatone Arenelles de Jalandoni, dating back to 1927 and Isla Bank form a nice ensemble with the house set at an angle on Jalandoni St. Not far, you can see a small house hidden in the vegetation at 14 Washington Street; a superb residence on 20 St. Isabelle was completely renovated. Stop on the way sample an *ensaimada* at the Biscocho Haus Bakery on Lopez Street. From the houses

Molo Old House

seen on random walks "La Bastilla" on Lopez Street, a beautiful house at the end of a garden and another on Bonifacio Drive with fine, wood fretwork are worthy of mention.

MOLO *(3 kilometers southwest of Iloilo)* The 18th-century church is in classic gothic renaissance style but, in front, on Lopez Jaena Street, there is a magnificent 1900 house in a sprawling, slightly wild flowery garden, hemmed in by beautiful wrought iron grills.

SINAMAY HOUSE *(6 kilometers southwest of Iloilo on Osmeña Street)* It is one of the old houses partially open to visitors. The owner, Mrs. Cecilia Villanueva, maintained the tradition of piña weaving on looms. Here, you can buy beautiful piña fabric at unbeatable prices.

GUIMBAL CHURCH *(29 kilometers southwest of Iloilo)* This surrealistic church of yellow sandstone has a very sober façade with an adjacent bell tower.

Dinagyang Festival, Iloilo

NADSADJS FALLS *(Igbaras, 39 kilometers southwest of Iloilo)* A guide is necessary to reach the 16-meter high waterfalls. You must walk five kilometers, making several river crossings. From the waterfalls start Mount Napulac. It is more accessible by jeepney up to barangay Bagay, higher up. However, this is only possible during the dry season. If you want to make the climb, you must stay overnight at one of the simple resorts on the coast. Banatayan Beach Resort has a few air-conditioned cottages. Tel. No.: (033) 512-0013.

Guimbal Church

MIAG-AO CHURCH *(40 kilometers south-west of Iloilo)* Miag-ao is arguably the most amazing and beautiful church of the Philippines—mainly because of its two asymmetric pyramidal towers and its finely sculptured, yellow sandstone façade. The latter represents papaya trees surrounding a fan-shaped palm tree as the central motif. A low relief adorns the towers, the same motif you will see inside the sober church. The construction dates back to 1797 when the church served as a fortress against the Muslim raids. Restored on several occasions, Miag-ao is on the UNESCO World Heritage List.

SANTA BARBARA CHURCH AND CONVENT *(16 kilometers north of Iloilo)* The buildings, dating back to 1845, have been renovated several times. However, the exterior remains pleasing. The wood and brick convent opens onto a flowered interior patio.

Isla Naburot, Guimaras

Guimaras

Guimaras, 45 minutes by *banca* from Iloilo, is an ideal spot for relaxation and, depending on your budget or your mood, you can stay at one of the charming, romantic houses at Isla Naburot or in the small resort of Baras. Guimaras has a jagged coastline with numerous coves. You can snorkel at certain places, especially in front of Isla Naburot.

There is also Costa Aguada on the east coast of Guimaras which is best accessed from Bacolod, on the island of Negros Occidental.

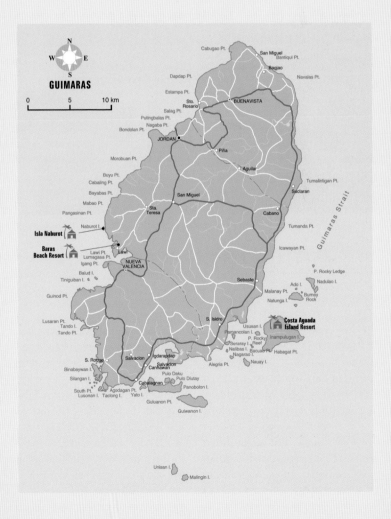

Amigo Terrace Hotel

The Amigo Terrace Hotel, located in the town center of Iloilo, is a large modern five-story building which, when viewed from the exterior, seems very ordinary. You are agreeably surprised, therefore, when you enter and discover the elegant reception area with its gleaming marble floor, large comfortable rattan sofas and antique pieces. A beautiful flower arrangement adds a touch of color and gaiety to the place.

The reception area opens onto the slightly elevated restaurant-bar, Café Chichirico. Here, the décor is warm and pleasant with beautiful rattan or wrought iron furniture, green plants in large jars and little bouquets of flowers on the tables. A grand piano stands in the corner.

A large staircase leads to the rooms on the fourth and fifth floors but you can also go up using an elevator.

The interiors are very comfortable with soft wall-to-wall carpeting and bamboo furniture, but the décor is simpler than that of the reception area. The rooms are bright because of the bay windows. The superior deluxe rooms, slightly more expensive, are a better choice as they are more spacious and include such facilities as a minibar and a coffee maker.

AMIGO TERRACE HOTEL

Corner Iznart and Delgado Streets, Iloilo City, Panay

Tel   (033) 335-0908 to 17
Fax   (033) 335-0610
E-mail amigo@iloilo.net
       amigohtt@mozcom.com
Web   www.amigohotel-iloilo.com

 By air and land (2 hours)
Sixty-five-minute daily flights on Philippine Airlines, Air Philippines or Cebu Pacific from Manila to Iloilo. Ten minutes by car from Iloilo airport to the hotel.

Note: *Transfer from Iloilo airport can be arranged by the hotel.*

Superferry (Tel. No.: 528-7979) and Negros Navigation (Tel. No.: 245-4395) also operate ferry service from Manila to Iloilo.

 100 Units
75 Standard Rooms • 10 Deluxe Rooms • 15 Suites
All rooms have air-conditioning, a bathroom with hot water, telephone and cable TV.

Indoor Facilities and Services
Gym • Business center

 Food and Beverage Outlets
Restaurants: Islands
Cuisine Offered: Filipino • International
Quality: Good

 Watersports and Other Activities
Swimming pool. See Iloilo's points of interest.

 Per room per night

Note: *The Days Hotel close by also offers a very good degree of comfort. All of its 20 rooms have air-conditioning, hot water, TV, a safe, a minibar, and tea/coffee-making facilities. However, most of the rooms have no windows, and the six that do, look into the atrium of the commercial center where the hotel is located.*

Days Hotel, fourth and fifth floors of the commercial center "The Atrium at the Capital", corner General Luna, Bonifacio Drive, Iloilo.

Tel   (033) 337-3297 • 336-8801 to 10
Fax (033) 336-8000
Web www.dayshotel.com

Isla Naburot

sla Naburot on the west coast of Guimaras is sheer paradise. It is a little wooded islet, with a semi-circular, golden beach that leads to a coral lagoon. The main attraction of Isla Naburot, apart from its setting, is the uniqueness of its architectural style.

Anne Saldaña, the daughter of the owners, is there to welcome you upon your arrival. She lives on the island and supervises the operations of the resort. Warm and discreetly attentive to the needs of the guests, she is also an excellent cook, as you will experience when you try the restaurant.

The houses, dispersed among frangipani trees, hibiscus, bougainvillea and cycads were constructed in the 1970s. Initially conceived as family vacation house, the architecture was mostly the brainchild of Anne's mother, Mrs. Alice Saldaña. A doctor by profession, and an antique collector, she has a wealth of imagination—and taste. The best use was made of natural, unusual, organic materials: pebbles and shells, roots and knotted tree trunks, driftwood retrieved from the beach, fragments of blue and white Chinese porcelain. She also recovered odd pieces from old houses: wooden doors, floors and shutters. What may seem eccentric is in fact a charming, alluring ensemble. The houses are furnished with beautiful antique furniture: planter's armchairs, cupboards and benches. The floors are made of either beautifully polished wood or 1920s tiles. In the bathrooms, towels and sarongs are laid out for you in giant clam shells. Mirrors bordered with tiny shells and pegs fabricated from roots decorate the walls. At night, with the exception of a mosquito net swaying in the breeze, there is nothing to separate you from the starry sky and sound of the waves.

You have a choice between the stone houses, distinctly different but equally superb, and the wooden cottages on a promontory over the dining area. The cottages, smaller and less impressive compared to the houses, are very welcoming and quite independent. Cottage 1, with a bathroom overlooking the lagoon is extraordinary. A little house is right on the beach, but is too close to the kitchen and the dining area.

If you need more spacious lodgings, you can stay at the family house facing the main beach. The ground floor houses the resort's library and a piano. The main rooms on the second floor have balconies that look out to the sea. A few meters away, tucked into a cove, is another house with its own private beach. It has a billiard table on the ground floor and rooms upstairs overlooking the beach. The inconvenience is that it cannot be concealed from the exterior by either windows, shutters or curtains.

On the other side of the island, five minutes on foot, are two houses perched on a cliff that enjoy a fabulous view. The "house on the cliff" is particularly dramatic on its rocky spur, resembling a sentry on guard. It can only be occupied on special request, as the owners prefer to leave it open to guests keen on watching the sunset or relaxing in one of the hammocks. The other house is accessible from the family house by a mossy stone staircase. It is very pleasant with a terrace on the ground floor and a spacious room on the first floor with a view of the sea. The restaurant/dining area is an open wood structure right on the beach. The sand itself serves as flooring. Everything is cooked in large earthenware pots over woodfire. Mealtimes are veritable feasts—a moment of the day to savor!

ISLA NABUROT ISLAND LIFE ADVENTURE

Jordan, Guimaras island
No phone. Only radio communications and cellphones.

Booking Office in Iloilo
Saldaña Compound, Tabucan, Mandurriao, Iloilo
Tel (033) 321-1654
Fax (033) 321-0880

By air, land and sea (3 hours)
Sixty-five-minute daily flights on Philippine Airlines, Air Philippines or Cebu Pacific from Manila to Iloilo. Fifteen to thirty minutes by car from Iloilo airport to the pier. One hour by *banca* from the pier to the resort.

Note: *Transfer from Iloilo airport can be arranged by the resort.*

Superferry (Tel. No.: 528-7979) and Negros Navigation (Tel. No.: 245-4395) also operate ferry service from Manila to Iloilo.

4 Units
1 Family House (near the restaurant—living room and 2 bathrooms on the ground floor; on the second floor, 4 bedrooms and 1 attic) • 1 Small House (on the beach near the restaurant, with 1 bedroom and bathroom) • 1 House (on another small beach—on the ground floor, 1 bedroom, 1 bathroom; on the second floor, 1 big bedroom and 2 smaller ones with 2 bathrooms; 3 cottages with bathroom) • 1 House (with a terrace and one huge bedroom with one bathroom)
There is no electricity on the island, therefore no air-conditioning. At night, oil and kerosene lamps; battery-operated portable lights. Extra beds can be added.

Food and Beverage Outlets
Restaurant on the beach
Cuisine Offered: Filipino • Seafood
Quality: Excellent and plentiful

Watersports and Other Activities
Beach (white sand) • Snorkeling (by the beach) • Island hopping • Boats for hire

Per room per night on full board basis (inclusive of Island Hopping)

Baras Beach Resort

This is another little hidden resort on the western coast of Guimaras, one hour by banca from mainland Iloilo. The resort nestles in a very pretty interior bay from the midst of which jut out rocky islets. The bay is very sheltered and serves as a mooring place for yachts and sailing boats in the region. Nothing along the coast of Guimaras gives you a clue of Baras' existence—unless you enter the bay. The white sand beach of Baras contrasts strikingly with its mantle of luxurious green foliage teeming with bird life.

The Englishman, Peter Harper-Bill, who owns the resort with his Filipino partner Mike Araneta, lives there all year round. On a property covering 17 hectares, he constructed nine bamboo bungalows on stilts, with *nipa* roofs bringing to mind those in Indonesia. The cottages have the advantage of being quite detached, each perched on the coast overlooking the sea. Each has a lovely terrace but those of the family cottages are particularly impressive. The interior of the cottages is simple with wood flooring, plaited bamboo walls and basic furniture. Each has a bright, white-tiled bathroom.

The activities of Baras are all water-oriented. A fleet of boats including a banca, a catamaran and sailboat are available for rent...though not always. (These do not belong to Peter.)

It is pleasant to sail around Guimaras, as it is a fairly large island with an area of 579 square kilometers. In the countless bays around the little coral islets, you can stop on the tiny, golden deserted beaches. Some of the areas are favorable for snorkeling.

Mountain biking is a popular sport in Guimaras. Bikes can be rented in Baras.

BARAS BEACH RESORT

Barangay Lawi, Jordan, Guimaras
Iloilo City
Tel (0917) 241-1422
(0917) 940-1501
E-mail *barasguim@yahoo.com*
Web *www.baras.willig-web.com*

 By air, land and sea (3½ hours)
Sixty-five-minute daily flights on Philippine Airlines, Air Philippines or Cebu Pacific from Manila to Iloilo. Fifteen to thirty minutes by car from Iloilo airport to the pier. One hour by resort *banca* from the pier to the resort.

Note: *Transfer from Iloilo airport can be arranged by the resort.*

Superferry (Tel. No.: 528-7979) and Negros Navigation (Tel. No.: 245-4395) also operate ferry service from Manila to Iloilo.

 9 Units
3 Double Cottages • 6 Family Cottages (3 or 4 people)
All rooms have a fan, mosquito net, and bathroom. Generator from 6 a.m. to midnight.

Indoor Facilities and Services
Table tennis

 Food and Beverage Outlets
Restaurant and bar
Cuisine Offered: Filipino • Malaysian • Indonesian • European • Grilled Seafood

 Watersports and Other Activities
Beach (white sand) • Snorkeling (in other places) • Island hopping (Catamaran—maximum of 4) • Boats for hire • Sailing • Hiking • Birdwatching • Mountain biking

 Per room per night inclusive of breakfast

Note: *Cash payment only.*

Costa Aguada Island Resort

osta Aguada resort is on the island of Inampulugan, off the west coast of Guimaras. It is best accessed from Bacolod.

The island offers an interesting blend of marine and natural pleasures. With a surface area of 1,067 hectares, it is partially covered by coconut and bamboo plantations on one side and by jungle on the other. White sandy coves hug the length of coast fringed by beautiful mangroves. You can in

fact snorkel by swimming out from the mangroves.

The island and the resort belong to Tony Oppen who launched an extensive eco-tourism project there. The first phase of this project, Bamboo Beach, was opened to the public in 1992. This comprised a hotel complex, a kitchen garden, an orchard, a mini zoo, a handicraft village and walking trails. A once existing turtle park has not been re-established since the turtles returned to the sea after a typhoon destroyed their enclosure.

Two types of lodging are offered: individual cottages at the back of the hotel each with a spacious room good for one family and a dining room where meals can be served; and equally spacious duplex cottages, on the edge of the beach (deluxe rooms), or higher up with a good view of the sea (standard rooms).

The cottages and their furniture are made from locally available bamboo and *nipa*. All the rooms have a balcony with armchairs.

The very pretty and spacious restaurant, made of bamboo and *nipa*, offers excellently-cooked seafood.

You can tour the island by tram, on foot, on horseback or on bicycle. If you like walking, an interesting track goes through a tropical forest with gigantic trees. This leads you to Mount Pulanggurao, the summit of the island. From there, you have a clear view of the gulf of Panay and its many neighboring islands.

COSTA AGUADA ISLAND RESORT
Inampulugan Island,
Sibunag, Guimaras
Tel   (0917) 300-9942
       (0917) 928-2558

Booking Office in Bacolod
24 Lacson St., Citihardware Bldg.,
Mandalagan, Bacolod City
Tel   (034) 433-7373
       (034) 434-4541

Booking Office in Makati
G/F Oppen Building
349 Sen. Gil J. Puyat Ext.
Makati City
Tel   890-5333 loc. 513/514
       896-5422 • 752-3688
Fax   890-5543
E-mail *orinc@itextron.com*
Web   *www.costa.com.ph*

By air, land and sea (3 hours)
Seventy-minute daily flights on Philippine Airlines, Air Philippines or Cebu Pacific from Manila to Bacolod. Twenty minutes by mini-bus from Bacolod airport to Pulupandan boat terminal (24 km south of Bacolod). Forty-five minutes by *banca* from Pulupandan boat terminal to Inampulugan Island.

Note: *Transfer from the airport can be arranged by the resort with its own minibus and banca. As the crossing can be bumpy and scary in the afternoon or in bad weather, it is advisable to cross early morning (both ways).*

Superferry (Tel. No.: 528-7979) and Negros Navigation (Tel. No.: 245-4395) also operate ferry service from Manila to Bacolod.

64 Units
20 Beachfront Cottages • 18 Creekside Cottages • 12 Roadside Cottages • 14 Hillside Cottages
All rooms and cottages are fan-cooled and have a private balcony and a bathroom.

Indoor Facilities and Services
Medical services • Foreign currency exchange

Food and Beverage Outlets
Restaurant: Coconut Pavilion
Cuisine Offered: Seafood • Filipino • American
Quality: Excellent
Bars: Orchid Bar

Watersports and Other Activities
Swimming pool (with kiddie pool) • Beach • Snorkeling (by the resort) • Island hopping • Kayaking • Other boats for hire • Fishing • Mountain biking • Hiking • Horseback riding • Tennis • Badminton • Volleyball • Children's playground

 Per room per night

Boracay

Climate   Seasons not very pronounced, relatively dry from November to June; wet during the rest of the year

Typhoons   July to October

Ati-Atihan, Kalibo, third week of January, culminating on the weekend. The festival commemorates the 13th-century buying of land in Panay from its inhabitants, the Ati or Aeta, by the Datus of Borneo. To celebrate this event, a feast is organized and the merrymakers, in order to resemble the Ati, cover their faces in soot. The feast of the Infant Jesus is also associated with more pagan festivals. There is a parade of different "tribes" in their colorful costumes and dancing to the piercing sound of drums.

Boracay

Opinions differ about this paradise island. Some adore the place while others, nostalgic about the Boracay of days gone by, find that it overindulges tourists.

No one really hates Boracay, as everyone is aware that its long beach of powdery white sand, crystal-clear waters that change from translucent topaz to deep sapphire, glorious sunsets and endless summer atmosphere are unique. Despite the overcrowding and problems affecting the environment, this island still attracts more tourists every year. Tourism began to develop here in the 1970s and by now, Boracay has 180,000 visitors a year, a third of them foreigners. Together with Mactan, it is one of the most visited islands in the Philippines.

Boracay is on the northwestern end of Panay Island and is serviced by two airports. Caticlan, only 20 minutes away by *banca*, and Kalibo, 60 kilometers away. Traveling through Kalibo, though longer, allows you to fly bigger, more comfortable aircrafts; the bus ride from Kalibo takes you through rice fields bordered by banana and coconut trees framed by mountains in the distance. The last stretch of this trip culminates in a cliff road overlooking the sea. Crossing to the island by *banca* from Caticlan can sometimes be rough during the rainy season. This is the reason why the passage to the island is done through the eastern coastline.

The island is only seven kilometers long and one kilometer wide at its narrowest. It is fairly flat with its highest point at a mere 100 meters. It is on the west coast, on the spectacular White Beach, that the hotels are located. The eastern coastline of the island has remained very much untouched.

Boracay is dotted with more than 200 hotels, many of which are small in comparison to those in Mactan. Singling out nine resorts of different categories and varying price ranges is difficult and subjective. With the exception of Lorenzo Grand Villa, which is quite unusual because of its location and its architectural style, we have favored those hotels inspired by the traditional architectural styles of the region and using natural materials in harmony with Boracay. Other hotels like Club Panoly and Boracay Regency, which are very comfortable, were therefore not included here.

White Beach

WHITE BEACH White Beach extends its almost 4 kilometers of powdery white sand along Boracay's western coast. Very few beaches in the Philippines have sand as fine in texture or as sparkling white as that in Boracay. With its colored *bancas* and rows upon rows of coconut trees along its border, White Beach is the typical tropical island paradise. In spite of constant construction work, and the number of hotels, restaurants, souvenir shops, and aqua activity centers of all kinds that are spread all around, there is no denying its beauty. The beach is wider and more peaceful in the northern part of the island, from Willy's Rock where a path ends. In the extended portions of White Beach, you will find small serene beaches like Diniwid and Punta Beach, a little further on. In February and March, green weeds invade the beach.

PUKA SHELL BEACH This very nice, wild beach of gold sand stretching up to a kilometer in length is located at the northern tip of the island. Its name was derived from tiny puka shells that were once found on this beach and which were used for pendants and necklaces. Other than a few vendors selling trinkets and the sound of passing *bancas*, nothing disturbs the peace here. You can also do some snorkeling around the rocks at the end of the beach.

LIVE CORAL BEDS AND CORAL GARDEN These are the two best spots for snorkeling near White Beach. You can get there by *banca*. Snorkeling is also possible between Lorenzo South and the southeastern tip of the island, but there is nothing really extraordinary to see.

WILLY'S ROCK This is the rock formation about 100 meters from White Beach facing Willy's Resort. With a little imagination, it takes on a slightly frightening shape at sunset. It has very often been photographed and is, without any doubt, always associated with Boracay.

BORACAY'S EAST COAST Untamed and less visited because of the inhospitable sweeping winds, the east coast is the ultimate paradise for ardent windsurfers. At the southeastern tip of the island facing Crocodile Island, you will find pretty, almost deserted beaches where picnics are indeed a pleasure.

SHOPPING The pathway parallel to White Beach is strewn with shops selling clothes, handicrafts, shells and baskets. The little pleasures of Boracay include a stroll here, a stop for a drink in one of the many small bars along the way and lunch or dinner in the different restaurants that are plentiful on the island. You have a wide choice

Willy's Rock

of handicrafts in the Boracay Shopping Center not far from the Tourist Center.

RESTAURANTS Along White Beach, there are many restaurants and bars offering various cuisines.

French cuisine:
LA RÉSERVE, located between boat stations 1 and 2, offers excellent dishes from the south of France, flavored with herbs and olive oil. There is a wide choice of seafood dishes and French wines.

RED COCONUT, close to La Réserve, serves different kinds of delectable sweet and savory crepes.

Italian cuisine:
FLOREMAR at Angol.

Indian cuisine:
TRUE FOOD, not far from boat station 2, offers authentic Indian food served on low tables. You can enjoy the food sitting on floor cushions.

Philippine and international cuisine:
MANGO RAY serves excellent seafood dishes while you admire a lush garden and quiet surroundings.
SEVERO at Angol also serves good seafood dishes right on the beach.

Friday's Resort Boracay

Friday's Resort Boracay, managed by Australians and Filipinos, was opened in 1986 and is undoubtedly the loveliest resort in Boracay. It enjoys the privilege of being in the best area of the island, the extreme north of White Beach where the beach is widest. You can make the most of your stay in this idyllic side of the island and yet be near the center of activity.

The resort is built in a dense coconut grove. You can at times see the trees growing out of ceilings and stairways! Masses of greenery and flower beds outlined with pebbles surround the cottages. The architecture is inspired by the local style using natural materials like bamboo for walls and *cogon* for the rooftops. Elegance and simplicity are artfully combined in a unique style.

The rooms are in bamboo cottages painted in stained green. Set in two floors, these are linked by an exterior staircase with wide terraces or balconies provided with mattresses and hammocks. The spacious Premier Rooms along the sea are on either side of the reception area. Direct access to the beach and its turquoise waters is no doubt a plus point. The Deluxe Rooms are set back from the beach right in the middle of the coconut grove; some look out onto a swimming pool. Their interiors and terraces are smaller than the Premier Rooms, but they are comfortable enough for three persons.

The rooms are tastefully decorated, blending modern comfort and tradition with artful mastery. The parquet floor, shutters and furniture are made of a fine tropical wood while the walls and ceiling are covered with panels of braided wicker. The warm colors blend into a harmonious palette with touches of bold colors—like colored throw pillows on immaculate white bedcovers. However, note that the white Deluxe Rooms are more simply furnished.

The restaurant on the beach is very elegant and pleasant, with comfortable wicker armchairs and white tablecloths on tables adorned with flowers. Besides the usual menu, you may discover other dishes during the peak season as a themed menu is introduced during this period. You can stay on the beach and have a drink while admiring the unforgettable Boracay sunsets.

A bulletin board displays the resort's activities for the day.

FRIDAY'S RESORT BORACAY

Boracay Island, Malay, Aklan
Tel (036) 288-6200
Fax (036) 288-6222
E-mail info@fridaysboracay.com
Web www.fridaysboracay.com

Booking Office in Makati
Friday's Resort, Manila Sales Office
UG 32 Alfaro Place,
146 L.P. Leviste Street,
Salcedo Village, Makati City
Tel 892-9283 • 810-1027
810-2101
Fax 892-9118
E-mail info@fridaysboracay.com
reservations@fridaysboracay.com

Both by air, land and sea
1. (3 ½ hours) Fifty-five-minute daily flights on Philippine Airlines or Cebu Pacific from Manila to Kalibo (Panay Island). Ninety minutes by air-conditioned bus on Southwest Tours from Kalibo airport to Caticlan Jetty Port. Departures depend on flight schedules. Twenty-five minutes by *banca* from Caticlan Jetty Port to the resort.

2. (2 ½ hours) Thirty-five-minute daily flights on Seair (Dornier 328 planes) or sixty-five-minute daily flights on Asian Spirit or Seair or ninety-minute daily flights on Pacific Air from Manila to Caticlan (Panay Island). Five minutes by tricycle from Caticlan airport to Caticlan Jetty. Twenty-five minutes by *banca* from Caticlan Jetty Port to the resort.

Note: *Transfer from Kalibo or Caticlan airport is arranged by the resort.*

Interisland Airlines also flies from Manila to Caticlan. For more information, you can call tel. nos. 852-8010 to 13.

34 Units
18 Premier Rooms • 16 Deluxe Rooms
All rooms have air-conditioning, cable TV, minibar, telephone, laptop modem access and are equipped with a king size bed and either one or two single beds. Bathrobes and slippers are provided. Only premier rooms have coffee and tea facilities. Five sets of rooms are interconnected.

Indoor Facilities and Services
Business center • Babysitting • Asian language interpreters • Massage and beauty services • In-house library • Game room • Tour desk • Pool table • Table tennis • Video room

Food and Beverage Outlets
Restaurants: Friday's Restaurant
Cuisine Offered: European • Seafood • Asian • Filipino
Bars: Friday's Beach Bar

Watersports and Other Activities
Swimming pool • Beach (white sand) • Diving • Hobie cat sailing • Snorkeling (in other places) • Dive center • Fishing • Sunset cruises • Jet skiing • Water skiing • Windsurfing • Sailing • Parasailing • Island hopping (with picnic) • Mountain biking

Per room per night including round trip transfer from Caticlan airport

Lorenzo Grand Villa

Lorenzo Grand Villa is perched atop a small cliff facing Caticlan on Boracay's southern tip. It lies on a two-and-a-half-hectare property and has a spectacular view of the ocean and the Panay mountain range. This is an ideal place for snorkeling as the water is clear and shallow and protected from currents. It is the perfect place to celebrate a special occasion or to simply spoil yourself.

Opened in 1996, it is the latest addition to the chain of Lorenzo Resorts that include Lorenzo South and Lorenzo Main. If you stay at Lorenzo Grand Villa, you can in fact, avail the facilities offered at the others.

The villa's extravagant architecture, flouting all rules of art, is a motley mix of both oriental and Filipino design in the 1930's style. The façade, composed of semi-circular balconies with a lacework design, and the rooms, in pastel shades of pink, orange, mauve and green, are in a long, two-story building.

The reception area is a surprising mix of marble floors, an imposing white staircase with a spiralled balustrade, an exquisite braided bamboo ceiling with a base decorated with geometric motifs, an indoor pond and attractive wall-hangings.

The rooms on opposite sides of the reception overlook the ocean and the swimming pool down below. They open onto balconies through arched panels by means of sliding capiz door. Bright and spacious with huge bathrooms, the rooms are equipped with all modern comforts. The floors and furniture are made of fine wood and the ceiling repeats the braided foliage of the reception dome. The interior decoration is overwhelming, clearly a trademark of the Villa's style.

The swimming pool, spawned by with wooden bridges, is surrounded by a beautiful tropical garden of palm trees, hibiscus and goldfish ponds. The stone pathway leading to the sea has imprints of leaves.

Steep staircases lead down to the centerfront. One of these leads to the pontoon from where you take the shuttle boat to the other Lorenzo resorts. Another one ends with a ladder leading directly to the water, where you can go swimming and the last one takes you to the tiny beach of Calirojan.

LORENZO GRAND VILLA

Sitio Cagban, Brgy. Manoc-Manoc, Boracay Island
Tel   (036) 288-3512 to 15

Booking Office in Quezon City
10 John F. Kennedy Street,
Project 8, Quezon City
Tel   926-4152 • 926-3958
         928-0719 • 456-9162
Fax   926-1726
E-mail *reservation@e-boracay.com*
Web   *www.e-boracay.com*

 Both by air, land and sea
1. (3 ½ hours)   Fifty-five-minute daily flights on Philippine Airlines or Cebu Pacific from Manila to Kalibo (Panay Island). Ninety minutes by air-conditioned bus on Southwest Tours from Kalibo airport to Caticlan Jetty Port. Departures depend on flight schedules. Fifteen minutes by resort *banca* from Caticlan Jetty Port to the resort.

2. (2 ½ hours)   Thirty-five-minute daily flights on Seair (Dornier 328 planes) or sixty-five-minute daily flights on Asian Spirit or Seair or ninety-minute daily flights on Pacific Air from Manila to Caticlan (Panay Island). Five minutes by tricycle from Caticlan airport to Caticlan Jetty Port. Five minutes by *banca* from Caticlan Jetty Port to the resort.

Note: *Transfer from Kalibo or Caticlan airport can be arranged by the resort.*

Interisland Airlines also flies from Manila to Caticlan. For more information, you can call tel. nos. 852-8010 to 13.

 20 Units
4 Premiere Rooms • 16 Superior Rooms
All rooms have air-conditioning and have a bathroom with hot water and bathtub, cable TV, minibar, telephone, fan and a private balcony.

Indoor Facilities and Services
Babysitting • Massage • Foreign currency exchange • Shuttle service • Medical services • Billiards • Table tennis

 Food and Beverage Outlets
Restaurant: La Azotea Restaurant
Cuisine Offered: American • Filipino
Bar: Poolside bar

Watersports and Other Activities
Swimming pool • Beach (tiny, white sand) • Snorkeling (by the resort) • Dive shop • Island hopping • Tennis court (Lorenzo Main) • Shuttle boat service to other Lorenzo Resorts • Motorbiking • Mountain biking • Playground

 Per room per night inclusive of lunch and dinner

Lorenzo South

In the 1930s, struck by the beauty of Boracay's beaches and anticipating the island's great potential as a tourist getaway, a young couple named Lorenzo and Titay Lumbo began buying plots on the island. It was their daughter Elizabeth, however, who designed the three Lorenzo resorts that exist today: Lorenzo Main, Lorenzo South, and more recently, Lorenzo Grand Villa.

Lorenzo South, ringed by rocks, is directly on the beach along White Beach's south end. The stretch of white sand lined with coconut trees is narrower in this area, but since it is away from the crowds and noise of central Boracay, you have the privilege of total tranquility. A few meters from here, you can reach the pathway going to other parts of the island by strolling along White Beach or by riding a tricycle.

The resort's architecture combines the rustic and the elegant. From the beach, you can see its pointed green rooftops reminiscent of Batak houses with the inverted prow-shaped roofs. Blending with the cliff just behind the resort, the two-story cottages are made of natural materials, mainly bamboo and anahaw. The posts, with geometric motifs painted in pastel colors, add a bright note.

The rooms on the ground floor have the advantage of direct access to the beach but those on the upper floor, reached via an outside stone stairway, are just as pleasant, hidden among the trees. The rooms are all very comfortable and can house a family with three children. They have high ceilings, with large capiz windows that open onto a balcony overlooking the sea. Rooms 201 to 208, in particular, which are slightly elevated, have extra second balconies that look out toward the rocky wall of vegetation behind the resort.

Café Lorenzo, the resort's only restaurant, directly on the beach right at the resort's entrance, is very attractive. The resort's private beach is cleaned every morning and deck chairs and towels are readily available. You can actually swim in a coral reef right in front of the resort…even if it is nothing to rave about. The resort's *banca* can take you to the other Lorenzo resorts, where you can avail of the facilities and partake in the activities being offered.

LORENZO SOUTH

Sitio Angol, Boracay Island,
Malay, Aklan
Tel   (036) 288-3558 • 288-3560
Fax   (036) 288-3402
E-mail *lrsouth@yahoo.com*

Booking Office in Quezon City
10 John F. Kennedy Street,
Project 8, Quezon City
Tel   926-3958 • 926-4152
Fax   926-1726
E-mail *reservation@e-boracay.com*
Web   *www.e-boracay.com*

Both by air, land and sea
1. (3 ½ hours)   Fifty-five-minute daily flights on Philippine Airlines or Cebu Pacific from Manila to Kalibo (Panay Island). Ninety minutes by air-conditioned bus on Southwest Tours from Kalibo airport to Caticlan Jetty Port. Departures depend on flight schedules. Twenty minutes by *banca* from Caticlan Jetty Port to the resort.

2. (2 ½ hours)   Thirty-five-minute daily flights on Seair (Dornier 328 planes) or sixty-five-minute daily flights on Asian Spirit or Seair or ninety-minute daily flights on Pacific Air from Manila to Caticlan (Panay Island). Five minutes by tricycle from Caticlan airport to Caticlan Jetty. Twenty minutes by *banca* from Caticlan Jetty to the resort.

Note: *Transfer from Kalibo or Caticlan airport can be arranged by the resort.*

Interisland Airlines also flies from Manila to Caticlan. For more information, you can call tel. nos. 852-8010 to 13.

26 Units
24 Deluxe Rooms • 2 Premiere
All rooms have air-conditioning and have a bathroom with hot water, cable TV, minibar, telephone, fan and a private balcony.

Indoor Facilities and Services
Babysitting • Massage • Foreign currency exchange • Shuttle service • Medical services • Billiards • Table tennis • Library

Food and Beverage Outlets
Restaurant: Café Lorenzo
Cuisine Offered: American • Filipino
Quality: Good

Watersports and Other Activities
Swimming pools • Beach (white sand) • Snorkeling (by the resort) • Island hopping • Tennis • Motorbiking • Mountain biking • Playground • Shuttle boat service to other Lorenzo Resorts • Aqua sports arrangements with Tommy's sea sports (near Boat station 2 at Bazzura Bar)

 Per room per night inclusive of breakfast

3-5-7 Boracay Beach Resort

3-5-7 Boracay is a well-appointed 600 square-meter resort facility at Station 3 of Boracay island in Kalibo, Aklan.

Upon reaching the resort, you may have an odd feeling about its pink and white façade and its concrete construction, but its charm will definitely be felt when you enter any of its 10 well-appointed rooms (executive, family or suite classifications). Each of them exudes the warmth of tropical island luxury while also underscoring the comfort of modern living. Bamboo, fine abaca, local weaves and other native materials are used to achieve tasteful interior decoration while air-conditioning, cable TV and hot running water plus a stand-by generator complete the excellent experience.

3-5-7 Resort offers aquasport activities such as diving, snorkeling, windsurfing and parasailing. An island hopping tour and a one-hour banana boat ride is usually given free with accommodation packages.

The resort's corporate membership to the prestigious Fairways and Bluewater Golf Club also allows access to guests who might want to tee off at the greens. Any fees incurred however, are charged to the accounts of visiting golfers and guests.

The resort also has its own bar/restaurant, which serves Filipino and International cuisine. Foreign guests might find the prices quite reasonable, but local tourists might find them a bit steep. A house specialty is the Fish and Chips, with the fish cutlets cooked as fresh as the day they were caught. The resort owner, a past franchise holder of a popular pancake house, takes pride in the resort's pancakes since the 3-5-7 chef had been with him since the franchise days.

A particular standout that the resort offers is its second-story veranda from which a romantic dining experience may be enjoyed.

3-5-7 BORACAY BEACH RESORT

Manoc, Manoc, Boracay Island, Malay, Aklan
Tel   (036) 288-3473 to 74
Fax   (036) 288-3034
E-mail 357brcy@skyinet.net
Web   www.357boracay.com

Booking Office in Makati
9460 Baticulin Street,
San Antonio Village, Makati City
Tel   899-1943 to 44
        899-1793 to 94
Fax   897-5052

 By air and land
1. (3 ½ hours)   Fifty-five-minute daily flights on Philippine Airlines or Cebu Pacific from Manila to Kalibo (Panay Island). Ninety minutes by air-conditioned bus on Southwest Tours from Kalibo airport to Caticlan Jetty Port. Departures depend on flight schedules. Twenty minutes by *banca* from Caticlan Jetty Port to the resort.

2. (2 ½ hours)   Thirty-five-minute daily flights on Seair (Dornier 328 planes) or sixty-five-minute daily flights on Asian Spirit or Seair or ninety-minute daily flights on Pacific Air from Manila to Caticlan (Panay Island). Five minutes by tricycle from airport to Caticlan Jetty Port. Twenty minutes by *banca* from Caticlan Jetty Port to the resort.

Note: *Transfer from Kalibo or Caticlan airport can be arranged by the resort.*

Interisland Airlines also flies from Manila to Caticlan. For more information, you can call tel. nos. 852-8010 to 13.

 9 Units
7 Executive Rooms • 1 Family Room • 1 Suite Room
All rooms have air-conditioning with tiled bathrooms and hot shower

Indoor Facilities and Services
Game room • Videoke bar

 Food and Beverage
Bar/Restaurant
Cuisine Offered: Filipino • International • Seafoods

Watersports and Other Activities
Beach (white sand) • Snorkeling • Jet skiing • Diving • Banana boat ride • Paddle boating • Island hopping

 Per room per night inclusive of breakfast

Tirol and Tirol Beach Resort

Tirol and Tirol Beach Resort is located in a wide area of the beach shaded by many coconut trees. It is right at the center of Boracay, at the edge of the pathway that runs along the White Beach. Named after its owners, it has been in operation for over 20 years. An unpretentious resort, it is a pleasant place where you can get good value for the money.

Apart from the two beachfront cottages, the rest are on each side of an enclosed garden perpendicular to the sea. The rooms are spacious and the garden, dotted with coconut trees, makes a pleasant and restful spot.

The Balinese-style *nipa* and bamboo cottages have an elegant look. Bamboo is used in many diverse forms: narrow slats for the terrace flooring, as railings with geometric motifs. Thicker bamboo poles are used for the walls, while thin strips of braided bamboo were used for the hammocks. You can choose between the individual cottages that are just right for one or two persons, or the more spacious rooms in the duplex cottages, ideal for families.

The interior design is simple and functional. The ceiling and walls are simply painted in white and brightened up with checked curtains. The floors and furniture are made of wood while the bathroom has ceramic tiles.

Tirol and Tirol does not have restaurant service but a light breakfast can be provided on the terrace, and you can always go to the neighboring Nigi Nigi Nu Noos 'e' Nu Noos Beach Resort for a generous breakfast. The resort has its own tennis courts and can also arrange *banca* rentals for your excursions.

TIROL AND TIROL BEACH RESORT

Station 2, Sitio Manggayad,
Boracay Island, Malay, Aklan
Fax (036) 288-3165
E-mail tandt@boracay.i-next.net
tiroltnt@philwebinc.com
Web www.tirolandtirol.com

Both by air, land and sea

1. (3½ hours) Fifty-five-minute daily flights on Philippine Airlines or Cebu Pacific from Manila to Kalibo (Panay Island). Ninety minutes by air-conditioned bus on Southwest Tours or Boracay Island Star from Kalibo airport to Caticlan Jetty. Departures depend on flight schedules. Twenty minutes by *banca* from Caticlan Jetty Port to the resort.

2. (2 ½ hours) Thirty-five-minute daily flights on Seair (Dornier 328 planes) or sixty-five-minute daily flights on Asian Spirit or Seair or ninety-minute daily flights on Pacific Air from Manila to Caticlan (Panay Island). Five minutes by tricycle from Caticlan airport to Caticlan Jetty Port. Twenty minutes by *banca* from Caticlan Jetty Port to the resort.

Note: *Transfer from Kalibo or Caticlan airport can be arranged by the resort through a travel agent.*

Interisland Airlines also flies from Manila to Caticlan. For more information, you can call tel. nos. 852-8010 to 13.

24 Units

8 Beachfront Cottages • 8 Non-Beachfront Hotel-type (new bldg.) • 6 Non-Beachfront Cottages • 2 Standard Cottages
Except for standard rooms which are fan-cooled, all rooms have air-conditioning, fan, cable TV, a bathroom with hot water and a private terrace.

Food and Beverage Outlets

No restaurant. Only a light breakfast is served.

Watersports and Other Activities

Beach (white sand) • Snorkeling (in other places) • Boats for hire • Tennis

Per room per night inclusive of light breakfast

Red Coconut Beach Hotel

What started out as a restaurant wanting to offer one of the more decent foods in the island of Boracay in the early 1980s has come full circle. Today, Red Coconut Beach Hotel's seaview rooms, tastefully designed with Filipino motifs and found in a three-story building fronting the beach, offers luxurious accommodations not easily found in the other resorts in the area.

The façade of the main building, designed and made to look like they are of wooden logs and similar materials, add to the feeling of warmth of the resort. The small pool surrounded by lush greens and palms makes it so inviting especially on hot summer days or nights.

A few steps from the beachfront property will take you to the garden view cottages. These cottages are set around a well-manicured garden, hence the term. Here you can find the family cottage, which can accommodate up to 15 people. It has a huge master's bedroom on the first level and two big loaf rooms on the second level with king-size beds. The other cottages are furnished with queen-size beds specifically catering to couples or honeymooners, while the rest are with two double-sized beds.

For obvious reasons, the seaview rooms are always preferred to the garden view rooms.

As with many hotels in Boracay, booking way ahead of time is recommended during peak periods, especially New Year's Eve and Easter.

The hotel aspires to make sure that its guests get the feeling of being in their home away from home during their stay in the resort. Not surprisingly, its managers and staff undergo training aimed at achieving this. There are times, however, that travel-savvy and discriminating guests find themselves wanting a bit more from such an acclaimed getaway.

RED COCONUT BEACH HOTEL
Station 1, Malay, Aklan
Tel   (036) 288-3507
Fax   (036) 288-3770
Web   *www.redcoconut.com.ph*

Booking Office in Manila
Domestic Rd. beside Domestic Airport, Pasay City
Tel   852-7789 to 92
Fax   852-7793
E-mail   *info@redcoconut.com.ph*

 By air, land and sea
1. (3 ½ hours)   Fifty-five-minute daily flights on Philippine Airlines or Cebu Pacific from Manila to Kalibo (Panay Island). Ninety minutes by air-conditioned bus on Boracay Island Star from Kalibo airport to Caticlan Jetty Port. Departures depend on flight schedules. Twenty minutes by *banca* from Caticlan Jetty Port to the resort.

2. (2 ½ hours)   Thirty-five-minute daily flights on Seair (Dornier 328 planes) or sixty-five-minute daily flights on Asian Spirit or Seair or ninety-minute daily flights on Pacific Air from Manila to Caticlan (Panay Island). Five minutes by tricycle from airport to Caticlan Jetty Port. Twenty minutes by *banca* from Caticlan Jetty Port to the resort.

Note: *Transfer from Kalibo or Caticlan airport can be arranged by the resort.*

Interisland Airlines also flies from Manila to Caticlan. For more information, you can call tel. nos. 852-8010 to 13.

 43 Units
17 Garden View Rooms • 26 Sea View Rooms
Rooms are equipped with cable TV, minibar, IDD and NDD telephone, hot shower, a private veranda/balcony, and uninterrupted power (220v).

Indoor Facilities and Services
Gym • Spa

 Food and Beverage
Bar and Restaurant
Cuisine Offered: Filipino • International • Seafoods

 Watersports and Other Activities
Swimming pool • Beach (white sand) • Kayaking • Windsurfing • Snorkeling (in other places) • Diving (in other places) • Mountain biking • Island hopping • Jet skiing

Per room per night

Nigi Nigi Nu Noos 'e' Nu Noos Beach Resort

Set on the fringes of the pathway that runs through White Beach, Nigi Nigi Nu Noos 'e' Nu Nu Noos Beach Resort occupies a central location on the beachfront. Opened over 10 years ago, it is managed by Filipino, English and Canadian nationals.

The resort is architecturally enchanting. In the garden, with stone statues of vigilant divinities, are nine Balinese-style bamboo pagodas built close to one another. These pagodas, with pointed *nipa* roofs, house the rooms. Each has two rooms except in the two-story pagoda, which has four.

You can choose between air-conditioned and fan-cooled rooms, or between standard rooms, which are not very large, and family rooms, which have a mezzanine.

The rooms are bright due to wide, picture windows. Bamboo is used as the major decorative element for the interiors—thick bamboo poles on the ceiling and braided bamboo on the walls. The huge beds, also made from bamboo, are fitted with mosquito netting. Philippine and Balinese handicraft articles like fans, *batik*, carpets, wooden sculptures, wicker and pottery create a warm ethnic atmosphere. The attached bathrooms are just as pleasant and comfortable.

The rooms are extended on to the terraces furnished with benches and double-seats from where you can admire the garden. Privacy from the neighboring room is ensured by a dividing panel.

The spacious bamboo restaurant is built along the pathway leading out toward the sea. Here, you will find brightly-colored wooden Balinese statues and the tables are covered with batik cloths. A domesticated kalaw bird might just keep you company as you dine. The restaurant's cuisine enjoys a good reputation while the Nigi Nigi Jazz Blues Bar right next door is famous for its cocktails.

The resort has a cyber café. It also offers many services including a *banca* for excursions around the island.

NIGI NIGI NU NOOS 'E' NU NOO[ ] BEACH RESORT

White Beach, Malay,
Boracay Island, Aklan
Tel (036) 288-3101
Fax (036) 288-3112
E-mail *niginigi@pworld.net.ph*
Web *www.niginigi.com*

Booking Office in Manila
Filipino Travel Center
G/F, Doña Ramona Apartment Bldg.,
1555 M. Adriatico Street,
Ermita, Manila
Tel 536-1705

 By air, land and sea

1. (3½ hours) Fifty-five-minute daily flights on Philippine Airlines or Cebu Pacific from Manila to Kalibo (Panay Island). Ninety minutes by air-conditioned bus on Boracay Island Star from Kalibo airport to Caticlan Jetty. Departures depend on flight schedules. Twenty minutes by *banca* from Caticlan Jetty Port to the resort.

2. (2½ hours) Thirty-five-minute daily flights on Seair (Dornier 328 planes) or sixty-five-minute daily flights on Asian Spirit or Seair or ninety-minute daily flights on Pacific Air from Manila to Caticlan (Panay Island). Five minutes by tricycle from Caticlan airport to Caticlan Jetty Port. Twenty minutes by *banca* from Caticlan Jetty Port to the resort.

Note: *Transfer from Kalibo or Caticlan airport can be arranged by the resort.*

Interisland Airlines also flies from Manila to Caticlan. For more information, you can call tel. nos. 852-8010 to 13.

 21 Units

12 Standard Cottages (10 with air-conditioning and 2 with fan) • 8 Family Rooms (4 with air-conditioning; 4 with fan) • 1 Air-conditioned Studio Apartment with kitchenette.
All rooms have a bathroom with hot water and a private veranda.

Indoor Facilities and Services
Business center • Babysitting • Tour desk • Foreign currency exchange • Telephone and fax service

 Food and Beverage Outlets
Restaurant: Nigi Nigi Restaurant
Cuisine Offered: Seafood • Asian • International

Watersports and Other Activities
Beach (white sand) • Snorkeling (in other places) • Diving (in other places) • Island hopping (with picnic) • Bike rental

 Per room per night inclusive of breakfast

Angol Point Beach Resort

Angol Point Beach Resort is ideal if you are looking for privacy. "Peaceful" is the word that describes the resort best, as it is located along the pathway in the southern part of White Beach—away from the noisy areas. It has just eight cottages to offer, which in a way guarantees privacy.

The resort is owned by Francis Tayengco, a Filipino-Chinese architect who divides his time between New York, where he lives and work for half the year restoring historical monuments and the Philippines, where he shuttles between Iloilo and Angol Point. Besides being an architect, Francis is also an ardent environmentalist, who designed the resort in 1990 to blend harmoniously with its surroundings and a magnificent, perfectly-maintained coconut grove.

Since the Chinese considers 8 as a lucky number, the eight octagonal cottages are built on the lawns at a considerable distance from one another, amidst the lush greenery and coconut grove. The surrounding exudes a deep sense of peace and tranquillity, something quite rare in Boracay.

The wooden cottages with *nipa* roofs are spacious and the interiors are tastefully decorated. Beautiful wood flooring, bamboo furniture, braided bamboo ceiling and walls make up the room. Capiz windows with mosquito screens look out onto the garden while cottages 1 and 5 look out to the sea. The marble bathrooms are pleasant despite the absence of hot water. All the cottages have large terraces with armchairs and hammocks.

Angol has no restaurant. Only tea and coffee are served in the terraces in the mornings. However, there are many restaurants nearby where you can get meals. For breakfast, English Bakery 3 is just a few steps away. For the other meals, you can try the Italian restaurant Floremar de Mano or the Thai restaurant Sulutha and Jazz Up Café for music in the evening.

The resort offers services such as organizing your airport transfers or helping you plan *banca* excursions around the area.

ANGOL POINT BEACH RESORT
White Beach, Malay,
Boracay Island, Aklan
Tel (036) 288-3107

Booking Office in Manila
1221 A. Mabini Street,
Ermita, Manila
Tel 522-0012

Both by air, land and sea
1. (3½ hours) Fifty-five-minute daily flights on Philippine Airlines or Cebu Pacific from Manila to Kalibo (Panay Island). Ninety minutes by air-conditioned bus on Southwest Tours from Kalibo airport to Caticlan Jetty Port. Departures depend on flight schedules. Fifteen minutes by *banca* from Caticlan Jetty Port to the resort.

2. (2 ½ hours) Thirty-five-minute daily flights on Seair (Dornier 328 planes) or sixty-five-minute daily flights on Asian Spirit or Seair or ninety-minute daily flights on Pacific Air from Manila to Caticlan (Panay Island). Five minutes by tricycle from Caticlan airport to Caticlan Jetty Port. Fifteen minutes by *banca* from Caticlan Jetty Port to the resort.

Note: *Transfer from Kalibo or Caticlan airport can be arranged by the resort through a travel agent.*

Interisland Airlines also flies from Manila to Caticlan. For more information, you can call tel. nos. 852-8010 to 13.

8 Units
8 Individual Bungalows
All bungalows have a bathroom (no hot water), a private terrace and fan.

Food and Beverage Outlets
No food and beverage service except for morning coffee or tea.

Watersports and Other Activities
Beach (white sand) • Snorkeling (in other places) • Boats for hire

  Per room per night

Sand Castles Resort Boracay

S and Castles Resort Boracay is at the edge of the pathway along White Beach. Greg Hutchinson, an Australian and his Filipina wife, Viveca, run the resort.

A well-planned bamboo structure is the main building that houses the reception area and a restaurant. In the reception area, guests can use a small lounge with a TV set, a refrigerator and books. Tea and coffee are also available. The restaurant—with elevated alcoves that you can reserve for intimate dinners—specializes in Thai cuisine.

Some of the rooms are located on the second floor of the main building. These are furnished with wood furniture which is more elaborate than in the cottage rooms. There is also a luxurious, exquisite honeymoon suite with large picture windows that open directly onto the ocean—very romantic and tastefully decorated with colonial style furniture, exposed roof beams, attractive fabrics, colored mats, clay vases and plants.

The other rooms are in bungalows behind the main building. These are spread out, facing one another on each side of the garden.

Three are individual rooms while the six others are duplexes. The bungalows are elevated, each one with its own terrace that looks out to a garden of talisay and coconut trees. The cottages open to this garden through sliding doors and capiz windows. In a shaded alley is a pergola covered with bougainvillea creepers. All the structures use *nipa*, bamboo and wood. The bamboo work on the terraces is delicate—fine slats for flooring and thicker poles with geometric motifs for the railings.

The interiors of the bungalows are done in traditional style with pinkish wood for the floor, *sawali* (rectangles of braided wicker) walls and ceiling, and bamboo furniture. The décor make use of handicrafts from various regions of the Philippines. The handwoven bedcovers and murals come either from Ifugao or Mindanao. Pottery, mats and colored straw hats adorn the walls. Green plants and gauzy white curtains on the windows make for a picture perfect effect. The bathrooms are bright and comfortable.

The Hutchinsons manage Tribal Adventure Tours that organizes off-the-beaten-track excursions.

SAND CASTLES RESORT BORACAY

White Beach, Boracay Island, Malay, Aklan
Tel/Fax (036) 288-3207
Fax (036) 288-3449

Booking Office in Makati
Shop #6 G/F New World Hotel
Makati Ave., Makati City
Tel 755-6849
Tel/Fax 752-7575
E-mail *info@tribaladventures.com*
Web *www.tribaladventures.com*

 Both by air, land and sea

1. (3 ½ hours) Fifty-five-minute daily flights on Philippine Airlines or Cebu Pacific from Manila to Kalibo (Panay Island). Ninety minutes by air-conditioned bus on Southwest Tours from Kalibo airport to Caticlan Jetty Port. Departures depend on flight schedules. Twenty minutes by *banca* from Caticlan Jetty Port to the resort.

2. (2 ½ hours) Thirty-five-minute daily flights on Seair (Dornier 328 planes) or sixty-five-minute daily flights on Asian Spirit or Seair or ninety-minute daily flights on Pacific Air from Manila to Caticlan (Panay Island). Five minutes by tricycle from airport to Caticlan Jetty Port. Twenty minutes by *banca* from Caticlan Jetty Port to the resort.

Note: *Transfer from Kalibo or Caticlan airport can be arranged by the resort.*

Interisland Airlines also flies from Manila to Caticlan. For more information, you can call tel. nos. 852-8010 to 13.

 20 Units
8 Duplex Air-conditioned Bungalows • 2 Honeymooners Air-conditioned Bungalows • 1 Family Air-conditioned Bungalows • 7 Air-conditioned Villas • 2 Fan-cooled Beachview Villas
All rooms have a bathroom with hot water.

Indoor Facilities and Services
Library

 Food and Beverage Outlets
Restaurant: Asian Castles Restaurant and Bar
Cuisine Offered: Asian • Seafood

 Watersports and Other Activities
Beach (white sand) • Snorkeling (in other places) • Diving (in other places) • Island hopping • Kayaking • Windsurfing • Tribal adventure tours

 Per room per night

Negros

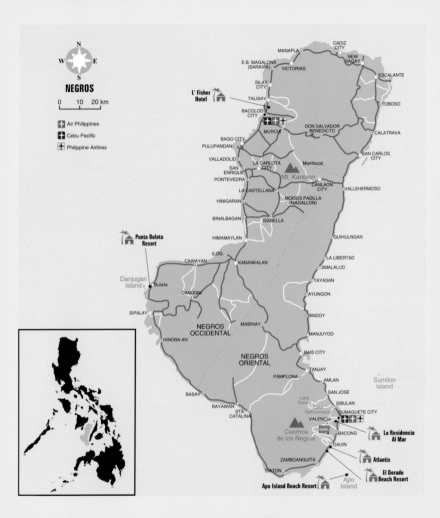

NEGROS

0   10   20 km

 Air Philippines
 Cebu Pacific
 Philippine Airlines

Climate		**Bacolod, Dumaguete and Apo Island:** Seasons not very pronounced, relatively dry from November to April; wet during the rest of the year
		Southwest coast – Hinoba-an: Dry from November to April, wet during the rest of the year
		Siquijor: Rainfall more or less evenly distributed throughout the year
Typhoons		December to April

Masskara Festival, Bacolod City, the weekend closest to the 19th of October. The festival is marked by parades of masked and elaborately costumed dance troupes from schools, companies and other city organizations. On this occasion, the whole city sells *papier-mâché* masks.

Negros Oriental – Dumaguete

Dumaguete is the capital of Negros Oriental and is distinguished from the other towns of the Visayas by its cultural and administrative dynamism. Controlled urbanism allows access to the sea along Rizal Boulevard, where the cafés and restaurants are congregated. With the mountains as a backdrop and its extensive coastline at the fore, Dumaguete enjoys a privileged natural setting which has been well-preserved.

Dumaguete has a large population of students. One indication of its juvenile population and its keeping up with the times is the proliferation of internet cafés, in addition to its numerous schools. The Silliman University is one of the oldest Protestant universities in the Philippines, named after the missionary who founded it in 1901. It houses the Silliman University Marine Laboratory, which takes part in research programs along with other foreign universities. The Foundation University, initially known as Foundation College was established in 1949. The main campus of the university is only a few minutes' walking distance from the heart of the city. In Dumaguete itself, you can visit the **Bell Tower** that once served to alert the population from impending pirate attacks. At the impeccably clean and picturesque market, you can find agricultural produce, the main livelihood of the region, and handicrafts like *banig*, the finely-plaited palm frond mats. The **Anthropological Museum** within the Silliman University is also worth a visit.

Sumilon Island

VALENCIA *(7 kilometers west of Dumaguete and 1ž hours by car from Dauin—one day tour)* Valencia, at the foot of Mount Talinis is the jump-off point for several excursions. From **Camp Look Out**, you can enjoy the views of Dumaguete and the nearby islands, Cebu and Siquijor. The 40-meter high **Casiroro Falls**, 30 minutes on foot from Valencia, are hidden in lush tropical vegetation in the middle of rocks. The 1,900-meter high **Mount Talinis** is for seasoned mountaineers, as scaling it requires several days. It is a dormant volcano covered in dense forest and is also known as "Cuernos de los Negros."

TWIN LAKES *(25 kilometers northwest of Dumaguete, 2 kilometers from San Jose)* Danao and Balinsasayao are crater lakes surrounded by dense rainforests at an altitude of 800 meters. The four-hour climb (15 kilometers) is well worth it as a breathtaking view awaits you. It may be very difficult to complete this trek in one day, though.

BAIS *(one hour by car north of Dumaguete, in the Strait of Tañon)* From March to May, dolphins and whales can be observed from Bais. The La Planta Hotel can organize whale-watching excursions.

DAUIN *(15 kilometers south of Dumaguete)* Dauin is one of the oldest towns in the region, established in the 18th century, with an appealing little church. Dauin also has a wide black sand beach where the resorts of El Dorado and Atlantis are located.

APO ISLAND *(15 minutes from Dumaguete to Dauin; 1 hour by banca or 45 minutes by car up to Zamboanguita, and then half an hour by banca)* With a surface area of 12 hectares, it was transformed into a marine sanctuary under the auspices of the Silliman University. It is an exceptional diving and snorkeling site. It may be difficult to reach the island in adverse weather and the strong currents necessitate being guided by members of the diving club. The resorts on Dauin organize dives at Apo, but it is possible to stay on Apo itself, at the Apo Beach Resort.

SUMILON ISLAND *(1 hour and a half from Dumaguete by banca)* Once a marine sanctuary, this area was damaged by cyanide fishing. The situation has since improved with areas now already good for diving and snorkeling.

Dumaguete Festival

Negros Occidental

The province of Negros Occidental is the main center of sugar production in the country. A destination still unknown to tourists though easily accessible by frequent flights, Bacolod and its region is rich in history.

Masskara Festival

Bacolod City

Bacolod, capital of the province of Negros Occidental, offers diverse attractions.

THE NEGROS MUSEUM Constructed in 1931, it is a sugar museum, located in the old building of the Provincial Capitol. A good example of colonial architecture, it overlooks a lagoon surrounded by vegetation.

THE SHOWROOM OF THE ASSOCIATION OF NEGROS PRODUCERS (ANP) It displays a wide variety of the beautiful handicraft products from the region. It is located on No. 9 Lacson Street, not far from the L'Fisher Hotel.

THE SAN SEBASTIAN CATHEDRAL Completed in 1882, it is located near the Bacolod City Plaza, the main square of the town. The cathedral is made of coral stone from the Guimaras Islands and is crowned by two pinnacles.

THE SANTA CLARA CHAPEL Constructed entirely in wood and *capiz* shell, this chapel in Sta. Clara subdivision has a mosaic wall entirely made from shells.

Pontevedra Church

Antiques You will find several antique shops such as the Casa Grande Antique Shop at No. 29, 17th Street corner Lacson Street, where some *objets d'art* and furniture belonging to rich owners of plantations or sugar refineries are sold.

Old Steam Locomotives They can still be observed at the Central Azucarera de la Carlota in the south of Bacolod, the Hawaiian Philippines Company, the Lopez Sugar Central or the Sagay Sugar Central. Make inquiries at the Department of Tourism office in Bacolod regarding the organization of these visits during harvest season (October to April).

Cuisine Bacolod would not be complete without mentioning its cuisine, justifiably well-known throughout the country. Sample the famous *inasal*, barbecued chicken flavored with lemongrass. There are many good restaurants where you can discover the specialties of the region, including Manokan Country, in the reclamation area, where you will also find a number of food stalls; and Chicken Deli, with a slightly dim interior on No. 8

Lacson Street, next to the ANP Showroom. If you want a change, try the Chinese restaurant L'Sea on No. 14 Lacson Street, a few steps from L'Fisher Hotel and Kaisei on No. 10 Lacson Street, with its beautiful and warm Japanese wood décor.

North Bacolod

The old houses in North Bacolod are generally two-story edifices, with the ground floor made of stone and the upper floor made of wood. The villas are very elegant with their *calados*—wooden dividers in sculpted wood with floral motifs—and their *ventillas* in delicately worked wrought iron under the windows. These contain beautiful furniture and *objets d'art* accumulated over the years.

Talisay *(7 kilometers to the north)* Two villas can be admired from the exterior only. Lacson House on No. 36 Rizal Street, is really beautiful despite its being in a state of abandonment. Its first floor in stone is decorated with superb lintel circular arcs. The Lizares House, at the corner of E. Lizares and Bonifacio Streets, constructed in the 1880s, is a slightly eccentric house, immense with its multiple wings, balconies. Gothic windows and a tower. It was completely renovated and repainted in a beautiful pink-beige.

Silay *(14 kilometers north of Bacolod)* The little tranquil town of Silay, like Vigan and Taal, has old colonial Spanish houses that have also been well-preserved. Silay has the particularity

Lizares House, Talisay

of having these villas located along wide, flower-lined streets where it is very pleasant to take a stroll. The town built its fortune from sugarcane, which the Frenchman Yves Leopold Germain Gaston introduced for commercial culture at the end of the 19th century. These villas bear witness to the prosperous era from the end of the 19th century up to the Second World War, when Silay was the economic and cultural capital of Negros, and was nicknamed "The Paris of Negros." Still belonging to the descendants of their rich owners, the villas have been transformed into museums and can be visited by appointment.

Balay Negrense Museum, Silay

Old structures in Silay which deserve a visit:

CINCO DE NOVIEMBRE STREET (*Green House*) This little villa painted in green was constructed in 1935 by Manuel Severino Hofileña and is still inhabited by Ramon, one of his descendants. To be a lover of art is part of family tradition: the eight brothers and sisters of Ramon are all in the artistic profession. Ramon has an incredible collection of paintings by Filipino and foreign artists. He is also a fervent defender and promoter of the culture of this region and has, for the last few decades, annually organized guided tours which have become famous. Inform him of your visit in advance at Tel. No.: (034) 495-4561; Fax: 441-2508.

BALAY NEGRENSE MUSEUM (*Gaston House*) This magnificent villa dating back to 1901, reputed to be haunted in the olden days, was restored and transformed into a museum in 1987. It is surrounded by a beautiful garden planted with frangipani trees. It is one of the biggest colonial houses in Silay, comprising two large reception halls and 12 rooms—one for each child. It belongs to the eldest son of Yves Leopold Germain Gaston, who lived here from 1901 to 1927. Visits may be conducted from Tuesday to Sunday, 10 a.m. to 6 p.m.

RIZAL STREET On Rizal Street, the main road, are two interesting buildings: the Rizal Commercial Bank and the Bernardino and Ysabel Jalandoni House and Museum (Pink House). This beautiful and spacious house was constructed in 1908 with Mindoro wood and sculpted steel ceilings from Germany. It is the property of the heirs of Antonio J. Montinola and his wife. Visits may be made from Tuesday to Sunday, between 10 a.m. and 5 p.m. After a visit, take a snack at the oldest bakery in town, El Ideal, famous for delicious pastries such as the guapple tart, made from the fruit which is a cross between an apple and a guava.

Victorias Milling *(34 kilometers from Bacolod)* This is one of the main sugar refineries in the province, which began its operations in 1928. It may be visited from Tuesday to Friday (except at lunchtime). German steam locomotives dating back to 1912 are still in use. The son of the sugar refinery's founder was responsible for the mural paintings in Saint Joseph's Chapel, constructed in the 1960s.

The Cartwheels Chapel *(45 kilometers from Bacolod in Manapla)* Located within the grounds of the Hacienda Rosalia that once belonged to Yves Leopold Germain Gaston, this chapel was entirely constructed with the wheels of carabao-drawn carts.

East Bacolod

East Bacolod is dominated by the Kanlaon volcano, one of the most active in the Philippines. The climb is begun at the foot of the volcano from Mambucal, 31 kilometers southeast of Bacolod. You can also stroll up to the sulphur spring, source of Mambucal Hot Springs, surrounded by luxurious vegetation. A little resort is located there and is called the Mambucal Summer Resort.

South Bacolod

If you stay at Punta Bulata Resort, you can visit these sites on the way:

Montilla-Tomkins Hacienda *(Ubay, Pulupandan, 28 kilometers from Bacolod)* Surrounded by sugarcane fields, the house was constructed in 1852 by the hacendero Don Agustin Montilla de Cordoba and is still family property. You can visit it by making an appointment with Ernest Baker, Casa Grande Antique, No. 29 17th Street corner Lacson Street, Tel. No.: (034) 432-1128. The villa contains hundreds of wooden statues representing saints, and antiques of diverse origins such as porcelain from the Sung and Ming dynasties, Chinese camphor chests, canopy beds fashioned by a Chinese master cabinet-maker, Viennese furniture and family portraits.

Hinigaran *(60 kilometers from Bacolod)* You will see the Church of Saint Mary Magdalene and its adjoining bell tower with two bells in alloyed silver dating back to 1896.

Danjugan Island

DANJUGAN ISLAND *(150 kilometers from Bacolod, 20 minutes by banca from Punta Bulata)* Danjugan is a marine sanctuary launched in 1994 by Professor Bellamy in collaboration with the scientists of the Negros Forests and Ecological Foundation and the Philippine Wetlands and Wildlife Conservation Foundation (Silliman University). For a visit, a permit must be obtained from the person in charge, Mr. Gerry Ledesma at Tel. No.: (034) 441-1658.

The island covers a surface area of 42 hectares. You can go around it by *banca*, stopping on the numerous white sand coves which dot its coast. It is possible to snorkel in front of Beach Camp. A track leads to five little lagoons filled with mangroves and bat caves.

HINOBA-AN *(200 kilometers south of Bacolod, 30 minutes from Punta Bulata)* At Hinoba-an is a beautiful gold sand beach fringed with coconut trees. You can snorkel directly from the coast. Located halfway between Bacolod and Dumaguete, the beach is very popular with the residents of the capitals of the two Negroses. It is from Hinoba-an that you can also visit the Obong Caves. The restaurant of the Brazaville Beach House resort serves good local and international food at reasonable prices. Two comfortable rooms are available for rent in this holiday resort. Tel. No.: (034) 433-2515 or e-mail: *pgdavid@lasaltech.com* or web: *www.lasaltech.com/~pgdavid.*

Punta Bulata

La Residencia Al Mar

L a Residencia al Mar is one of the oldest hotels in Dumaguete. A beautiful, old house that was once the family home of Governor Escaños of Negros Oriental, this single-story residence on the Rizal Boulevard sea front was built in the old colonial Spanish style. Its present owners, Mr. and Mrs. Hilado, renovated it in a clever, tasteful manner preserving its charm while providing it with all the necessary modern amenities.

The small reception is warm with its well-polished red-tile floors and its Chinese porcelain jars. On either side of the reception are two restaurants, considered among the most elegant in town—the Don Atilano which serves good food in a pleasant Spanish setting, and the other which serves Filipino cuisine. You can also have breakfast here with the view of the sea through the bay windows.

A polished wooden staircase leads from the reception area to the rooms on the upper floors. On the first floor, there is a little drawing room with a warm and congenial atmosphere.

It is decorated with engravings on the walls, antique furniture, statues of Thai Buddhas, and vases with dry-flower arrangements. There are guestrooms on either side of this drawing room, the most charming of which have balconies that look out toward the sea. These are cozy, with wrought iron beds, replicas of antique furniture, pretty earthenware lamps and retro coat hangers. The white walls are decorated with nice engravings and the floors are of polished wood. Each room has a tiled bathroom. The standard rooms, are not as recommended, as they are only slightly cheaper but do not have any windows.

Note: *If La Residencia Al Mar is fully booked, the next best place in town, also on the seafront a few blocks away, is the Bethel Guesthouse. Managed by Protestants and run by a very efficient staff, it is a small, all-white building with 67 immaculately clean rooms.*

- *Bethel Guesthouse*
  Tel (035) 225-2000
  422-8000 (Islacom)
  Fax (035) 225-1374
  E-mail bethel@mozcom.com

LA RESIDENCIA AL MAR

Rizal Boulevard, Dumaguete City, Negros Oriental
Tel (035) 225-7100
(035) 422-0888 to 89
Fax (035) 422-8449
E-mail
lresidencia_ygh@yahoo.com

1. By air and land (2 hours) Seventy-five-minute daily flights on Air Philippines, Cebu Pacific or Philippine Airlines from Manila to Dumaguete. Ten minutes by car from Dumaguete airport to the hotel.

2. By air, land, sea and land (5 ½ hours on the first morning flight) Seventy-five-minute daily flights on Philippine Airlines, Air Philippines or Cebu Pacific from Manila to Cebu. Twenty minutes by car from Cebu Mactan airport to the pier. From Cebu to Dumaguete, three hours and thirty minutes by SuperCat Fast Ferry (Tel. No.: (032) 234-9600). One daily service at 8:00 a.m. or by Oceanjet (Tel. No.: (032) 255-7560). One daily service at 6:00 a.m.

Walk Two minutes from Dumaguete harbor to the hotel.

Note: *With prior notice, the hotel will arrange for a car waiting for the guest at the airport.*

Superferry also operates ferry service from Manila to Dumaguete. For more information, you can call tel. nos. 528-7979 or 528-7171.

16 Units
1 Family Room • 3 Executive Suites • 4 Executive Deluxe Rooms • 6 Deluxe Rooms • 2 Standard Rooms (no windows)
All rooms have air-conditioning, a bathroom with hot water, TV. The Family Room, Executive Suites and Executive Deluxe Rooms have a minibar.

Food and Beverage Outlets
Restaurants: Don Atilano Steakhouse, Wakagi Japanese Restaurant • Seafoods & Filipino Restaurant
Cuisine Offered: Native dishes • European • Mexican • Italian • Japanese
Quality: Average

Watersports and Other Activities
Tours to Dumaguete points of interest

Per room per night inclusive of breakfast

El Dorado Beach Resort

The atmosphere in El Dorado Beach Resort is casual and friendly. The mood is set as soon as you arrive at the airport—a vividly painted van awaits you and after a short drive through town, takes you to the resort in 20 minutes through a pleasant countryside.

High white walls surround El Dorado and you enter through a massive, imposing wooden door. The owner, Markus Kalberer, of Swiss origin, is well-acquainted with the art of building, as he worked in the construction sector for several years. He managed to make the best of the narrow terrain that has only a limited beach frontage.

Along a flower-lined alley is a long building with low white walls and *nipa* roof, housing most of the rooms. These, though quite small, have a terrace and are well furnished. Markus' eye for detail is evident in the many functional minutiae. The interior decoration makes use of materials from the region: bamboo for the beds and shell for the lamps. If children accompany you, it is recommended that you rent a second room as it is difficult to put in an extra bed.

Near the swimming pool, framed by bougainvilleas, is the bar where divers get together to talk about their day. Here, you will notice a large outdoor screen where films are shown in the evenings. Occasionally, divers present their films here.

On the area near the sea are three, fairly spacious double cottages and a restaurant. Each cottage is different. One, accessible only by ladder, is perched on a tree with branches emerging from its roof; the other has a *nipa* roof, which goes right down into the ground. The open-air restaurant faces the sea and it is not rare, on rainy days, for the water to come right into the restaurant.

El Dorado is a dive resort; its black sand is not that appealing. Sea Explorers, a club integrated into the resort, specializes in excursions to Apo Island, one of the major dive sites in the Philippines. You can also have your first night dive here from the beach. For snorkeling, there is the marine sanctuary of North Masaplod, which is very close to the resort. The sea can get quite rough, making the beach impassable. In this case, you need only to walk along the shore right up to the sheltered beach of the fishing village of Dauin. Here you can watch the fishing boats go out to sea at the end of the day.

Apart from diving and snorkeling, it is also possible to hire mountain bikes—take the track parallel to the beach and pedal to the market and Dauin Church.

EL DORADO BEACH RESORT

Washington Road, Lipayo, Dauin, Negros Oriental
Tel   (035) 425-2274
Fax   (035) 424-0238
E-mail
info@eldoradobeachresort.com
Web
www.eldoradobeachresort.com

 1. By air and land (2 ½ hours) Seventy-five-minute daily flights on Air Philippines, Cebu Pacific or Philippine Airlines from Manila to Dumaguete. Twenty minutes by van from Dumaguete airport to the resort.

2. By air, land, sea and land (6 hours on the first morning flight) Seventy-five-minute daily flight on Philippine Airlines, Air Philippines or Cebu Pacific from Manila to Cebu. Twenty minutes by car from Cebu Mactan airport to the pier. From Cebu to Dumaguete, three hours and thirty minutes by SuperCat Fast Ferry (Tel. No.: (032) 234-9600) One daily service at 8:00 a.m. or by Oceanjet (Tel. No.: (032) 255-7560). One daily service at 6:00 a.m. 20 minutes by van from Dumaguete harbor to the resort.

Note: *Transfer from Dumaguete airport/harbor can be arranged by the resort.*

Superferry also operates ferry service from Manila to Dumaguete. For more information, you can call tel. nos. 528-7979 or 528-7171.

 26 Units
1 Dormitory Room • 3 Cottage Rooms • 16 Standard Rooms • 3 Deluxe Rooms • 1 Family Room • 1 Garden House • 1 Santol House
Except for the cottages, which are fan-cooled, all rooms have air-conditioning, a bathroom with hot water, TV.

Indoor Facilities and Services
Foreign currency exchange • Pool table • Massage service • Internet and business services • Shuttle service • Library • Billiards • Table soccer

 Food and Beverage Outlets
Restaurant: Beachside Restaurant
Cuisine Offered: International
Quality: Good

Bars: Bellringer Bar • Beach Bar • Pool Bar

 Watersports and Other Activities
Swimming pool • Beach (gray sand) • Snorkeling (in other places) • Diving (Sea Explorers Dive shop) • Island hopping • Boats for hire • Mountain biking • Children's playground • Open-air movie screening at night

 Per room per night

Atlantis Resort Dumaguete

Atlantis Resort Dumaguete was formerly the resort of Aquavit, under the management of German national Bernd Scheuer, who, for more than 30 years, has traveled in different places as a professional diver. It was recently associated with Atlantis at Puerto Galera whose name it now bears.

Located on the black sand beach of Dauin, not far from El Dorado Beach Resort, this resort is possibly the most pleasant of the resorts along this coast where visitors come mainly for the fabulous diving on Apo Island, just an hour away by *banca*.

Atlantis is set in a veritable oasis filled with beautiful trees and flowering plants. A pretty pond brimming with water lilies is set among the plants. A tiled alley bordered by *nipa-*

capped lanterns leads, through a green lawn, to where the spacious bungalows are found.

The bungalows are superb—white walls decorated with brown geometric designs and *nipa* roofs in the form of pagodas. Each has a terrace opening onto the garden. Two independent duplex bungalows face the sea and it is quite relaxing to stretch out on the hammocks, looking at the beach bordered with periwinkles and bindweed. The rooms are very restful with immaculate white walls contrasting with red tile floors. The bamboo furniture is original in design. A splash of color is achieved with the bedcovers and the wall hangings.

The restaurant with its little bar is pleasantly located in front of the sea. At the back of the restaurant is a nice bamboo building, which houses the dive center and the library.

A recent extension work has not diminished the charm of the resort in any way, as the new building, sheltering the additional rooms, is at the back of the resort. These rooms, however, though as comfortable as the cottages, have the disadvantage of being further from the sea. Fortunately, the swimming pool is just close by.

ATLANTIS RESORT DUMAGUETE (FORMERLY AQUAVIT)
Lipayo, Dauin, Dumaguete City, Negros Oriental
Tel   (035) 425-2327
Tel/Fax   (035) 424-0578
E-mail   georg@atlantishotel.com
Web   www.atlantishotel.com
www.diving-philippines.com

Booking Office in Makati
Tel   817-2883

 1. By air and land (2 ½ hours)
Seventy-five-minute daily flights on Air Philippines, Cebu Pacific or Philippine Airlines from Manila to Dumaguete. Twenty minutes by car from Dumaguete airport to the resort.

2. By air, land, sea and land (6 hours on the first morning flight)   Seventy-five-minute daily flights on Philippine Airlines, Air Philippines or Cebu Pacific from Manila to Cebu. Twenty minutes by car from Cebu Mactan airport to the pier. From Cebu to Dumaguete, three hours and thirty minutes by SuperCat Fast Ferry (Tel. No.: (032) 234-9600) One daily service at 8:00 a.m. or by Oceanjet (Tel. No.: (032) 255-7560). One daily service at 6:00 a.m. from Cebu to Dumaguete. Twenty minutes from Dumaguete harbor to the resort.

Note: *Transfer from Dumaguete airport/harbor can be arranged by the resort.*

Superferry also operates ferry service from Manila to Dumaguete. For more information, you can call tel. nos. 528-7979 or 528-7171.

 36 Units
30 Deluxe Rooms • 4 Sea View Deluxe Rooms • 1 Honeymoon Hut • 1 Family Suite
All rooms have air-conditioning, a bathroom with hot water, cable TV and minibar.

 Food and Beverage Outlets
Restaurant: Toko's Restaurant
Cuisine Offered: Filipino • International
Quality: Good
Bar: Pool Bar

 Watersports and Other Activities
Swimming pool • Beach (black sand) • Diving (dives on Apo Island) • Kayaking • Motorbike rental • Tours to: Casiroro waterfalls (full day), Mount Talinis (3 days) and Twin Lakes (2 days)

 Per room per night

Apo Island Beach Resort

Picture a little white sand beach on an isolated island, hemmed in by rocks at the foot of a wooded cliff. This is Apo, a haven for lovers of solitude and, of course, for divers who are on the site of the fabulous coral reef.

The cove is accessible by a narrow passage on the beach through the cliff, and as the resort has only eight cottages, you are assured of complete privacy. You have a choice between the cottages on the beach or the slightly elevated ones overlooking the sea. All are made of bamboo and *nipa* with wooden floors and wicker furniture, but differ slightly in style.

The largest, known as The Residence, is perched high on a cliff and is the home of the owner, an Australian, who lives here only occasionally.

It is a circular house, devoid of windows, opening directly onto the trees and the sea. It is furnished with antique Philippine furniture: a planter's armchair, a bench, tables and a sideboard, sculpted and decorated with assorted objects.

The Lower Triton, also circular and built directly on the beach at the foot of the cliff, is the most pleasant of the cottages. It has a nice terrace with sliding *capiz* panels and two lounge chairs. Upper Triton is an elevated cottage on the beach while Surf 1 and Surf 2 are smaller semi-detached cottages also on the beach.

On the beach, composed of white coral debris, are plastic lounge chairs and *nipa* parasols. The comfort of Apo Beach is basic—there is no electricity; the bathrooms are cramped and can, during the dry season, lack water. For this purpose, two buckets of water are distributed per day. This can be quite inconvenient if you have small children. Apart from these minor shortcomings, this beach resort is really a heavenly spot, which you would like to keep secret. As it is on the dive site of Apo itself, it is very convenient to stay here if you are mainly interested in diving and snorkeling.

APO ISLAND BEACH RESORT

Dauin, Negros Oriental
No phone. Only radio communications.

Booking Office in Dumaguete
Paradise Travel Center,
3 Noblefranca Street,
Dumaguete City, Negros Oriental

Tel	(035) 422-9663
	422-9820
Tel/Fax	(035) 225-5490
E-mail	*paradise@glinesnx.com.ph*

If the office in Dumaguete is closed, call Coco Grove Beach Resort which is under the same management and has radio contact with Apo Island Beach Resort.

Tel	(035) 481-5008
Fax	(035) 481-5006

 By air, land and sea (3–3 ½ hours) Seventy-five-minute daily flights on Air Philippines, Cebu Pacific or Philippine Airlines from Manila to Dumaguete. Thirty minutes by car from Dumaguete to Malatapay pier. Forty-five minutes by *banca* from Malatapay pier to Apo Island.

Note: *Transfer from Dumaguete or Siquijor (1 ½ hours by banca) can be arranged by the resort.*

Superferry also operates ferry service from Manila to Dumaguete. For more information, you can call tel. nos. 528-7979 or 528-7171.

 8 Units
Lower Triton • Upper Triton • Surf I • Surf II • 4 Golden Cowrie Rooms
All cottages have a bathroom with cold water only. Beds have mosquito nets. There is no electricity, only oil lamps are used.

 Food and Beverage Outlets
Restaurant and Bar
Cuisine Offered: Filipino
Quality: Good

Note: *There is also the nearby restaurant of Paul Rhodes who owns Liberty, the other resort on Apo Island, more basic but very clean and friendly with a good dive center.*

Watersports and Other Activities
Beach (white sand) • Snorkeling (in front) • Diving • Island hopping

 Per cottage per night

L'Fisher Hotel

Located on the main road in the heart of Bacolod, only fifteen minutes from the airport, L'Fisher Hotel is an excellent starting point for visiting the town.

You can easily walk to the plaza, the reclamation area, the showroom for the handicraft producers of Negros, and the antique shop areas. Moreover, several restaurants are situated in the immediate neighborhood of the hotel.

L'Fisher Hotel hides behind a conventional exterior with its window-paned façade and the pretentious awning of its entrance. In fact, the hotel's interior is quite modern unlike the regular provincial hotels. The lobby is pleasantly surprising, consisting of an atrium around which the rooms are located on three levels. Galleries with balustrades decorated with artificial plants link the rooms. A gigantic chandelier and recessed light bulbs illuminate the slightly dark area, making the attractive gray marble flooring sparkle. Comfortable white sofas are available for visitors. Tourists are rare in Bacolod and you will generally encounter businessmen and executives attending seminars.

The carpeted rooms are spacious and very comfortable. These are decorated in a classically elegant fashion in soft, pistachio-green tones with nice wood furniture. The bathrooms, tiled in beige with a large glass-enclosed shower are well-designed. Each suite has its strong point: a view of the swimming pool for the Junior Suites; luxurious bathrooms in red marble for the Senior Executive Suites, and an apartment-sized area for the Royal Suite.

The little swimming pool on the ground floor, though a bit narrow, is quite pleasant after a tour of the town, as there is no nice beach around. The hotel can also organize a round of golf, as well as a tour to the different points of interest in the region.

The hotel has two restaurants—Café Marinero and Don Ricardo in the lobby extension. The coffee shop is open 24 hours and has a warm atmosphere with its pink marble floor and its pretty, green lacquered bamboo furniture. It is here that breakfast is served. Don Ricardo, a more formal restaurant with a quiet air, adjoins the coffee shop. Its décor evokes a Spanish tavern with its brick walls and gray marble floor.

L'FISHER HOTEL

14 and Lacson Streets, Bacolod City, Negros Occidental
Tel   (034) 433-3731 to 39
Fax   (034) 433-0951
E-mail   lfisher@philonline.com

Booking Office in Makati
Unit 1-C Torre de Salcedo Condominium, 184 Salcedo Street, Legaspi Village, Makati City
Tel   892-2119 • 813-7477
Fax   892-3328
E-mail   lfisher@globelines.com.ph

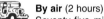

By air (2 hours)
Seventy-five-minute daily flights on Philippine Airlines, Air Philippines or Cebu Pacific from Manila to Bacolod. Fifteen minutes by the hotel's shuttle bus service from Bacolod airport to the hotel.

Superferry (Tel. No.: 528-7979) and Negros Navigation (Tel. No.: 245-4395) also operate ferry service from Manila to Bacolod.

100 Units
72 Deluxe Rooms • 19 Super Deluxe Rooms • 1 Junior Suite • 2 Honeymoon Suites • 1 Senior Executive Suites • 1 Royal Suite • 4 Executive Rooms
All rooms have individually controlled air-conditioning unit, telephone, cable TV, mini-bar, and a bathroom with hot water. Suites have a bathtub and piped-in music.

Indoor Facilities and Services
Medical services • Car rental • Foreign currency exchange

Food and Beverage Outlets
Restaurants: Café Marinero • Don Ricardo
Cuisine Offered: International • Filipino • Continental
Quality: Average

Watersports and Other Activities
Swimming pool • Golf arrangements with nearby golf courses • Tours to Bacolod points of interest

Per room per night inclusive of breakfast

Punta Bulata Resort

Architect Miren Zayco and her husband Bomber, both residents of Bacolod, fell in love with the charming site of Punta Bulata —a peaceful cove of white sand fringed with coconut, palm and papaya trees in the middle of a lawn surrounded by green hills. The welcome is warm and personal. You can reach the place after a two-and-a-half hour drive down a decent road, passing by pleasant countryside composed mainly of sugarcane plantations.

Just before arriving at Punta Bulata, the road meanders through a more hilly landscape with a view of the jagged coastline. From the Punta Bulata cove, you will see the large island of Danjugan quite close by, a smaller neighboring island on the right and on the left, Turtle Island. The white sandy beach in front of Punta is extended by another beach, also part of the resort.

Punta Bulata was once a place where the owners' family came for visits, a fact which explains its rather haphazard style. It was opened only recently as a resort. All the rooms have a view of the sea. The Family Beach suite and the two beach cabanas, completely made of bamboo and *nipa*, are the closest to the beach. The rooms open, through a large sliding door, onto the terrace, provided with blinds and mosquito netting. The spaces are not very roomy though, as large wooden platforms on which the mattresses are placed take up the space.

The Hillside Suite is quite charming. Leaning against a hill and accessible via a metal spiral staircase, it offers a nice view of the cove which you can admire at leisure from the large bamboo terrace nestled in the trees. The room is very romantic and bright with its two bay windows. A huge mirror whose frame is painted in marine motifs occupies a whole wall. The bathroom is particularly big and nice.

The large yellow tent, more suitable for youngsters, has a bathroom and even air-conditioning. The room however, is reduced to mattresses laid out on the floor. Two narrow rooms with bunk beds, in the aluminum Turtle Van at the entrance of the resort are not recommended, as you are sure to feel suffocated.

The meals are served either in the little octagonal *nipa* and bamboo pavilion on the beach, or on your terrace. Deck chairs are available and the shallow waters are ideal for children.

You have several excursion possibilities on the islands in front of the resort. A visit to the marine sanctuary of Danjugan Island may also be organized by the resort, including the permit to visit from Gerry Ledesma, the person in charge of Danjugan. The beach of Hinoba-an is only half an hour away from Punta Bulata Resort.

PUNTA BULATA RESORT

Brgy. Elihan, Cauayan,
Negros Occidental
No phone. Only radio communications.

Booking Office in Bacolod
Tel/Fax (034) 433-5160
E-mail info@puntabulata.com
Web www.puntabulata.com

 By air and land (5 hours)
Seventy-five-minute daily flights on Philippine Airlines, Air Philippines or Cebu Pacific from Manila to Bacolod. Two hours and 45 minutes by car from Bacolod airport to the resort.

Superferry (Tel. No.: 528-7979) and Negros Navigation (Tel. No.: 245-4395) also operate ferry service from Manila to Bacolod.

 21 Units
2 Beach Cabanas (good for 4) • 1 Beach Family Suite (good for 3) • 2 Hillside Suites (good for a couple) • 1 Air-conditioned Tent (good for a group) • 2 Turtle Vans (not recommended) • 1 Beach Casita • 1 Hillside Casita • 1 air-conditioned bus (good for 8) • 10 Spa Rooms
Except for Beach Casita which is fan-cooled, all rooms including the tent have air-conditioning, fan and a bathroom with cold water. Only the Hillside Suites have hot water and a bathtub.

 Food and Beverage Outlets
Restaurant: La Verandah
Cuisine Offered: Filipino • Continental • American
Quality: Average
Bar: El Toco Bar Latino

 Watersports and Other Activities
Beach (white sand) • Snorkeling (at Danjugan Island) • Island hopping • Kayaking
With prior permission from Gerry Ledesma, the Project Manager, a visit to the marine sanctuary project of Danjugan Island can be arranged.

 Per room per night

Siquijor Island

Filipinos often associate Siquijor Island with witchcraft and sorcery. Upon arrival, the visitor is filled with some apprehension and curiosity. The reality is quite reassuring… or disappointing, depending on what you came looking for.

The magic of Siquijor lies in its being a little, timeless island. It takes only one and a half hours to go around the 340-square-kilometer island via the well-maintained main road. On the island, you will only encounter tricycles, motorbikes and a few jeepneys. This makes a pleasant change from the traffic jams of Manila.

MOUNT BADILAAN   The most picturesque part of the island is that which surrounds the only 600-meter high Mount Badilaan. Leaving the coast, you cross an uninhabited countryside dotted by coconut groves and a few beautiful trees. Then the road is reduced to a mud track before it enters the dense 244-hectare national park. On a gray, misty morning, the Stations of the Cross may lead you to the summit. It may look like a magical trail… you expect a goblin or an elf to leap out at any moment. You must register at the DENR office located at the entrance of the road. And with a permit, you can also go trekking and camping in the park.

THE VILLAGE OF SAN ANTONIO   This village near Mount Badilaan is where most of the *mananambals* (medicine men) live. You can ask to meet them, notably Juan Pons, one of the most well-known in Siquijor. At Easter, the medicine men gather certain plants, roots and tree barks for concocting their secret potions. They use these to cure patients throughout the year. The extracted oil is burned on a charcoal fire, then placed near the patients in order to cure them and eliminate negative influences. The oil which can be bought for this purpose must then be applied regularly. Faith in this treatment is necessary for its effectivity.

THE CONVENT OF SAN ISIDRO LABRADOR AND THE CHURCHES   The tour of the island continues on to Lazi, at the convent of San Isidro Labrador constructed in 1891. It is a large building, but unfortunately rundown and disfigured by its corrugated iron roof. In front of the convent is the Church of St. Francis of Assisi with its bell tower dating back to the 1870s. From Lazi and Sandugan, and then at San Juan, the road is not as pretty,

The Convent of San Isidro Labrador — Lazi

strewn with a number of little dwellings. The coast, which you will be able to see from time to time, is lined with mangroves. At San Juan is also an old church with a watchtower.

THE BEACHES The white sand beaches of San Juan and Salang Do-Ong are pretty enough without being exceptional. There is no place for snorkeling but you can go diving from the beach of Paliton, near San Juan Beach on the west coast of Siquijor, at Tonga Point, a little more to the north, or at

Apo Island an hour and a half's drive from here. Be careful before making the crossing to Apo, as the sea can be quite turbulent at certain periods of the year. There is a good dive center managed by a Swiss national— Splash Diving Center—at Tubod, San Juan, not far from Coco Grove Cell No.: (035) 481-5007, e-mail: *siquijor@sea-explorers.com*. It is on San Juan Beach that you will find two of the most pleasant resorts in Siquijor— Coco Grove Beach Resort and Coral Cay Resort and Dive Shop.

Coral Cay Resort and Dive Shop

Coral Cay Resort and Dive shop opened in 1997. It is managed by an American, David Gerdin and his wife, who hails from Siquijor. The resort is very pleasant and well-maintained as it is. But its owner, David, a former building specialist, never run out of ideas for improving it, (particularly the construction of a swimming pool). The resort was constructed with utmost care, keeping eye on details: bright reading lights in the bedrooms, fans that actually work, a safety box in the air-conditioned cottage and a sliding panel separating the terraces of certain semi-detached cottages.

The garden is planted with coconut trees, orchids and hibiscus. The resort has a large beach frontage where the restaurant, a big building completely open to the outdoors, is located. A bar made of bamboo has high stools arranged to face the sea. Green plants in earthenware jars decorate the area. A big, stone barbecue grill nearby promises grilled fish and seafood caught the day itself.

The bamboo cottages on the beach are the most pleasant. On the whole, the cottages are spacious with the exception of the standard ones which are a little smaller. Each differs slightly in style and décor. The floors are made of beautiful wood, the walls blending plaited bamboo and white pebble-washed walls. The beds, covered in gaily colored blankets, are made of intertwined bamboo poles. The bathrooms have white tile floors with gray or beige marble walls. There is also the superb and huge Beach Aircon Deluxe room with its subtle décor and furnishings.

The economy rooms are in a low building at the back of the garden. Although they are small and a bit dark, they are also immaculately clean and functional.

The four-kilometer long gold sand beach in front of the resort is particularly pretty, the hammocks suspended between the palm trees inviting relaxation. The warmth and enthusiasm of the owner is indeed a plus for this resort.

CORAL CAY RESORT AND DIVE SHOP

Solangon, San Juan, Siquijor
Tel (0919) 269-1269
Tel/Fax (035) 481-5024
E-mail *scoralcayresort@yahoo.com*
Web *www.coralcayresort.com*

From Manila, by air, land, sea and land (4 hours on the first morning flight) Seventy-five-minute daily flights on Air Philippines, Cebu Pacific or Philippine Airlines from Manila to Dumaguete. Ten minutes by car from Dumaguete airport to Dumaguete harbor. Forty-five minutes by ferry from Dumaguete to Siquijor Island. There are two ferries: Delta I arriving in Larena (departure at 6 a.m. and 4:30 p.m.) and Delta Car Ferry arriving in Siquijor town (departure at 6 a.m. to 2:30 p.m.). Delta Fast ferries (Tel. No.: (035) 420-0888 • 420-1111). Fifteen minutes by car from Siquijor town, thirty minutes from Larena.

Note: *Transfer from the pier by the resort's own jeepney can be arranged. SuperCat Fast Ferry and Oceanjet occasionally service the Cebu-Larena route. Check shipping line schedules.*

Superferry also operates ferry service from Manila to Dumaguete. For more information, you can call tel. nos. 528-7979 or 528-7171.

13 Units
4 Economy Rooms (with cold water and fan only) • 1 Standard Deluxe Cottage • 2 Garden Duplex Cottage • 2 Beach Duplex Cottage • 2 Beach Deluxe Cottages • 1 Beach Aircon Deluxe (2 adjoining rooms with air-conditioning, hot water and minibar) • 1 Story Duplex
All rooms have hot water (except for the economy rooms) and fan (except for the air-conditioned deluxe cottage).

Indoor Facilities and Services
Mini-gym • Foreign currency exchange • Massage • Library • Billiards • Table tennis

Food and Beverage Outlets
Beachfront restaurant
Cuisine Offered: Seafood • Filipino • Continental

Watersports and Other Activities
Swimming pool • Beach (white sand) • Snorkeling (in other places: Paliton beach but not too good) • Diving (Splash Dive center in Tubod; dives in Paliton Beach, Tonga Point and Apo Island—1 ½ hours with the big *banca* of the resort) • Kayaking • Other boats for hire • Hiking in Mount Badilaan • Mountain biking • Jeepney for island tour

 Per room per night

Coco Grove Beach Resort

Coco Grove Beach Resort is on the edge of a beach, in a beautiful garden enclosed by a pebbled wall. The well-maintained garden is full of coconut trees, bougainvillea, fragrant frangipani trees, philodendrons clinging to knotted tree trunks, ficus trees and hibiscus. Little stone pathways lead to the different buildings.

The cottages are at the back of the beach on a slight elevation obscured by the vegetation. These are constructed from natural materials like wood, bamboo, with roofs and walls made of plaited *nipa*. The interior of each room, though a bit dark, is pleasant with wood flooring and wicker furniture covered with floral printed fabrics. Each one has a terrace with a little bamboo sofa. Although the cottages are semi-detached, the privacy of each one is preserved through bamboo partitions that separate the terraces.

The most pleasant cottage in the resort is the only one on the beach—very spacious, with a drawing room and a second room in the mezzanine. The décor is better planned: mother of pearl lamps, colored wall hangings. It has a nice marble bathroom.

Along the beach are the Garden Bar, the swimming pool and the restaurant. The Garden Bar, with high stools and wicker tables was built with little beach pebbles, its interior is painted in a bright yellow.

The nearby swimming pool is pretty, surrounded by multi-colored bougainvilleas. It is pleasant to stop by here and have a drink as there are lounge chairs and tables scattered around. Above the swimming pool is a stone terrace bordered with frangipani trees and two dove cotes.

The restaurant, which also houses the reception area and the bar, is at the bottom of the garden, directly on the beach. The meals are served on a covered terrace overlooking the sea.

The sea, however, does not have any exceptional coral—just a few little fish—but there are starfish of incredible forms and colors. On the right side of the beach begins the rocky coast with small coves to explore.

COCO GROVE BEACH RESORT

Tubod, San Juan, Siquijor
Tel   (035) 481-5008
Fax   (035) 481-5006

Booking Office in Dumaguete
Paradise Travel Center
3 Noblefranca Street,
Dumaguete City, Negros Oriental
Tel/Fax (035) 422-9663 • 225-5490
E-mail   paradise@glinesnx.com.ph

From Manila, by air, land, sea and land (4 hours on the first morning flight)   Seventy-five-minute daily flights on Air Philippines, Cebu Pacific or Philippine Airlines from Manila to Dumaguete. Ten minutes by car from Dumaguete airport to Dumaguete harbor. Forty-five minutes by ferry from Dumaguete to Siquijor Island. There are two ferries: Delta I arriving in Larena (at 6 a.m. and 7pm.) and Delta Car Ferry arriving in Siquijor town (at 8:30 a.m. and 12 p.m.). Delta Fast ferries (Tel. No.: (035) 420-8888 • 420-1111). Thirty minutes by car from Larena.

Note: *Transfer from the pier by the resort's own jeepney can be arranged. SuperCat Fast Ferry and Oceanjet occasionally service the Cebu-Larena route. Check shipping line schedules.*

Superferry also operates ferry service from Manila to Dumaguete. For more information, you can call tel. nos. 528-7979 or 528-7171.

25 Units
Main: 2 Beachside Rooms • 1 Orchid Villa-Superior Family Room • 1 Deluxe Room • 1 Family Deluxe Room • 4 Deluxe Rooms (hillside) • 2 Standard Rooms (hillside); **Sunset Beach:** 6 Sunset Family Rooms • 6 Sunset Deluxe Rooms • 1 Bougainvilla-Family Room (beachfront) • 1 Hibiscus-Family Room (farthest & no air-conditioning)
All rooms have air-conditioning, with private marble bathroom with hot shower, with minibar (except in standard rooms) and with private veranda.

Indoor Facilities and Services
Table tennis • Billiards

Food and Beverage Outlets
Restaurants: Sunset Restaurant
Cuisine Offered: Filipino • International • Seafood
Bar: Cocktail Restaurant

Watersports and Other Activities
Swimming pool • Beach (white sand) • Splash Dive center in Tubod (dives in Paliton Beach, Tonga Point and Apo Island (1 ½ hours with the big *banca* of the resort) • Snorkeling (Paliton Beach) • Kayaking • Windsurfing • Other boats for hire • Trampoline • Motorcycling • Tours to neighboring areas (waterfalls, mountains, caves) • Soft-top Wrangler jeeps for hire • Siquijor tour (½ day or full day) by jeepney • Trekking in Bandilaan National Park

 Per room per night

Bohol

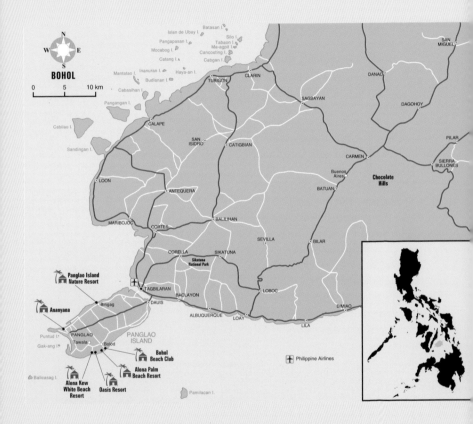

Map labels (clockwise / by region):

SAN MIGUEL, DANAO, DAGOHOY, PILAR, SIERRA BULLONES, CARMEN, Chocolate Hills, Buenos Aires, BATUAN, BILAR, LOBOC, DIMIAO, LILA, LOAY, ALBUQUERQUE, BACLAYON, DAUIS, TAGBILARAN, SIKATUNA, Sikatuna National Park, CORELLA, SEVILLA, BALILIHAN, CORTES, MARIBOJOC, ANTEQUERA, LOON, CATIGBIAN, SAN ISIDRO, CALAPE, CABILAO I., Sandingan I., Pangangan I., Cabasihan I., Mantatao I., Inanuran I., Budlanan I., Haya-an I., TUBIGON, CLARIN, SAGBAYAN, Islan de Ubay I., Batasan I., Pangapasan I., Silo I., Mocabog I., Tabaon I., Ma-agpit I., Catang I., Cancosting I., Cabgan I.

BOHOL

N W E S

0 5 10 km

Panglao Island Nature Resort

Ananyana

Bingag

Puntud I.
Gak-ang I.

Tawala

PANGLAO

Bolod

PANGLAO ISLAND

Bohol Beach Club

Alona Palm Beach Resort

Alona Kew White Beach Resort

Oasis Resort

Balicasag I.

Pamilacan I.

Philippine Airlines

Climate   Dry from December to May, coolest from December to February, warmest from March to May

Typhoons   From August to October, though very infrequent

272

Bohol

The Strait of Bohol separates the province of Bohol from Cebu. It is an oval-shaped island with 3,865 square kilometers of undulating, verdant land with a few remaining forests. Here, life moves at a snail's pace to the rhythm of nature. Tagbilaran, the capital, is an equally quiet town, unlike Cebu, its more cosmopolitan neighbor.

A long coastal road of 160 kilometers borders the island. The distances between the different points of interest are never very great, so even if your time is limited, you can see quite a lot by simply planning your excursions. You can visit old churches, go diving, collect seashells or explore the countryside.

THE ISLAND OF PANGLAO *(30 minutes from Tagbilaran)* This island is connected to Bohol by bridge. It is on the south coast that most of the resorts are located, notably along the famous white sandy beach of Alona. These are resorts that cater to divers and have a casual ambiance.

Near the little market town of Panglao is a shop with an impressive collection of seashells. Some are rare specimens that will interest collectors. Most of the exquisite pieces are for export.

THE DIVING SPOTS Fifteen dive sites may be counted in this region, some of which are quite far from Alona Beach. The closest ones are the Alona House Reef and Arco Point, near Bohol Beach Club. Further away is the marine sanctuary of Balicasag Island and its famous black coral (45 minutes); Duljo Point (30–50 minutes); Pamilacan Island, known for its manta rays (45–60 minutes); Cabilao Island and its hammerhead sharks (3 hours). Balicasag and Cabilao are considered to be among the most exceptional dive sites. On Balicasag is a small resort run by the Department of

Chocolate Hills

Laoay River

Tourism. For diving in Cabilao, it is preferable to stay at the resort of Inanuran, only 30 minutes from the site.

THE SIKATUNA NATIONAL PARK AND THE TARSIER *(Corella, 10 kilometers from Tagbilaran)* This little park contains a well-preserved forest not easy to explore, as there are few accessible tracks. The tarsier, an endangered species that lives in the forest, is a curious little primate: a tiny ball of fur with enormous round eyes. These are timid, nocturnal animals and you can have the opportunity of observing them if you go at night to the Study Center at the Department of Environment and Natural Resources in Barrio Cancatac, a few kilometers from Corella.

THE LAOAY RIVER *(about 15 kilometers east of Tagbilaran)* It is pleasant, towards the end of the afternoon after a visit to the Chocolate Hills, to stop on the road going back to Tagbilaran and take a motorboat trip on the Laoay between Loboc and Busay Falls. You can see the caged tarsiers near the wharf.

THE BASKET MARKET OF ANTEQUERA *(about 19 kilometers north of Tagbilaran)* This picturesque market is held very early on Sunday mornings and you will miss the best part if you arrive after 9 a.m. You will be astounded by the variety of baskets on sale. These range from miniature baskets, stacked on top of each other, decorative jars, and other more traditional and useful articles. After the market, you can refresh yourself under the waterfalls of Mag-Aso, two kilometers away.

THE OLD CHURCHES Bohol has a number of coral stone churches constructed and renovated by the Recollects between 1768 and 1855. The triple arched portico is a characteristic of these churches with sober façades.

BACLAYON CHURCH *(7 kilometers southeast of Tagbilaran, on the road to Loboc and*

Baclayon Church

Carmen) Considered to be the oldest stone church in the country, it was constructed in 1595 by the Jesuits and renovated by the Recollects. This is a truly magnificent church with a fortified bell tower. You cannot fail to admire the gilded altars that are its crowning glory.

LOBOC CHURCH *(15 kilometers east of Tagbilaran, to be combined with a visit of the River Laoay)* This church possesses a fresco depicting the floods that hit the town in 1876. These were painted by an artist from Cebu. The belfry is separate from the church.

LOON CHURCH *(20 minutes northwest of Tagbilaran, to be combined with Antequera)* The church of Loon (1855) is considered to be one of the most beautifully constructed churches by the Recollects in Bohol. It has two bell towers which make up the integral part of its elegant baroque façade.

CHOCOLATE HILLS *(2 hours from Tagbilaran)* More than 1,000 hillocks, sometimes brown, sometimes green, depending on the season, lift their rotund and magical silhouettes from a plateau in the center of Bohol. Rings of trees in the middle of prairies surround them. It is a rural and peaceful landscape to be discovered on foot. Many trails in the countryside lead to the heart of these hills, sometimes crossing small woods inhabited by multicolored butterflies. It is best to park your car at the parking area of the Chocolate Hills Complex in Buenos Aires, on top of the hill. There is a small hotel, as well as a terrace restaurant looking out to the hills. It is, in fact, the best place to survey the hills in their totality—unless the more courageous actually climbs one of them! The view is splendid, especially at the break of dawn, when a light coat of mist floats at their feet—or toward twilight. From the complex, you can simply go down on foot up the first track on the left. The Chocolate Hills can be part of an excursion but, in fact, they deserve to have one whole day reserved for their exploration.

Note: *All these excursions can be organized by Tagbilaran's Office of Tourism, by the hotels presented in this guide or through Danny Nazareno, an independent guide who can be contacted at Cell No.: (0921) 327-2977.*

Bohol's tarsiers

Bohol Beach Club

The big attraction of the Bohol Beach Club is its setting in a vast wooded area, far from the animation of Alona Beach and its particularly superb beach stretching over four kilometers of white sand. It is the only resort in Panglao that has a really attractive beach, as the frontage of some resorts is often reduced to narrow strips of sand. The resort belongs to the Tambuli Resorts that also own the Tambuli Beach Club and Villa in Mactan, Cebu.

After crossing the garden, you enter a large building with an impressive *nipa* ceiling that houses the lobby and the restaurant. Constructed with a high bamboo framework, the building opens onto the swimming pool, and further on, to the sea. To the right of the reception area, a sandy track lined with large clay jars, is shaded by a magnificent arbor of fuchsia bougainvillea, up to the bungalows.

The *nipa*-roofed bungalows lie side-by-side, facing the beach. Each one has three or four rooms. Since they were renovated, they have unfortunately lost their rusticity, the white walls, marble floors and modern beige furniture giving them a rather cold look. The only local material is the woven *nipa* ceiling. Nevertheless, the rooms are comfortable and bright due to the large bay windows. Each room has its own private terrace, separated from that of its neighbor by a partition. You can get a glimpse of the sea through the palm trees.

The main swimming pool with a Jacuzzi in the middle of a tiled terrace facing the sea is a very pleasant area. Not far from here is the beach with its *nipa* parasols, deck chairs and hammocks where you can lie in complete tranquillity.

A lot of activities are proposed by the Aqua Sports Club, one of which is diving. Arco Point, a dive site, and the coral reef of Alona are less than 10 minutes away by *banca*. You can also rent a taxi for the day with a driver-cum-guide to visit the many interesting spots of Bohol.

BOHOL BEACH CLUB

Panglao Island, Bohol
Tel (038) 411-5222 to 24
Fax (038) 411-5226
Web *www.tambuli.com*

Booking Office in Manila
Tambuli Beach Resorts
Suite 1401 Victoria Building,
U.N. Avenue, Manila
Tel 522-2302 to 03
Fax 522-2304
E-mail *reservations@tambuli.com*

 1. By air, land, sea and land (5 hours on the first morning flight) Seventy-five-minute daily flights on Philippine Airlines, Air Philippines or Cebu Pacific from Manila to Cebu. Twenty minutes by car from Cebu Mactan airport to the SuperCat Terminal. From Cebu to Tagbilaran, one and a half hours by SuperCat Fast Ferry Corporation (Tel. No.: (032) 234-9600). Two daily services (at 8 a.m. and 4:30 p.m.) or by Oceanjet (Tel. No.: (032) 255-7560). Four daily services (at 6 a.m. and last trip at 5:30 p.m.) Thirty minutes by car from Tagbilaran pier to the resort.

2. By air and land (2 hours) Seventy-minute daily flights on Philippine Airlines from Manila to Tagbilaran. Thirty minutes from Tagbilaran airport to the resort.

Note: *Transfer from Tagbilaran airport/pier can be arranged by the resort.*

Superferry (Tel. No.: 528-7979) also operates ferry service from Manila to Cebu and Manila to Tagbilaran; Negros Navigation (Tel. No.: 245-4395) from Manila to Tagbilaran.

 88 Units
36 Beachfront Standard Rooms • 20 Superior Poolside Rooms • 24 Superior Beachfront Rooms • 6 Executive Suites • 1 Two-bedroom Family Suite • 1 Premium Suite
All rooms have a bathroom with hot water, air conditioning and a small terrace.

Indoor Facilities and Services
Babysitting • Car rental • Foreign currency exchange • Massage • Business center • Medical services • Table tennis

 Food and Beverage Outlets
Restaurants: Kalubihan Restaurant
Bars: Coco Bar Café • Pool Bar 2
Cuisine Offered: Filipino • International
Quality: Average

Watersports and Other Activities
Swimming pools with Jacuzzi • Beach (white sand) • Snorkeling (60 meters off shore) • Island hopping • Dolphin- and whale-watching • Diving (see Bohol's points of interest) • Kayaking • Other boats for hire • Tours to Bohol points of interest • Tennis

Per room per night

Alona Kew White Beach Resort

Alona Kew White Beach resort is on Alona Beach, along with many other medium-sized resorts set in a very congenial atmosphere. If you enjoy diving, this is a good place to stay. Moreover, the resort is very comfortable and its cottages have been fashioned with excellent taste.

The property is not very large but the owners have tried to make the most of it by maintaining the coconut trees and by paving the flower-lined alleys—along which the bungalows have been built—with beach pebbles.

The bungalows are quite spacious, but do not have a direct view of the sea as they are laid one after the other.

They are built with woven bamboo and have *nipa* roofs. The interiors are cozy and warm; the pale wooden paneled walls contrast well with the nice wooden furniture and *capiz* lamps. In front of each bungalow is a little terrace hemmed in by bougainvilleas. Apart from the bungalows, the resort also has rooms, though not as charming, in a two-story building behind the beach.

You enter the resort through an attractive arch and you can see, near the reception, the large, pleasant circular restaurant which is open on all sides. On fine nights, you will surely prefer to dine at the tables that are set directly on the beach facing the sea. Candles create a romantic atmosphere and you can ask the musicians to come and serenade you. The cuisine and the ambiance of the resort during mealtimes are so well known that it attracts clients from the neighboring hotels.

The white sandy beach in front of the resort is quite narrow; a few deck chairs are set on the grass. It is enjoyable to walk along Alona Beach and see the many handicrafts stalls selling souvenirs or to have a drink at one of the numerous little resorts that border it.

For more active recreation, the resort can arrange diving expeditions for you or a visit to the various attractions of Bohol.

Note: *Alona Kew White Beach Resort's next-door neighbor, Oasis Resort, is a good alternative. It has 6 duplex cottages, which comprise of 12 rooms. All the cottages are made out of bamboo and wood, with nipa as roofing. Two single beds and a pullout bed are provided in each room. Each room has a veranda overlooking the thick foliage and the swimming pool. It also has a restaurant, which offers Filipino and European cuisines. The resort offers safari trips to Apo Island and Siquijor; there is also a dive center.*

Oasis Resort
*Alona Beach, Tawala,
Panglao Island, Bohol
Tel/Fax (038) 502-9083
E-mail* seaquest@seaquestdivecenter.com
Web www.seaquestdivecenter.com

Oasis Resort

ALONA KEW WHITE BEACH RESORT

Tawala, Panglao Island, Bohol
Tel (038) 502-9042 • 502-9027
Fax (038) 502-9029
E-mail *kewbeach@mozcom.com*
Web *www.alonakew.com*

 1. By air, land, sea and land (5 hours with the first morning flight) Seventy-five-minute daily flights on Philippine Airlines, Air Philippines or Cebu Pacific from Manila to Cebu. Twenty minutes by car from Cebu Mactan airport to the SuperCat Terminal. From Cebu to Tagbilaran, one and a half hours by SuperCat Fast Ferry Corporation (Tel. No.: (032) 234-9600). Two daily services (at 8:00 a.m. and 4:30 p.m.) or by Oceanjet (Tel. No.: (032) 255-7560). Four daily services (at 6:00 a.m. and last trip at 5:30 p.m.) Thirty minutes by car from Tagbilaran pier to the resort.

2. By air and land (2 hours) Seventy-minute daily flights on Philippine Airlines from Manila to Tagbilaran. Thirty minutes from Tagbilaran airport to the resort.

Note: *Transfer from Tagbilaran airport/pier can be arranged by the resort.*

Superferry (Tel. No.: 528-7979) also operates ferry service from Manila to Cebu and Manila to Tagbilaran; Negros Navigation (Tel. No.: 245-4395) from Manila to Tagbilaran.

 50 Units 3 Suites (air-conditioned) • 27 Superior Deluxe Rooms (air-conditioned) • 3 Bungalow Cottages (fan) • 10 Standard Rooms (fan) • 6 Standard Rooms (air-conditioned) • 1 Executive Room (air-conditioned)
All rooms have a bathroom with hot/cold water.

Indoor Facilities and Services
Tour desk • Car rental • Foreign currency exchange • Babysitting • Massage

 Food and Beverage Outlets Restaurant: Alona Kew White Beach Restaurant
Cuisine Offered: International • Filipino • Seafood
Quality: Good

 Watersports and Other Activities Beach (white sand) • Snorkeling (in other places) • Dive shop • Island hopping • Swimming pool • Kayaking • Other boats for hire • Fishing • Sunset cruise • Tours to Bohol points of interest • Mountain biking

 Per room per night inclusive of breakfast

Panglao Island Nature Resort

A nature-friendly retreat far from the clutter of Manila is Panglao Island Nature Resort—20 minutes from the airport of Tagbilaran City in Bohol. It is built on 14 hectares of tropical allure, a secluded spot where you can bask in the warmth of the sunshine and be cooled by the turquoise blue water that surrounds the island.

The resort's structures were designed to adapt to the natural features of the terrain and even enhance its surroundings, very pronounced in the thatched roof bungalows built alongside the mountain. From a good vantage, they can even be seen looking like the world-famous Chocolate Hills of Bohol. Similarly, the resort's Infinity Pool seems to merge with the sea from a certain angle despite its being about 15 meters above sea level.

All the different rooms in the resort, while featuring luxurious amenities, also have that natural and local touch, especially in its furniture and fixtures—small patches of greenery are in the bathrooms and even the closet and drawer handles are made of guava tree twigs. Among the interesting modern features in the bungalows, however, are their outdoor Jacuzzis.

The resort has practically very little beach to offer. Nonetheless, it has white sand but not as fine and as white as that in Boracay. The resort itself was built on top of a cliff. To get to the small stretch of beach, you need to go down some steps, some 15 meters below.

The resort offers numerous aqua and non-aqua daytime activities and may also arrange tours of the different places of interest found in the islands of Panglao and Bohol.

At night, guests can be ferried to a man-made island where drinks are served and music is played. You would have to ride a boat to get to the man-made island, though. Curiously, a huge rope which hangs between the two islands is sometimes employed to pull your boat to the man-made facility from the main island instead of having it rowed. The experience is also rather awkward since you actually see an electric line also making the crossing to supply power to the unique entertainment center.

The resort has a restaurant offering Asian cuisine. An elevated gazebo which can house 20 people is available for guests to have their meals in while enjoying a spectacular view of the sea. Business functions are sometimes held in the conference facilities of the resort.

PANGLAO ISLAND NATURE RESORT

Bingag, Dauis, Bohol
Tel (038) 411-2599 • 411-5875
(038) 411-5878 • 411-5982
Fax (038) 411-5866 • 411-5879
E-mail metroctr@mozcom.com
Web www.panglaoisland.com

Booking Office in Quezon City
1 Sacred Heart Street,
Horseshoe Village, Quezon City
Tel/Fax 724-0538

 By air and land (5 hours)
Seventy-five-minute daily flights on Philippine Airlines, Air Philippines or Cebu Pacific from Manila to Cebu. Twenty minutes by car from Cebu Mactan airport to the SuperCat Terminal. From Cebu to Tagbilaran, one and a half hours by SuperCat Fast Ferry Corporation (Tel. No.: (032) 234-9600). Two daily services (at 8:00 a.m. and 4:30 p.m.) or by Oceanjet (Tel. No.: (032) 255-7560). Four daily services (at 6:00 a.m. and last trip at 5:30 p.m.) Thirty minutes by car from Tagbilaran pier to the resort.

Superferry (Tel. No.: 528-7979) also operates ferry service from Manila to Cebu and Manila to Tagbilaran; Negros Navigation (Tel. No.: 245-4395) from Manila to Tagbilaran.

 48 Units
18 Bungalows • 6 Deluxe Rooms • 12 Superior Duplex Rooms • 12 Superior Quadruplex Rooms
Each guest room has a veranda with drying rack, coffee table and chairs, and is equipped with air-conditioning, satellite cable TV, IDD/NDD telephone facility, refrigerator, in-room coffee and tea, private bathroom (bathtub in Deluxe rooms, outdoor Jacuzzi in Bungalow), hair dryer, personal safe.

Indoor Facilities and Services
Gym • Sauna • Jacuzzi • Foreign currency exchange • Car rental service • Babysitting • Massage

 Food and Beverage Outlets
Restaurants: Panglao Island Restaurant • Sea View Gazebo • Garden View Gazebo
Cuisine Offered: Filipino • Continental • Oriental

 Watersports and Other Activities
Snorkeling • Diving • Kayaking • Windsurfing • Mountain biking • Children's playground

 Per room per night inclusive of breakfast

Ananyana Beach Resort

The small road leading to Ananyana Beach Resort, amidst lush vegetation, does let you expect a natural setting, with a resort featuring local materials such as bamboo, *nipa* or *sawali*. But as you pass the wooden gate, adorned with the fertility symbol that is the logo of Ananyana, you reach a place that is also both exotic and romantic.

The garden resembles a tamed jungle forest with its tall plants, strewn with red and orange flowers, where earthen jars and *anitos,* the carved figures of forefathers and spirits, are scattered. Vegetation reaches the border of the appealing, small white sand beach.

Set in the midst of the garden, as in a glade, are the few buildings of this intimate resort, housing the reception area, the restaurant, the dive shop and the suites. All have thatched, two-level roofs. The adjoining swimming pool is entirely made of natural stones, and its clear water is inviting and soothing with bluish-green hues, whose sight induces a feeling of calmness.

One building houses the eight suite rooms, four in each of the two levels. The façade of the first story is covered with stone and the second with wood. Each room has a balcony, whose flooring is, together with the interior area, made of warm reddish Vigan tiles. Shutters are made of wood. The simple but elegant native furniture comprises a big bamboo bed and a wooden bureau-cum-dresser, while the bathroom makes use of the same stone and wood theme that permeates the resort.

Two family suites share another small building with a thatched roof, and have the same red tiles, bamboo, stone and wood materials as the other structures, with wood and *capiz* shutters that diffuse the light and allow a warm glow in. Each suite has a living room with a spacious divan that can be used as a bed, and a mezzanine with the bedroom and its king-size bed. The suites have a garden; open-air bathroom covered with natural stones, loose pebbles and bamboo slats, decorated with plants and earthen jars. In those jars, water is stored and kept cool, for a refreshing shower on a hot summer day. It is pleasant to take a bath while stargazing under the very clear skies of Bohol.

The open-air restaurant, set beside the pool, has a view of the beach as well, with fresh flowers decorating each table. The Asian fusion-cuisine food is simple, but the restaurant prides itself of choosing ingredients for their freshness, spicing them with local herbs and ingredients.

ANANYANA BEACH RESORT

Doljo Beach, Panglao Island
Tel (038) 502-8101
E-mail info@ananyana.com
Web www.ananyana.com

 By air (3 hours)
Seventy-minute daily flights on Philippine Airlines from Manila to Tagbilaran. Thirty minutes from Tagbilaran airport to the resort. Another 20 minutes of paved road ride by car to the resort.

By sea and land (2 ½ hours)
From Cebu to Tagbilaran, one and a half hours by SuperCat Fast Ferry Corporation (Tel. No.: (032) 234-9600). Two daily services (at 8:00 a.m. and 4:30 p.m.) or by Oceanjet (Tel. No.: (032) 255-7560). Four daily services (at 6:00 a.m. and last trip at 5:30 p.m.) Another 20 minutes paved road ride by car to the resort.

Superferry (Tel. No.: 528-7979) and Negros Navigation (Tel. No.: 245-4395) also operate ferry service from Manila to Tagbilaran.

 10 Units
8 Suites • 2 Family Suites
All suites have air-conditioning, minibar, spacious bathroom and either a balcony or a garden terrace.

 Food and Beverage Outlets
Asian fusion style open-air restaurant

Indoor Facilities and Other Services
Internet access • Motorbike rentals • Babysitting • Massage

 Watersports and Other Activities
Beach (white sand) • Swimming pool • Diving • Snorkeling • Kayaking • Beach volleyball • Island hopping • Dolphin watching • Sunset cruising and tours to the nearby Chocolate Hills, Hinagdanan Cave and Magaso Falls

 Per room per night

Alona Palm Beach Resort and Restaurant

Alona Palm Beach Resort and Restaurant is a 2.5-hectare resort, part of a sprawling 6-hectare property, with the rest of the property being planted with coconut trees, mango trees and other fruit-bearing trees. The pleasant beach across Alona is wide and well-maintained, raked every morning; unlike with other resorts in Panglao, it is a wide, clear expanse free of any obstacle and con-

struction. A winding walkway extends from the resort to the fringes of the beach filled with coconut trees. The lush garden completes the impression that natural beauty has been given prime importance by the owners, Angie, who stems from Bohol and her husband, Swiss architect Marcel Brunner.

Tables dot the perimeter of the big, irregularly shaped swimming pool, which is also highlighted by a sunken bar. On one side of the bar at pool-level, guests may enjoy their drinks sitting on stools while dipped in the refreshing waters.

The 12 tastefully designed villas of the resort consist of one big and spacious room, with an entrance at the back and a veranda in front. In the front-row villas, the king-sized bed is placed diagonally across the room so that it faces the French window of the veranda, thus offering a view of the pool or the garden. Modern architectural designs play with a Filipino motif, and it is interesting to note the use of *sinamay* (abaca fiber) weave work to border frames in the rooms and tiles and local wood in the bathrooms. The rooms have modern amenities, including satellite TV and Internet facilities.

The restaurant, amidst the greenery and lush vegetation of the Alona Palm Beach, is one of the attractions of the resort, with both varied and tasteful international cuisine, and attentive service. We enjoyed the creamy but light Cream of Tomato soup, the tasty and plentiful Fettuccini Marinara, the perfectly cooked Peppered Steak served with Penne; and the huge, colorful, almost crunchy Apple Pie, with its cream and fruit toppings, was just sinful. Even local non-guests of the resort, from as far as Tagbilaran, patronize this restaurant, which is one of their favorite dinner venues.

ALONA PALM BEACH RESORT AND RESTAURANT

Alona Beach, Tawala,
Panglao Island, Bohol
Tel   (038) 502-9141
Fax   (038) 502-9142
E-mail *info@alonapalmbeach.com*
Web   *www.alonapalmbeach.com*

 1. By air and land (5 hours)
Seventy-five-minute daily flights on Philippine Airlines, Air Philippines or Cebu Pacific from Manila to Cebu. Twenty minutes by car from Cebu Mactan airport to the SuperCat Terminal. From Cebu to Tagbilaran, one and a half hours by SuperCat Fast Ferry Corporation (Tel. No.: (032) 234-9600). Two daily services (at 8 a.m. and 4:30 p.m.) or by Oceanjet (Tel. No.: (032) 255-7560). Four daily services (at 6 a.m. and last trip at 5:30 p.m.) Thirty minutes by car from Tagbilaran pier to the resort.

2. By air and land (2 hours) Seventy-minute daily flights on Philippine Airlines from Manila to Tagbilaran. Thirty minutes from Tagbilaran airport to the resort.

Note: *Transfer from Cebu Mactan airport can be arranged by the resort.*

Superferry (Tel. No.: 528-7979) also operates ferry service from Manila to Cebu and Manila to Tagbilaran; Negros Navigation (Tel. No.: 245-4395) from Manila to Tagbilaran.

 12 Units
6 Luxury Villas (with 1 king-size bed each) • 6 Luxury Villas (with 2 double-size beds each)
All rooms have large bathrooms with hot water. Other facilities includes air-conditioning, ceiling fan, satellite TV, telephone with data port, minibar, tea/coffee maker.

Indoor Facilities and Services
Massage

 Food and Beverage Outlets
Restaurant: Alona Palm Restaurant
Cuisine Offered: International • Filipino
Quality: Good and plentiful

Watersports and Other Activities
Beach (white sand) • Swimming pool (big) • Kayaking • Badminton • Miniature golf • Table tennis • Local tours (countryside, whale and dolphin watching) • Mountain biking

 Per room per night inclusive of breakfast

Samar and Leyte

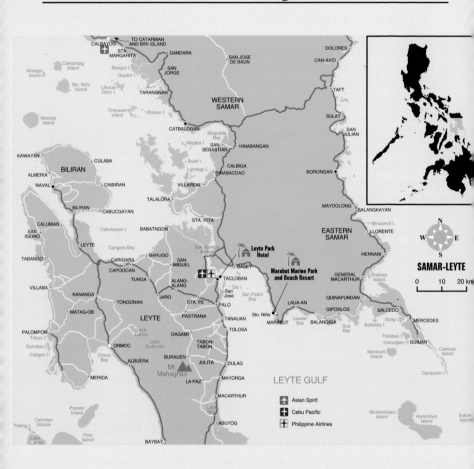

Leyte

Climate   **Tacloban and major part of Leyte:** Rainfall more or less evenly distributed throughout the year
South East coast: No dry season with a very pronounced maximum rainfall from November to January

Typhoons   November to December

Samar

Climate   **West coast:** Rainfall more or less evenly distributed throughout the yea
East coast: No dry season with a very pronounced maximum rainfall from November to December

Typhoons   **South Samar:** November to December
North Samar: June to December

Samar and Leyte

Samar (13,429 square kilometers) and Leyte (6,268 square kilometers) are two large islands that make up Eastern Visayas, slightly developed and still very forested. It is a region for forest and trekking enthusiasts. The point of entry to the sites on these two islands is Tacloban, the provincial capital of Leyte. It is a bustling town linked by daily flights to Manila. Once in Tacloban, it is easy to go to the neighboring island of Samar by crossing the San Juanico Bridge, a spectacular winding route of two kilometers.

The Leyte Park Hotel in Tacloban is a good place from which to discover this magnificent region relatively untouched by tourism and, if given advanced notice, it can organize individual and group tours. The principal excursions organized by this hotel are described here. Note that the Leyte Park Hotel was the local liaison during the ELF Authentic Adventure endurance test in 1999.

Samar

SOHOTON NATURAL BRIDGE NATIONAL PARK *(one day)* The national park covers a surface area of 840 hectares of well-preserved forest. The *banca* leaves the pier of Leyte Park Hotel. On the way, you need to get a permit from the office of the DNR in Basey. The trip to the caves is a superb two-and-a-half hour crossing through the *nipa*-bordered river. You come across little fishermen's dwellings —vividly painted wooden boats— and kingfishers, herons and egrets if you make the trip very early in the morning. At a certain point in the river, the shallow waters make it impossible to continue in the

banca which you must leave for a smaller boat. You are hemmed in by high rocky walls before arriving at the spectacular caves of Panhulugan, composed of several chambers with stalactites and stalagmites. One of the rangers of the little post at the entrance of the national park will give you a guided tour of these caves armed with a torch. A few trails have been cleared into the interior of the jungle and one of them takes you to the cave of Sohoton. Here you can see the natural bridge of Sohoton, a big limestone archway spanning the river. You can go down to the river and bathe in its cool, refreshing waters.

THE RAPIDS OF THE CALBIGA RIVER AND THE WATERFALLS OF LULUGAYAN *(one day)* The town of Calbiga is one and a half hours from Tacloban, north of the town of Basey, on the west coast of Samar. The waterfalls, though only 15 meters high, permit rafting along 12 kilometers. The life along the river is the main attraction of the excursion.

Marabut, Samar

Mahagnao Volcano Mountain Park, Leyte

THE DISCOVERY OF SAMAR BY JEEPNEY *(two to ten days)* The Leyte Park Resort offers an original way to discover Samar—by jeepney for two persons with a driver who also acts as a guide. After a night in one of the little guesthouses offering basic amenities, you begin the discovery of a region wonderfully untamed. You need at least 10 days to considerably discover what Samar has to offer. The difficulty is that the road between Catarman on the northwest coast and Borongan on the southeast coast is not yet completed. If you want to see both coasts, you need to go back the way you came. For the trip to the southeastern coast, you can spend the night at Guiuan, then at Borongan. For the trip to the northwestern coast, you can stop at Calbayog and Catarman.

BORONGAN *(three days and two nights)* From Tacloban, a four-hour trip by car brings you to the village of Borongan on the southeast coast of Samar. You cross green ricefields interspersed with forest and beautiful mangroves border the beaches. The night is spent at the Borongan Pensionne House of Father Ryan Lopez. The next day, you can go trekking in the jungle on one of the tracks used by the ELF Authentic Adventure endurance test. You can reach the island of Makati in 45 minutes and snorkel or go back up the Suribao River by boat, leaving from the mouth of the river. In one hour, you arrive at the waterfalls and can bathe in deliciously cool, clear waters.

GUIUAN AND THE SOUTHERN ISLANDS OF SAMAR *(three days minimum)* From the Tanghay Pensionne House, you cut across the surrounding islands with beautiful white sandy shores and turquoise-blue lagoons. Some of these are the island of Limasawa with its good diving sites, the superb and serene Suluan island and Homonhon where Magellan landed in March 1521 after a four-month voyage.

CALBAYOG *(two and a half hours from Tacloban, 2 days)* You can visit the waterfalls of Blanca Aurora at San Jorge and the bizarre ruins of the village constructed by the Spanish, now overrun by nature. The stopover is Eduardo's Hotel.

CATARMAN *(five hours from Tacloban, two days)* The coastal road between Calbayog and Catarman is very striking because of its scenic beauty. You can stay at the Villa Alvado Resort. The high point of the trip is the island of Biri, a part of the islands of Balicuatro at the northern tip of Samar, facing the Pacific. This island is composed of fantastic rock formations that are not found anywhere else in the Philippines. Nature has created a strange unreal world, the winds sculpting wave formations, gigantic mushrooms and amphitheaters in sandstone.

Note: Asian Spirit flies to Catarman and Calbayog from Manila

Leyte

RED BEACH AND PALO *(12 kilometers from Tacloban)* It is difficult not to mention the island that General MacArthur made famous during the Second World War. He and his troops landed here to capture the important military base held by the Japanese. Many Japanese tourists, as well as Americans and Filipinos, visit this site and the commemorative monument erected here.

THE ISLAND OF BILIRAN *(one or ideally, two days)* Biliran, north of Leyte, is a mountainous island with a summit of 1,300 meters. It is reached after three hours of driving from Tacloban and has numerous waterfalls in the midst of dense forest where you can go trekking. Half an hour from Biliran is the island of Maripipi where you can go snorkeling.

MAHAGNAO VOLCANO MOUNTAIN PARK *(one hour 30 minutes from Tacloban, two days)* This park at an altitude of 400 meters is located 66 kilometers from Tacloban. The Leyte Park Resort transports you here with a guide, camping material and provisions. You must have at least a weekend to fully explore the area and the numerous hiking trails. The camp is at the edge of a lake with green, opaque waters surrounded by virgin forest. At night, the cries and calls of the jungle creatures lull you to sleep. A few fishermen's dwellings have been constructed around the lake where you can canoe. Quite a few well-marked tracks go into the dense forest. You can climb up the volcano above the lake where you will discover hot water springs. This will take about two hours.

Leyte Park Hotel

Leyte Park Hotel, the largest hotel in Tacloban, occupies a prime spot on a slight promontory facing the bay of San Pedro. From here, you can get a glimpse of Samar Island on the opposite side. An energetic, spirited atmosphere often reigns here, as the hotel is the venue for numerous conferences and is the place where local residents go for the restaurants, bars and discotheque.

You can take part in several activities and excursions from here. It is notably the jump-off point for Marabut Marine Park and Beach Resort and the Sohoton National Park. If given sufficient notice, the resort can organize camping in Lake Magnano, a jeepney tour of Samar, or a ride in a catamaran to discover the coastal areas.

The hotel is made up of two large three-story buildings. The first of these buildings houses the reception area with its high bamboo ceiling. It is huge and very pleasant, and it opens directly onto the outdoor area. You can relax here, comfortably installed in one of the wicker sofas surrounded by green plants. A few steps lead to the bar and the restaurant—The Verandah Café—which offers a good view of the swimming pool and the sea through large bay windows. The restaurant has coconut wood furniture designed in Cebu. The other parts of the building are used as conference halls.

The second building, also accessible from the reception, houses the rooms, all of which look onto the sea, with their little terraces. Dreary long corridors lead to the rooms, but the antique furniture that decorates them is quite attractive. It is better to book in the recently renovated rooms, as the others are a bit lackluster with their red carpeting and dilapidated furniture. The new ones are quite pleasant with beautiful coconut wood floors, white walls contrasting with a bamboo plaited ceiling, functional bamboo furniture and all other required comforts. The little adjoining bathrooms are tiled in white and have bathtubs. The interior decoration and furnishing of the spacious Executive Rooms are a little more imaginative and stylish.

Other rooms are housed in cottages, which can be found in the garden. The Supreme cottages are excellent, with nice terraces facing the sea. These are huge, completely paneled in beautiful red wood with high plaited bamboo ceilings. The very attractive bathrooms open partially onto the rooms by inclining wooden shuttered windows. The wood, bamboo and palm furniture is tastefully original. The new Quadruplex cottages are more reasonably-sized but are equally nice.

There are two large swimming pools—one is for children, hemmed in by trees and plants facing the sea. There is a pleasant circular bar with a double *nipa* roof just on the side. San Pedro, the seafood restaurant, is just a 10-minute walk away, or you can wait for the shuttle bus to take you there.

LEYTE PARK HOTEL

Magsaysay Boulevard,
Tacloban City, Leyte
Tel (053) 325-6000
Fax (053) 321-1099
(053) 325-5587
E-mail
leyteparkhotel@yahoo.com
Web
www.geocities.com/leyteparkhotel

Booking Office in Pasig
Unimasters Conglomeration, Inc.
Unit 1002 Orient Square Building,
Emerald Avenue, Ortigas Center,
Pasig City
Tel 633-9727
Fax 687-5884

By air and land (2 hours)
Seventy-five-minute daily flights on Philippine Airlines or Cebu Pacific from Manila to Tacloban. Fifteen minutes by car from Tacloban airport to the resort.

Note: *Transfer from Tacloban airport can be arranged by the resort.*

94 Units
Main Building: 48 Standard and Executive Rooms
Cottages: 42 Rooms in cottages (Supreme Suites, Quadruplex) • 4 Pool Villa
All rooms have air-conditioning, a private bathroom with hot water, cable TV.

Indoor Facilities and Services
Business center • Fitness and aerobics center • Billiards • Table tennis

Food and Beverage Outlets
Restaurants: The Verandah Café • San Pedro Bay Seafood • Lobby Sala Grill • Pool Patio Pizzeria • Food Plaza
Cuisine Offered: International • Filipino

Bars: Tavern Videoke Bar • Paris Saint Tropez Disco and Bar

Watersports and Other Activities
Swimming pools (with kiddie pool) • Snorkeling (in other places) • Diving (in other places) • Kayaking (in other places) • Other boats for hire • Diving • Jet skiing • Island hopping (with picnic) • Firing range • Trekking • Tours to Leyte and Samar's points of interest

Per room per night

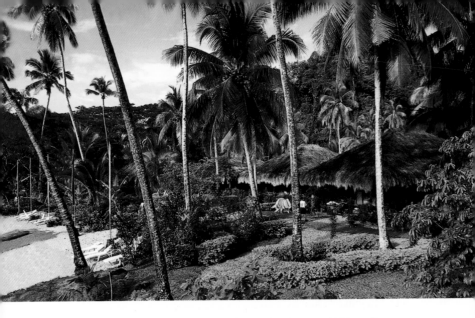

Marabut Marine Park and Beach Resort

From Leyte, as you travel to Marabut by *banca* through the scenic route linking Leyte and Samar, you will already feel a little bit of paradise—a feeling that endures once you are there. The site, with its subtle charm, evokes unexpectedly the landscapes of El Nido. On this area of the coast, very flat everywhere else, rocky sandstone peaks suddenly emerge covered with an abundance of tropical pandanus vegetation, cycas and ficus. These formations also extend into the shore all along the river, just before Marabut.

The resort is set in a stunning natural site. A peaceful bay with tranquil waters encircles the cliffs on the edge of a white sandy beach. Strange rock peaks in the form of sugar loaves make up the face of the resort. Marabut is composed of only six double bungalows but the owner

plans to expand. Though this promises to be a successful undertaking, it will necessarily diminish some of the family atmosphere of the resort. It is advisable you get there before that happens.

The bungalows facing the sea, accessible through a flower-bordered alley, are only a few meters from the sea. Polynesian architecture inspires these bungalows, as the former resort's manager. Mounted on piles and extended by a terrace, these are vast and airy due to the many wooden shutters protected by mosquito nets. The materials used are local—wood, cogon and walls in plaited bamboo. The interior is simple and pleasant with high ceilings, beautiful varnished wood floors, bamboo furniture and bright reading lights. The sink is inside the room, encased in tree trunks. There is an enclosed, separate, fairly large shower.

The restaurant is, for the moment, merely a cogon roof on wooden pillars decorated with leaves. The tables face the sea and a little bar and barbecue are at the back. A larger restaurant will soon be constructed but even now the place is perfect.

Sunset at the resort is a wondrous spectacle of coves swathed in intense orange and soft purple gray hues, enigmatic silhouettes of looming cliffs, the stillness of the night disturbed only by the cry of the seagulls. At Marabut, you can indulge in several activities: simply relax on the lounge chairs scattered along the shore; stroll along the little coconut grove on the right of the resort which leads to the cliffs; trek with a guide through the surrounding countryside, or go by kayak or rubber boat to the nearby rocky peaks facing the resort and take a break at their sandy coves. You can snorkel around the rocky peaks. A bit further, you can reach a vast lagoon through a cleft in the cliff. The lagoon has the particularity of being partially filled by mangroves with twisted roots. The only site where you can dive is on Tooth Island, 40 minutes away by *banca*.

The cliffs around Marabut are covered with wild vegetation, and only a cacao or an eagle breaks the calm of the setting. Even further on you can go up the river first aboard a boat, then by canoe and finally on foot to reach the waterfalls. The road is difficult and requires 12 hours of your time! However, you can try to make only a part of the journey, superb even as soon as you leave Marabut.

MARABUT MARINE PARK BEACH RESORT

Brgy. Macarato, Marabut, Samar
Tel   (053) 325-6000 • 520-0414
Fax   (053) 321-1099 • 325-587
E-mail *leyteparkhotel@yahoo.com*
Web
www.geocities.com/leyteparkresort

Booking Office in Pasig
Unimasters Conglomeration, Inc.
Unit 1002 Orient Square Building,
Emerald Avenue, Ortigas Center,
Pasig City
Tel   633-9727
Fax   687-5884

 1. By air and land (3 hours)
Seventy-five-minute daily flights on Philippine Airlines or Cebu Pacific from Manila to Tacloban. Fifteen minutes by car from Tacloban airport to Leyte Park Hotel. One hour by car/van from Leyte Park Hotel to Marabut.

2. By air, land and sea (2 ½ hours)
Plane and car as described in 1. Forty-five minutes by *banca* from Leyte Park Hotel to Marabut.

Note: *Transfer from Leyte Park Hotel to Marabut is arranged by Leyte Park Hotel who will also arrange for pick up of guests from Tacloban airport.*

 5 Units
5 Duplex Cottages
All cottages have fans, a bathroom with cold water only and a private terrace.

Indoor Facilities and Services
Table tennis

 Food and Beverage Outlets
Restaurant in an open bungalow facing the sea, small bar in the restaurant
Cuisine Offered: Filipino

Watersports and Other Activities
Beach (white sand) • Snorkeling (10 minutes by Kayak) • Diving (to be arranged in advance through Leyte Park Hotel—40 minutes by *banca*) • Island hopping • Kayaking • Other boats for hire • Fishing • Trekking • Rock climbing • Beach volleyball

 Per room per night

Mindanao

The Hidden Bay, Camiguin

Painting by Lily Yousry-Jouve

Mindanao

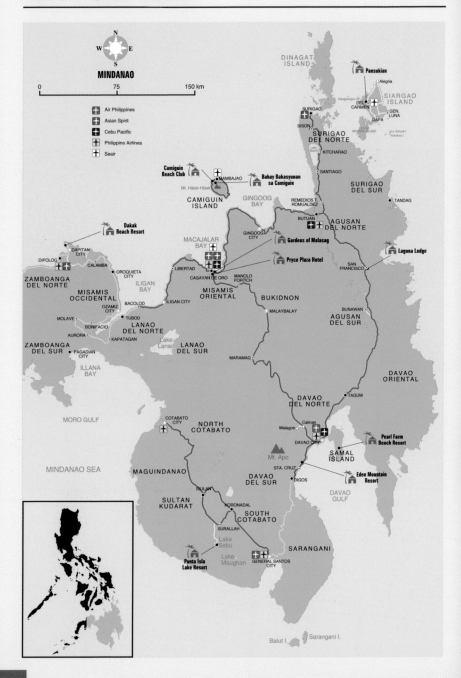

MINDANAO

0   75   150 km

Air Philippines
Asian Spirit
Cebu Pacific
Philippine Airlines
Seair

DINAGAT ISLAND

Pansukian
Alegria
SIARGAO ISLAND
GEN. LUNA
DAPA
DEL CARMEN
Kanguangan I.

SURIGAO
SISON
SURIGAO DEL NORTE
KITCHARAO
SANTIAGO
SURIGAO DEL SUR
TANDAG

Camiguin Beach Club
MAMBAJAO
Bahay Bakasyunan sa Camiguin
Mt. Hibok-Hibok
CAMIGUIN ISLAND
GINGOOG BAY
REMEDIOS T. ROMUALDEZ
BUTUAN
AGUSAN DEL NORTE

Dakak Beach Resort
DAPITAN CITY
DIPOLOG
CALAMBA
OROQUIETA CITY
ZAMBOANGA DEL NORTE
MISAMIS OCCIDENTAL
OZAMIZ CITY
BACOLOD
MOLAVE
BONIFACIO
AURORA
KAPATAGAN
ZAMBOANGA DEL SUR
PAGADIAN CITY
ILLANA BAY

MACAJALAR BAY
GINGOOG CITY
Gardens of Malasag
LIBERTAD
Pryce Plaza Hotel
CAGAYAN DE ORO
MANOLO FORTICH
MISAMIS ORIENTAL
ILIGAN BAY
ILIGAN CITY
LANAO DEL NORTE
TUBOD
Lake Lanao
LANAO DEL SUR
MARAMAG

SAN FRANCISCO
Laguna Lodge

BUKIDNON
MALAYBALAY
BUNAWAN
AGUSAN DEL SUR

MORO GULF

MINDANAO SEA

DAVAO ORIENTAL

DAVAO DEL NORTE
TAGUM

COTABATO CITY
NORTH COTABATO
Malagos
Calinan
DAVAO CITY
Mt. Apo

MAGUINDANAO
ISULAN
SULTAN KUDARAT
KORONADAL
DAVAO DEL SUR
STA. CRUZ
DIGOS

Pearl Farm Beach Resort
SAMAL ISLAND
Eden Mountain Resort
DAVAO GULF

SURALLAH
SOUTH COTABATO
Lake Sebu
Lake Maughan

Punta Isla Lake Resort
GENERAL SANTOS CITY
SARANGANI

Balut I.
Sarangani I.

296

THE SECOND LARGEST ISLAND IN THE PHILIPPINES, Mindanao is in the southernmost end of the archipelago—a neighbor of Malaysia and Indonesia.

Mindanao is a world of contrasts. Its proximity to Malaysia and Indonesia explains the very early installation of migrants. The conversion to Islam of the island began in Sulu at the end of the 14th century. Jolo became the flourishing commercial center of Mindanao at that time, extending up to the end of the 16th century, notably in the region of Lake Lanao. The arrival of the Spaniards in the 16th century prevented the spread of Islam. Since then, the Muslims have resisted different attempts at cultural integration. Land which was part of ancestral Muslim territory was given to migrants from other areas of the country. Tensions developed, culminating in conflicts that continue even today. The rebel groups prospered—Moro National Liberation Front separatists were joined by the Communist New People's Army; Muslim extremists from the Moro Islamic Liberation Front and the Abu Sayyaf Group unfortunately made headlines a few years ago. For these reasons, simple logic will keep you away from the areas of Cotabato, Zamboanga, Jolo and Basilan, where much of the conflict is concentrated. Should you really find a need to visit these areas, make inquiries about security conditions first.

The diversity of Mindanao on the climatic and geographic levels, the unique character of its fauna and flora (still vibrant despite intensive logging); the abundance of natural resources; the diversity of the population and their cultures; all these make Mindanao an island apart.

DAVAO is a cosmopolitan city where Muslims, Catholics, Japanese, Visayans, Tagalog, Chinese and Spanish live together. The region also shelters numerous ethnic tribes such as the Tagacaolos, Guiangans, B'laans, Aetas, Bagobos and Mandayas.

APO, the highest mountain in the country at 2,954 meters, has plant species which cannot be found anywhere else in the world, including the exotic waling-waling orchid.

THE BUKIDNON REGION, with Cagayan De Oro as its point of entry, is rich in forested mountains favorable for trekking. The peaceful island of Camiguin and its volcanoes are also in this region.

The remote region of Lake Sebu, north of General Santos, is the cradle of the T'Boli and B'laan tribes, the dream weavers.

The fabulous "enchanted" marshlands of Agusan, with a surface area of 20,000 hectares, represents the largest humid zone of the country in the basin of the Agusan River, south of Butuan.

SIARGAO AND DINAGAT, north of Mindanao, are magical and extraordinary places with untamed coastlines, limestone cliffs and immense lagoons. This area is close to the Philippine Trench in the Pacific Ocean, the world's deepest spot at more than 10,000 meters below sea level.

Seven Falls, Lake Sebu

Davao

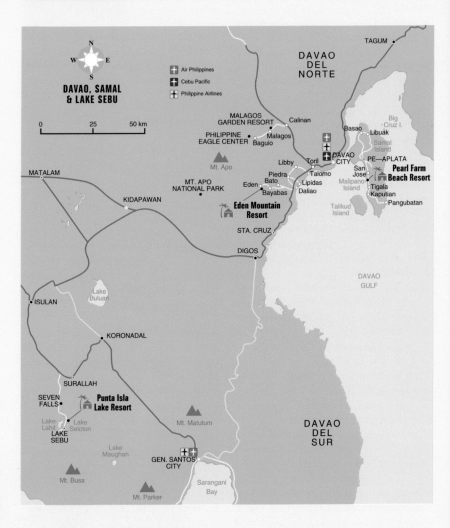

DAVAO, SAMAL & LAKE SEBU

Air Philippines
Cebu Pacific
Philippine Airlines

TAGUM

DAVAO DEL NORTE

MALAGOS GARDEN RESORT
Calinan
PHILIPPINE EAGLE CENTER
Malagos
Baguio
Mt. Apo
MATALAM
MT. APO NATIONAL PARK
KIDAPAWAN
Libby
Toril
DAVAO CITY
Talomo
Piedra
Bato
Eden
Lipidas
Bayabas
Daliao
Eden Mountain Resort
STA. CRUZ
DIGOS

Basao
Libuak
Samal Island
Big Cruz I.
PE—APLATA
San Jose
Pearl Farm Beach Resort
Malipano Island
Tigala
Kaputian
Pangubatan
Talikud Island

DAVAO GULF

ISULAN
Lake Buluan
KORONADAL
SURALLAH
SEVEN FALLS
Punta Isla Lake Resort
Lake Lahit
Lake Seloton
LAKE SEBU
Lake Maughan
Mt. Busa
GEN. SANTOS CITY
Mt. Matutum
Mt. Parker
Sarangani Bay

DAVAO DEL SUR

0   25   50 km

Climate   Rainfall more or less evenly distributed throughout the year

Typhoons No typhoons

Kadayawan Festival, Davao City, third week of August. This festival celebrates the harvesting of fruits, flowers and other agricultural products particularly abundant this time of the year. The festival includes dances in the street with participants in ethnic costumes, to the sound of tribal music. A river parade of boats decorated with flowers and fruits as well as an agro-industrial exhibition are also part of the festivities. Do not miss the chance to admire the splendid orchids, in particular the Waling-Waling and the section dedicated to the particularly rich regional handicrafts.

Davao

Located in southeastern Mindanao, Davao is a huge province, and its capital—Davao City—is a cosmopolitan city. The third most populated in the Philippines and the largest in terms of size, Davao City is a gateway to many discoveries involving culture and nature.

Davao City

THE DABAW MUSEUM AND THE DABAW ETNICA *(in the premises of the Waterfront Insular Hotel)** The museum exhibits the handicrafts and costumes of the Bagobos, Mandayas, Manobos, Atas, T'Boli and B'la-an tribes. Etnica is a workshop where you can observe the different stages in the creation of the very beautiful traditional fabric of the T'boli tribe, woven with geometric motifs.

THE ALDEVINCO SHOPPING CENTER Located on C. M. Recto Avenue, one of the principal commercial arteries of the city, this is a gigantic bazaar where you can find antiques, Indonesian batiks, tribal handicrafts, traditional Muslim objects in bronze and superb hand-painted pottery.

THE ISLAND OF SAMAL *(15 to 30 minutes by banca from the Santa Ana Wharf situated in front of the Magsaysay Park)* Samal Island is part of the group of islands in the Gulf of Davao comprising the islands of Talikud, Big and Small Ligid and Malipano. These islands are endowed with very pretty white sand beaches. Here you will find several resorts, notably the well-known and luxurious Pearl Farm Beach Resort.

THE PHILIPPINE EAGLE CENTER *(at Malagos, Baguio District, 45 kilometers from Davao City, on the road to Bukidnon/Cagayan de Oro City)* The Philippine Eagle Center was created in 1987 to safeguard the great Philippine Eagle. The largest eagle species in the Philippines is endangered, its natural habitat destroyed by deforestation. You can observe them here along with other species of eagles, as well as spot cockatoos, crocodiles, pythons, monkeys, hornbills and wild boar,

all in captivity. The site is the departure point for a number of trekking trips. If you need more information, Tel. No.: (082) 224-3021, Fax No.: (082) 224-3022 or e-mail: *phileagl@pldtdsl.net, info@philippineeagle.org* Web: *www.philippineeagle.org*

MALAGOS GARDEN RESORT Close to the Philippine Eagle Center, the Malagos Garden Resort is a place to admire orchids, plants and tropical fruits of the region, such as the famous durian. It is also a butterfly observation spot.

MOUNT APO *(three to four days)* Mount Apo, a national park, is the highest summit of the Philippines at 2,954 meters. The lowest areas have been deforested, but dense forest remains higher up. The easiest way to climb it is via Kidapawan, 110 kilometers from Davao (two hours by road). You must register at the Municipal Hall of Kidapawan before taking the one-hour jeepney trip to Agko. You hire a guide and spend the first night on the bluish banks of Lake Agko, an area surrounded by tree ferns. There are basic lodgings here. A mist over the lake, due to the hot springs, gives the place an unreal aura.

On the second day, you go across the Marbel River before entering deep forest. The night is spent on the banks of Lake Venado, at an altitude of over 2,000 meters. The final, very steep ascent requires three hours. For more information, contact the Davao Department of Tourism or the Mount Apo Climbers' Association at Digos, 57 kilometers south of Davao.

Mount Apo

*Waterfront Insular Hotel may be the best place to stay in the center of Davao because of its prime location by the sea, facing the island of Samal. Tel. No.: (082) 233-2881.

Pearl Farm Beach Resort

Constructed on the 11-hectare site of a former pearl farm, the Pearl Farm Beach Resort nestles at the farthest point of a white sand beach surrounded by hills covered with exuberant plant life. It is the creation of Francisco Mañosa, who is also the architect of the Amanpulo Resort. The resort is a successful blend of the traditional Samal, Mandaya and Maranao architecture with all the necessities of modern comfort.

The shapes of the structures, notably their roofs covered with bamboo tiles, are particularly innovative.

The Parola Bar, an imposing round structure with a double roof, stands guard at the entrance. A little path bordered with sampaguita plants winds across the garden. It links the various cottages—the Samal Houses along the beach, the Balay Houses on the hills and the Mandaya Houses around the swimming pool. If you are going to stay at Pearl Farm, it is better to opt for the more luxurious Samal Suites or the Malipano Villas, as the lower categories are less original.

The Samal Suites are spacious two-story cottages on stilts remarkably made only of bamboo and magnificent tropical woods—ipil-ipil, molave and yakal. They are arranged in a line facing the sea in such a manner as to maintain privacy. Inside, the rooms have wood flooring, woven wicker walls and elegant rattan furniture that are superb. These suites are spacious, with a bedroom, a drawing room convertible into another room, two marble bathrooms and a wide terrace looking out to the sea. The décor makes use of handicrafts and the colorful fabrics of the ethnic Muslim tribes of the region, contrasting with the immaculate white of the sofas. You have direct access to the sea by a staircase. A jar of water with a coconut shell ladle is placed at your door for rinsing off.

The Malipano Villas, isolated on the island in front of Pearl Farm, were originally built by the owners of the Pearl Farm—Mr. and Mrs. Floirendo—for their children. Very tastefully decorated, these are three octagonal structures with a roof in the form of *salakot*, the traditional *nipa* palm hat. Each is composed of a wide terrace where you can organize a barbecue party, a living room, a dining room, and three or four bedrooms each with its own bathroom. Each villa, furnished with antiques, is decorated with ethnic motifs.

The Maranao Restaurant by the swimming pool, is a very beautiful and tall bamboo structure furnished with elegant furniture. The swimming pool is exceptional, its waters flowing down to the sea. On the other hand, the diving and snorkeling are nothing extraordinary. However, the white sand beaches of the resort and Malipano Island—accessible in a few minutes by shuttle boat—are very pleasant. Small boats can also be rented from the aquatic club. At sunset, it is pleasant to walk around Malipano Island to discover the mangrove, or to have a drink at the Parola Bar.

PEARL FARM BEACH RESORT

Kaputian, Island Garden City of Samal, Davao del Norte
Tel (082) 221-9970 to 76
Fax (082) 221-9979

Booking Office in Davao
G/F, Damosa Complex, Lanang, Davao City
Tel (082) 235-0876 • 234-0601
Fax (082) 235-0873

Booking Office in Makati
Unit 804, Corporate Center 139 Valero St., Salcedo Village, Makati City
Tel 750-1896/98 • 890-2093
Fax 750-1894

By air, land and sea (3 hours)
One-hundred-five-minute daily flights on Philippine Airlines, Air Philippines or Cebu Pacific from Manila to Davao City. Five minutes by car from Davao airport to the Waterfront Insular Hotel. Forty-five minutes by *banca* from the Waterfront Insular Hotel to the resort.

Note: *Transfer from Davao airport can be arranged by the resort.*

Superferry also operates ferry service from Manila to Davao. For more information, you can call tel. nos. 528-7979 or 528-7171.

73 Units
19 Standard Rooms (Balay House/ Hilltop Room) • 21 Superior Rooms (Samal House) • 20 Deluxe Rooms (Mandaya House) • 6 Executive Suites (Samal Suite) • 7 Villas (Malipano Villas—five have three bedrooms and two have four bedrooms.)

All rooms have air-conditioning, private bathroom with hot water, cable TV, telephone, and minibar. Except for standard rooms, hair dryer, coffee/tea maker are also provided. Samal Suites and Malipano Villas have a bathtub. All rooms have either a balcony or a veranda or a small pocket garden.

Indoor Facilities and Services
Business center • Medical services • Helipads • Game room

Food and Beverage Outlets
Restaurant: Maranao Restaurant
Bar: Parola Bar
Cuisine Offered: International
Quality: Good

Watersports and Other Activities
Swimming pools with Jacuzzi • Beach (white sand) • Snorkeling • Diving • Island hopping • Kayaking • Windsurfing • Hobie cat sailing • Water skiing • Other boats for hire • Coral garden tour • Children's playground • Sunset cruise • Biking

Per room per night including roundtrip airport transfer, breakfast and lunch

Eden Mountain Resort

Eden Mountain Resort, with its 80 hectares of pine groves, is a haven of peace, greenery and coolness where it is enjoyable to walk and feel the crunching of the pine needles beneath your feet. Nestled on the slopes of Mount Talamo, with an altitude of about 830 meters, it offers a magnificent view of the gulf of Davao and the island of Samal.

In the '70s, the region was primarily known for its orchid cultivation and excessive forest exploitation. A Davao-based businessman named Jesus V. Ayala, and his wife Fe Misa, bought the property in 1974 and decided to undertake the ambitious eco-tourism project of reconverting the area into a young, vigorous forest. They imported pine seedlings from Benguet and Bukidnon, replanted 30% of the land and constructed forest trails. After over 30 years, they have achieved a big part of their objective.

A botanical garden, an orchard, and a kitchen garden allow their visitors to discover the flora and fruit trees of the region. White parrots and mynahs can also be found in the resort's little aviary. You can also visit a breeding area that shelters various animals such as deer, monkeys and Indian peacocks. There is also a stable for those who love horseback riding. Going around the resort's ground is done either by foot or by riding on a jeep.

A path, well-lighted at night, links the Vista Cottages, which are grouped in twos and set among the pine trees. These are made of wood but have corrugated iron roofs. The interior is bright and comfortable with rattan furniture. In the evenings, the only sounds that you will hear from the forest are the songs of the nocturnal birds and from crickets.

For larger groups, the Hidden Cottage or the Log Cabin is recommended. The Hidden Cottage is tucked among the pine trees. It is suitable for a group seeking privacy. On the other hand, you can enjoy the lovely view of the pine forest in the 25-year old Log Cabin, which has a fully equipped kitchen, a drawing room, and a dining room complete with a fireplace.

The children's playground, remarkably well equipped, is a model of its kind. The restaurant, Holiday Terraces, is constructed on five levels under an impressive archway of tall trees. Bordered by mini waterfalls, it is particularly pleasant because of the coolness. In the evenings, you may be invited to sit down on the grass-covered benches of the Amphitheater, a place for family gatherings and shows, where each family prepares an entertainment number. Certainly, this resort has much to offer not just to individuals but to the whole family as well.

EDEN MOUNTAIN RESORT

Brgy. Eden, Toril District, Davao City

Booking Office in Davao City
Eden Nature Park & Resort, Inc.
Sales and Marketing Office
Matina Town Square
MacArthur Highway, Matina,
Davao City
Tel   (082) 299-1020
             (082) 296-0791
Tel/Fax (082) 299-0313
E-mail
       info@edennaturepark.com.ph
       Web *www.edennaturepark.com.ph*

By air and land (3 ½ hours)
One-hundred-five-minute daily flights on Philippine Airlines, Air Philippines or Cebu Pacific from Manila to Davao City. Ninety minutes by car from Davao airport to the resort.

Note: *Transfer from Davao airport can be arranged by the resort.*

Superferry also operates ferry service from Manila to Davao. For more information, you can call tel. nos. 528-7979 or 528-7171.

52 Units
Suites: 10 Vista Cottages (with fan, mini-bar, private bathroom with hot water) • 8 Holiday Lodges (with mini-bar, private bathroom with hot water) • 8 Camelia Rooms; **Family Cottages:** • 1 Hidden Cottage (two-bedroom unit with 2 bathrooms, kitchen, sala and dining area, good for 10 persons) • 1 Log Cabin (four-bedroom unit with 3 bathrooms, kitchen, sala and dining area, good for 12 persons) • 1 Pine Lodge (two-bedroom unit with verandah, kitchen, sala and dining area, good for 10 persons); **Standard:** 6 Begonia Rooms (good for 4) • 12 Aster Rooms (good for 2 with common toilet-and-bath facilities); **Mountain Villas:** Mountain Villa 1 (four-bedroom unit for 11 persons) • Mountain Villa 2 (two-bedroom unit for 5 persons); **Outdoor Accommodations:** 2 Campsites • 1 Mountain Hall

Food and Beverage Outlets
Restaurants: Vista Kiosk
Cuisine Offered: Filipino • Continental
Quality: Average

Watersports and Other Activities
Hiking along walking trails • Horseback riding • Children's playground, skating (with skates rental), botanical garden, tour ride within the park

Per room per night inclusive of breakfast

Lake Sebu, South Cotabato

Lake Sebu

You might have in mind the traditional image of Lake Sebu teeming with pink water lilies, dotted with frail boats carrying T'boli women adorned in their magnificent square head-dresses and colorful fabrics. That was a reality until recently. But today, modern life has caught up with the T'boli tribes and comfortable jeans and t-shirts have replaced the cumbersome traditional costumes. Despite this, you will discover a very interesting region inhabited by gentle people. The ceremonial costumes are still worn at marriage rites; the ancestral fabrics still of abaca fiber inspired by their dreams. Perhaps, if you venture deeper into the mountains, you might encounter more protected tribes with their traditions still in practice. However, prior inquiries about security conditions.

Lake Sebu is another out-of-this-world region. The spectacle of *tilapia* fish traps bristling on the lake, with its surrealistic geometric design, gives a bizarre impression. Bamboo poles, some of which still grow despite having been cut, divide the fish breeding area. The lake itself is made up of little islets where the fishermen live in precarious dwellings on stilts, made of bamboo, with *nipa* roofs. To the right of the resort of Punta Isla, you can admire the water lilies that only bloom very early in the morning. The T'bolis crisscross the lake in boats that are often merely dug-out tree trunks.

At the market place on Saturday mornings, you will be lucky to see some of the elderly T'boli wearing the traditional costume, though this is quite exceptional. Another market day takes place on

Wednesday when the B'laans descend from the mountains.

Tours in the area of Lake Sebu

THE TOUR OF THE LAKE BY BOAT *(one or two hours)* The Punta Isla boat is adequately comfortable for a tour of the lake. You can observe the fish breeding areas and see some interesting dwellings on the riverbanks or on the islets.

SEVEN FALLS *(a good half day)* You can only reach two of the seven waterfalls, but these are already superb. To do this, you rent a motorbike (with or without a driver; three can ride on the motorbike) and travel six kilometers on the main road. Then, dismounting, you walk through two kilometers of pleasant countryside surrounded by mountains—an easy walk. The first waterfall is not very high but it is wide, with a fine rock face enveloped in tropical vegetation. The second waterfall is more spectacular, crashing 70 meters down into the rainforest.

TRANGIKINI FALLS *(two hours)* The waterfalls may not seem very interesting. What is particularly pleasant though, is the surrounding forest and the countryside you pass to reach them. The waterfalls are just two kilometers away from Punta Isla.

THE WEAVERS' WORKSHOPS The T'bolis are reputed for their T'nalak fabric, woven from abaca fibers with geometric motifs, usually in black, red, and beige. In some villages, you can still observe women weaving: it takes them one month to weave 12 meters of cloth. These fabrics may be purchased either at the Santa Cruz Mission School or on the main road of the village, a few minutes from Punta Island.

Lake Sebu

Punta Isla Lake Resort

You cross a cheerful countryside with many orchards and plantations, notably the immense Dole pineapple plantation. Etched from a distance is the imposing silhouette of the Matutum Volcano (2,293 meters). The last part of the route from Surullah onwards takes you up on the mountain trail. The atmosphere changes as soon as you leave the agricultural plain—the air gets cooler and the light becomes brighter. Finally, about two-and-a-half hours trip from General Santos, you arrive at Lake Sebu where you will notice the *tilapia* fish-breeding enclosures.

There are several small, similarly styled hotels offering basic amenities around the area but Punta Isla Lake Resort is the only one with a good view of the lake. You can, of course, visit Lake Sebu by spending a night at Gen. Santos, although the length of the trip will not allow you to see much of the region, which would be a pity.

The resort is up on a cliff overlooking the lake. It is very popular among the locals who come here to spend the day, especially to have lunch in the little wood pavilions floating near the shoreline. The restaurant is situated on top of a hill with a pleasant terrace having a superb view of the lake. From the top, you can also view the *tilapia* fish-breeding enclosures that form interesting pattern of squares. The *tilapia* is served in all possible culinary preparations: *kinilaw* (raw in vinegar), *adobo* (stewed, in vinegar and soy sauce) grilled (the dishes are cooked on over charcoal fire) and then hauled up to the restaurant by an ingenious system of pulleys!

The resort is made up of a double bungalow and some rooms located in a nearby building. Obviously the double bungalow is the best choice, as it has a very pleasant terrace with a view of the lake. You can even have your meals served there in complete privacy. The interior brings to mind a simple, tiny—though neat—mountain refuge.

It is clear that Punta Isla Lake Resort does not have the comfort of a five-star hotel but the welcome is warm and the staff is efficient when asked to organize excursions, which include boat rides, renting a bike or visiting the nearby waterfalls and the weavers' workshops.

Note: *According to the latest information, Estares Lake Resort, a little resort located just at the side of Punta, has recently been renovated and its cottages with bathrooms are deemed to be more comfortable than those of Punta. However, it was not possible to visit this resort. Estares Lake Resort Tel. mobile: (0910) 604-5498.*

PUNTA ISLA LAKE RESORT
Lake Sebu, South Cotabato
Tel (0919) 485-2910
Tel/Fax (083) 238-8503
Fax (083) 238-3398
Note: *You need to be patient; call repeatedly as the number is difficult to access.*

 By air and land (5 ½–6 hours)
One-hundred-five-minute daily flights on Philippine Airlines or one-hundred-eighty-minute daily flights (via Cebu) on Air Philippines from Manila to General Santos. Two to two and a half hours by the resort's jeepney from General Santos to Lake Sebu (92 km).

Note: *It is recommended to take the jeepney arranged by the resort as it takes a lot more time by public transport. However, if you arrive without prior notice, you have to take a Yellow Bus bound for Koronadal (an hour from Gen. Santos), then in Koronadal take a Yellow Bus, minibus or jeepney bound for Surallah (an hour from Koronadal) and from the market at Surallah, take a jeepney bound for Lake Sebu.*

Superferry also operates ferry service from Manila to General Santos. For more information, you can call tel. nos. 528-7979 or 528-7171.

 11 Units
1 Double Bungalow (with two rooms and two bathrooms)
There is hot water. There is no air-conditioning or fan but you don't need it as it is cool in the mountains. The two rooms share a terrace.
In a building: 4 Single Room (with bathroom; good for 1 or 2) • 4 Double Room (with bathroom; good for 4) • 1 Family Room (with bathroom; good for 8) • Dormitory-type [double deck (18 beds) with common bathroom]

Indoor Facilities and Services
Car rental • Foreign currency exchange

 Food and Beverage Outlets
Restaurant: Lemlunay Bar and Restaurant
Cuisine Offered: Filipino Dishes • American • International
Quality: Average

 Watersports and Other Activities
Fishing boat on the lake • Trekking to Seven Falls or to Trangikini Falls • Bike rental

 Per room per night

Note: *Cash payment only.*

Northeast Mindanao

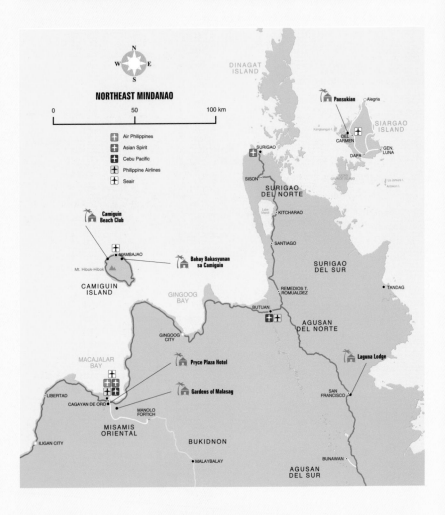

Climate	**Cagayan de Oro:** Seasons not very pronounced, relatively dry from November to April; wet during the rest of the year
	Camiguin: Rainfall more or less evenly distributed throughout the year
	Agusan: No dry season with a very pronounced maximum rainfall from November to January
Typhoons	**Cagayan de Oro:** Not visited by typhoons
	Camiguin: October to January
	Agusan: December to January

Cagayan de Oro

Cagayan de Oro, the capital of the province of Misamis Oriental, is a pleasant town because of its green zones, surrounded by mountains. It is located along the Bay of Macajalar and is bordered on the west by the Cagayan river. It is also an important university center. Located here is the Xavier University, which also houses a small archeological museum exhibiting the traditions of the Mindanao tribes. It is necessary to pass by Cagayan de Oro in order to reach the island of Camiguin.

MAKAHAMBUS CAVE *(14 kilometers southwest, half-an-hour)* The cave has an impressive view of the Cagayan River which is more than 100 meters below.

THE DEL MONTE PINEAPPLE PLANTATION AT CAMP PHILLIPS *(34 kilometers, one day)* This plantation covers 90 square kilometers, (one of the largest in the world) and can be visited with permission from Del Monte.

GARDENS OF MALASAG ECO-TOURISM VILLAGE *(12 kilometers, 30 minutes)* These gardens are set in a 7.2-hectare wooded area where animal and plant lives are protected. A project of the Department of Tourism, it aims to present the cultures of the different tribes of north Mindanao.

NOSLEK CANOPY WALK AT CLAVERIA *(43 kilometers northeast, one hour 45 minutes)* At the heart of the verdant Magbais rainforest is a rope bridge suspended at an equal level with the tree canopy—more than 20 meters above the ground. It permits you to discover the vegetation and wildlife at the peaks. It is an unforgettable experience, though not recommended if you are afraid of heights. The trip is organized by the Department of Tourism of Cagayan de Oro. Danfil Discovery Tours (Tel. No.: 524-8703 in Manila) offers a two-day program with a guide. You can combine the canopy walk with a trek to the neighboring forest the first day, and rafting on the Magbais river and its waterfalls on the second day. You can sleep in the guesthouse in the middle of the forest.

The Marshes of Agusan

THE MARSHES

Lost in the middle of Mindanao, in a relatively unknown region, are the fabulous marshlands of Agusan. Stretching over an area of 20,000 hectares, a greater part of the marshes has been classified a Wildlife Sanctuary, sheltering an abundance of intriguing plant and wildlife. The marshes are composed of nine lakes, the most well known of which being the Lakes Dinagat, Binahaon, Mihaba, Mahauan and Dagan, accessible by a boat trip up several rivers.

Strips of grassland punctuated by trees separate the lakes. Submerged forests occupy more than half of the marshlands. The marshes of Agusan are imbued with the melancholic, mysterious atmosphere associated with swamps. The vastness makes you lose all sense of time.

On the riverboat trip, you may be caught unaware by the flight of an iridescent kingfisher. Then, making your way through narrow waterways under mossy arched trees, you have the vision of bluish lakes covered in purple hyacinths.

The Manobos who inhabit the marshlands live far from civilization and in

Agusan Marsh, Manobo Village

primitive floating dwellings that balance precariously on enormous tree trunks. These only float during the rainy season, resting on the riverbanks for the rest of the year.

The marshes are an ideal spot for bird watching, notably during the migration period from October to January, which is also the rainy season. You can also navigate better by boat during this season, as the water level is higher. More than a hundred species have been accounted for here. Outside the migration season, you can observe kingfishers, ducks, egrets and purple and gray herons all along the way.

ORGANIZING THE VISIT (*one day*) The greater part of the marshes can be visited in one day, on condition that you spend the night at San Francisco, 45 minutes from Bunawan—the point of entry into the marshlands, but where the lodgings are extremely basic. The marshes have only just been opened to visitors.

To visit the marshes, the fastest and most reliable way is to rent a pumpboat at the Bunawan pier. You can then go up the river in 20 minutes to the Department of Environment and Natural Resources (IPAS office), register and get a guide (compulsory) after having made a small donation. It is not advisable to go directly to the IPAS office, which can at first seem the simplest thing to do. The only boat they have is rarely available and you will, in any case, be sent to Bunawan to hire one. Then begins the journey up the Agusan River that takes about two hours, before arriving in a marshy zone. You can visit a number of lakes from here. It is possible to reach Lake Dinagat—the nearest—in one hour.

Note that during the dry season, it is difficult to navigate the pump boat, and as such, not all the lakes are accessible. At one of the villages, a Manobo boat—in fact a narrow tree trunk with a precarious balance—is offered for rent. The ideal mode of transportation would be a kayak.

Camiguin

Camiguin is a volcanic island with no less than five volcanoes, one of which is Mount Hibok-Hibok (1,250 meters) with a surface area of 294 square kilometers. Its towering mountainous silhouette, often obscured by clouds, emerges from the midst of the Mindanao Sea fringed with charcoal-gray beaches. The island, with the exception of a few pockets of forest notably around Mount Hibok-Hibok, is covered with palm trees that rustle wildly in the winds that frequently blow at certain periods of the year. Island of volcanoes and waterfalls, Camiguin is also an island of *la dolce vita,* where daily life unfolds at a leisurely pace, where the inhabitants are friendly and the alleys and lanes are lined with flowering bougainvillea and orchid gardens adorn the front of little wooden houses. You will meet very few tourists,

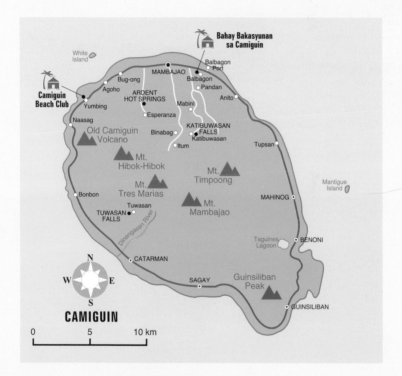

Festival of the Lanzones, end of October. The festival celebrates the harvest of this small, delicious, yellow fruit which tastes like a cross between a lychee and a lemon, and grows in bunches along the foothills of Mount Hibok-Hibok. The atmosphere is good-natured, rich in colors and perfectly orchestrated. The two days of festivities are marked by parades by dance groups wearing traditional costumes of the different tribes of North Mindanao. They set off from the Town Hall Square and go to Mambajao.

as it is not very easy to reach. In fact, you need at least six hours to come here from Cagayan de Oro.

You can tour the island in a day by hiring a jeepney or a motor bike. The 64-kilometer road is in good condition. The side roads, on the other hand, are transformed into quagmires as soon as the first rains fall.

MAMBAJAO *(17 kilometers from the pier of Benoni, 30 minutes by jeepney)* Mambajao, capital of the island, is a nice little town with well-preserved, old wooden houses dating back to the period of Spanish colonization. Observe the house occupied by the Landbank of the Philippines and, outside the village on the main road going to Agoho, the Paradiso restaurant.

THE OBSERVATORY OF THE INSTITUTE OF VOLCANOLOGY AND SEISMOLOGY *(three and a half kilometers above Mambajao)* It is accessible by car and offers a superb view of the coast and the volcanoes covered by coconut trees.

KATIBUWASAN FALLS *(five kilometers southeast of Mambajao)* This impressive waterfall, 50 meters high, is surrounded by lush vegetation. You can swim in the large natural pool and rent large rubber tubes for the children's pleasure.

MAGSAYSAY ISLAND *(three kilometers from Hubangon)* This five-hectare island, inhabited by fisherfolk, can be reached by *banca*. The island is wooded and endowed with a pretty, gold sand beach. From the beach, you can snorkel and dive all along the cliff. It is one of the best diving and snorkeling sites of Camiguin.

TUASAN FALLS *(six kilometers northeast of Catarman)* Less spectacular than the waterfalls of Katibuwasan and only 25 meters high, the Tuasan waterfalls have nonetheless the advantage of being more peaceful,

Women of North Mindanao in Traditional Costume

surrounded by jungle with a natural swimming pool. The falls are accessible by trekking through the forest for four kilometers from the main road. Two kilometers before Catarman, there is a sign showing the entrance of the track to the waterfalls.

THE SITE OF THE ANCIENT VOLCANO AND THE MARINE CEMETERY *(13 kilometers west of Mambajao)* Following the Stations of the Cross along the path, you will easily reach the summit of Daan Volcano, with an altitude of 800 meters. It erupted in 1871, burying the little village of Bonbon. A cross marks the cemetery which sank into the sea with a part of the church. These remains are visible at low tide.

WHITE ISLAND *(15 minutes by jeepney from Mambajao and 10 minutes by banca)* White Island is a strip of white sand beach on the sea, facing the village of Agoho where the resorts are situated. Because of the strong currents, it is advisable to make this excursion after consulting the timetable, through one of the two selected resorts. The view of Camiguin Island from White Island is spectacular. The contrast between this shining white islet and the black sandy

Katibuwasan Falls

coast of Camiguin dominated by Mount Hibok-Hibok is astonishing.

ARDENT HOT SPRINGS *(six kilometers southwest of Mambajao)* It is ideal to go for a swim in the hot water springs toward the end of the afternoon or even early into the evening to be able to make the best of the fresh air and relax after a busy day.

MOUNT HIBOK-HIBOK *(one day, four-hour climb to the summit)* Mount Hibok-Hibok, at an altitude of 1,250 meters, is the most active of the volcanoes in Camiguin, last erupting in 1951. The jump-off point for the trek up the volcano is at Ardent Hot Springs Resort where the amenities are simple. It is preferable to stay here overnight if you want to make the climb very early in the morning. The trek does not require any particular skills but be wary of the frequent mists that can cause you to lose your way as you approach the summit. It is advisable to take a guide since the trail is not very well marked. You cross a part of the forest, then bushy moorland. The view from the summit is superb, but often hidden by clouds. If you want to climb down the crater, you must spend the night there. You can book through the Philippine Tourism Authority in Manila, Room 522, DOT Building, T. M. Kalaw Street, Ermita, Tel. No.: 524-2495 or 524-2502, Fax No.: 525-6490.

Siargao

To the north of Mindanao, facing the Pacific Ocean lies a secret island, solitary and isolated, breathtakingly stunning… Siargao. It has been known as the best place for surfing in the Philippines and one of the best in Asia since around the 1970s. Cloud 9, with breaks of nine and 12 feet, and Tuason Point are some of the most renowned surf spots.

However, the lure of Siargao and its surrounding islands goes way beyond surfing. You discover magical, fascinating landscapes with high limestone cliffs, bringing to mind those of El Nido. You will pass through cliffs that are totally isolated, embracing immense lagoons, some of which constitute genuine labyrinths. Siargao's beauty, verging on fantasy, is an absolutely bewitching mermaid's chant to which you totally surrender.

If your budget permits, the discovery of these islands from the resort of

Lagoon in Siargao

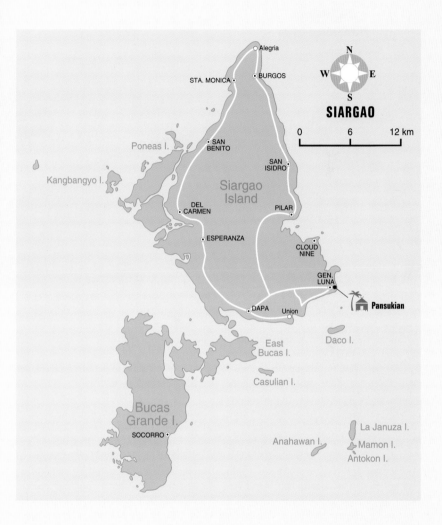

Climate	No dry season with a very pronounced maximum rainfall from November to January
Typhoons	November to December

Best season for surfing: July to November

Pansukian Mangroves

Pansukian will long after haunt your memory as an exceptional moment. Moreover, it is not very easy to organize these excursions from the other more surf-oriented resorts. There are many sites to discover but here are some of those you should not miss:

SOHOTON CAVES ON BUCAS GRANDE ISLAND *(one day)* The island of Bucas Grande is a one-hour-and-forty-five-minute *banca* journey from Pansukian. The island has two wide emerald-green lagoons encircling high cliffs covered in jungle. The *banca* stops at the first lagoon and the trip is made via kayak (approximately two hours). You enter in awe and admiration, a hushed world whose tranquillity is disturbed only by the cries of kalaws and kingfishers. The access to the second lagoon is as mysterious as you can imagine. You enter a dark cave hidden in a cliff and then, discover the scale of the second lagoon. At a certain spot in

the lagoon is a cave that you can discover while swimming. Be advised however, that it is quite possible to get lost in the inner sections of the lagoon.

CAOB ON THE ISLAND OF KANGBANGYO *(one day)* The island is a one-and-a-half-hour *banca* ride from Pansukian. You can visit the village of Caob in an area of the mangroves inhabited by man-eating crocodiles. This visit is possible only at certain times, depending on the rise of the tide. Nearby are two magical lagoons—the first not far from the village and the second accessible after crossing an amazing canyon. The best means of transportation here is the kayak.

THE TWIN ISLES OF LA JANOZA AND MAMON *(half-day)* The inhabited isles are one hour away from Pansukian. They face each other and are separated only by a narrow channel rich in corals, fish and shells. It is a marvelous area for snorkeling. Although the visit can be finished in one morning, bringing along a picnic is not a bad idea.

LAGOON *(25 minutes from Pansukian)* Off General Luna are several little islets comprising coral reefs that you can also visit by *banca* and kayak: Guyam, Daco and Pansukian.

THE PANSUKIAN MANGROVE Just behind the Pansukian resort is a really amazing mangrove stretch that you can discover by kayak. It is advisable to be accompanied by a guide so as not to lose your way. You will enjoy observing the variety of birds.

TREKKING IN THE FOREST OF BUCAS GRANDE *(one day)* A track which can become quite slippery during the rainy season goes through a dense rainforest clinging to the cliffs. The stunning view of the lagoons is your well-earned reward.

Dinagat Island

Equally as beautiful as Siargao though different, the mysterious and mystifying island of Dinagat is still well off the beaten track. If you are an avid explorer, the island will fascinate you. Pansukian can organize discovery expeditions as Dinagat is only an hour and a half away from the resort.

The west coast of Dinagat is made up of several sharply inclined limestone cliffs that seem like astounding sculptures, with forms sometimes shredded and torn, sometimes round and soft. The cliffs hug the expansive, deserted lagoons traversed only by a rare fishing boat.

The river branches go deep into the island. The most remarkable areas are Hagakak, Kotkok Island and Pigot Site. Beyond Cape Desolation, the east coast of the island facing the Pacific is strikingly desolate and wild. In Sangay, 1,000-meter-high mountains covered with rainforest reach down to the white sand riverbanks before the river finally empties into the ocean.

Dinagat

Dakak Park Beach Resort

akak is a huge resort, set within a wooded, 15-hectare property. Surprisingly, despite its size, Dakak is well integrated into the natural environment that it fully respects. This environment is quite spectacular—a serene bay fringed by a 750-meter beach with fine, golden sand, encircled by rocks and boulders on one side, and a towering limestone spur on the other. The beach gently pushes into the sea making it ideal for children. You can, in 20 minutes, scale the cliff through a well-marked trail and enjoy the superb view of the beach and the sea.

The bamboo bungalows with *nipa* roofs are well concealed in the vegetation and from the beach, it is difficult to imagine that a resort of such dimension is hidden there. The bungalows are laid out in tiers from the seafront to the top of the hill and are distributed over different sections— from section A at the rear end of the beach, to the most distant section E.

The last sections, quite high up and far from the beach and the restaurant, are not recommended for elderly people. The bungalows on the seashore are better located, the best being those at the foot of the cliff.

The duplex bungalows are well set apart and soundproof. Each is enclosed by vegetation and has a generally good view. All the rooms are spacious, furnished with every comfort and beautiful bathrooms. The décor is pleasant: *nipa* wall tapestries, *capiz* windows and wicker drawing rooms. The private terraces have beautiful planter's armchairs in wood and a small table.

The resort has several restaurants. The one at the end of the beach is surrounded by a profusion of orchids from the resort's greenhouse. Breakfast and lunch are always served here, but in the evening, dinner may be taken in any of the other restaurants ... depending on the mood of the manager.

Dakak has three superb swimming pools, one of which is reserved exclusively for children. A pleasant little bar is near the swimming pool close to the sea.

Dakak is a place suitable for families with children. It has a safe beach and a variety of activities are possible within the area—watersports, golf, tennis and horseback riding. An hour away by boat, snorkeling is possible in Aliguay and Sinilog, two islands that belong to the resort.

Climate Rainfall more or less evenly distributed throughout the year

DAKAK PARK BEACH RESORT

Taguilon, Dapitan City, Zamboanga del Norte
Tel (065) 213-6813

Booking Office in Mandaluyong
State Financing Center
Ortigas Avenue, Mandaluyong City
Tel 721-2726
Fax 721-1461
E-mail dakak28@yahoo.com
Web www.dakak.com.ph

 By air and sea (2 ½ hours)
Ninety-minute daily flights on Philippine Airlines from Manila to Dipolog. Forty-five minutes by minibus from Dipolog airport to Dapitan.

Note: *Transfer from Dipolog airport is arranged by the resort.*

Superferry also operates ferry service from Manila to Dipolog. For more information, you can call tel. nos. 528-7979 or 528-7171.

 156 Units
48 Standard Bungalow • 96 Deluxe Villas • 12 Super Deluxe Villas
All rooms are duplex bungalows in clusters. All bungalows are spacious and have air-conditioning, minibar, TV, intercom, a bathroom with hot water, a private veranda, a king size bed and one single bed.

Indoor Facilities and Services
Cellular phone room (open 24 hours) • Babysitting • Medical services • Massage • Sauna • Foreign currency exchange • Car rental • Billiards • Table tennis • Bowling

Food and Beverage Outlets
Restaurants: Port Orient Terrace
Cuisine Offered: International • Filipino
Quality: Good
Bars: Pirate's Bar

Watersports and Other Activities
3 Swimming pools with Jacuzzi • Beach (white sand) • Snorkeling (in other places) • Dive center • Island hopping (45 minutes to Aliguay Island) • Kayaking • Other boats for hire • Fishing • Sunset cruise • Horseback riding • 3-hole golf course

 Per room per night

Pryce Plaza Hotel

The Pryce Plaza Hotel, perched on a green cliff of Carmen, overlooks Cagayan de Oro. It offers a nice panorama of the town and the bay of Macajalar further away. Less than 15 minutes from the airport and the town center, the hotel is essentially a business hotel though it is also an excellent stopover en route to Camiguin from Manila.

A four-story white building with a green-tiled roof, the hotel is composed of rooms and suites with equal standards of quality and comfort. These are bright and spacious, decorated in shades of salmon contrasting with the sober wood furniture.

The best rooms are those that have a view of the swimming pool, as well as those on the upper floors as these have the most open views.

The pool area is situated at the foot of the building. Aside from the large rectangular swimming pool, there is a little paddling pool with a water slide for younger children.

Pryce Plaza has two restaurants, Café Cagayan (has a splendid view of the city) and Josefina's Seafood & Grill (with a variety of fresh seafood). Enjoy refreshments and cocktails while listening to soothing sounds of live music, one can relax and unwind at the Compadres Bar.

Hotel amenities include tennis, basketball, badminton courts and a fully equipped gym with sauna and massage facilities. A few minutes away are Pueblo de Oro Golf & Country Club, and the classic Del Monte Golf Club is in nearby Bukidnon. For those interested in sight-seeing, Nissan-Rent a-Car is located at the front desk of the hotel. Airport transfers, tours out of town or excursions to nearby towns may be arranged.

PRYCE PLAZA HOTEL
Carmen Hill, Cagayan do Oro City, Misamis Oriental
Tel (088) 858-4536 to 37
(088) 858-3111 • 858-3131
Web www.pryceplaza.ph

Booking Office in Makati
17/F Pryce Center,
Don Chino Roces Avenue,
Makati City
Tel 899-4401
(ext. 711/712/706)
899-9430
Fax 899-6862
E-mail
reservations@pryceplaza.ph

By air and land (2 hours)
Ninety-minute daily flights on Philippine Airlines, Air Philippines or Cebu Pacific from Manila to Cagayan de Oro City. Fifteen minutes by car from Cagayan de Oro airport to the hotel.

Note: With prior notice the hotel can arrange for airport transfers through Nissan-Rent-a-Car.

Superferry (Tel. No.: 528-7979) and Negros Navigation (Tel. No.: 245-4395) also operate ferry service from Manila to Cagayan de Oro.

81 Units
34 Standard Rooms • 40 Superior Rooms • 3 Deluxe Rooms • 1 Junior Suite • 2 Executive Suites • 1 Presidential Suite
All rooms and suites are centrally air-conditioned with individual thermostat control and have cable TV, a bathroom with hot water, telephone, radio and minibar.

Indoor Facilities and Services
Business center • Airport transfer • Car rental • Babysitting • Foreign currency exchange • Medical services • Gym • Sauna

Food and Beverage Outlets
Restaurants: Japanese Corner • Josefina's Seafood and Grill • Café Cagayan
Cuisine Offered: Filipino • International • Japanese • Seafood • Barbecue
Quality: Good
Bars: Compadres Bar (live piano music)

Watersports and Other Activities
Swimming pool (with kiddie pool) • Tennis • Golf arrangements with two nearby golf courses • Children's playground • Tours to Camiguin Island

 Per room per night inclusive of breakfast

Gardens of Malasag

Also known as Eco-Tourism Village, the Gardens of Malasag, 12 kilometers from Cagayan de Oro, were conceived by the Philippine Department of Tourism. Inspired notably by the Gardens of Grenada in Spain and the Bouchart Gardens of Canada, these gardens aim to present the cultures of tribes of north Mindanao in a natural environment, while protecting the animal and plant life. The site is in a wooded area of 7.2 hectares offering impressive views of the bay of Macajalar.

The area is crossed by several tracks along which can be found numerous traditional huts of the main tribes of the region exhibiting tribal musical instruments, costumes, agricultural tools and handicrafts. Several exhibitions are held beneath the trees, surrounded by the lush plant life, which present different varieties of orchids, bananas, bamboos and frangipani trees. An area of the garden is devoted to birds, butterflies, monkeys and deer.

A stay in the gardens of Malasag is a pleasant experience. The *nipa* cottages have a nice view of the bay. Children will certainly enjoy swimming in the pool as well as learning about tropical plants and making of handicrafts.

GARDENS OF MALASAG

Eco-Tourism Village
Malasag, Cagayan de Oro,
Misamis Oriental
Philippines Tourism Authority
Cugman, Cagayan de Oro City
Tel (0919) 291-3464
Tel/Fax (088) 855-6183
Fax (088) 855-6183

Booking Office in Manila
Reservation/Sales Division
Marketing Department
Philippine Tourism Authority
5/F, DOT Building
T.M. Kalaw Street, Ermita, Manila
Tel 524-2495 • 524-2505
Fax 525-6490
E-mail
marketing@philtourism.com
Web *www.philtourism.com*

 By air and land (2 ½ hours)
Ninety-minute daily flights on Philippine Airlines, Air Philippines or Cebu Pacific from Manila to Cagayan de Oro City. Thirty minutes by car from Cagayan de Oro airport to the resort.

Note: *The resort does not arrange for airport transfer. You will have to hire a taxi at the airport.*

Superferry (Tel. No.: 528-7979) and Negros Navigation (Tel. No.: 245-4395) also operate ferry service from Manila to Cagayan de Oro.

 22 Units
4 Standard Rooms • 14 Deluxe Rooms • 2 Camiguinon (fan-cooled) • 2 Cagayanon (fan-cooled)
All rooms have air-conditioning, private bathroom with shower or bathtub, and refrigerator.

Indoor Facilities and Services
Shuttle jeepney inside the village

 Food and Beverage Outlets
Restaurant: Higaunon Café
Cuisine Offered: Filipino

 Watersports and Other Activities
Swimming pool • Hiking through the forest • Badminton

 Per room per night

Camiguin Beach Club

When you finally reach Camiguin Beach Club from the pier of Benoni, you would have practically completed almost half the tour of the island and during the 40-minute trip, absorbed the charm of its tranquil atmosphere. Camiguin Beach Club has its own beach, its big advantage over the other resorts on the island.

The resort, which is owned by a Cebu-based businessman named Jacinto L. Romero, was constructed in 1996. The resort is composed of six main rooms on the ground floor of a white building facing the swimming pool. You will be welcomed by a warm and friendly ambiance. The rooms are bright, with white walls and wooden furniture. The bathrooms with hot water are large and impeccably clean. Each room has its own terrace with a sea view, where you can curl up with a book while keeping an eye on the children splashing in the pool or, simply let yourself be soothed by the peaceful atmosphere.

The lagoon-shaped swimming pool, on the edge of the beach, is fringed with green lawns and flowers. haded by impressive century-old trees, it is very pleasant. It is so big that it is almost out of proportion to the small size of the resort. Meals are served in the large, sea-view restaurant.

Like the majority of beaches on this volcanic island, the resort's beach is made up of black sand, though just in front of the resort is the beautiful white sand beach of White Island. If you are at least four adults staying at the resort, the trip to White Island is complimentary. A complete guided tour of the town is free, provided you are in a group with at least eight people.

CAMIGUIN BEACH CLUB

Yumbing, Camiguin Province, Camiguin Island
Tel/Fax (088) 387-9028
E-mail pcrbank@skyinet.net

Booking Office in Cebu
Tel/Fax (032) 344-0960

Booking Office in Cagayan de Oro
Tel/Fax (088) 856-4152

By air, land, sea and land (5 ½ hours) Ninety-minute daily flights on Philippine Airlines, Air Philippines or Cebu Pacific from Manila to Cagayan de Oro City. Ninety minutes by car/van from Cagayan de Oro airport to Balingoan port, Misamis Oriental. A taxi can be hired from the airport or you can take a bus on Bachelor Express or Ceres Liner headed for Butuan from the Bus Terminal located at the Agora Market. One to one and a half hours by ferry from Balingoan port to Benoni wharf of Mahinog on Camiguin Island. There are at least 5 vessels (Kalinaw, Hijos, Shuttle Ferry 1 & 6, Yuhum, Royal Princess) with departures almost every hour from 7:15 a.m. to 3 p.m. Forty minutes by private van service arranged by the resort from Benoni wharf of Mahinog. You may also take a public jeepney.

Superferry (Tel. No.: 528-7979) and Negros Navigation (Tel. No.: 245-4395) also operate ferry service from Manila to Cagayan de Oro.

16 Units
6 Deluxe Rooms • 2 Standard Rooms (along the pool) • 6 Air-conditioned Economy Rooms • 2 Fan-cooled Rooms in the annex building (good for 4) All rooms have a bathroom with hot water, cable TV, refrigerator and a choice of twin beds or matrimonial bed. Extra beds can be added in all rooms.

Food and Beverage Outlets
Restaurants: Fine Dining Restaurant • Open Boardwalk Restaurant at Poolside and Beach side
Cuisine Offered: Filipino • International
Quality: Average

Watersports and Other Activities
Swimming pool (with kiddie pool) • Beach (gray sand) • Snorkeling (at Magsaysay Island) • Diving (in other places) • Island hopping to White Island or Magsaysay Island • Camiguin Island discovery tour • Golf at Camiguin Golf Club

Per room per night inclusive of breakfast

Note: *Cash payment only. Special packages available*

Bahay Bakasyunan
sa Camiguin

Bahay Bakasyunan sa Camiguin, which in English means "Vacation House in Camiguin," was conceived by its owner, Mr. Efren Uy, as a place for accommodating visiting family members. In 1994, the house was transformed into a resort preserving its hospitable, family atmosphere. The keys to your room are handed over to you without any formality as you arrive at the central pavilion housing the reception area and the boutique.

The six duplex bungalows, each with two rooms, are aligned at a good distance from each other on half of the terrain. The other half has been left in its natural state. There is an impressive coconut grove on the meticulously maintained lawns.

The resort has the advantage of having better ventilation than in the other resorts on the island where the structures are a bit too compact.

The ensemble is relaxing, neat and clean. The architecture is resolutely traditional with *nipa* roofing, bamboo walls and furniture. An extra bed may be added without any difficulty, as the rooms are comfortably spacious. All the rooms have individual terraces that look out onto the coconut grove.

While it is possible to swim in the sea after walking over large pebbles, Bahay Bakasyunan sa Camiguin does not have a beach—its only weak point. However, this is largely compensated by the big swimming pool situated on the edge of the shore. It is pleasant, surrounded by green lawns, with a special pool for children and a separate Jacuzzi. You will especially appreciate it if you go to Camiguin during the cool season, which is also the time for the Lanzones Festival.

You can also rent a van or a *banca* belonging to the resort and accomplish all the excursions to the points of interest in Camiguin, without being obliged to go to Mambajao where the travel agents are located. If you prefer a motorbike, you can rent one in Mambajao.

The Café Cecilia is a well-ventilated structure in traditional style, opening onto the sea. It is advisable to order in advance so as to avoid an interminable wait.

BAHAY BAKASYUNAN SA CAMIGUIN

Balbagon, Mambajao,
Camiguin Island
Tel (088) 387-1057
Tel/Fax (088) 387-0131
Fax (088) 387-0278

**Booking Office in
Cagayan de Oro City**
c/o Universal Hardware
108 Gomez Street, Cagayan de Oro
Tel (088) 857-4244

By air, land, sea and land (5 hours)
Ninety-minute daily flights on Philippine Airlines, Air Philippines or Cebu Pacific from Manila to Cagayan de Oro City. Ninety minutes by car/van from Cagayan de Oro airport to Balingoan port, Misamis Oriental. A taxi can be hired from the airport or you can take a Bachelor Express or Ceres Liner bus headed for Butuan from the Bus Terminal located at the Agora market. One to one and a half hours by ferry from Balingoan port to Benoni wharf of Mahinog on Camiguin Island. There are at least 5 vessels (Kalinaw, Hijos, Shuttle Ferry 1, Yuhum and Royal Princess) with departures almost every hour from 7:15 a.m. to 4 p.m. Twenty minutes by private van service arranged by the resort from Benoni wharf of Mahinog. You may also take a public jeepney.

Superferry (Tel. No.: 528-7979) and Negros Navigation (Tel. No.: 245-4395) also operate ferry service from Manila to Cagayan de Oro.

12 Units
12 Deluxe Air-conditioned Rooms in 6 Duplex Cottages
Each room has a private bathroom, cable TV, telephone, private terrace and twin beds.

Indoor Facilities and Services
Car rental for Island tours • Motorized boat/ Speedboat rental

Food and Beverage Outlets
Restaurants: Café Cecilia (overlooking the sea) • Amakan Restaurant (open during peak season and conventions, seminars and weddings)
Cuisine Offered: Filipino
Quality: Average

Watersports and Other Activities
Swimming pool (with kiddie pool and Jacuzzi) • Snorkeling (in other places) • Diving (in other places) • Children's playground • Island hopping to White Island or Magsaysay Island • Tours to Camiguin Island

Per room per night inclusive of breakfast

Almont Inland Hotel Resort

Laguna Lodge

The little town of San Francisco, the nearest point of entry to the marshes of Agusan, is a few minutes from the main road going from Davao to Butuan, which actually is a very good road. You can find a good number of decent lodgings in the town offering basic amenities—usually one room with a bathroom—including the pleasant De Asis Lodging House and Diwata. Arguably, the best among these is the Laguna Lodge.

Laguna Lodge is conveniently located a short distance from the bus station in a quiet street away from the noise. It is a low white building made up of 45 rooms. These are air-conditioned, relatively spacious with attached bathrooms. They are clean though furnished in a rather meager manner—

two beds, a linoleum-clad floor and walls painted green.

On the ground floor is a little room that serves as a restaurant, but it is better to have your breakfast in one of the cafés near the bus station and buy warm, freshly baked bread from the corner bakery. A 10-minute walk takes you to Christina's Café, where you can dine in an old, pretty little wood house set in a garden courtyard. It serves the best cuisine in town, but make sure you go there early, as it closes at 8:30 p.m.

LAGUNA LODGE
San Francisco, Barangay 2,
Agusan del Sur, Mindanao
Tel (085) 839-1125
(0919) 693-9447

Both by air and land
1. Manila/Butuan/San Francisco
(4 ½ hours) Ninety-minute daily flights on Philippine Airlines or Cebu Pacific from Manila to Butuan. Two and a half hours by car/van from Butuan to San Francisco by private car or public bus. The best bus companies are Bachelor Express, LCI and Reyno Express.

2. Manila/Davao/San Francisco (6 hours)
One-hundred-five-minute daily flights on Philippine Airlines, Air Philippines or Cebu Pacific from Manila to Davao. Four hours by Bachelor Express or private car from Davao to San Francisco.

Superferry also operates ferry service from Manila to Davao. For more information, you can call tel. nos. 528-7979 or 528-7171.

45 Units
7 Rooms (with own toilet, no air-conditioning) • 7 Rooms (with own toilet, air-conditioning) • 31 Rooms (with common toilet, no air-conditioning)

Food and Beverage Outlets
Small Restaurant
Restaurant: Christina Café in town is the best choice

Watersports and Other Activities
The resort is the best starting point to visit Agusan Marsh in Bunawan, 45 minutes from San Francisco by bus.

Per room per night

Note: *Another way to go to the Agusan marshes is through Butuan, although you will need to travel three hours by road. A good place to stay along this route is the Almont Inland Hotel Resort on J.C. Aquino Avenue, halfway between the airport and Butuan. This is a comfortable hotel with deluxe bungalows placed around a nice swimming pool.*

Note: *Cash payment only.*

Tel *(085) 342-7414*
Fax *(085) 342-9524*
E-mail *almontinlandresort@yahoo.com*

While in the region, you might also want to visit the Northern Mindanao Regional Museum, located near the town hall.

Pansukian Tropical Resort

Pansukian, a resort of charm *par excellence*, is the realization of a rather mad dream of Nicolas Rambeau. Succumbing to the charms of Siargao, he gave up his law practice in Paris, transformed himself into an architect and landscape, artist and made his dream a reality in 1994 with the construction of the resort.

Depending on the tide, you arrive either by the side open to the sea or by a tributary filled with mangroves. Either way the astonishment is the same. You find it difficult to imagine the existence of such perfect serene beauty in a remote place. The approach from the mangrove is particularly spectacular—from the pier resembling an Indonesian temple, meanders a long wooden footbridge.

Pansukian is set in a former white-sand bank between the Pacific Ocean and a part of the mangroves, which has become a tropical paradise of palm and coconut trees, *pandanus* tree, crotons, ferns, orchids and heliconias. Four wooden pavilions on piles enclose a garden patio around which are the reception area, an indoor restaurant and kitchen, a dining room facing to the sea, a library, a boutique and a billiard room.

The restaurant is very pleasant. Delicious dishes inspired by Asian and

French cuisines are served in generous portions by an attentive, cheerful staff. A bar is in a separate pavilion, protected by an unusual three-tiered roof and you can have coffee in the pavilion facing the sea while snugged in a hammock.

Some of the ocean-view cottages are located along a circular wooden gangway well concealed in the vegetation. Each cottage has a large private terrace with comfortable armchairs and hammocks, as well as exterior bathrooms. The other cottages are to the rear of the beach, completely hidden in the garden and have all the desired comforts and amenities. The huge bathrooms are quite remarkable with an interesting combination of dark polished wood and white tiles. There is also a completely circular, first class honeymoon suite secluded within the green mantle of vegetation.

Only natural quality materials have been used in the structures and the interior décor—superb wood floors, bamboo for the furniture and *nipa* for the roofs. The latter are particularly well-designed, their silhouettes blending with those of the strangely inclined coconut trees in the background to form what looks like a step from a baroque dance. Indonesian *batik*, woven baskets from Palawan and baskets of flowers and fruits decorate the interiors. A small dish of fresh flowers, placed in your room every evening, shows a real attention to detail.

You will certainly find it difficult to tear yourself away from this idyllic resort, to enjoy some of the activities and excursions, proposed with the service of a guide, that you can organize from the resort (see general presentation of Siargao).

PANSUKIAN TROPICAL RESORT

General Luna, Siargao Island, Surigao Del Norte
Tel (0920) 901-2072
E-mail *mail@pansukian.com*
Web *www.pansukian.com*

1. By air and sea (5 hours) Ninety-five-minute daily flights on Asian Spirit from Manila to Surigao. Three hours by resort *banca* to Siargao.
2. Via Cebu, by air, sea and sea (8 ½–9 hours on the first morning flight). Seventy-five-minute daily flights on Philippine Airlines, Air Philippines or Cebu Pacific from Manila to Cebu. Four hours by Philippine Fast Ferry from Cebu to Surigao. Departure at 8:30 a.m. Tel. No.: (032) 234-9600) Three hours by resort *banca* to Siargao.
3. Via Butuan, by air, land and sea (7 hours) Ninety-minute daily flights on Philippine Airlines and Cebu Pacific from Manila to Butuan. Two hours by air-conditioned minibus/car arranged by the resort or by public bus on Bachelor Express or on Philtranco headed for Manila from Butuan to Surigao. Three hours by resort *banca* to Siargao.
Note: *Options by chartered flight or helicopter arranged by the resort. The sea can be rough at certain times of the year, specially during the surf period.*

Superferry also operates ferry service from Manila to Cebu and Manila to Surigao. For more information, you can call tel. nos. 528-7979 or 528-7171.

9 Units
5 Garden cottages (with detached private bathrooms, cold water, air-conditioning, verandah) • 4 Tropical Villas (with private garden, verandah, ensuite bathroom with hot showers, air-conditioning, mini-refrigerators)
Indoor Facilities and Services
Billiards • Table tennis • Library

Food and Beverage Outlets
Restaurant/Bar
Cuisine Offered: Filipino with a French touch
Quality: Excellent

Watersports and Other Activities
Beach (white sand) • Snorkeling (in other places) • Island hopping (with picnic) • Kayaking • Other boats for hire • Surfing • Deep sea fishing (marlin) • Trekking (in the forest) • Mountain biking • Tour to the village (by motorbike or jeepney)

 Per room per night on full board basis

PLACES WITH A HEART

PHILIPPINES

Appendices

Intramuros, Manila

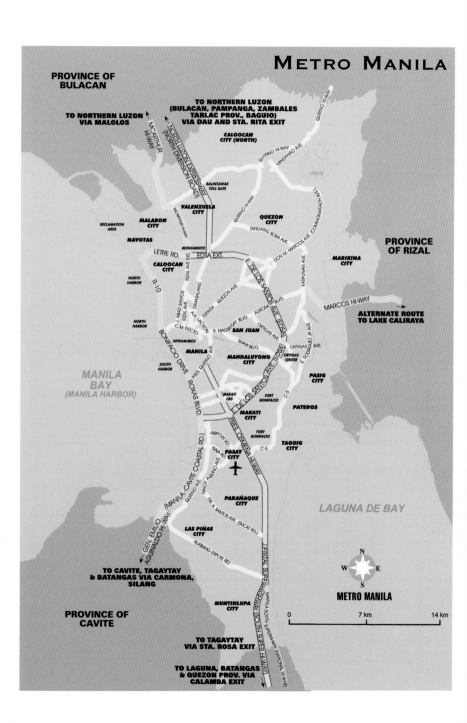

METRO MANILA

PROVINCE OF
BULACAN

TO NORTHERN LUZON
(BULACAN, PAMPANGA, ZAMBALES
TARLAC PROV., BAGUIO)
VIA DAU AND STA. RITA EXIT

TO NORTHERN LUZON
VIA MALOLOS

CALOOCAN
CITY (NORTH)

MCARTHUR HI-WAY

NORTH LUZON EXPRESSWAY
(NORTH DIVERSION ROAD)

QUIRINO HI-WAY

BALINTAWAK
TOLL GATE

VALENZUELA
CITY

QUIRINO HI-WAY

MINDANAO AVE.

QUEZON
CITY

PROVINCE
OF RIZAL

RECLAMATION
AREA

MALABON
CITY

TANDANG SORA AVE.

DON M. MARCOS AVE. (COMMONWEALTH AVE.)

MARIKINA
CITY

NAVOTAS

MONUMENTO

LETRE RD.

EDSA EXT.

KAIPUNAN AVE.

CALOOCAN
CITY

RIZAL AVE. EXT.

DIMASALANG

E. DE LOS SANTOS AVE. (EDSA)

QUEZON AVE.

MARCOS HI-WAY

NORTH
HARBOR

R-10

C. J. ABAD SANTOS

RIZAL AVE.

A. H. LACSON

ESPAÑA

ALTERNATE ROUTE
TO LAKE CALIRAYA

NORTH
HARBOR

C.M. RECTO

R. MAGSAYSAY BLVD.

AURORA BLVD.

SAN JUAN

E. RODRIGUEZ JR. AVE.

ORTIGAS AVE.

BONIFACIO DRIVE

INTRAMUROS

SHAW BLVD.

ORTIGAS
CENTER

MANILA

PRES. QUIRINO AVE.

MANDALUYONG
CITY

E. RODRIGUEZ JR. AVE.

MANILA
BAY
(MANILA HARBOR)

SOUTH
HARBOR

ROXAS BLVD.

E. DE LOS SANTOS AVE. (EDSA)

C-5

PASIG
CITY

MAKATI
CBD

FORT
BONIFACIO

MAKATI
CITY

PATEROS

PRES. OSMEÑA HI-WAY

AIRPORT RD.

NAIA RD.

FORT
BONIFACIO

C-5

TAGUIG
CITY

MANILA-CAVITE COASTAL RD.)

QUIRINO AVE.

NINOY AQUINO AVE.

PASAY
CITY

PARAÑAQUE
CITY

DR. A. SANTOS AVE. (SUCAT RD.)

LAGUNA DE BAY

GEN. EMILIO
AGUINALDO HI-WAY

LAS PIÑAS
CITY

ALABANG-ZAPOTE RD.

J. P. RIZAL SUPERHIGHWAY

N
W   E
S

METRO MANILA

TO CAVITE, TAGAYTAY
& BATANGAS VIA CARMONA,
SILANG

MANILA & SOUTH SUPERHIGHWAY (NATIONAL HI-WAY)

MUNTINLUPA
CITY

0   7 km   14 km

PROVINCE OF
CAVITE

TO TAGAYTAY
VIA STA. ROSA EXIT

TO LAGUNA, BATANGAS
& QUEZON PROV. VIA
CALAMBA EXIT

HOTELS IN METRO MANILA

There are few hotels with charm in Metro Manila, a metropolis of well over 10 million people that non-residents will use only as a jump-off point to provincial destinations. The list we have here is only based on the choice of a comfortable hotel, which may usually be expensive.

Reservations made through a travel agency or the Internet is advised to ensure bookings in these hotels, as well as to get cheaper rates. The "++" that comes after the rates "for taxes and services" range from 20% to 25%.

MAKATI CITY

Makati City is the foremost business, shopping and entertainment district of Metro Manila. Following is a list of the best hotels in Makati City. All of them are located in the heart of Makati City, close to prime shopping areas such as the Ayala Center. The Ninoy Aquino International Airport is 30 minutes away (provide some allowance for delays in traffic). Published room rates (for double/twin occupancy in the lowest category) for the year 2003 are within the US$ 235-330 range.

THE PENINSULA MANILA
Corner of Ayala and Makati Avenue,
Makati City
Tel: 887-2888
Fax: 815-4825
       498 rooms
       9 restaurants/bars
Room rate: from US$ 150++
E-mail: tpm@peninsula.com
The group's website: www.peninsula.com

The Peninsula Manila is one of the most elegant hotels in Makati. Its marble lobby is spectacular, with a very elegant and impressive staircase. An orchestra plays classical music and creates a relaxing ambiance. From the outside, the hotel is distinguished by an imposing fountain that separates the two buildings housing the rooms. It has two very fine restaurants, Old Manila for modern European cuisine amidst an ambiance of Manila's old world charm, and Spices for Asian cuisines.

MAKATI SHANGRI-LA, MANILA
Ayala Avenue corner Makati Avenue,
Makati City
Tel: 813-8888
Fax: 813-5499/813-5059
       699 rooms
       7 restaurants/bars
Room rate: from US $230++
E-mail: slm@shangri-la.com
The group's website: www.shangri-la.com

Makati Shangri-La, Manila—not to be mistaken with the Edsa Shangri-La, Manila located at Ortigas Center—is one of the most luxurious hotels in town, together with the Peninsula Manila. The two hotels face each other. The Makati Shangri-La, Manila also has a marble lobby with an impressive staircase, only slightly more ornate than that of the Peninsula Manila. From outside, the hotel can be recognized through its pink facade. Cheval Blanc serves fine French cuisine, and Shang Palace offers delicious Cantonese/Chinese specialties in a superb setting evoking an old Chinese house.

HOTEL INTER-CONTINENTAL MANILA
1 Ayala Avenue, Makati City
Tel: 815-9711
Fax: 817-1330 • 815-1948
       338 rooms
       6 restaurants/bars
Room rate: from US$ 220++
E-mail: manila@interconti.com
The group's website:
www.intercontinental.com

Hotel Inter-Continental Manila is also centrally located and prestigious. As it has a smaller room capacity than the other hotels in the list, its lobby is more modest in size and much less impressive. The Prince Albert Rotisserie in this hotel is one of the best French restaurants in Metro Manila.

MANDARIN ORIENTAL, MANILA
Makati Avenue corner Paseo de Roxas,
Makati City
Tel: 750-8888
Fax: 819-9689
       448 rooms
       7 restaurants/bars
Room rate: from US$ 165++
E-mail: momnl-reservations@mohg.com
The group's website:
www.mandarinoriental.com

Slightly at a distance from the first three hotels in the list, the Mandarin Oriental,

Manila is nevertheless centrally located. Its lobby is very small and therefore, not very impressive. However, services offered are equally good and it is worth mentioning that it has a Cathay Pacific check-in facility.

DUSIT HOTEL NIKKO, MANILA

Ayala Center Makati City
Tel: 867-3333
Fax: 867-3888
      542 rooms
      7 restaurants/bar
Room rate: from US$ 270++
E-mail: dusitmnl@dusit.com
Website: http://manila.dusit.com/

Without doubt, the Dusit Hotel Nikko Manila is the nearest hotel to Ayala Center. It has an elegant and wide marble lobby. It also has a fine Thai restaurant, Benjarong Royal Thai Restaurant.

NEW WORLD RENAISSANCE HOTEL

Esperanza Street corner Makati Avenue, Makati City
Tel: 811-6888
Fax: 811-6777
       599 rooms
       4 restaurants
Room rate: from US$ 250++
The group's website: www.marriott.com
www.renaissancehotels.com

The New World Renaissance Hotel belongs to the Marriott Group. It is also centrally located, close to Greenbelt Shopping Center and Ayala Center.

HERALD SUITES

2168 Chino Roces Avenue, Makati City
Tel: 759-6270 to 75 • 894-1193
Fax: 759-6282
       60 rooms
       1 Japanese restaurant
       1 coffee shop
Room rate: from US$ 50++
E-mail: reserve@heraldsuites.com
        enquiry@heraldsuites.com
Web: www.heraldsuites.com

The hotel has a tiny but elegant lobby dominated by a skylight. The interiors are mainly in wood and wrought iron–all rooms have beautiful wood floors and custom-made wood furniture. An excellent fine-dining Japanese restaurant with authentic tatami *rooms is on the second floor.*

ORTIGAS CENTER, MANDALUYONG CITY

Ortigas Center is the second largest business and shopping district of Metro Manila. It is 15-20 minutes away from Makati City and the Ninoy Aquino International Airport is 45 minutes away (given provisions for delays in transit). It is the area where the headquarters of Asian Development Bank is located. It probably has the highest concentration of shopping malls with SM Megamall, the prestigious Shangri-La Plaza Shopping Center and Robinsons' Galleria located within a short distance from each other.

EDSA SHANGRI-LA, MANILA

1 Garden Way, Ortigas Center,
Mandaluyong City
Tel: 633-8888
Fax: 631-1067 • 632-6549
      658 guest rooms and suites
      7 restaurants/bars
Room rate: from US$ 240++
E-mail: esl@shangri-la.com
The group's website: www.shangri-la.com

Edsa Shangri-La, Manila is set in lush tropical gardens. All of the hotel's guestrooms are spacious and delightfully appointed, combining a distinct cosmopolitan flair with traditional Filipino style. For the business executive, there is a fully-equipped business center, and for the sports-buff, a complete fitness center, tennis and outdoor swimming pool.

ROXAS BOULEVARD, PASAY CITY

Many hotels are along or close to Roxas Boulevard, facing the sea. It is also a central location, 30 minutes from the international and domestic airports, near the historical site of Intramuros, museums, galleries, the Cultural Center of the Philippines, the Metropolitan Museum of Manila, the GSIS Theatre and the antique shops on Mabini Street and Malate with its numerous restaurants and cafés open until late at night.

MANILA HOTEL

One Rizal Park,
Manila (along Roxas Boulevard)
Tel: 527-0011
Fax: 527-0022 to 24
      500 rooms
      7 restaurants/bars
Room rate: from US$ 250++
E-mail: resvn@manila-hotel.com.ph
Web: www.manila-hotel.com.ph

Opened in 1912, it is the oldest and the most prestigious hotel in Manila because of its historical background. It lies on 3.5 hectares of lush green shoreline and some of the rooms overlook Manila Bay and Rizal Park. The Champagne Room has a romantic ambiance and a beautiful art nouveau decor.

THE WESTIN PHILIPPINE PLAZA

CCP Complex, Roxas Boulevard, Pasay City

Tel: 551-5555
Fax: 551-5610
       645 rooms
       9 restaurants/bars
Room rate: from US$ 225++
E-mail: bscenter@westin.com
Web: www.westin.com/manila

Right on the seafront, it is the only resort-hotel in Manila. It has a very nice swimming pool close to the seashore where open air buffet-style dinners are served on Sundays.

HYATT REGENCY MANILA
2702 Roxas Boulevard, Pasay City
Tel: 833-1234
Fax: 831-8076
       260 rooms
       3 restaurants/bars
Room rate: from US$ 110++
E-mail: reservations@hyatt.com.ph
The group's website: www.hyatt.com /
       www.manila.regency.hyatt.com

The haciendas of Spain were the inspiration for the pleasing and warm decor of the rooms. The café Al Fresco offers fine Italian cuisine.

THE HERITAGE
Roxas Boulevard corner EDSA Extension,
Pasay City
Tel: 854-8888 • 854-8648
Fax: 854-8833
       467 rooms
       3 restaurants
Room rate: from US $240++
E-mail: inquiry@heritagehotelmanila.com
The group's website:
       www.millenniumhotels.com

Most of the rooms have a nice view of Manila Bay. Connoisseurs say that Hua Ting Cantonese restaurant serves very good and authentic Chinese cuisine.

GRAND BOULEVARD HOTEL
1990 Roxas Boulevard, Manila
Tel: 526-8588
Fax: 526-1701
       500 rooms
       4 restaurants/bars
Room rate: from US$ 160++

TRADERS HOTEL
3001 Roxas Boulevard, Pasay City
Tel: 523-7011 to 20
Fax: 522-39852
       290 rooms
       2 restaurants
Room rate: from US$ 110++

E-mail: thm@shangri-la.com
The group's website: www.shangri-la.com

MANILA PAVILLION HOTEL
United Nations Avenue, Ermita, Manila
Tel: 526-1212
Fax: 526-2552
       590 rooms
       6 restaurants/bars
Room rate: from US$ 165++

THE PAN PACIFIC MANILA
Gen. Malvar Street corner Adriatico Street
Malate, Manila
Tel: 536-0788
Fax: 536-6220
       236 rooms
       13 restaurants/bars
Room rate: from US$ 210++
E-mail: reserve.mnl@panpacific.com
The group's website: www.panpac.com

ORCHID GARDEN SUITES MANILA
620 Pablo Ocampo Sr. Street,
Malate, Manila
Tel: 523-9870
Fax: 523-9829
       88 rooms
       3 restaurant/bars
Room rate: from US$ 60

The hotel has a huge fitness center and spa.

CENTURY PARK HOTEL
599 P. Ocampo Street, Malate, Manila
Tel: 528-8888 • 528-5814 to 16
Fax: 525-3209
       500 rooms
       7 restaurants/bars
Room rate: from US$ 218++
E-mail: information@centurypark.com.ph
Web: www.centurypark.com

The hotel has a big atrium in the ground floor lobby where instrumentalists perform from 6 p.m. to 9 p.m. everyday. Across the hotel is Harrison Plaza, a major shopping mall.

QUEZON CITY

SULO HOTEL
Matalino Road (at the back of Quezon City Hall, beside Philippine Heart Center) Diliman, Quezon City
Tel: 924-5051 to 71
Fax: 922-2030
       68 rooms
       6 restaurants
Room rate: from US$ 52
E-mail: frontoffice@sulohotel.com.ph
Web: www.sulohotel.com.ph

This transportation section gives the necessary information on the various modes of transportation available to the traveler who wants to go—within a reasonable amount of time—to the destinations mentioned in this book. It also indicates the existing connections between cities other than Manila so as to enable the traveler to continue the trip without having to go back to Manila.

Note: The frequency of service is indicated as follows: 2d. means twice daily; 1w. means one weekly service. The duration of the trip is indicated in minutes for airlines, in hours for other means of transportation.

TRANSPORTATION BY AIR

As of March 2005, eight domestic airlines have regular flights. These are the five major airlines—Philippine Airlines, Air Philippines, Cebu Pacific, Asian Spirit and Interisland Airlines—and the three smaller ones: Seair, Pacific Airways and Island Transvoyager, which service a few routes only.

Most airlines offer discounts known as "advance promo package" for tickets purchased in advance.

Groups of a minimum of 10 persons are also eligible for a discount. There are also seasonal promotions.

In most cases, children from two to 12 years of age are charged 50% off the regular fare—except on small aircraft in which all passengers pay full fare. Infants below two years of age get 90% off from the regular fare.

Payments are made either in cash or by credit card. If you do not want to go personally to a ticketing office to buy your ticket, you can make your booking through a travel agent who will purchase and deliver your tickets.

Except for Philippine Airlines which has its own terminal, NAIA Centennial Terminal 2; and Air Philippines, Cebu Pacific and Asian Spirit which use Manila Domestic Terminal 1; other airlines have a specific check-in facility, the details of which have to be requested prior to departure.

AIRLINE DIRECTORY

AIR PHILIPPINES

Main office:	Air Philippines Corporation, R-1 Hangar, APC Gate 1, Andrews Avenue, Nichols, Pasay City
	Tel: 851-7601
	Fax: 851-7922
Airport terminal:	Manila Domestic Airport Terminal 1, Domestic Road, Pasay City
Reservations:	**Tel:** 855-9000
E-mail:	reservations@airphilippines.com.ph
Web:	www.airphils.com

ISLAND TRANSVOYAGER, INC.

Reservations:	**Tel:** 851-5674 • 854-1417
	Fax: 854-1418
Airport terminal:	A. Soriano Aviation Terminal, Andrews Avenue, Pasay City
E-mail:	marismacahilig@elnido.resorts.com

ASIAN SPIRIT

Main office:	Asian Spirit Airlines, Delta Air Hangar P.O. Box 7593, Manila Domestic Airport, Pasay City
	Tel: 853-1957
	Fax: 851-1804 • 05

Airport terminal:	Manila Domestic Airport Terminal 1,
	Domestic Road, Pasay City
Domestic ticketing office:	Corner Domestic Road and Andrews Avenue,
	Pasay City
Sales and Promotion	**Tel:** 851-1795 • **Fax:** 851-1794
Express Ticketing Office	Along Domestic Road, Pasay City
	Tel: 514-4311 to 12
Reservations:	**Tel:** 851-8888 • 851-1810
E-mail:	aspirit@asianspirit.com
Web:	www.asianspirit.com

CEBU PACIFIC

Main office:	Robinsons Place, Fuente Osmeña, Ground Level, Cebu
	Tel: (032) 255-4040
	Tel/Fax: (032) 253-9433
Office in Manila:	Level 1 Robinsons Galleria, EDSA
	corner ADB Avenue, QuezonCity
	Tel: 632-7026 • **Fax:** 632-7028
Airport terminal:	Manila Domestic Airport Terminal 1, Domestic Road,
	Pasay City
Reservations:	**Tel:** 636-4938
E-mail:	ceb.reservation@cebupacificair.com
Web:	www.cebupacificair.com

PACIFIC AIRWAYS

Airport Terminal:	3110 Domestic Airport Road, NAIA, Pasay City
Reservations:	**Tel:** 851-1509 • 851-1501 • 854-7431
	Fax: 833-7430 • 853-8393
E-mail:	pacificair@netasia-mnl.net

INTERISLAND AIRLINES

Airport Terminal:	Domestic Airport Road (beside Old Domestic
	Terminal), NAIA, Pasay City
Reservations:	**Tel:** 852-8010 to 13 • **Fax:** 852-7793

ISLAND AVIATION

Main Office:	**Tel:** 833-3855
	A. Soriano Hangan Andrews Avenue, Pasay City

PHILIPPINE AIRLINES

Airport terminal:	NAIA Centennial Terminal 2, Mia Road, Pasay City
	Tel: 877-1109
Reservations (open 24 hours):	For all passengers **Tel:** 855-8888
	For Mabuhay Class passengers and
	Mabuhay Club Members **Tel:** 855-7888
	Note: Group bookings must be requested by fax.
	Fax: 551-2378
Flight status information:	**Tel:** 855-9999
E-mail:	webmgr@pal.com.ph
Web:	www.philippineairlines.com

SEAIR

Main office:	Seair, Hangar 7224, Clark International Airport,
	Clark Field, Pampanga
	Tel: (045) 599-2384 to 86 • **Fax:** (045) 599-2383
Airport terminal:	Air Ads Terminal, adjacent to the Manila Domestic
	Airport Terminal 1 across the ALPAP Building,
	Pasay City
Reservations:	**Tel:** 884-1521 • **Fax:** 891-8711
E-mail:	info@flyseair.com or tickets@flyseair.com
Web:	www.flyseair.com

DESTINATION	AIR PHILIPPINES CORPORATION	ASIAN SPIRIT AIRLINES	CEBU PACIFIC AIR	PHILIPPINE AIRLINES	SEAIR	OTHERS
From MANILA						
Bacolod (Negros)	70min./1d		60min./3d	70min./3d		
Baguio		50min./1d				
Basco		120min./4w				
Busuanga		60min./1d			65min./7w	90min./1d**
Butuan			85min./1d	90min./1d		
Cagayan de Oro	85min./1d		85min./2d	90min./4d		
Calbayog (Samar)		70min./3w				
Catarman (Samar)		65min./4w				
Caticlan (Panay)		60min./14d			70min./10d	90min./1d**
(*Dornier 328 planes*)					35 min./4d	
						45min./1d****
Cebu	70min./3d		70min./9d	75min./7d		
Clark		30 min./3w			30min./1d	
Coron						90min./1d**
Cotabato				95min./1d		
Cuyo						90min./1d**
Davao	100min./2d		100min./6d	105min./3d		
Dipolog				90min./1d		
Dumaguete (Negros)	75min./1d		75min./2d	75min./2d		
El Nido					115min./3w	75min./1d*
Gen. Santos	180min./1d***			105min./1d		
Iloilo (Panay)	65min./3d		60min./4d	65min./3d		
Kalibo (Panay)			50min./1d	55min./2d		
Laoag				55min./4w		
Legaspi				55min./1d		
Puerto Princesa (Palawan)	70min./1d	75min./1d	70min./1d	75min./1d		
(via Busuanga and El Nido)						
San Jose (Mindoro)		50min./1d				
Sandoval					90min./1d	
Subic			30min./1d			
Surigao		95min./1d				
Tacloban (Leyte)			70min./3d	75min./3d		
Tagbilaran (Bohol)			70min./1d	70min./1d		
Virac		75min./1d				

FLIGHT DURATION / FREQUENCIES

DESTINATION	AIR PHILIPPINES CORPORATION	ASIAN SPIRIT AIRLINES	CEBU PACIFIC AIR	PHILIPPINES AIRLINES	SEAIR
From BUSUANGA:					
El Nido					30min./3w
Puerto Princesa (via El Nido)					95min./3w
From CEBU:					
Bacolod	35min./1d		30min./1d	35min./1d	
Butuan			40min./3w		
Cagayan de Oro		60min./1d			60min./3w
Camiguin					35min./3w
Caticlan		60min./1d			60min./1d
Davao	55min./1d		55min./2d	55min./1d	
Dipolog		40min./4w			
General Santos	65min./1d			65min./1d	
Iloilo	40min./1d		40min./1d	40min./1d	
Siargao					50min./2w
Surigao		40min./3w			
From ILOILO:					
Cebu			35min./1d	40min./1d	
Davao	135min./1d[***]		135min./1d[***]		
General Santos	145min./1d[***]				
From BACOLOD:					
Cebu				35min./1d	
Davao	160min./1d[***]				
General Santos	170min./1d[***]				

[*]   Island Transvoyager, Inc.

[**]   Pacific Airways

[***]   via Cebu

[****]   Interisland Airlines

341

DELTA FAST FERRIES

Terminal in Dumaguete:	Pier 3, Port area **Tel:** (035) 420-0888 • 420-1111 Delta I : 6:00am, 9:00am, 1:30pm, 4:30pm Delta Car Ferry : 6:00am, 10:30am, 2:20pm

OCEANJET

Terminal in Cebu:	Pier 1, North Reclamation Area, Cebu City **Tel:** (032) 255-7560 **Fax:** (032) 255-0115
Web:	www.oceanjet.net

MOUNT SAMAT FERRY EXPRESS, INC.

PTA Bay cruise Terminal:	CCP Complex, Roxas Boulevard, Manila **Tel:** 551-5290
Manila to Orion (Bataan):	1 hour (6:30am, 8:30am, 10:30am, 1:00pm, 3:00pm, 5:15pm)

NEGROS NAVIGATION COMPANY, INC.

Main Office:	Pier 2, North Harbor, Manila **Tel/Fax:** 245-4395
Web:	www.negrosnavigation.ph

SUPERCAT FAST FERRY CORPORATION*

Main office:	Pier 4, North Reclamation Area, Cebu City **Tel:** (032) 234-9600
Web:	www.supercat.com.ph

SuperCat Fast Ferry is a sister company of WG&A which operates SuperCats. SuperCats are twin-hulled fast ferry catamarans measuring an average of 35 to 45 meters in length, cruising at speeds of up to 34 knots (63 kilometers per hour). This means cutting travel time between ports by more than 50%. All SuperCat vessels boast of comfortable airline-type seats, air-conditioning, wall-to-wall carpeting and a canteen/minibar. A 35-meter SuperCat has an average seating capacity of 245 passengers and a 40-meter catamaran can carry as much as 306 passengers. The 50-meter TriCat has a seating capacity of 403 passengers.

There is only one type of fare. However, senior citizens are entitled to a 20% discount, disabled citizens 20% discount, students 15% and children ranging from four to 11 years of age are charged 50% off the regular fare.

Within the Visayas

Cebu to Tagbilaran	1 hour 30 min.	2d (8:00am, 4:30pm)
Cebu to Dumaguete (via Tagbilaran)	3 hours 30 min.	1d (8:00am)
Cebu to Larena (via Tagbilaran)	3 hours 45 min.	1d (8:00am)
Cebu to Ormoc (Leyte)	2 hours	3d (6:00am, 11:00am, 4:00pm)
Iloilo to Bacolod	1 hour 45 min.	3d (9:55am, 2:15pm, 6:45pm)

Between the Visayas and Mindanao

Cebu to Dapitan via Dumaguete	5 hours 30 min.	1d (8:00am)

WILLIAM, GOTHONG ABOITIZ, INC. (WG&A) / SUPERFERRY

Main Office:	12/F Times Plaza Building, United Nations Avenue corner Taft Avenue, Manila
Reservations:	**Tel:** 528-7979 • 528-7171
E-mail:	customerinteraction@superferry.com.ph
Web:	www.superferry.com.ph

WG&A operates a fleet of 10 passenger ships, measuring an average of 123 to 185 meters in length, cruising at speed of 15 to 20 knots. The following fares are available: super-value, megavalue, tourist, business class, cabin, stateroom and suiteroom.
Tickets may be purchased in different outlets nationwide or online via the website.

CONNECTIONS AVAILABLE FROM MANILA
Trips out of Manila are available to almost all the destinations mentioned in this book. Traveling by sea takes a lot more time (for example, it takes 21 hours to go to Cebu) and frequency of service, except for Cebu, is limited at most to three times a week. However, there is the very convenient 11-hour night trip between Manila and Coron (Palawan) and vice-versa, especially convenient for divers who want to spend a weekend in Coron.

CONNECTIONS AVAILABLE WITHIN THE VISAYAS
From Tagbilaran to Dumaguete	4 hours/2w

CONNECTIONS AVAILABLE WITHIN MINDANAO
From Surigao to Nasipit/Butuan	5 hours/1w
From Davao to General Santos	8 hours/3w

CONNECTIONS AVAILABLE BETWEEN THE VISAYAS AND MINDANAO
From Cebu to:	
Nasipit/Butuan	14 hours/1w
Surigao	9 hours/1w
From Tagbilaran to Dipolog	10 hours/1w
From Iloilo to:	
Cagayan de Oro	13 hours/2w
General Santos	13 hours/1w
From Bacolod to Cagayan de Oro	15 hours/4w

CONNECTIONS AVAILABLE WITHIN PALAWAN
From Coron to Puerto Princesa	13 hours - 1w

Contact numbers of WG&A in:

Visayas
Cebu	Tel: (032) 233-7000 • 232-0499
Dumaguete	Tel: (035) 225-0734 • 226-1075
Tagbilaran	Tel: (038) 411-3651 • 411-3048
Bacolod	Tel: (034) 435-4965 • 434-2531
Iloilo	Tel: (033) 337-7151 • 335-0812
Ormoc	Tel: (053) 561-9818

Mindanao
Davao	Tel: (082) 221-1390
Cagayan de Oro	Tel: (08822) 725-406 • 231-4800
General Santos	Tel: (083) 553-5974 • 52-4461
Dipolog	Tel: (065) 212-5574
Iligan	Tel: (063) 221-1327 • 223-3415
Surigao	Tel: (086) 231-9645 • 826-3804
Nasipit/Butuan	Tel: (085) 343-3366 • 342-8529

Palawan
Puerto Princesa	Tel: (048) 434-5734 • 434-5736 to 38

TRANSPORTATION BY LAND AND SEA

BUS AND FERRY SERVICES BETWEEN BATANGAS AND MINDORO

SIKAT LTD.   **Tel:** 521-3344 • **Fax:** 526-2758

Sikat Ltd. operates a daily bus and ferry service from Manila to Puerto Galera. The bus departs daily from City State Tower Hotel, 1315 Mabini Street, Ermita, Manila and has a direct connection with a ferry at the ferry terminal in Batangas Harbor. The ferry arrives at Muelle pier at Puerto Galera. The trip takes 4 ½ hours.

CCL SHIPPING LINES   **Tel:** 523-8545

CCL Shipping Lines operates a daily van and ferry service from Manila to Puerto Galera. The van departs from Swagman Hotel located at Flores Street, Ermita, Manila and has a direct connection with the Island Cruiser at the ferry terminal in Batangas Harbor. The ferry arrives at Muelle pier at Puerto Galera. The trip takes 4 ½ hours.

MONTENEGRO LINES also operates ferries from Batangas to Abra de Ilog. For more information you may check with the Passenger Terminal in Batangas: (043) 723-8294.

Ferry services within BICOL

MV BICOLANDIA LINES   **Tel:** (052) 830-1187

REGINA SHIPPING LINES   **Tel/Fax:** (052) 811-1345

TRANSPORTATION BY LAND

Bus connections within LUZON

VICTORY LINER BUS COMPANY

Terminals:
#561 Edsa, Pasay City   **Tel:** 833-5019 • 833-5020 • 833-4403
#683 Edsa near Aurora Boulevard, Quezon City **Tel:** 727-4534 • 727-4688
#713 Rizal Avenue Extension, Caloocan   **Tel:** 361-1506 to 10 • 364-2926
#1310 España corner Galicia Street,   **Tel:** 921-3296 • 741-1436
       Sampaloc, Manila   **E-mail:** sales@victoryliner.com
                                               Web: www.victoryliner.com

Victory Liner services the following destinations: Olongapo City, departure every 30 minutes starting 5:30 a.m., Baguio City, departure every hour in the morning, Alaminos in Pangasinan, Bagac in Bataan, Agoo in La Union and Tagaytay City.

DANGWA TRANCO

Dimasalang, Manila   **Tel:** 731-2879
Dangwa Tranco services the following destinations: Out of Manila: Banaue (10 hours), daily departure at 7:30 a.m. Tickets cannot be purchased in advance. From Baguio, Bus Terminal: Sagada (6 to 7 hours) and Bontoc (5 hours).

DAGUPAN BUS COMPANY

Cubao, Quezon City   **Tel:** 727-2330 • 727-2287
Dagupan Bus Co. services the following destinations: Baguio (6 hours), Alaminos (6 hours), Dagupan (5 hours), Tugegarao (12 hours), Pangasinan (5 hours)

PHILIPPINE RABBIT

EDSA, Quezon City
Sta. Cruz, Manila   **Tel:** 734-9836
Philippine Rabbit services the following destinations: Baguio (7 hrs.), Vigan (8 hrs.), Laoag (10 hrs.), Angeles City (2 hrs.), Alaminos, Pangasinan (6 hrs.), San Fernando, La Union (6 hrs.) with daily trips from 5:30 a.m. to 8:30 p.m. With one-hour intervals.

PHILTRANCO

Pasay City	**Tel:** 853-3218 to 20
Cubao, Quezon City	**Tel:** 911-2523

Philtranco services Legazpi (12 hours), daily trips at 9:00 a.m., 7:00 p.m., 9:00 p.m.

PARTAS

Cubao, Quezon City	**Tel:** 725-7303 • 725-1740
Pasay, City	**Tel:** 851-4025

Partas services the following destinations: Baguio (7 hrs.), Vigan (9 hrs.), Laoag (10 hrs.), San Fernando, La Union (6 hours) with daily trips from 1:00 a.m. to 12 midnight.

MARIA DE LEON

Manila   **Tel:** 731-4907

Maria de Leon services the following destinations: Ilocos Norte (8 hrs.), Laoag (10 hrs.), San Fernando and La Union (6 hours) with daily trips at 6:30 a.m. to 12 noon.

DOMINION BUS LINES

Cubao, Quezon City	**Tel:** 727-2350
Manila	**Tel:** 743-3612

Dominion services the following destinations: Cubao-Vigan (9 hrs.) daily trips at 3:30 to 8:00 a.m., 1:30 to 10:30 p.m. San Fernando, La Union (6 hrs.) daily trips at 4:30 to 6:30 a.m., 3:30 to 11:45 p.m. Manila to Vigan (9 hrs.) daily at 12:30 p.m. and 10:30 p.m. and San Fernando, La Union (6 hours) daily at 7:30 a.m. Departures are at one-hour intervals.

JAM TRANSIT

Manila   **Tel:** 831-3178

Jam Transit services the following destinations: Batangas (2–3 hrs.), daily trips at 1:30 a.m. to 10:30 p.m., with 15-minute intervals. Sta. Cruz, Laguna (2 hrs.) daily trips from 3:00 a.m. to 11:00 p.m., Lucena (4–5 hours) daily trips from 3:00-8:00pm. Kalawag, Quezon (6 hours) with daily trips from 3:00am-8:00pm.

FARIÑAS TRANSIT

Manila   **Tel:** 743-8580

Fariñas Transit services the following destinations: Vigan (9 hrs.), Laoag (10 hrs.), San Fernando La Union (6 hrs.) daily trips at 5:30 am to 5:30 pm. with one-hour intervals and 6 p.m. to 1:30 a.m. with 30-minute intervals.

TRITRAN TRANSIT

Cubao, Quezon City	**Tel:** 925-1758
Buendia, Pasay City	

Tritran Transit services the following destinations: Batangas (3 hrs.), Lucena (4 hrs.) daily trips at 1:00am-11:30pm with 30-minute intervals.

Bus connections within NEGROS

CERES LINER has two daily services between Bacolod and Dumaguete. It takes 5 hours via Mabinay. From Bacolod Terminal, the first departure is at 3:10 a.m., the second and last one at 1:30 p.m., Tel: (034) 446-0681. From Dumaguete Terminal, the first departure is at 3:10 a.m., the second and last at 6 p.m., Tel: (035) 225-9030.

Bus connections within MINDANAO

BACHELOR EXPRESS	
In Davao:	Ma-a, Davao City
	Tel: (082) 244-0637
In Butuan:	J.C. Aquino Avenue, National Highway, Butuan City
	Tel: (085) 225-3521

Davao-Butuan	7 hours - Every hour
Davao-Cagayan de Oro	11 hours - Every hour

air-conditioned (first trip at 3 a.m., last trip at 9 a.m.)
non-air-conditioned (first trip at 10 p.m., last trip at 9 a.m.)

Davao-Surigao   9 hours - Every hour
air-conditioned/non-air-conditioned (first trip at 6 p.m., last trip at 12:45 p.m.)

YELLOW BUS LINE COMPANY

In Davao: Ma-a, Davao City **Tel:** (082) 298-0045
In Koronadal: **Tel:** (083) 228-2511 • 228-2240
In General Santos: Bus Terminal • **Tel:** (083) 552-2148

Davao-General Santos   3 hours
Davao-Koronadal   5 hours - Every hour
    Deluxe (first trip at 1:30 a.m., last trip at 6:30 p.m.)
    Air-conditioned (first trip at 4 a.m., last trip at 5 p.m.)

BUS CONNECTIONS WITHIN PANAY

CERES LINER has a daily service between Iloilo and Kalibo. It takes 4 hours.

Provided below are other connections between Cebu and Tacloban and between Cebu and Dumaguete, which are neither mentioned in the domestic airlines, shipping companies sections nor mentioned in the practical date sheets.

CONNECTION BETWEEN CEBU AND TACLOBAN/CEBU AND DUMAGUETE

CONNECTION BETWEEN CEBU AND TACLOBAN

By sea and land (5 hours): Ferry – 2 hours by Philippine Fast Corporation from Cebu to Ormoc, on Leyte Island. **Bus** – 2 hours from Ormoc to Tacloban (108 km). Several bus companies available. Hourly intervals.

CONNECTION BETWEEN CEBU AND DUMAGUETE

By land, sea and land (4 hours): **Taxi** - 2 ½ hours from Cebu to Liloan, at the southern tip of Cebu Island. **Banca** - 30 minutes from Liloan to Sibulan (North of Dumaguete). Every hour interval. **Taxi or jeep** - 15 minutes from Sibulan to Dumaguete.

CAR RENTAL COMPANIES

AVIS-RENT-A-CAR

Central Reservations Office in Manila   **Tel:** 851-9274
                                        Web: www.avis.com

RENTAL LOCATIONS IN THE PHILIPPINES:
Manila: Ninoy Aquino International Airport, The Peninsula Manila Hotel and Holiday Inn Hotel

Cebu: Mactan International Airport

Davao City: Apo View Hotel

Subic: Subic Bay International Airport and Olongapo City

Pampanga: Holiday Inn Resort Clark Field and Balibago, Angeles City

NISSAN RENT-A-CAR

Central Reservations Office in Manila   **Tel:** 894-5979 • 894-4820
                                        Web: www.nissanrentacar.com

BUDGET RENT-A-CAR

Tel: 831-8247
E-mail: budget@vasia.com
Web: www.budget.com
RENTAL LOCATIONS IN MANILA: Ninoy Aquino International Airport and Hotel Intercontinental Manila

HERTZ RENT-A-CAR

Tel: 812-1529
Web: www.hertz.ph
RENTAL LOCATIONS IN MANILA: Ninoy Aquino International Airport and G/F Sunette Tower, Durban Street, Manila

DOLLAR RENT-A-CAR

Tel: 893-3233
E-mail: rentacar@info.com.ph
Web: www.dollarrentacarph.com
RENTAL LOCATIONS IN MANILA: Ninoy Aquino International Airport and New World Hotel